Nuclear Rites

Nuclear Rites

*A Weapons Laboratory
at the End of the Cold War*

Hugh Gusterson

UNIVERSITY OF CALIFORNIA PRESS
Berkeley   Los Angeles   London

University of California Press
Berkeley and Los Angeles, California

University of California Press
London, England

First Paperback Printing 1998

Library of Congress Cataloging-in-Publication Data
Gusterson, Hugh.
    Nuclear rites : a weapons laboratory at the end of the Cold War /
Hugh Gusterson.
        p.   cm.
    Includes bibliographical references and index.
    ISBN 978-0-520-21373-9 (pbk : alk. paper)
    1. Nuclear weapons—Research—Social aspects—California—
Livermore.   2. Lawrence Livermore National Laboratory—Employees.
3. Antinuclear movement—Social aspects.   I. Title.
U264.4.C2G87   1996   96-7234
306.2'7—dc20   CIP

Printed in the United States of America

10   09   08   07   06
    12   11   10   9   8   7   6

The paper used in this publication meets the minimum requirements of
ANSI/NISO Z39.48-1992 (R 1997) (*Permanence of Paper*). ∞

To Lynn and Joan, my family in Livermore

CONTENTS

PREFACE

I am often asked why an anthropologist would study a nuclear weapons laboratory. The risk of being labeled deviant by colleagues in anthropology and irrelevant by arms control specialists is high, and the difficulties in carrying out fieldwork are substantial: nuclear weapons scientists are very busy people who do not suffer fools gladly; because their work is top secret, most of their daily life is inaccessible to participant observation, traditionally the cultural anthropologist's principal research technique; and their work is not only virtually impossible to observe but also, for the person lacking several years training in physics, virtually impossible to understand.

Despite these obstacles, I chose to do an ethnographic study of a nuclear weapons laboratory for three reasons. First, I believe the American public debate on defense policy in general—and on nuclear weapons policy in particular—has been sorely in need of a cultural perspective. Discussions have hitherto been dominated by scientists, political scientists, and politicians, who construe defense policy questions as problems that, like those in mathematics, have one correct answer. I believe that policy problems are rarely like math problems, and my own interest is less in finding the one true answer to the conundrums of nuclear policy than in understanding how people become so profoundly convinced that their answer is the only one. It is my belief that if more people looked at defense policy in this light, our public discussions might be more generous and imaginative.

Second, I believe that it is important to invigorate and extend anthropology as a discipline by conducting ethnographic studies of institutions of power in the West and, in particular, by developing a cultural analysis of Western science. If the first wave of anthropologists in the early twentieth century documented the lifeways of "traditional" peoples whose cultures were rapidly disappearing and the second wave documented the effects of colonialism and the struggle for decolonization after World War II, the third wave must investigate the functioning of power and the flux of identities within an integrated global system at the end of the second millennium. We now live in a world where money, people, and ideas flow liberally across local and national boundaries and where our lives are profoundly affected by the practices of multinational corporations, scientific laboratories, and television studios. This does not mean that anthropologists should abandon their traditional objects of study; rather, it means they should extend them, by adding such people as bond traders, bureaucrats, biologists, migrant factory workers, tourists, airline attendants, and soap opera fans to the anthropological archive of shamans, traders, nomads, and peasants.

This study is part of an emergent genre in the anthropological literature of investigations of powerful institutions and of fundamental political conflicts in the West.[1] Traditionally, ethnographic studies in Western settings have been quite peripheral in anthropology: they have often been excluded from anthropology's list of its own classics; they have tended to focus on marginal, relatively powerless populations, such as ghetto dwellers, ethnic minorities, or hippies; and they have often been carried out somewhat casually in later life by anthropologists whose primary training and fieldwork were in entirely different culture areas. This is changing as traditional foreign fieldwork sites dry up, as the population of practicing anthropologists becomes more demographically diverse, and as anthropologists reflect critically on their historical fascination with the exotically primitive and the socially marginal. More anthropologists now accept the importance of subjecting Western institutions, particularly powerful ones that deeply affect the lives of millions of people, to sustained and rigorous anthropological scrutiny.

One powerful Western institution that is particularly understudied by anthropologists is science.[2] This is because scientists are a relatively inaccessible population in our society and because in Western thought science has tended to be construed as somehow outside culture, so that shamans, for example, seemed to embody cultural knowledge while scientists did not. But it is vitally important that ethnographic studies of science be undertaken, because of the material and political power that scientists now wield within Western society and because of the ideological power of scientific and scientistic discourses in Western society. Technology is omnipresent in our lives, literally from birth to death, and our understanding of ourselves and our world in the West is profoundly shaped by the tropes of science. It is important that we understand this understanding.

Finally, I undertook this study for quite personal reasons. I began following nuclear weapons issues closely in the early 1980s when, as a young man who had for some years feared that he would one day die in a nuclear war, I joined the antinuclear movement in the San Francisco Bay Area. It was at this time that I first met a weapons scientist from Lawrence Livermore National Laboratory, the nuclear weapons laboratory that is the subject of this book. I was invited to represent the San Francisco Nuclear Freeze Campaign in a debate with the scientist at a San Francisco high school. I soon became much less interested in winning the debate than in understanding what was obvious but, in my frame of mind at the time, startling to me: the man I was debating believed passionately that his work, far from being dangerous, was important and honorable. He was sick with a cold and the liberal San Francisco teenagers in the class were being unremittingly unkind, heckling him and even, at one point, accusing him of a perverse sexual attraction to weaponry. Still he earnestly attempted to explain why he believed it was important to develop new kinds of nuclear weapons. Although the teenagers were on "my side," I found myself wishing they would be quiet so I could hear what he had to say.[3] It was when I realized that I was more interested in understanding the scientist than in arguing with him that I knew my career as an activist was ending, and I began to feel the inexorable pull of the fieldwork I would eventually do. Three years later, in 1987, I moved to Livermore to commence field research among the weapons scientists.

ACKNOWLEDGMENTS

The practice of anthropology would be impossible but for the openness and generosity of the people we anthropologists study. Most of the nuclear weapons scientists and antinuclear activists I interviewed had as much to lose as to gain by talking to me, and I am enormously grateful to them for their willingness to take the risk. I hope that they will find in this book an unexpected but illuminating perspective on their lives. If it is, as it should be, an unfamiliar perspective, I trust it will be thought-provoking rather than thoughtlessly provocative. The appropriate style for cultural analysis lies somewhere between the bland and the offensive—a zone that is not always wide. Space does not permit me to thank all the people who helped me in the field individually, but some do deserve special mention. In particular, I would like to thank Jackie Cabasso, David Dearborn, Hugh DeWitt, Alex Forman, Art Hudgins, Sun-Wouk Kang, Marylia Kelley, Cynthia Nitta, Sue Olesen, Leslie Peeters, Tom Ramos, Dennis Raunig, Elizabeth Selle Jones, Lynn and Joan Seppala, September, Bob Several, Starhawk, David Solnit, Johana Thomson, and Bill Zagotta.

Several people have been kind enough to comment on various drafts of this book. Thanks go to my dissertation committee—Bart Bernstein, Mary Pratt, Renato Rosaldo, and Sylvia Yanagisako—for supervising the dissertation from which this book grew and for their skilled and compassionate guidance throughout my graduate student career. I also want to extend special thanks to Lynn Eden: in addition to providing voluminous written comments, she was kind enough to organize a special meeting in which a group of scholars and Livermore scientists went over the manuscript with me. I am also grateful to the following people for taking the time and trouble to comment on all or part of the manuscript: Steve Becker, Laura Benkov, Barbara Blumenthal, Jim Campbell, Paul Chilton, Elizabeth Cousens, Paul Craig, James Der Derian, Sid Drell, Leon Drummer, Michael Fischer, Steve Flank, Sybil Francis, John Futterman, Paul Gelles, Faye Ginsburg, Chris Gray, Lizbeth Gronlund, Jim Howe, Jean Jackson, Evelyn Fox Keller, Marylia Kelley, Ray Kidder, Jonathan Ladinsky, Michael MacCracken, John Mack, Sharon Marsh, Priscilla McMillan, Greg Mello, Laura Nader, Lisa Peattie, Leslie Peeters, Ted Postol, Tom Ramos, Mary Riseley, Ron Robertson, Seymour Sack, Charlotte Sheedy, Nina Tannenwald, Sharon Traweek, Celeste Wallander, Charlie Weiner, Bill Zagotta, and especially David Dearborn. Thanks also to the Harvard University dissertation writers group for their critical response to an early draft of chapter 5; to the Center for Psychological Studies in the Nuclear Age Academic Council and MIT Sloane School Organizational Studies Group for their comments on early presentations of chapter 6; to the SSRC-MacArthur fellows in Budapest and everyone at two presentations at the School of American Research in Santa Fe for their responses to a summary presentation of the entire manuscript; and to Western Massachusetts Psychotherapists for Social Responsibility for their responses to part of the argument in chapter 1.

Portions of chapter 3 appeared as chapter 9, "Becoming a Weapons Scientist," in George Marcus, ed., *Technoscientific Imaginaries: Conversations, Profiles, and Memoirs* (Chicago: University of Chicago Press, 1995).

Special thanks to Sheila Berg for her fine editing, to Elizabeth McClenahan for her superb help with tape transcription, to Charlotte Sheedy for her negotiating skills, to Stan Holwitz and the University of California Press for their extraordinary patience, and to Parth Domke and Kathleen Spinale for secretarial assistance. Thanks also to Andy Christenson for expert indexing.

For moral support as I worked on this project, I am grateful to Barbara Blumenthal, Margo Davis, Shirley Katz, Matthew Kohrman, Vladimir Matijasevic, Leslie Peeters, John Smolowe, and especially Allison Macfarlane.

Finally, this book would have been impossible without the financial and institutional support of the Center for Psychological Studies in the Nuclear Age and the Center for International Affairs at Harvard University, MIT's Center for International Studies, a Mellon New Directions Fellowship, an SSRC-MacArthur Fellowship in International Peace and Security, a MacArthur summer arms control grant at Stanford, and a Weatherhead postdoctoral fellowship at the School of American Research. I am grateful to the Dean's Fund at MIT for providing funds for indexing. My thanks also to Stanford University for many years of financial support and the best education I could ask for.

A NOTE ON NAMES

Anthropologists have traditionally worked in settings where the identity of individual interviewees was of little interest to the outside world. This, together with A. R. Radcliffe-Brown's famous opinion that individuals' names had no business in an ethnography, led to a convention of either burying individual identities in descriptions of abstract roles or—out of deference to the privacy of those whose lives had been intruded upon—the invention of pseudonyms. These conventions present unique problems in the context of my own fieldwork since the subjects of my study are both more urgently in need of anonymity and more legitimate objects of the naming gaze than the subjects of traditional ethnographies. Many of the people I interviewed offered confidences that could have compromised their relationships with friends, colleagues, and superiors or changed perceptions of them in the local community. The traditional ethnographic convention of referring to people by pseudonyms is vital in protecting their privacy, especially since this book may be read by people who know them personally. At the same time, many of the people I interviewed are, however modestly, public figures whose views and actions are a matter of public record—legitimately so since what they do or say has an impact on our lives. They are often named, quoted, and analyzed as individuals by journalists, policy analysts, and members of their community.

In this ethnography I have chosen to use a mixture of real names and pseudonyms. Some people appear under their real names while others appear only under pseudonyms. Others appear at one moment under their real name and later under a pseudonym. This is done, not to confuse the reader, but to maximize documentary verisimilitude and at the same time honor the privacy that properly lies at the heart of the ethnographic contract. If the information I am using about someone (say, a director of the Livermore laboratory) is a matter of public record (reported, say, in a newspaper), then I use his or her real name. If I acquired the information in the context of a formal interview or an informal conversation, then I use a pseudonym, unless I have specifically been given permission to use the person's real name. Throughout, real names include surnames while pseudonyms take the form of first names only.

Some of the characters have been not only renamed but also restructured. When I thought someone's identity, even with a false name, too obvious, I have taken the liberty of changing aspects of his or her identity. This means, for example, that a few female weapons scientists have been presented as male in circumstances where, owing to the male-female ratio in parts of the laboratory, identifying them as women would have been functionally equivalent to naming them as individuals. In instances where I cite them precisely in the context of their experience as women, I have tried to disguise them in other ways.

It has always seemed to me that inventing pseudonyms in exotic foreign languages is one of the most entertaining privileges of being an anthropologist. It dismays me that I have peopled an ethnography with "Johns" and "Janes." I trust that they will seem no less extraordinary for that.

CHAPTER I

Introduction

The bomb first was our weapon. Then it became our diplomacy. Next it became our economy. Now it's become our culture. We've become the people of the bomb.
E. L. DOCTOROW

NUCLEAR WEAPONS: A CULTURAL PERSPECTIVE

In a context in which policy makers, international relations experts, nuclear weapons scientists, and antinuclear activists have sought to persuade us that there is only one way to understand the world and that they knew what it is, the contribution of anthropology is to disturb comfortable understandings of the world by showing the simultaneous plausibility and arbitrariness of multiple ways of understanding and living in it. George Marcus and Michael Fischer (1986: 39), pleading for "anthropology as cultural critique," argue that the power of anthropology lies in its ability to jar understanding by "relativizing . . . taken-for-granted concepts" and making fleetingly visible the constructedness of our cultural worlds. As Renato Rosaldo (1989: 39) puts it, "If ideology often makes social facts appear natural, social analysis attempts to reverse the process. It dismantles the ideological in order to reveal the cultural." This is precisely my aim here: to take what has appeared to many to be common sense and reveal the cultural.[1]

My starting point for the development of a cultural analysis of the nuclear arms race is the presumption, which is as much a cliché in some anthropological circles as it is an affront to the worldview of many policy makers and political scientists, that reality is a social construction. I do not mean to suggest that presidents, missiles, and mushroom clouds are figments of our imagination. Clearly they are not. But groups of people have to share and communicate about entities in the world—whether these are physical entities such as nuclear missiles or abstract entities such as nuclear deterrence—through language and other mediating forms of representation, and in the process of representing the world, we construct it.

To take a simple example, there are many ways to see a missile: it can be a Peacekeeper or an MX, a token of security or of vulnerability, a technical diagram or an image in a nightmare, a small pointy dot seen from above or a massive metallic phallus seen from the side, a number in a chart or a reason for not having children. It is possible to represent anything in the world, from a missile to the notion of peace, in a number of different ways. Our often unthinking representations of the world are partial constructions of it. These partial constructions are not only produced by us; they also, as social entities that precede us, produce us as people.[2]

Take the example of risk. In *Risk and Culture*, Mary Douglas and Aaron Wildavsky ask, "Can we know the risks we face, now or in the future?" Their answer: "No, we cannot; but yes, we must act as if we do" (1982: 1). According to Douglas and Wildavsky, although we know from experience that some things are dangerous, it is in the contingent nature of life that we cannot predict all the risks we face, and, despite the brave attempts of some mathematicians, it is hard to rank and compare different kinds of risks. When we do feel confident in our fears, this is not so much a sign that we have correctly divined the ontology of the world as it is a reflection of our embeddedness in particular social relationships of power, solidarity, and meaning. Whether we are antinuclear activists afraid of a nuclear holocaust, environmentalists afraid of the greenhouse effect, or conservative Republicans afraid of the decay of moral values at home, our perceptions of risk are always cognitively selective, always socially mediated, and always inextricably entangled with social relationships and with ideological systems of representation that shape our understanding of the world. Perceptions of risk, however much they present themselves as objective or unquestionable, are inherently social.

What is true of risk in general is particularly true of risk in regard to nuclear weapons. Not only do we not have any definitive, scientific way to compare the risks nuclear weapons create and the risks they alleviate—of knowing finally whether to see nuclear weapons as objects that protect us from the risk of conventional war or rather as themselves the risk from which we need to be protected—but also the very logic of nuclear deterrence is inherently, profoundly paradoxical and self-contradictory since it is the essence of deterrence to prevent disaster by threatening it.[3] In the ironic words of General Wilmer, a character in Arthur Kopit's play *End of the World with Symposium to Follow* (1984), "In order to *prevent* a nuclear war, you have to be able to *fight* a nuclear war at *all levels*, even though they're probably unwinnable and unfightable." Nuclear deterrence is premised on a paradoxical—to its opponents, Orwellian—logic whereby resolve and credibility are communicated by threats that, since they are almost certainly suicidal, are incredible. Nuclear deterrence creates a situation in which it may be rational to act a little crazy and crazy to be too rational. It can quite plausibly be argued—and equally plausibly disputed—that every technical innovation and change in strategic doctrine that makes it more feasible to fight a nuclear war thereby makes a nuclear war less likely. Michael May, a former director of the Livermore laboratory, caught this fundamental irony in the logic of nuclear deterrence in his assessment of the stabilizing and destabilizing effects of nuclear testing.

> The changes in nuclear weapons and the nuclear tests that made submarine-launched nuclear missiles possible extended the arms race, but made deterrent forces far more survivable against attack. The changes and tests that made MIRVs[4] possible made first strikes against fixed ICBMs[5] more effective, but they also made ABM[6] systems less effective and helped pave the way for the ABM Treaty of 1972. The changes and the nuclear tests that might make strategic defenses possible could be used to help deterrence, but they could also be used to help an aggressor. A tested, reliable stockpile can serve both deterrer and first-striker. (May 1986: 98)

As Debra Rosenthal (1990: 229) has written, "logic reaches a dead end with mutual assured destruction."

A number of postmodern theorists have written in recent years about the impossibility of achieving, as they put it, "totalizing discourses." These are accounts of the world that are undeniably true for all people-political narratives and ideological systems that can compose the contradictory heterogeneity of the world and of language itself without being internally inconsistent and vulnerable to deconstruction.[7] For postmodernists, this shows the impossibility of the Enlightenment project of redemption through rationality. We might say that the situation created by nuclear weapons, in which logic has been left impaled on itself, represents a particularly piquant crisis of modernity, a hyper-postmodern situation in which the terror of the weapons lies not only in the damage they can do to millions of human bodies but in the violence they have already inflicted on our sense of logic, rationality, and progress. They have brought into being a situation from which, apparently, no game theorist or scientist can satisfactorily rescue civilization.

In this tormented situation we have not so much a problem with a solution as a predicament. The nuclearist and antinuclear worldviews are both plausible constructions of the world that are unable to defeat one another. Neither can, in Jean-François Lyotard's (1984) terminology, transform itself from a mere local narrative into a global metanarrative—an account of the world that is compellingly true for all people. In this book I ask how, given this situation, people have arrived at different but deeply held convictions about nuclear weapons. How did some people come to believe, so completely that the fears and doubts of others genuinely puzzled them, that the development of nuclear weapons made both superpowers more secure? And how did others come to believe, so profoundly that they sometimes even accused those who disagreed with them of being mad, that the stockpiling of nuclear weapons by the superpowers was a terrifying act of lunacy?

This is the same question that Douglas and Wildavsky ask: How is it that particular social constructions of risk acquire compelling ideological and emotional force in people's lives? In answering this question, Douglas and Wildavsky focus on the issue of recruitment: Why are people from particular kinds of social settings drawn toward certain ideologies of risk? This is an important issue, and in later chapters I ask why members of certain religious denominations are likely to support or oppose the continued development of nuclear weapons, and why many women and members of the humanistic middle class have been attracted by the antinuclear movement. However, I believe that Douglas and Wildavsky err in focusing so heavily on recruitment and that we must look not only at the ways institutions recruit people but also at the ways they socialize them (Downey 1986). We cannot fully understand the hold on the heart of ideologies of risk without looking at the practices[8] through which people are culturally re-produced by institutions and social movements so that they find particular ideologies meaningful. In this book I examine how weapons scientists are socialized by means of such practices as being interviewed for a job, learning the language of nuclear weapons science, being investigated for a security clearance, going to church, participating in nuclear tests, reading laboratory publications, and telling jokes. In explaining how people become antinuclear activists and how their convictions deepen over time, I emphasize the importance of learning the language of fear and emotion, of being exposed to certain kinds of films, writings, and presentations, and of participating in demonstrations and, in some cases, civil disobedience.

It is my contention that an understanding of such practices is vital to the analysis of politics and power. Traditional forms of social and political analysis, which are mostly structuralist in derivation, tend to analyze political power in terms of institutions rather than practices. Looking at the structural relationships between institutions and individuals within institutions, they ask who is structurally located so as to have access to the levers of power. Thus many sociologists and political scientists have asked me why, if I was interested in understanding the arms race, I chose to study a nuclear weapons laboratory rather than, say, the Senate Armed Services Committee or senior officers at the Pentagon—groups of people who, as they see it, have had more power over nuclear weapons policy. Within the framework of the institutional analysis of politics, one possible response is that it is important to study Lawrence Livermore National Laboratory because it, along with the other American weapons laboratory, Los Alamos, is so positioned within the structural processes of the American defense establishment that its scientists and administrators are the ones who have *really* driven the arms race by lobbying for new weapons and using their influence to block certain arms control treaties—and indeed this has been argued quite plausibly, if also sometimes a little simplistically, by some (DeWitt 1986; McLean 1986: 37–41; Miall 1987: 11–28; Zuckerman 1983: 109–125).

Although it is irrefutable, in my view, that the Livermore laboratory has influenced American government decisions to procure new weapons, the arms race has been a complex process that cannot be reduced to a few key sites of origin or impetus. I have chosen to study the Livermore laboratory not so much because of its position, central or otherwise, as an institution in the national pyramid of power but because of the importance of looking at the production and contestation of power, knowledge, and belief at the local level in order to understand national and global political processes. This is because, to prosper, institutions do not just need material resources and structurally assured leverage over decision-making actors. They also need legitimacy. Thus to understand the vigor, until recently at least, of the arms race, we must understand not only those central institutions and actors dominant in our society—presidents, political action committees, Senate committees, and defense contractors, for example—but also the importance of discourses and practices that permeate all corners of society and whose power may lie in their dispersed and routine ordinariness (Foucault 1980*b*).

My main focus in this book is on the ways "regimes of truth," as the French political philosopher Michel Foucault calls them, are produced. This is not to say that government politics are unimportant, and I do pay attention in the account that follows to the evolution of government policy, the relationship of the laboratory to its local and national political environment, and the overarching context of U.S.–Soviet relations. However, I am more interested in the production of ideology than in the production of policy per se, and so I look at nuclear policy through the lens of a cultural analysis that investigates social power by following Clifford Geertz's (1983: 69) admonition to practice a "continual dialectical tacking between the most local of local details and the most global of global structure in such a way as to bring them into simultaneous view."

My thinking about the cultural politics of nuclear weapons policy has taken shape in reaction to two other schools of thought: that of a group of political scientists and policy makers who have immodestly called themselves "realists" or "neorealists" and that of a group of psychologists who have depicted American nuclear weapons policy as a form of psychopathology. I find myself in substantial disagreement with both. To give some sense of the intellectual landscape within which this study is located and to sharpen the distinctiveness of my own approach, I give below a brief sketch of these perspectives, emphasizing areas of divergence from my own.

THE "REALIST" PERSPECTIVE

In the 1980s, as détente collapsed, discussions of defense policy in government, think tank, and university circles were largely dominated by international relations theorists known as "neorealists" and by nuclear weapons experts who were sometimes called "realists." Although neorealism and nuclear realism are by no means the same thing, their proponents share to some degree an underlying worldview. Hence, in my deliberately schematic discussion here, I lump both groups together for heuristic purposes under the umbrella term "realism." The realist worldview has been articulated by a number of thinkers, but my account here draws strongly on Kenneth Waltz's *Theory of International Politics* (1979)—the locus classicus of neorealist thinking among international relations theorists—and on the various writings on nuclear weapons by members or associates of the Harvard Nuclear Study Group.[9]

There are four main components to what I am calling the realist point of view. First, realists assume that the international system is characterized by a "state of nature" or anarchy. Within the nation-state the disciplinary power of government prevents the strong from picking on the weak and keeps relationships orderly and relatively free from violent strife, but this is not the case in interstate relations. Here there is no international government to regulate and discipline the relations between states so that, in Waltz's (1979: 102) words, "the state among states . . . conducts its affairs in the brooding shadow of violence. . . . Among states, the state of nature is a state of war."

Second, since the international system is anarchic, realists assume that states must rely on self-help measures for their security. "States have to do whatever they think necessary for their own preservation, since no one can be relied on to do it for them. . . . Self-help is necessarily the principle of action in an anarchic order" (ibid., 109, 111). This means that states must rely for their security on military force and on alliances with other states against potential predator states. Some realists have argued that bipolar international systems, such as the one that arose during the cold war, are the most likely to assure peace—or, to use a word preferred by security specialists, stability.[10] Others have maintained that multipolar systems, such as the one that existed in nineteenth-century Europe, are more stable.[11]

Third, nuclear realists see nuclear weapons as the ultimate form of self-help. States that are able to threaten potential aggressors with nuclear retaliation greatly increase the costs of aggression against themselves and, hence, become more secure. If, as in the case of the two superpowers through the last two decades of the cold war, the nuclear arsenals of opposed states are balanced by one another so that neither dares attack the other, nuclear weapons can have a stabilizing effect on international relations. Within the framework of realist thinking, nuclear weapons, although they are indisputably dangerous, are not so much the problem as the (at least temporary) solution. The real problem is the anarchic international system with its tendency to generate conventional wars.

Finally, realists have tended to presume that relatively little can be done to transform the fundamentally anarchic nature of the international system, at least in the near term—and it is the near term that largely preoccupies realists (Holt 1986). Realists may hope that the international system can gradually be transformed into a more cooperatively structured whole over the long term, but they tend to focus on what they see as the inescapable necessity of military self-help in the short term. Thus, in the words of Stanley Hoffmann (1986: 5), realists' support for the nuclear state "comes from their conviction that the very nature of international reality rules it [disarmament] out. . . . They see the contest between Washington and Moscow . . . [and] they believe that it . . . cannot be transcended . . . because it is the very essence of international politics that the two biggest actors must be rivals, that the growth of the power of one must cause fear in the other."

Consequently, unlike many in the antinuclear camp, realists have not expected too much from arms control treaties besides some agreements that help contain the costs of maintaining the nuclear arsenals and some measures that enhance crisis stability while diminishing the likelihood of accidental nuclear war.[12] Realists on the whole distrust appeals for disarmament. The Harvard Nuclear Study Group (1983: 255), for example, criticizes what it calls "atomic escapism," saying that "living with nuclear weapons is our only hope. . . . This challenge will be both demanding and unending."

The strengths of the realist perspective consist in its realization that nations together form a system with its own structural logic, in its ability to provide plausible explanations for many recent wars, and in its sensitivity to the dangers of disarmament. However, within the community of international relations theorists and defense specialists itself, recent years have seen the tentative emergence of a critique of the realist paradigm. This critique has focused in particular on the realists' presumption of anarchy in the international system and on their assumption that domestic politics is largely irrelevant in the analysis of international security issues. This book is in part intended to push that critique further.

Among international relations theorists, for example, some have begun to argue that the international system is not so completely anarchic as has been claimed. They suggest that the war of all against all in the international system is partly moderated by the existence of fragile incipient regimes of cooperation, particularly in regard to trade. These regimes consist, in Stephen Krasner's (1983a: 2) words, of "implicit or explicit principles, norms, rules, and decision-making procedures around which actors' expectations converge in a given area of international relations."[13] Rephrasing this more anthropologically, we might say that, against the putative "state of nature" in the international sphere, an international society is in the process of being created with its own transnational culture—a shared set of norms and meanings that facilitate and constrain interactions across national boundaries.

A number of writers have also broken with the realists' assumption that national and international political systems are disarticulated from one another and that state behavior in the international system tends to be constrained by the structure of the state system itself much more than it is determined by the internal structure of individual states. Within political science circles, this argument has largely been phrased in terms of the importance of intrastate bureaucratic rivalries.[14] Neo-Marxists, looking at the situation more in terms of dominant classes and interests, have drawn attention to the importance in decisions to design and build new weapons of what is popularly, if somewhat nebulously, known as the "military-industrial complex."[15] Feminist writers have suggested that the three levels of political practice in neorealist thinking (international, national, and individual) are integrated by the masculine identity of the men who dominate at each level. They argue that to understand the international behavior of states and statesmen, we should look as much at the gender system within and across states as at the structure of the international system.[16] Finally, poststructuralists have argued that war, balances of power, and nuclear deterrence are not forced responses to anarchy but elaborate social institutions produced by an international system that has evolved over many centuries and is sustained by complex, powerful, and deeply rooted discourses and practices. Where the realists claim to simply describe the world as it is, the poststructuralists accuse them of using the language of positivism to reify it and to legitimate the prevailing order.[17]

In this book, in line with these heterogeneous critiques of realism, I take it as axiomatic that the international security system is a cultural phenomenon and that national and international politics are deeply articulated with one another. I suggest, for example, that struggles within American society over class and gender relations produced movements that contested American nuclear weapons policy and, arguably, helped draw down the cold war, and I show how international relations can be profoundly interconnected with, for example, domestic marital relationships, church politics, and local real estate markets—all phenomena that lie far beyond the territory that interests most international relations scholars. My presumption is that, to paraphrase Tip O'Neill, international politics is, in part at least, local politics and that it is also cultural politics. Many realists, drawing on Hobbes and Machiavelli, sometimes speak of "power politics" as if there were some domain where the exercise of power exists in a pure form disconnected from ideas, norms, and ideologies. Power is, however, inextricably enmeshed with ideology: power is always sustained and constrained by it; power constantly generates and regenerates it; and the exercise of power is always interpreted and predicted in terms of it.

Such an approach will no doubt mark me out as, in some sense of that problematic term, a postmodernist. Realists have recently complained, not entirely without reason, that the postmodern critique of realism has taken the form of abstract argumentation about philosophy and social theory rather than empirical case studies. Stephen Walt (1991: 223), for example, complains that "post-modern approaches have yet to demonstrate much value for comprehending world politics. . . . [I]ssues of war and peace are too important to be diverted into a prolix and self-indulgent discourse that is divorced from the real world." What, the realists have asked in exasperation, would an empirical postmodernist case study of international relations look like? This book is intended, in part, as an answer to their question.

THE PSYCHOLOGICAL PERSPECTIVE

In the 1980s, within the American antinuclear community, folk and academic versions of a psychological critique of the arms race became highly influential. This critique was particularly identified with the writings of the humanistic psychologist Robert Jay Lifton. In its own way, it is as problematic as the realist perspective.

The psychological critique consists of three main claims. First, Lifton and the antinuclear psychologists have construed the nuclear relationship between the superpowers in terms of psychopathology. Where the realists saw nuclear weapons as potential instruments of stability and security, the psychologists saw them as manifestations of dementia. Lifton (1982*a:* ix–x, 18), for example, tells us that the arms race is "an objective social madness," a "disease," and "something on the order of a psychotic fantasy." Another leading antinuclear psychologist, John Mack (1985: 292), says that "the nuclear arms competition fulfills the conditions of a severe collective psychiatric disorder in a formal, literal, or scientific sense" and "is quite literally psychotic." Joel Kovel (1983: 84) calls the arms race "paranoid madness," and Robert R. Holt (1984: 212) calls it "certifiably pathological."

Second, antinuclear psychologists have argued that those who design nuclear weapons, or devise strategies that might involve their use, could not carry out such potentially genocidal work unless they were in a state of numbness or denial. Lifton repeatedly makes an analogy between working in a nuclear weapons laboratory and working in a Nazi death camp.[18] Accusing weapons professionals of psychodynamic rigidity, he has also claimed to find among them a "fundamentalist" mode of thinking involving unquestioning faith in the protective power of nuclear weapons (Lifton 1982*a*, 1982*b*, 1983; Lifton and Markusen 1990).[19]

Third, Lifton and others have argued that the nuclear arms race is based on a distorted psychology of enmity—a stark demonization of "the Other," polarizing the world between the American "we" who are good and the Soviet "they" who are evil. They argue that we have enemies at least partly because we need and create them. In this view, the psychology of enmity draws its energy from "disavowed elements of the self" (Stein 1985: 257) and from unresolved childhood conflicts and fears that unscrupulous national leaders are able to tap into and manipulate.[20]

The psychological critique of the arms race is important. It reminds us that nuclear weapons are dangerous and potentially genocidal. It warns us that people can become numb in response to the overwhelming destructive force and apparent immovability of such weapons. And it tells us that we must pay attention to emotions and the unconscious mind as well as the rational calculations of the conscious mind when we discuss nuclear policy. In this context, however, I want to concentrate on gaps and problems in the psychologists' arguments.[21]

To begin with, they often fail to take seriously what is important in the realist view of the world, namely, that, as Stanley Hoffmann (1986: 9) puts it, "enemies are not mere projections of negative identities; they are often quite real." Given the way the world is currently organized, states do indeed have enemies and are sometimes attacked by them if they are weak. The psychologists are often so eager to find the pathology in the arms race that they do not take seriously enough nuclear professionals' own rationales for their positions. For example, in his book *Minds at War*, Steven Kull, one of the more influential antinuclear psychologists, criticizes strategists' scenarios for winnable nuclear wars as unrealistic and maladaptive— and therefore hunts down unconscious motives for them—without seriously addressing their rationale: they know nuclear wars should not be fought but must still somehow communicate to potential enemies the credibility and resolve that, they believe, deter aggression. Whether or not one agrees with the strategists' solution, it is important to take account of the problem the strategists see themselves as trying to solve.[22]

The psychological critique of the arms race also tends to confound psychological and social processes. Although some psychologists embroider their analyses with caveats that individual and collective processes are different, the incessant discussion of international relations in terms of individual pathology and the frequent comparisons of national politics and personal psychology encourage the reduction of national and international politics to individual psychology. However, the individual and the national are not only, as the jargon of political science would phrase it, different "levels of analysis"; they also involve different processes requiring different *kinds* of analysis. Understanding the psychology of Edward Teller, the "father of the hydrogen bomb," may illuminate the arms race, but it does not explain it.[23] Although institutional processes are enmeshed with individual psychological processes, neither kind of process can be reduced to the other, and societies cannot be analyzed as if they were giant personalities. In this book, proceeding more in the spirit of Emile Durkheim than of Sigmund Freud, I show how institutions and processes of cultural production act on individuals to produce certain normative structures of feeling while at the same time I try to respect the partial autonomy of individual psychological processes.[24]

Finally, the psychological critique, just like the realist position it attacks, uses the rhetoric of positivist science to contract the space for political debate. If the realists invoke notions of the "realistic" and the "natural" to reduce our sense of the possible in international relations and to bolster their own expert authority, the psychologists achieve the same effect by labeling certain policies pathological. The rhetoric of psychopathology, although it is a useful weapon in the armory of critique, becomes a way of closing off debate and silencing opponents, who can then be accused of being "in denial" if they fight back. In this book, viewing the nuclear debate through the lens of relativism rather than psychopathology, I present the recent struggle over nuclear weapons policy in America as a struggle between different cultural values and political orders rather than in terms of a choice between sanity and insanity. Instead of presuming an Archimedean point from which people can be declared to be "in denial," "paranoid," and "psychotic"—labels that can, in any case, without too much effort of the imagination, be thrown back at the labelers—it is my presumption that such diagnoses are themselves stratagems of power and that a more self-aware approach might eschew normative labeling while exploring how different psychological states are made real for different people. If there is critique here, it takes the form of what Marcus and Fischer (1986) call cultural critique—the deconstruction of ideology— rather than psychiatric labeling.

CULTURAL CRITIQUE AND ETHNOGRAPHIC AUTHORITY

Since this is an exercise in "cultural critique," I want to end this introductory chapter with a brief note bearing on the nature of cultural critique itself and on the question of ethnographic authority. I attempt to demonstrate here that the cultural worlds inhabited by nuclear weapons scientists and antinuclear activists are constructed and how this is so. It goes without saying, of course, that my own interpretation of their constructions is itself a construction. This does not mean that it is a fabrication: my argument is based on carefully researched facts subjected to the standard rules of logic and evidence. These facts are, however, interpreted from a point of view, filtered through my own preoccupations and theoretical presumptions. There is knowledge here, but it is what Donna Haraway (1991: 183–202) calls "situated knowledge," shaped not only by the nature of the situation I studied but also by my own positional relationship with that situation. A different anthropologist, no more or less competent than me, would doubtless have asked different questions, would have been struck by different facts, and, filtering them through a different theoretical framework perhaps, would have written a different book. If the people anthropologists study can construct the world in different ways, it should not surprise us that anthropologists can also.

One problem for the anthropologist studying his or her own society is, in Emily Martin's (1987: 11) words, "how solidly entrenched our own cultural presuppositions are and how difficult it is to dig them up for inspection." If the ethnographer of foreign cultures has the problem of making the strange familiar, the ethnographer's problem at home is how to make the familiar strange. Here I have tried to use the juxtaposition of two radically opposed groups within American society, showing how each looks from the estranged vantage point of the other, as a means of creating the relativizing effect that comes more easily in ethnographies of faraway peoples (see Clifford 1981).

That I have tried to make sense of the struggle between weapons scientists and antinuclear activists as one who was once an active partisan of one side in the struggle surely affects the interpretation offered here. It helps me to see some things just as, doubtless, it obstructs me from seeing others so clearly. Yet the reader might be surprised at what I had difficulty understanding. As one whose former activism was confined to that electorally oriented corner of the antinuclear movement known as the Nuclear Freeze Campaign, I found the attitudes and beliefs of many antinuclear activists, particularly those in the anarchist, religious, and New Age parts of the movement, just as unfamiliar as the attitudes and beliefs of the weapons scientists, and I often had to work just as hard to make sense of them. The study is informed by this attempt, which is the basis of ethnography, to simultaneously achieve empathy with and distance from the diverse people I set out to understand. If I have succeeded, I expect it to disturb the conventional wisdom of activists as well as weapons scientists.

CHAPTER 2

Beginnings

I was once asked by a group of protestors, "How can we make an impact in Livermore?" And my response was, "Come live among us. Pitch your tent in our midst and live with us. Mourn with us. Celebrate. And then tell us what you think. You listen to what we've said, and then we'll listen to you."

THE REVEREND BILL NEBO,
LIVERMORE PRESBYTERIAN CHURCH

AN ANTHROPOLOGIST ARRIVES

I moved to Livermore on November 27, 1987. That night a bomb was planted, and exploded, beneath a car parked at the weapons laboratory.[1] It seemed like an inauspicious start to fieldwork.

Livermore is a small, unprepossessing town roughly forty miles east of San Francisco (fig. 1).[2] It is the kind of town at which few people stop unless they need gas. Until the 1970s, it was not even served by a freeway. Livermore's logo consists of a bunch of grapes, an atom, and a cowboy on a bucking bronco superimposed on one another (fig. 2). Until the weapons laboratory was established in 1952, the town largely relied for its livelihood on horse ranches and vineyards—especially the Wente and Concannon vineyards. Today the vineyards are prospering as much as ever, despite rumors that their wine contains high levels of radioactive tritium, and the wineries are still important players in local politics. There are also still horse ranches on the grassy fringes of town, though a number of ranchers have sold their land to developers eager to raise up condominiums, industrial parks, and shopping malls. But even if the cowboy economy is in decline, a commercialized cowboy culture lives on in local country and western saloons and the ever-popular annual Livermore rodeo.

By the time I arrived in Livermore in 1987, its population had grown to about 56,000,[3] but Livermore and the neighboring towns of the Livermore Valley were still insulated from the urban sprawl around San Francisco by a huge swath of undeveloped land, and Livermore itself was widely

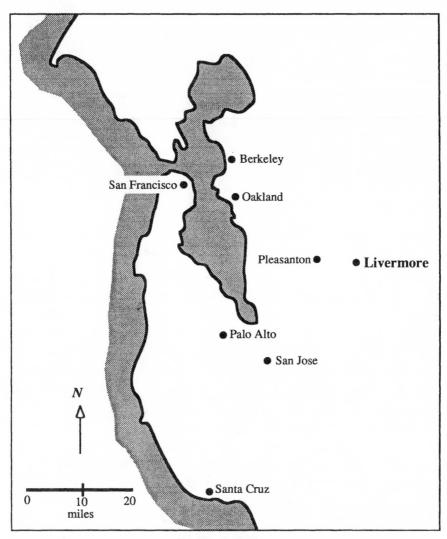

Figure 1. The location of Livermore in the San Francisco Bay Area. (Map created by Allison Macfarlane)

regarded as a remote cultural backwater in the San Francisco Bay Area. The *New York Times* science writer William Broad (1985: 23) describes Livermore as "the sort of place that might wear thin after a few weeks." In the late 1980s it was a town without first-run movie theaters, dance clubs, exercise clubs, department stores, gourmet restaurants, bookstore-cafés, or any of the other hallmarks of yuppie metropolitan life. For

Figure 2. The logo of Livermore, California. (Courtesy City of Livermore)

recreation its citizens either went elsewhere or to the bowling alley, the pizza or ice-cream parlors, one of the local Chinese restaurants, the country and western bars, or the $2.50 movie theater on First Street. Yet if Livermore was not a good place to be young and single (as I was), it was a good place to raise a family: it had many parks and churches, a low crime rate, a very good school system, and an excellent library for a town of its size. It also had the second-highest proportion of Ph.D.'s per capita of any community in the country. (The community with the highest is New Mexico's Los Alamos, home to America's first nuclear weapons laboratory [Bartimus and McCartney 1991: 109].) The Ph.D.'s were sometimes referred to by some of the town's other residents, with a mixture of disdain and affection, as "propeller-heads."[4]

On the eastern edge of Livermore, just beyond the new tract homes and the vineyards that look so beautiful in the late afternoon light, is Lawrence Livermore National Laboratory (fig. 3), where half of America's nuclear weapons were designed during the 1980s. Across the street lies the smaller Sandia National Laboratory, which provides engineering support for nuclear weapons design.[5] About fifteen miles farther east is Site 300, where Livermore scientists test high explosives.

Although a number of high-tech companies (including Intel, Hexcel, and Triad) have recently moved to Livermore, nuclear weapons are still the biggest business in town.[6] As one writer put it, "Livermore is a company town. The local economy and, more importantly, the social and political character of the city is shaped by the lab. The biggest questions

Figure 3. An aerial view of Lawrence Livermore National Laboratory. (Photo courtesy Lawrence Livermore National Laboratory)

facing the world today wrap themselves in and around daily life in Livermore like a ball of snakes" (Tompkins 1990). The Livermore laboratory is estimated to infuse $450 million in wages alone into the local economy each year. Laboratory employees dominate the boards of local schools and churches and, even as late as 1990, two out of five Livermore city councillors were laboratory employees and another was married to one (Albro 1990*a*, 1990*b*).

About half of the laboratory's employees live in the Livermore Valley. Of the rest, many technicians live farther east in Tracy and Stockton, where housing is cheaper. Most of the scientists who do not live in Livermore itself live in more upscale towns such as Pleasanton and Danville to the west.[7] A few live farther west still in the livelier environment close to the university at Berkeley and commute to the laboratory by car.

People in neighboring towns know, for the most part, that the laboratory works on nuclear weapons—they sometimes joke, for example, that people from Livermore glow in the dark—but they often have only a vague understanding of the specifics. In 1989 a reporter for a local newspaper stopped people on the street in Dublin, about ten miles from Livermore, to ask, "Do you know what they do at Lawrence Livermore National Laboratory?" One teenage student said no. Another said, "No, but I've heard a lot about radioactive waste in the water out there." A bank teller said, "I know they work on nuclear stuff because people have to wear badges." A department manager said, "They work on defense programs and do something with colliders." (The laboratory has no colliders.) A realtor said, "They do a lot of research on nuclear energy and research on Star Wars and build the bombs." (Livermore designs, but does not build, bombs.) Finally, a banker said, "They research the Star Wars defense. Only thing else I think they do is explore wind power" (*Tri-Valley Herald* 1989). (Livermore does no research on wind power, though there is a clump of windmills, which has nothing to do with the laboratory, on the nearby Altamont Pass.)

I lived in the town of Livermore for over two years. I first moved to one of the less salubrious parts of town close to the freeway, where I shared a house with a supermarket cashier and a technician in one of the laboratory's laser programs. Both were in their early twenties and, like most people in Livermore, white. The technician was a man and the cashier a woman. At the beginning of my second year in Livermore, I moved into an almost new tract home in a development popular with laboratory employees because it was only a few blocks from work. I shared the house with its owner, a computer programmer at the laboratory, and a young technician contracted by AT&T to the laboratory to help install their new multimillion-dollar telephone system. Both were, like me, white men. Finally, after nine months away from Livermore, I returned for the summer of 1990 and shared a house on the rural outskirts of town with a married couple. The husband, an engineer well respected in his field, worked on a number of projects at the laboratory, and his wife was an important figure in Livermore politics and business.

Anthropologists often like to stress the heroic privations they endured during fieldwork. Somewhat to my surprise, given my history of living in university communities and my background in the antinuclear movement, I found that I liked my housemates and enjoyed living in Livermore. I grew to appreciate the idiosyncratic intelligence and the straightforward small-town friendliness I found in Livermore's people, including many of its Ph.D.'s, and I came to love the play of light on the vineyards and the green-in-winter, parched-brown-in-summer hilly beauty of the country-side. Livermore is a town that was good to me, and I was sad to leave.

A LABORATORY IS BORN

Lawrence Livermore National Laboratory dates back to 1952. Until then all American nuclear weapons were designed at Los Alamos National Laboratory, high in the remote mountains of New Mexico. It was at Los Alamos during the Second World War that Robert Oppenheimer had brought together some of the most brilliant physicists of his day—Niels Bohr, Hans Bethe, Edward Teller, Richard Feynman, Victor Weisskopf, and others—to penetrate the secrets of the atom. Driven at first by fear of a German atomic bomb[8] and then by the sheer momentum of their research, the scientists of Los Alamos finally succeeded in testing the world's first atomic bomb at Alamogordo in the New Mexico desert just before dawn on July 16, 1945. The bomb had an explosive force equivalent to 18,600 tons of high explosive. Not long after, on August 6 and August 9, 1945, the United States dropped atomic bombs on Hiroshima and Nagasaki, largely obliterating both cities. The Japanese surrendered before a third atomic bomb could be dropped.[9]

At the end of the Second World War it was unclear what would become of America's fledgling nuclear weapons program, and differences of opinion had already begun to appear among its scientists. Leo Szilard—the Hungarian émigré who had first conceived the bomb and persuaded Albert Einstein to lobby President Franklin Roosevelt for an atomic bomb program—had gathered signatures on a petition to the president in 1945 aiming to avert the bombing of Hiroshima and Nagasaki. After the war, Szilard, Einstein, and others organized a short-lived scientists' movement warning of the perils of a nuclear arms race and advocating the international control of atomic energy (Lanouette 1992; Smith 1965).

Szilard and the arms controllers in the scientific community lost their battle to prevent an international arms race. As the cold war crystallized around crises in Berlin, Greece, and Czechoslovakia, and after the Soviets rejected the 1947 Baruch Plan to put nuclear weapons under international control, the Los Alamos laboratory continued its nuclear weapons work. After the Soviets stunned Americans by detonating their own atomic bomb in 1949, the Truman administration decided to mount a crash program to develop the hydrogen bomb. Together with the outbreak of the Korean War in 1950, the decision to pursue the H-bomb, opposed by Oppenheimer and a number of other leading physicists, signaled the eclipse of the arms controllers in American politics and the defeat of their vision of physics itself. The decision to build the hydrogen bomb was, in retrospect, an important milestone in the postwar militarization of American physics. It was soon followed by the establishment of a second weapons laboratory.[10]

The most visible pressure for a second laboratory came from Edward Teller, the charismatic Hungarian émigré physicist, staunch anti-Communist, and ardent advocate of continued weapons work who has been widely rumored to be the inspiration for Stanley Kubrick's Dr. Strangelove character (fig. 4).[11] In his book *Teller's War*, Broad (1992: 20) has called Teller "a major architect of the Cold War. With great skill and seemingly boundless energy, he did more than any other scientist, perhaps any other individual, to keep its structure intact and evolving."

By 1951, Teller felt that Los Alamos had not worked vigorously enough on the hydrogen bomb that he had been proposing since the earliest days of the Manhattan Project, and he was personally on increasingly bad terms with the director of Los Alamos, Norris Bradbury (York 1987: 63–64; Teller 1962: 54). Teller began to lobby vigorously for a second weapons laboratory and recruited some important allies, including Sen. Brien McMahon, Chair of the Joint Committee on Atomic Energy, and a number of senior air force officials. The debate within the government on the merits of a second laboratory shifted decisively in Teller's favor when the physicist Ernest O. Lawrence, a veteran of the original atomic bomb project who taught at the University of California, Berkeley, offered in early 1952 to establish a second laboratory as an adjunct to Berkeley's existing radiation laboratory (fig. 5). By offering to run the new laboratory as an extension of his own, thereby promising not to drain scientists away

Figure 4. Edward Teller in 1990. (Photo by Meridel Rubenstein, copyright 1990)

from Los Alamos, he made its establishment relatively easy and cheap, greatly increasing its attractiveness to the Washington bureaucracy. Lawrence suggested that the new laboratory should be sited at a former naval air base close to Berkeley where he had already built an accelerator. The naval air base was in a place called Livermore, "then a quintessential California cow town of 4,364 people" (De Wolk 1989). In September 1952, the new laboratory was established there. It was, like Los Alamos, under the oversight of the University of California.

Although Lawrence Livermore National Laboratory is often described as Teller's laboratory, in these early years it belonged to the physicist whose name it still bears: E. O. Lawrence. Teller had envisioned a laboratory modeled after Los Alamos during World War II which would enjoy generous resources and employ some of the leading scientists in the country in a crash program to develop hydrogen bombs. Lawrence, by contrast, envisioned a smaller number of bright but relatively unknown young scientists working with a loosely defined mission in a modest pro-

Figure 5. Ernest O. Lawrence. (Photo courtesy Lawrence Livermore National Laboratory)

gram that would gradually grow. It was Lawrence's conception of the laboratory that was implemented, and at one point in 1952, Teller withdrew completely when he saw that the Atomic Energy Commission (AEC) charter for the new laboratory did not even include work on the hydrogen bomb. The charter was changed, and Teller came back on board.

In these early years Lawrence oversaw the laboratory from a benign distance, working through the man he put in charge, Herbert York. (For the first year and a half, York was not actually called "Director." In fact, he had no formal title at all. He was simply known to have been selected by Lawrence to be in charge. [York 1987: 74–75].) Teller was made a member-at-large of the steering committee and, in recognition of his stature, was given power to veto any management decision—a power that, to the best of York's recollection, he never used. Meanwhile, the laboratory was largely run by a group of scientists from Berkeley whose average age was 30: for example, York, the director, was 31; Harold Brown, who ran the thermonuclear design division, was 24; John Foster, in charge of fission weapon design, was 29 (York 1975*b:* 12–13, 1987: 67–72).[12]

Geoffrey Sea (1992: 19–20) has said that "if ever there was an arms race, it was between the competing nuclear bomb design teams at Los Alamos and Livermore." Relations between Livermore and Los Alamos were prickly from the start. When the media gave credit for the first successful test of a hydrogen bomb (the Mike test) to Livermore—a misrepresentation the laboratory was prevented from correcting by national secrecy rules—Los Alamos scientists were deeply resentful (York 1975b: 13). The following year, 1953, Livermore staged its own first tests, Ruth and Ray, both of which were "fizzles"—the weapons scientists' term for failures. In the case of Livermore's first test, Ruth, "the metal tower, which normally would have been vaporized by the nuclear blast, was merely bent. Laughing Los Alamos scientists scurried for their cameras" (Broad 1992: 42). After this Los Alamos scientists liked to tease their Livermore counterparts by asking if they could borrow their tower after future tests. Livermore's third test, in the Pacific in 1954, was no more successful. The predicted yield of 1.5 megatons fell far short at 110 kilotons (Cochran et al. 1987: 153–154; Lawrence Livermore National Laboratory 1982: 6). When he heard about Livermore's failure in the Pacific, the mathematician John Von Neumann is said to have commented, "There will be dancing in the streets of Los Alamos tonight" (Easlea 1983: 133). Nearly forty years later, echoing Von Neumann's sentiments if not his loyalties, a Livermore weapons scientist told me, only half-jokingly, never to forget that "the Soviets are the competition, but Los Alamos is the enemy." From the start, then, Livermore, which has always represented itself as the more energetic and innovative of the two weapons laboratories, has consistently defined itself against the Los Alamos establishment.[13]

In March 1955, with the successful Tesla and Turk tests, the new laboratory finally showed that it had mastered the principles of nuclear weapons physics and began in earnest its career of successful nuclear weapons design (Cochran et al. 1987: 154). The laboratory's first major breakthrough came in the late 1950s when it succeeded in shrinking a warhead so that it could fit atop the submarine-based Polaris missile (Broad 1992: 45).

With success came growth. In 1953, the Livermore laboratory had a staff of 698 and an annual budget of $3.5 million. By 1958, it had a staff of over 3,000 and a budget of $55 million. By 1963, with a staff of over 5,000 and a budget of $127 million, it had slightly outgrown Los Alamos

(Senate Policy Committee 1984; York 1975*b:* 13–14). During the years of Ronald Reagan's defense buildup, the laboratory added another 1,000 to its staff and almost doubled its budget so that by the time I arrived in Livermore in 1987, it employed 8,000 people and had an annual budget of $1 billion (Senate Policy Committee 1984: 16).

THE LABORATORY TODAY[14]

Heading east from the center of Livermore, past the library and the high school, past the churches and the houses along East Avenue, just past the vineyards, on the eastern edge of Livermore where the town fades into farmland, Lawrence Livermore National Laboratory sprawls across one square mile of land. Although William Broad (1992: 19) calls it "the most feared laboratory on earth," the perimeter of the immense science facility is marked by a surprisingly flimsy and mostly unguarded wire fence.[15] The fence is dotted here and there with little yellow signs warning outsiders that loitering and trespassing are forbidden. In a few places there are cameras on the roofs of buildings and trailers so that the perimeter can be kept under surveillance.

When I first saw the laboratory, I was disappointed. Instead of the conspicuous high security, industrial landscaping, and impressive modern architecture I had expected, I found a ragged, nondescript sprawl of scrubland and trailers punctuated by the occasional modern concrete-and-dark-glass building.[16] One corporate visitor described it in these terms:

> Architecturally, Lawrence Livermore National Laboratory looks somewhat like an unkempt gulag or stalag. Actually, once you enter the barbed wire-topped fence you find there is less symmetry and landscaping than in the average gulag. Many of the buildings were built, wooden barracks style, after the second world war. Scattered on the grounds are a handful of modern buildings, along with the skeletons of odd-shaped structures that at one time or another housed some experiment. Other work areas are in rows of trailers. (daCosta 1990: 5)

For all its raggedness, the laboratory is not poor. It is home to some of the most advanced technology in the country, and its buildings and equipment are currently valued at $4 billion (*Valley Times* 1990).

It is hard to say with any certainty exactly how much of the annual budget of $1 billion went toward weapons research in the 1980s. According

TABLE 1.   Profile of Laboratory Employees, 1989

Staff	Ph.D.	M.S./B.A. B.S./A.A.	None	Total
Scientists and Engineers	1,177	1,637	59	2,873
Physicists	650	183	2	835
Chemists and material scientists	168	117	6	291
Engineers	250	815	34	1,099
Mathematicians and computer scientists	61	464	16	538
Environmental/biomedical scientists	48	58	1	106
Technical and crafts	2	1,150	1,841	2,993
Administrative and clerical	32	645	1,186	1,863
Total Laboratory	1,211	3,432	3,086	7,729

SOURCE: Laboratory transparency LO33.

to figures provided by the laboratory's public relations personnel, it was about $335 million each year, or a third of the overall budget.[17] However, the laboratory arrived at this figure by classifying programs, such as laser fusion, that have both military and civilian applications as nonweapons programs and by omitting overhead costs that contribute to weapons work. Most laboratory employees I spoke with, including one in the budget office, guessed that roughly two-thirds of laboratory resources were devoted to weapons research. The University of California's Special Committee to the Academic Senate, commissioned to investigate the laboratories, put the figure at 76 percent (Jendreson et al. 1989).[18] By the end of the 1980s, the laboratory was receiving $100 million a year for work on the Strategic Defense Initiative (SDI) alone (Wrubel 1990).

According to the laboratory's statistics, 86 percent of its employees are white. Asian-Americans and Hispanic-Americans each account for 5 percent of the workforce, and 3 percent are African-American. In 1989, the laboratory signed an agreement with the U.S. Labor Department to recruit more minorities after it was found deficient in that regard. As with most comparable institutions in the United States, there is a disproportionate concentration of minorities at the lower end of the laboratory's employment hierarchy (Rogers 1989b, 1990b).[19]

Laboratory employees encompass a broad range of scientific disciplines and levels of educational attainment (see table 1). Relations between staff are regulated by a number of hierarchies. The great divide within the laboratory social system is between the caste of scientists and engineers at the top and the caste of technicians and clerical workers who assist them. Mobility between castes is almost nonexistent. The scientists and engineers are better paid and have some degree of autonomy and control over their own labor, while technicians and clerical workers have little opportunity to initiate projects.[20] In the 1980s, the position of many technicians weakened as laboratory managers increasingly contracted their labor from outside companies so that the laboratory would not owe them benefits and could lay them off more easily if necessary.

Within the caste of scientists and engineers, those with Ph.D.'s carry more prestige and authority, and it is generally thought to be difficult, though not impossible, to win promotion to top administrative posts without a Ph.D.[21] Physicists are the elite within the elite, the laboratory brahmins who rank highest because their work, being the most abstract, is thought to be the most difficult and because, unlike the lower-ranking engineers, they are more preoccupied with thinking about things than with making them.[22] Although salary varies greatly with experience and achievement, and it is not hard to find engineers who are paid more than physicists, the physicists tend to be the most highly paid scientists at the laboratory and, with one exception, the director has always been a physicist.[23]

The arrangement of scientific disciplines into symbolic hierarchies is further illuminated by the employment patterns of women, who make up 26 percent of the laboratory's workforce (Rogers 1989b). Many are clerical staff. Of the women who are scientists and engineers, most are concentrated in "softer" fields such as biomedicine and environmental science, which are seen as relatively marginal (one warhead designer joked that the biomedical program had "Third World" status within the laboratory because its scientists always had to wait so long to get time on the Cray supercomputers). For example, 51 percent of employees in biomedicine and 30 percent of employees in computer science and environmental science are women. By contrast, in mechanical engineering, electrical engineering, and physics, the ratios are 7 percent, 6 percent, and 5.5 percent, respectively (LLNL Women's Association 1988). In addition to being concentrated in relatively low-prestige fields within the laboratory, women tend to be scarce in senior management circles.[24]

As the central mission of the laboratory is nuclear weapons design, the weapons scientists, especially the physicists, have the least obstructed

TABLE 2.   Nuclear Weapons Designed at Livermore, 1952–1989

Warhead No.	Type of Weapons System
W27	Regulus Cruise missile warhead
W38	Atlas/Titan ICBM (warhead)
B41	Strategic bomb for B-52
W45	Atomic demolition weapon and Terrier surface-to-air missile
W47	Warhead for Polaris submarine-launched ballistic missile (SLBM)
W48	155-mm nuclear artillery shell
W55	SUBROC antisubmarine weapon
W56	Minuteman II ICBM warhead
W58	Polaris SLBM warhead
W62	Minuteman III ICBM warhead
W68	Poseidon SLBM warhead
W70	Lance surface-to-surface missile
W71	Spartan surface-to-air missile
W79	8-in. artillery-fired atomic projectile
W82	155-mm artillery-fired atomic projectile
B83	Modern strategic bomb
W84	Ground-launched Cruise missile warhead
W87	MX ICBM warhead

SOURCES: Cochran et al. 1987: 47; LLNL fact sheet, "Nuclear Weapons Systems."

access to the resources that make energetic scientific work possible: supercomputer time, materials, technicians, and secretaries. Since its inception in 1952, the laboratory has designed eighteen warheads for the American nuclear stockpile (see table 2). (Los Alamos has designed 44 warheads.) The late 1980s found the laboratory's nuclear weapons designers working on a warhead for a new short-range attack missile (SRAM), an advanced Cruise missile warhead, an earth-penetrating warhead, a warhead for a new long-range missile, and a nuclear depth charge bomb (Cochran et al. 1987: 47).

Weapons design at Livermore is done by A and B divisions. B Division scientists design the "primary" (a fission device), which acts as the trigger in a thermonuclear device. A Division scientists design the "secondary," the fusion device that captures the energy of an atomic explosion and uses it to initiate a thermonuclear explosion.[25] There is some rivalry between

A and B divisions, and the scientists in each often claim that they do the most interesting physics. One A Division designer told me,

> The pressures and temperatures which are created [by a primary] are fundamentally always going to be limited by the nature of high explosive. However, once you have the amount of energy that you get out of a primary . . . already this thing operates like a miniature sun, and now the range of things you can do with that energy becomes much more open and flexible. And the people in A Division get to take advantage of that. They're the ones who can do innovative, add-on experiments. . . . They'd hate to hear me say that, but B Division almost performs a service, and A Division gets to reap all the glory in terms of physics. . . . I think that the more exciting physics tends to take place in A Division.

The same week a B Division designer told me,

> We get to do the most difficult physics in B Division. It's much easier to design a secondary than a primary that really works properly. I think the physicists in B Division tend to be of a higher caliber, and we have the most interesting and subtle design challenges.

In the 1980s L and W divisions at the laboratory were also involved in nuclear weapons development. L Division developed diagnostic equipment for underground nuclear tests at the Nevada Test Site and helped implement the tests. W Division engineered prototype nuclear devices for testing. L Division has now been disbanded.

In the 1980s there were three other weapons design projects at the laboratory based outside these four divisions. All three concerned SDI weapons intended to destroy enemy nuclear weapons in space, and all three programs were dismantled after I left the field. The most conspicuous of these was the program to develop a nuclear bomb-pumped X-ray laser,[26] a weapon that, scientists hoped, would focus a thermonuclear explosion into laser beams capable of shooting down enemy missiles in space. X-ray laser research at Livermore was conducted, mainly by a younger group of weapons designers, outside the bureaucratic structure of the regular weapons design divisions, through a new department called R Program that was lavishly funded and was even assigned $62.5 million for its own building in the late 1980s (Broad 1990a, 1992: 188–189, 208–209). It never got to use the building, however: in 1990, following disappointing test results, media allegations of impropriety, and the dramatic improvement of U.S.–Soviet relations, R Program was dismantled and its scientists repatriated to the regular design divisions.[27]

The laboratory also had a program, budgeted at $37 million a year, to develop the free electron laser, another SDI laser weapon. The free electron laser, of which there is a prototype at Livermore's Site 300, is an enormous accelerator capable of producing particle beams that might be able to destroy enemy missiles in space, if properly focused by orbiting mirrors. In 1990 this program was also essentially dismantled when the Pentagon chose the rival design of the Los Alamos laboratory as the b..sis for further research.[28]

The third SDI project was Brilliant Pebbles, a nonnuclear weapons system, whose ultimate feasibility was hotly disputed, planned to consist of fleets of orbiting space "rocks" ready to collide with enemy missiles and warheads in space.[29] Brilliant Pebbles became a centerpiece of the Bush administration's vision of strategic defense and, as the X-ray laser's fortunes declined, its research funding increased, reaching almost 10 percent of the laboratory's overall budget by 1991 until it too fell victim to military budget cuts at the end of the cold war (Weisman 1992). Brilliant Pebbles research at Livermore was the province of O Group, which did the original work on the X-ray laser before R Program was established. O Group was run as a sort of personal fiefdom by Lowell Wood, a controversial figure who was the protégé of the laboratory's director emeritus and co-founder, Edward Teller. Relations between O Group and the regular weapons divisions had been distant and strained for some years when I was in Livermore. (O Group saw itself as doing more creative physics than the regular weapons divisions. Some designers in A and B divisions complained that O Group diverted important resources from nuclear weapons work and that it did sloppy physics and then prevented other scientists from evaluating it by classifying it at the highest level of secrecy.)[30]

The four weapons divisions—A, B, L, and W—and the three SDI projects accounted for most of the weapons work at the laboratory when I was in Livermore, but there were still other projects that, although they had civilian applications, were weapons related. These included two more laser programs, the AVLIS facility and the inertial confinement fusion (ICF) facility, run by Y Division, the laser division at the laboratory. AVLIS is a new technology for enriching uranium. It vaporizes uranium, then shoots finely tuned laser beams at the uranium vapor so as to selectively ionize the fissionable uranium-235 used in nuclear reactor rods and nuclear weapons triggers, separating it from the less useful uranium-238. Livermore has also used the technology to separate different isotopes of plutonium.

The ICF program spends roughly $68 million each year on Nova, the most powerful laser in the world. Firing pulses of energy that last only a fraction of a second at tiny pellets of tritium and deuterium, the laser generates fusion reactions in the laboratory that share many of the characteristics of thermonuclear explosions and stellar interiors. Nova is used for basic physics, energy, and weapons research. If scientists could extract more energy from these reactions than it takes to generate them, as their calculations suggest they can, they would have the basis for a commercially viable fusion reactor. Even optimists place such a reactor at least forty years in the future, however. In the meantime, since the laser offers scientists a way to investigate the physics of thermonuclear explosions, it is funded by military sources and, in the 1980s, most results of Nova experiments were classified, though many experiments were declassified after the end of the cold war.[31]

The laboratory also operates a magnetic fusion facility, which experiments with a different technique for achieving fusion of deuterium and tritium—in this case, by using a magnetic field to compress a deuterium-tritium plasma. Since the government decided the magnetic fusion program's most prized machine, the tandem mirror facility, built at a cost of $246 million, was too expensive to run and closed it almost as soon as construction was completed in 1986, Livermore's magnetic fusion program has been less vigorous than expected.[32]

The laboratory's other programs include earth sciences, which conducts research on nuclear waste disposal, seismographic verification of arms control treaties, and oil shale production; G Division, which develops complex computer models of the greenhouse effect and nuclear winter scenarios; the biomedical division, which researches cancer, the composition of the human genome, and the effects of radiation on the human body; D Division, which uses computer simulations to explore nuclear and conventional war scenarios and arms control issues; Z Division, which analyzes intelligence data about foreign military capabilities; the Center for Technical Studies, which produces studies of national security issues; and the environmental restoration program, which develops new environmental cleanup technologies, monitors laboratory compliance with environmental regulations, and is responsible for cleaning up existing contamination at the laboratory.[33]

MAKING CONTACT

When I arrived in Livermore I had to figure out how to study, first, a laboratory with 8,000 employees whom I was forbidden by national security laws from observing at work; second, the relationship between that laboratory and a town of 56,000 people; and third, the relationship between the laboratory, the town, and a diverse collection of protest communities, most of which were based forty miles away in Berkeley and San Francisco. My training in a discipline originally devised for the study of small foreign villages and kin groups did not seem immediately helpful from the methodological point of view.[34] The size, geographic dispersal, and—in the case of the laboratory—secrecy of the communities I wanted to study, not to mention their sometimes strong mutual antipathy, made conventional techniques of participant observation problematic to say the least.[35] Yet I did not want to rely solely on formal interviews in which informants always watch their tongues; and, as an interpretive anthropologist interested in the complex nuances of discourse,[36] I had an acute skepticism about the value of questionnaires. I decided to mix formal interviews and the collection of documentary sources with a strategy of participant observation adapted to the demands and limitations of my own fieldwork situation. Since national security restrictions prevented me from learning about the scientists' lives by watching them at work and working beside them myself, I relied less on participant observation than most anthropologists in the field.

One way to monitor life at the laboratory was to read. The four major newspapers in the Bay Area—the *San Francisco Chronicle*, *San Francisco Examiner*, *Oakland Tribune*, and *San Jose Mercury News*—all cover the major stories at the laboratory. The *New York Times* also carries stories about the laboratory from time to time. The most extensive and consistent reporting on the laboratory, however, came from three local newspapers in the Livermore Valley—the *Tri-Valley Herald*, the *Valley Times*, and the weekly *Independent*—which provided detailed information about the laboratory's scientific projects, political struggles, personnel appointments, and embarrassments (ranging from drug scandals and misuse of public money to plutonium spills). About the time I arrived in Livermore, the laboratory's relationship with the local community became prickly and contentious in an unprecedented way, and the local press did a good job of documenting (many laboratory employees would say inciting) this development, which I was also able to follow by attending local public hearings.[37] There was also the laboratory's own newspaper, *Newsline*, an official publication that rarely alluded, even obliquely, to any controversy but was still a valuable source of information about laboratory policy, technical projects, and the apparently interminable bureaucratic reorganizations that were a constant feature of laboratory life.[38]

As for the laboratory itself, although I was not allowed to wander freely around areas where people do classified work, it was not entirely off-limits to me. Two of the laboratory's three cafeterias were open to the public, and I often ate lunch and met laboratory employees in them. The Visitors Center, where groups of students, Kiwanis, and so on, came to learn about the laboratory's work, was also open to the public and, despite the bureaucratic problems created by my British citizenship, the Visitors Center allowed me to join two of their tours of the Nova laser facility (where classified research is done). I also went on a tour of the free electron laser facility at Site 300. And toward the end of my fieldwork, one senior weapons designer was kind enough to take off the better part of a day to escort me around parts of the laboratory I would not otherwise have been permitted to see. We cycled around on the clunky old bicycles the laboratory leaves for anyone to use, visiting the magnetic fusion facility, the Cray supercomputers at the National Magnetic Fusion Energy Computer Center, the free electron laser center within the laboratory, and the Central Cafeteria. The day's schedule had been carefully planned beforehand, and at each location a senior scientist was waiting to discuss that facility with me in detail. This day was one of the high points of my fieldwork.

Meanwhile, around town I tried to meet as many people as I could in as many contexts as possible in an effort to understand their feelings and beliefs about the laboratory's work. I lived with laboratory employees and other members of the community and came to know them as friends. I attended a number of churches in Livermore, Catholic, Episcopalian, Presbyterian, and Unitarian; after a while Livermore's Unitarian Fellowship, which was somewhat divided about weapons work, became a home for me. The Fellowship invited me to mark my departure from Livermore by giving a Sunday address on how weapons scientists and protestors might talk to one another, and, since the end of my fieldwork, I have returned to give two more Sunday addresses. I also joined the basketball and softball teams at the laboratory, mistakenly supposing that scientists would be unathletic nerds; in retrospect, I can only marvel that both teams tolerated my athletic inadequacy as well as my insistent questions. I joined the Livermore Singles Group, through which I met a wide variety of people, many of them laboratory employees or former spouses of laboratory employees, at hikes, dinners, and other outings. And, in what can only be called a major faux pas, I blundered into the Valley Study Group, phoning to ask if I could join this elite group. The organization, in which membership is by invitation only, is for leading members of the Livermore Valley community. The press is barred from its meetings. Laboratory employees are technically ineligible to belong, but in practice many senior managers regularly attend as guests of their spouses who, by dint of their participation on hospital boards, and so on, are members. Although I was undistinguished by the standards of its other members and behaved entirely inappropriately in asking to join, the group made me welcome.

At the same time I tried to develop a deeper understanding of the various groups opposed to the laboratory's mission. Two of these were based locally in the Livermore Valley: Tri-Valley Citizens Against a Radioactive Environment (CAREs), an environmentally oriented group, and the Livermore Valley chapter of Beyond War, a New Age group. I attended some of the meetings organized by each and did participant observation in the classic mode with Tri-Valley CAREs as they tried to persuade local citizens outside Livermore's Safeway supermarket to sign a petition against the laboratory's planned incinerator.

Farther afield, I was interested in a number of groups based in San Francisco and Berkeley: the Ecumenical Peace Institute, Physicians for Social Responsibility, SANE/Freeze,[39] and the Bay Area Peace Test. The latter two allowed me to attend their planning meetings, and SANE/Freeze also allowed me to spend a day with two of their professional door-to-door canvassers observing the response of Bay Area citizens to their push for a comprehensive test ban treaty.[40] I also participated in two "peace pilgrimages" sponsored by the Berkeley Ecumenical Peace Institute.

The larger protests during my fieldwork were not in Livermore but at the Nevada Test Site. These were nationally coordinated weeklong events that attracted thousands of participants from all over the country, particularly from the San Francisco Bay Area. I attended two such protests, traveling to Nevada with an anarchist-oriented contingent from the Bay Area Peace Test who invited me to camp with them and experience the massive and complex protests from their vantage point. This was as different from life in Livermore as I could imagine.

The bulk of my information and understanding, however, came from relatively formal, often tape-recorded interviews, which usually took place in the interviewees' homes, though some also occurred at my home or in one of the laboratory cafeterias. Some were as short as one hour; others evolved into a series of interviews stretching over as many as fifteen hours. I invited people to recount their life histories, exploring the meaning of their decisions to become weapons scientists or antinuclear activists and the processes that followed from those decisions. In the interviews with weapons scientists—the people I interviewed in the greatest numbers and at greatest depth—I used the recollection of particular events and decisions to focus mainly on the ethics of weapons work and on the meanings invested in nuclear testing. In the interviews with antinuclear activists, I focused on the meaning of nuclear testing for them and on issues of tactical efficacy and personal empowerment. I collected a number of nuclear test narratives from weapons scientists and arrest narratives from antinuclear activists who had engaged in civil disobedience. Because of the classified nature of their work and my own fear that they would suspect me of spying for a foreign government, I largely avoided asking weapons scientists many questions about the technical side of their work.

The major problem I had to surmount in interviewing weapons scientists was that before I arrived in Livermore, I did not know any. For two reasons it seemed inadvisable to approach the laboratory management or public relations apparatus with a request that they supply me with interviewees: first, it was entirely possible that they would see my project as a danger or a nuisance and would, at best, refuse to cooperate or, at worst, actively discourage laboratory employees from participating; second, if they did decide to cooperate, there was the danger that they would be in a position to control my research to some degree by, for example, supplying me with carefully selected "model scientists." Instead of working through laboratory officials, starting from the top, I began at the bottom, arduously assembling my own network of personal contacts within the laboratory until, eventually, I worked my way up to some of the senior managers. At the beginning of my fieldwork I had a slight acquaintance with one person whose father worked at the laboratory. I went to see his father, intending only to discuss the feasibility of my project. To my surprise, almost as soon as I arrived, in a classic example of the subject teaching the anthropologist what to do, he asked me to take out my notebook, saying he was going to tell me his life story and explain why he believed in working on weapons. Three hours later he said he had enjoyed this experience and would call me the next day with the names and telephone numbers of six colleagues, if they agreed. True to his word, he called with six names and numbers. Each of them gave me more names, and so on.

At first I procrastinated considerably, finding it difficult to call the scientists and ask them for interviews. This was largely because I presumed they would feel embarrassed about their weapons work and would be reluctant to answer a stranger's nosy questions. I anticipated hostile or evasive rejections. I could not have been more wrong. Almost everyone I asked was happy to talk with me. One physicist told me, "I've thought for years that someone should do this. I'm glad someone's going to tell our story." I learned a valuable lesson, one of the most valuable in the entire experience of fieldwork: if I expected weapons scientists to be embarrassed or defensive about discussing their work, like fraudulent executives or drug dealers evading the "Sixty Minutes" camera crew, this was because of my own erroneous preconceptions. For the most part, these people wanted to talk about their work, what it meant to them, and why they believed in it. In all, only two scientists declined to be interviewed. Both, interestingly, were referred to me by their wives rather than, as was usually the case, their colleagues.

Over the course of two years I collected the names of far more people than I could possibly interview. At first I tried to make sure that I was talking to a broad cross section of laboratory employees, but, as my fieldwork progressed, I increasingly focused at first on the scientists and engineers in general and then on the elite physicists who design nuclear weapons and are the most deeply identified with nuclear weapons work as a vocation. I came to know some of them as friends outside the context of formal interviews, and a few were hospitable enough to my interest in the possibility of dialogue between weapons scientists and antinuclear activists that they agreed to come to dinner at my house on one occasion to talk to some activists.[41] Two years later, when I was living close to the Los Alamos laboratory while revising this book manuscript, some of the Livermore scientists put me in touch with their colleagues there.

As I became better known in Livermore, I was, in my turn, interviewed by the local newspapers and granted a certain authority as a local cultural commentator. And as I became better known among the warhead designers, I learned that they would compare their interview experiences with one another, joke about ways to mislead me, discuss my competence as a theorist and ethnographer, and generally traffic in gossip about me. The same was true of many antinuclear activists, though they tended to offer more vociferous opinions than the scientists on what they expected my conclusions to be.

In all, I conducted detailed interviews of one kind or another with sixty-four laboratory employees (52 men and 12 women) and forty-eight antinuclear activists (20 men and 28 women). I also spoke with twenty-three spouses or former spouses of laboratory employees, eight local ministers, five reporters, three former mayors of Livermore, and five psychotherapists or psychologists who counseled laboratory employees. I tried to speak not only to a large number of people but also to a large number of types of people, so as to get a sense of the laboratory as an institution from as many different perspectives as possible. What follows is an interpretation of the laboratory's culture and of the legitimation crisis it underwent in the 1980s, stitched together from my sampling of these perspectives.

CHAPTER 3

Becoming a Weapons Scientist

When life itself seems lunatic, who knows where madness lies?
DON QUIXOTE

WHO ARE WEAPONS SCIENTISTS?

When I arrived in Livermore I was curious to know what kinds of people chose to work at a nuclear weapons laboratory and how they were melded into a single community. I presumed that the laboratory was held together largely by the homogeneity of the people it recruited. From my reading before starting fieldwork, especially my reading of the antinuclear psychologists who dominate the social study of weapons professionals,[1] I had learned to think of weapons scientists in terms of types: the rational type, the numb type, the authoritarian type, the conservative type, and so on. And indeed the laboratory does recruit people who are very much alike in important ways: mostly white, male, and disposed by temperament to mistrust emotions. Still, one of the biggest surprises of my fieldwork was the discovery that Livermore scientists are heterogeneous in ways I had not expected.

Take politics, for example. I had assumed that nuclear weapons scientists would, by definition, be conservatives. In her study of nuclear weapons scientists in New Mexico, Debra Rosenthal (1990: 183) reports that the few liberals who endured at the Los Alamos and Sandia laboratories saw themselves as "besieged. They complained of diffuse and low-level persecution. . . . The cartoons they posted on their doors would be torn down the next morning. They were the butt of practical jokes." This was not the case at Livermore, where, although there was no shortage of conservatives, there were plenty of liberals who got on well with their colleagues. Clark, for instance, is a much-respected warhead designer at the laboratory. He had been a member of the Sierra Club, was an active supporter of women's rights, an opponent of U.S. intervention in Central America, a supporter of gun control, and, in the 1970s just before he came to the Livermore laboratory, an active protestor against the Vietnam War who wore his hair long and his ties wide. As he described himself just before he came to Livermore, "I had gone door-to-door collecting signatures against the Vietnam War and attended rallies and so on. I had my hair real long and wore beads and sandals for some time and was involved in the music and all that."

Clark's story is not so unusual. A number of the scientists I interviewed said they had been opposed to the Vietnam War. Others were environmentalists who had been active members of the local Sierra Club until it took a position in favor of a nuclear freeze in the early 1980s, at which point its Livermore membership plummeted. One woman who worked at the laboratory told me she was so enraged by the Exxon *Valdez* oil spill in Alaska that she cut her Exxon card in two, soaked it in oil, and mailed it back to Exxon. And Mark, a weapons designer on whose living room wall I could not help but notice a Gandhi poster, told me about his occasional daydreams of saving whales, a cause as classically liberal as his methods were not: "I had fantasies of being Captain Nemo in *20,000 Leagues under the Sea*, torpedoing the whaling ships. What the fuck's wrong with that? They're willing to kill whales, so why not blow up their ship and leave them to figure out where to go from there?"

Many laboratory scientists had also been active in the civil rights movement. One warhead designer had helped organize a campaign in Livermore in the 1960s to prohibit racial discrimination in jobs and housing. Another younger weapons scientist, who described herself as a feminist, had recently participated in the antiapartheid movement on her campus. Jeremy, a deeply religious weapons physicist, had spent part of the 1950s working with a worker-priest for racial integration in the American South before coming to the laboratory. And Phil, a warhead designer who had some union organizing experience and who liked to complain to me about the domination of American politics by corporate interests, told me he left his church because the minister opposed a social action program on behalf of minority inner-city residents. He also got into a row with some high-ranking military officials when they visited the laboratory.

> We had some colonels or lieutenant colonels over, and they were talking about something, and it was they were here to defend capitalism versus communism. And I called them on it. I said, "You've got things all screwed up. I'm not supporting this country because it's a capitalistic country. I'm supporting it because of its form of government, and to me that's what's important. . . . What are you guys talking about, 'protecting capitalism'? Am I paying your salaries just because that's what you're in here for?"

In 1988, one weapons designer took a straw poll of his colleagues to ascertain their preferences in the upcoming presidential election. He found that although Michael Dukakis had said he favored a nuclear test ban and a reduction of SDI research by about $3 billion a year (Bodovitz 1988*a*), his colleagues were split down the middle between George Bush and Dukakis. This was roughly the same spread I found in my own interview sample (two of whom told me they had voted for Jesse Jackson in the primary). In other words, the laboratory is a place where Reagan-Bush supporters, those with no great interest in politics at all, and liberals who had struggled for civil rights and against the Vietnam War all worked together in the development of nuclear weapons.

There was religious diversity as well. For example, in the course of my interviews with weapons scientists, I came across atheists, Jews, Catholics, Episcopalians, Presbyterians, Methodists, Lutherans, Unitarians, Baptists, Mormons, Evangelicals, and three Buddhists, all of whom worked on nuclear weapons.[2] These were people of varying religious worldviews, conventionally seen as ranging from liberal to conservative. Although their understandings of how to live a righteous life were grounded in different theologies, they were all integrated by the laboratory into a group capable of collaborative work on nuclear weapons.

As my fieldwork proceeded, I began to rethink my understanding of the grounds of this collaboration. How were conservative and liberal scientists able to work together on nuclear weapons in the context of a society that was contentiously divided, largely along liberal-conservative lines, about the need to keep building nuclear weapons? How were liberals—some of whom had participated in the peace movement of the 1960s and 1970s and were critical of Reagan's policy priorities in the 1980s—able to feel committed to developing nuclear weapons for Ronald

Reagan's arms buildup? And if the kinds of overt political ideologies—liberalism and conservatism, Democratic and Republican party political affiliation—celebrated by the media as the foundation of American politics did not undergird the laboratory's apparent political stability, what did? Evidently I had to think about political identity and ideology in new ways, not simply in terms of America's conventional political labels, if I was to understand the political integration of the laboratory that enabled its mission to proceed.[3]

Thus I also began to think about the practices through which the laboratory resocializes recruits and constructs itself as a moral and political community in which people with diverse overt political belief systems can participate. In thinking about weapons scientists as made rather than born, my gaze shifted from social or psychological types to integrative social practices and from overt political ideologies to less obvious kinds of political commitments. I began to think about the processes at the laboratory, and in the wider community in which the laboratory is embedded, that enable it to construct a community of people deeply convinced—so deeply convinced that they often asked me in puzzlement to explain why antinuclear activists were so afraid of nuclear weapons—that it is appropriate to develop nuclear weapons and that nuclear deterrence cannot fail. This in part involved thinking of science itself—the ideology that claims not to be one—as a source of binding energy capable of holding the scientists together despite their apparent political differences. It also involved a conceptual shift away from a static preoccupation with types toward an emphasis on dynamic social practices for the active production of new thinking, feeling, believing, acting selves (see Althusser 1971; Bourdieu 1977*a*, 1984; Foucault 1979, 1980*a*, 1980*b*).[4]

Insofar as other analysts have adopted a processual perspective on the making of weapons professionals, they have tended to present the processes involved as largely repressive or subtractive: ethical questions are avoided, feelings are denied, fears are repressed (Lifton and Markusen 1990; Mack 1986; Rosenthal 1990; Steiner 1989). In such analyses weapons professionals are defined as much in terms of what they lack as what they are. While part of the work of becoming a weapons scientist does indeed involve learning not to attend to particular fears, feelings, and questions—just as part of the work of becoming an antinuclear activist also involves learning inattention to particular questions—it also involves the active learning of discourses, feelings, and practices. To take the example of ethics: rather than ignore the ethical dilemmas of their work, weapons scientists learn to resolve these dilemmas in particular socially patterned ways. In other words, becoming a weapons scientist involves much more complex and creative social and psychological processes than repression and avoidance. As Foucault says, "Power would be a fragile thing if its only function were to repress" (1980*b*: 59). And further:

> We must cease once and for all to describe the effects of power in negative terms: it "excludes," it "represses," it "censors," it "abstracts," it "masks," it "conceals." In fact, power produces; it produces reality; it produces domains of objects and rituals of truth. The individual and the knowledge that may be gained of him belong to this production. (1979: 194)

Rosaldo (1989: 25) observes that "even those so-called realms of pure freedom, our fantasy and our 'innermost thoughts' are produced and limited by our local culture. Human imaginations are as culturally formed as distinctive ways of weaving, performing a ritual, raising children, grieving or healing." The power of the social processes sustaining the laboratory's work lies in their ability to actively, positively produce and reshape the identities and imaginations of its employees as they are transformed from neophytes into mature weapons scientists (see Traweek 1988: x–xi).

The process of social and psychological engineering involved here is ideological, but in a more fundamental way than we often mean when we use the term "ideology." The British social theorist and literary critic Raymond Williams (1977) has argued that we must think of ideologies not only in terms of discourses and ideas but also as "structures of feeling"— ways of experiencing and living in the world that profoundly reshape our emotions, bodily reflexes, and fantasies as well as our ideas and beliefs. As Michelle Rosaldo, another anthropologist, puts it, arguing against a separation of (private) feelings from (public) ideas and beliefs,[5]

> Recognition of the fact that thought is always culturally patterned and infused with feelings, which themselves reflect a culturally ordered past, suggests that just as thought does not exist in isolation from affective life, so affect is culturally ordered and does not exist apart from thought. . . . Affects, then, are no less cultural and no more private than beliefs. They are instead, cognitions—or more aptly, perhaps, interpretations—always cul-

turally informed, in which the actor finds that body, self, and identity are immediately involved. (1984: 137, 141)

As the laboratory re-produces its scientists, it not only works on their beliefs and their vocabularies; it also molds their fears, their joys, and their excitements, turning them to the service of nuclear deterrence.

CHOOSING THE LABORATORY

When scientists and engineers leave graduate school, they try to find a way to earn a living and, if possible, enjoy the kinds of freedom and intellectual stimulation they experienced at university, but within the context of a society where the practice of science is dominated by the military and by large corporations. Richard, a young weapons designer, told me, "You realize how big the military-industrial complex is when you graduate. If you get a degree in physics, there's almost nowhere to get a job where you're not part of the military-industrial complex. Even the universities are getting drawn in. It's too big."

A higher proportion of scientific and engineering jobs are military related in the United States than in any other Western country (Barnet 1991; Tsipis 1990). By the mid-1980s, after five years of the Reagan administration's defense buildup, two-thirds of U.S. federal research and development funding was directed to military projects (compared to 12.5% in Germany and 4.5% in Japan [Freiberger 1990]).[6] Forty-three percent of all American research and development funds, private as well as public, were going to military projects (FAS 1986: 8). As for the number of American scientists and engineers working on military projects, estimates in the 1980s ranged from 20 percent to 40 percent of the total number of scientists and engineers in America.[7] The Livermore and Los Alamos laboratories are the largest employers of physicists in the country. Between them, they employ 6 percent of all U.S. physicists (Schwartz 1988).

Some critics charge that many scientists are forced to work on weapons, even though they would rather not, because of the relative lack of jobs and funding in other areas of research.[8] The journalist Peter Carey has written,

They don't build bombs because of their values, because they love America or Jesus or both, or because they are patriotic Republicans or patriotic Democrats or whatever. That's merely what comes to us when they are asked to justify it, which was rare until the mid-1980s and the Nuclear Freeze movement.

They do it because they fell into it, or majored in physics and engineering, and could make good money at it. They do it even after they've gotten tired of it, because they have families to support, it's good money [and] moving is a hassle. (1990: 21)

Some of the critics, especially university physicists who tend to look on weapons physicists as members of a lower caste, told me it was their least gifted classmates, the ones with no alternatives, who went to work at Livermore and Los Alamos. One of them told me, for example, that "the people in the weapons physics programs are third-level in terms of physics." Livermore scientists do not see it this way, however. They agree with two local reporters who wrote of the laboratory,

In the galaxy of science research, Lawrence Livermore National Laboratory's star is one of the brightest. Its combination of enormous scientific tools, literally hundreds of the most brilliant scientists on Earth and almost unlimited resources gives the lab an edge that few others have. (A. Smith 1990*b*)

To many employees, Lawrence Livermore National Laboratory is an almost perfect playground for the mind. Research done at the lab consistently breaks new ground, scientists have the flexibility to try new approaches, and employees don't even have to wear a coat and tie or make it to their desk by 9 A.M. every day. (Albro 1991*a*)

We should bear in mind that Livermore recruits many of its scientists from prestigious universities such as MIT, Cornell, Princeton, UC Berkeley, and Stanford. Degrees from such universities tend to confer a certain freedom on their recipients, even if they cannot all find university jobs, and almost all the scientists I interviewed told me they had other opportunities but actively chose to come to the laboratory. They said they had found the laboratory an attractive employer. If the militarization of research and development in America did coerce their decisions, this was not the way they saw it.

So what reasons did scientists give for coming to work at Livermore? Although those I interviewed mostly felt that their work was making an important contribution to national and international security, they did not give this as a reason for taking the job in the first place. As Matthew, an older designer, put it, "I came to this more because of the physics than because of the Russians." Sylvia, a young warhead designer, said, "I thought about deterrence after the fact, more as rationalization than motivation." (Sylvia, unusually, said, "I took the job because the work is quite interesting, and because I was afraid the weapons weren't safe. I wanted to see what was going on rather than take other people's word.")

Few said that money was a decisive factor either, although the laboratory would surely have had more difficulty recruiting scientists and engineers if it did not offer competitive salaries. As Richard put it, "A good income was important to me, and the lab could offer me that, but that wasn't the main reason I came." Salaries vary not only with length of employment and experience but also with the academic qualifications and the distinction a scientist's work is judged to have by his or her superiors. Physicists tend to be the best paid, followed by engineers and then chemists, biochemists, and computer scientists. Two young physicists I knew who joined the laboratory as weapons designers in the 1980s were earning $55,200 and $56,400 per year, respectively. A new weapons designer with a Ph.D. earned about $50,000 a year. Two of the most senior and highly respected weapons designers were earning substantially more: $86,640 and $97,200. By contrast, a computer scientist of my acquaintance, employed at the laboratory for a decade, earned less than the physicists: $44,520. Lower paid still were technicians, who, on average, earned $33,300 after three years at the laboratory (Rogers 1990*d*). Of the laboratory's 8,000 employees, 168—mostly administrators—earned $100,000 or more per year, and the director earned $173,800 in 1991 (*Tri-Valley Herald* 1991).

A newly qualified scientist was able to earn substantially more at Livermore than he or she would have as an untenured professor at a university. A new weapons scientist at Livermore could earn almost double the salary of an untenured professor at a low-ranking university, though university jobs tend to be regarded as more prestigious by the national scientific community. As for other rival employers, the laboratory made sure that its salary offers to new scientists were roughly on a par with those they were likely to get from other national laboratories and almost as good as those they would get from private corporations such as Lockheed or TRW, though the laboratory finds it hard to keep up with the kinds of salaries private industry can offer employees later in their careers (Rogers 1990*e*). One senior manager told me it was not unusual for Livermore scientists to get a 25 percent salary increase if they moved into the private sector. Counterbalancing private industry's salary advantage, however, the laboratory can offer its scientists the opportunity to do basic research, whereas most scientists working for private industry, including physicists, end up doing more sales or engineering.

If Livermore scientists did not speak of ideology or salary as the decisive reasons for coming to Livermore, what reasons did they give? Most of those I interviewed articulated their decision to come to the laboratory in terms of an active dislike, even disdain, for university departments and corporations. They also stressed the genial atmosphere, research challenges, and facilities offered by the laboratory. Many scientists presented the laboratory as a workplace where, just like a university, they could do research, choose their own hours, and dress casually. Meanwhile, unlike their university colleagues, as long as their work is competent, they do not have to worry about tenure;[9] nor do they have to spend long hours teaching and writing grant proposals to fund their research. These scientists described the laboratory as having many of the advantages of the university without the disadvantages.

One professor at one of the country's most prestigious physics departments has trained many scientists who went on to work at Livermore. He characterized those who went to Livermore in these terms:

> They're not exactly intellectually less able than their peers. They're often people who just don't want to deal with the cutthroat competitiveness of a university department. I had a couple of students who, if they'd gone to teach at a university, probably wouldn't have got tenure, or would have ended up at a bad university. They went to Livermore and produced much better research than I would have expected because they felt nurtured by the place. It's very laid-back and puts a lot of emphasis on teamwork, on people working together to get the job done. I've often thought it's a sort of paradox that the weapons physicists often tend to be these gentler, less competitive types.

Eric, who came to Livermore in the early 1960s, had a choice between offers from the laboratory and Lockheed. He explained his decision this way:

> At MIT I had seen enough of young professors scrambling to achieve tenure and the tactics that were required or seemed to be required for them to receive good standing in the eyes of the department head, and so forth, and I thought that was really disgusting. I didn't like that at all. It seemed to me that there was an enormous jump-around-and-perform, but in a way that looked good to the elder members of the faculty. That didn't look good to

me. . . . At the same time, when I talked with people at Lockheed, I really felt uncomfortable about any sense of freedom; I really felt uncomfortable about the push based on the profit motive. That's what turned me against places like Lockheed—that profit was the bottom line, that you were going to be judged on the financial success of what you were doing. And that didn't seem very inspiring either. I had seen enough of Livermore to know that it seemed to offer quite a bit of academic freedom, quite a bit of time for self-improvement and for satisfying things that were interesting specifically for you—a characteristic of the university without that "after three years you will be put on the auction block and either accepted or rejected from this particular institution." . . . And there was a great deal of adventure here in those days. . . . With atmospheric testing, the way you collected samples was by climbing in the back seat of an air force airplane and taking off and having filter papers on either wing, and after the bomb goes off and you have a *lovely* mushroom cloud, then in an hour or so you make a quick pass through the cloud and expose the filter papers and collect samples and bring those back to the laboratory. . . . I thought that sounded *absolutely* wonderful.

Allison is a weapons scientist who taught at an Ivy League university for a while but found it "stodgy" and full of "snowheads." She went on to a West Coast university, where she experienced the only incident of sexual harassment in her professional career when a senior faculty member offered support for her continued employment in exchange for sexual favors. She also decided she disliked the rigidity and hierarchy she perceived in the academy:

I was getting turned off by what I would call the academic club I was working with. It's like an old man's club. You know the contrast between that and a national laboratory, where things are moving very rapidly, where things are very mission-oriented. . . . [the university department] has gurus. . . . People kowtow to them a lot. That kind of thing you don't see happening so much at Livermore. People are judged more on the merits of what they do.

Matthew is a weapons designer who came to Livermore in the 1970s. As an undergraduate he had expected to teach at a university one day, but he became increasingly disillusioned with the lack of freedom he perceived in the lives of university professors. Ironically, he likened the university to the military in its restraints on individual freedom:

I find writing hard, and I don't like the publish-or-perish business. It's not that I don't like pressure or hard work; I just like to impose my own deadlines rather than jump through other people's hoops. The university is like the military the way it confines you and arranges everyone in hierarchies. And then you're always scrambling to raise money. I have much more freedom at the lab.

Echoing this notion that there is more freedom at the laboratory, one middle-aged engineer told me,

> This is a very large place with a lot of jobs, a lot of managers. You can go around and interview. If you want a new job, you can go around and knock one up, see if you can find something that you like. Very few people are actually reassigned—unilateral reassignment to a new field—except at the very lowest group level. . . . It really is very free. There are very few things that people do against their will here.

Whereas many laboratory scientists also spoke of the excitement of weapons physics and the pleasure they derive from using the latest technology and working with gifted colleagues, university physicists often disparage weapons physics as more high-tech artisanship than science. One physics professor told me that the intellectual challenges in contemporary weapons design were minimal: "Weapons design now is just like polishing turds." Applying the physicist's greatest insult, namely, likening other physicists to engineers, he said of a weapons designer who is highly regarded at Livermore,

> He really knows his stuff, but he's not doing physics. He's just a bomb builder obsessing away about how to shave off a bit here and a bit there in a new bomb design. That's not physics. It's just an engineering problem. It's more complicated to design an integrated circuit board. Most of these guys are second-rate physicists who became important due to an accident of history.

Livermore scientists themselves, however, point out that their work involves 100,000-line computer codes, fantastic extremes of heat and pressure in experiments that replicate the conditions inside stars, and integrated knowledge of diverse areas of physics, chemistry, and engineering. They see their work as challenging and exciting and consider themselves fortunate to have free access to what one scientist described to me as "the ultimate toy shop": the very expensive, state-of-the-art equipment (supercomputers, lasers, spectrometers, etc.) available at the Laboratory.[10]

Matthew said the intellectual challenge of weapons physics was one of the reasons he came to Livermore:

> Mostly it's very challenging physics. It was and still is highly complex. It offers a lot of everything—computer work, engineering, going to the field,

doing academic studies. It blends theoretical and experimental physics, and it's work that's rich in diversity.

Jack, an older weapons designer who told me he was first attracted to Livermore by "the caliber of the people," said,

> This was a unique opportunity I just accidentally got into. I've never seen a collection of people like this before. I think the space effort would probably be a comparable thing. I think some of the things in medicine may be as exciting, but I think it tends to be more of an isolated research, not as much of a team effort as what we have here.

Clark, a younger warhead designer, said he was attracted to Livermore because

> there is a capability at Livermore to really be able to attack some of these problems in a more sophisticated way. . . . There is a strong infrastructure of code developers[11] . . . and there are big codes. There are huge computers to do these things on. Smart people to talk to. Plus the possibility at least in some physics areas to explore them with what they call add-ons, that is, additional experiments outside a nuclear weapon that take advantage of the environment created by the nuclear weapon. There are some very interesting things that can be learned by that.

When Allison ended her university career to come to Livermore, she worried that the work might not challenge her, but, like Jack, Matthew, and Clark, she came to feel that she was working in one of the most exciting areas of physics.

> I wasn't particularly worried about working on the weapons; I thought that one through pretty quickly. I'm fairly conservative about the need for a national defense. I was more worried that I wasn't going to be able to do forefront physics and that I wouldn't be able to talk about it. . . . [But] the work we do, the classified work, is so interesting, so fascinating, that people get so tied up with it they don't want to do any other kind of work.

ETHICS

Part of the process of socialization as a weapons scientist involves the internalization of a set of beliefs, attitudes, and feelings about the ethics of weapons work.[12] No matter how intellectually exciting nuclear weapons work may be, it brings with it moral dilemmas that laboratory employees must either confront or ignore as they go on with their work. In the West there have been two broad schools of thought about the moral issues raised by nuclear weapons: the deontological and the consequentialist. Deontologists, guided by what moral philosophers call "the wrongful intentions principle," argue that it is wrong to intend to do or to threaten to do that which it would be wrong to do. Saying that "one must not do evil as a means of doing good,"[13] they condemn threats to use nuclear weapons, even if the intended purpose of those threats is the prevention of war.[14] Consequentialists say that actions should be judged by their consequences rather than by the purity of the means involved: if in a system of mutual deterrence threats to incinerate millions of civilians prevent those millions of civilians from being incinerated, then it is moral to threaten to incinerate millions of civilians—and it may even be immoral not to.[15] It would be too simplistic to say that all antinuclear activists are deontologists and all those in favor of nuclear weapons work are consequentialists. There are, for example, antinuclear consequentialists who eschew the moral absolutism of deontological thinking but still argue in practical terms that the inevitable consequence of continued nuclear weapons work will be mass genocide and that the work is therefore immoral (see Lackey 1984). However, although antinuclear activists may be consequentialists or deontologists—or more commonly, given the messy nature of real life, may hybridize the two positions—nuclear weapons scientists are invariably consequentialists.[16] Approaching this fact as an ethnographer rather than as a moral philosopher, my interest here is not in whether they ought to be but in how they *become* consequentialists—or, more specifically, how they become pronuclear consequentialists. What are the social and psychological processes through which the consequentialist arguments undergirding weapons work come to acquire compelling force for nuclear weapons scientists?

Critics of the arms race tend to construe the social and psychological processes involved here largely in terms of avoidance and denial.[17] They criticize laboratory employees for not thinking about the moral issues involved at all, or for only thinking about them in terms of lame clichés that fail to probe the issue or stretch the mind. It was part of the rationale for the protests at the gates of the laboratory in the 1980s that the demonstrations would force weapons scientists to confront the moral dilemma they were presumed to be avoiding.[18] "It is my impression," said Donald King (1982: 19) a laboratory administrator who quit and joined the antinuclear movement, "that most employees took a job at the lab for the same reason I did—because they need work and were offered a job at good pay. Most employees have never given the matter of the morality of their activity much thought." And Debra Rosenthal (1990: 123) says of nuclear weapons scientists at Los Alamos and Sandia national laboratories in New Mexico, "The ethical dimensions of their own work was [sic] never a topic of conversation." She criticizes weapons scientists for failing to question the ethics of their vocation, for justifying their work with "the hackneyed phrases that accompany the tunes played by the blaring brass and tinkling cymbals of an all-American marching band," and for resorting to "platitudes like 'we are the good guys'" (ibid., 132).[19]

Many weapons scientists at Livermore deeply resent the "moralism" of laboratory critics and antinuclear activists. Bristling at charges that they are amoral, they say they have different ethics rather than no ethics. One warhead designer pointed out to me that before he came to the laboratory, he had lost his job in the army because he refused to obey an order, which he considered unethical, to alter a report. "The battalion commander got all upset, brought me the report, and wanted it changed. I refused to do it, gave him a pencil, and said, 'If we're going to lie, you're going to lie. I'm not going to do it.' . . . That was on a Friday. The following Monday I was out of my job."

Justin told me that although he felt comfortable designing nuclear weapons, there were jobs he considered unethical and could not do; for example, he would not work as a lawyer who defended murderers and drug dealers. And another weapons scientist, Luke, said that, on principle, he could never serve, as his brother had, as a Green Beret in Vietnam.

In an unpublished paper on the ethics of nuclear weapons work, Paul Brown, a senior scientist at the laboratory, acknowledges that protests at the laboratory have made some laboratory employees think more deeply about the ethics of their work. Still, contrary to the protestors' expectations, he argues that this has only deepened the scientists' commitment to their work.

> Do we, as weapons scientists, think about the implications of what we do? It would be difficult to avoid such thoughts in the face of continuing pressures against weapon research that resumed in a very intense way with the nuclear freeze movement in the early 1980s. My own thoughts became focused each time I had to pass through the barriers of protestors that periodically parade in front of the laboratory gates. Rather than dissuading

me and my fellow researchers from continuing to do what we do, I believe the demonstrators have caused us to consider the ethics more thoroughly. The result has been a reinforcing of personal convictions as to what our job is all about. In this sense, I personally believe the demonstrations have been a good thing. (Brown 1989: 3)

Most laboratory scientists do think about the ethics of their work at some point, but they tend to do it in private. While I did interview weapons scientists who told me that they never gave this matter much thought because their work seemed self-evidently appropriate, and while some scientists did recall conversations with colleagues about the ethics of nuclear weapons work, the more common, and startling, experience I had was finding scientist after scientist telling me I was lucky to be interviewing them because, unlike their colleagues, they had *really* thought about the ethical issues. It soon became obvious that a large number of people at the laboratory were thinking about the implications of their work in lonely privacy, all the time convinced that their colleagues were not, or at least not as deeply as they were—this in spite of the fact that the reasons people gave for doing weapons work were often strikingly similar.

Although collective discussions of the ethics of weapons work have become more common as a result of the antinuclear protests in the 1980s, laboratory culture mainly deals with the issue by privatizing it: "I sometimes have this sense that we're not supposed to discuss it," said one engineer.[20] Instead employees pick up hints from what they hear others say, but they largely work through the issue alone. There is a collective process here, but it is a process based on socialized individualism and collective privatization—a collective understanding that this issue is largely, though not entirely, to be confronted alone, that it is a matter for the private rather than the professional sphere.

There are exceptions, of course. One senior employee in the laboratory's budget office did host a series of small lunchtime meetings to discuss the ethical and psychological implications of weapons work while I was doing fieldwork, and the Catholic bishop of Oakland also sponsored a series of annual dialogues, over a period of years, between Catholic weapons scientists, theologians, and University of California faculty from his diocese. The meetings attracted about one hundred people. Such structured public discussions have, however, been more the exception than the rule.

The Livermore approach fits well with the norms of an American middle-class culture that, as many anthropologists and sociologists have observed, enforces and inculcates an extraordinary (by comparison with other cultures) independence and isolation of the individual in matters of conscience, choice, and identity while often producing a remarkable uniformity of behavior and belief.[21] Just as the struggles and choices—socialized as individual yet producing synchronized outcomes—of a sovereign, individual, privatized self lie close to the core of the American experience of love (Bellah et al. 1985; Varenne 1977), religious salvation (Tipton 1981; Weber 1958), and therapy (Bellah et al. 1985), so they are integral to the moral decision-making processes of nuclear weapons scientists. (They are also, incidentally, integral to the outlook of American antinuclear activists who, unlike their counterparts in Western Europe, developed a strongly psychological critique of the arms race that emphasized the importance of individual moral choice, denial, conversion, and empowerment.)

LEARNING THE CENTRAL AXIOM

The weapons scientists' process of moral self-definition begins with their interview at the laboratory—an experience that, in keeping with the privatization of the ethical issue, is structured in terms of an individual's lone encounter with the institution. The process usually begins with a screening interview by laboratory recruiters at the candidate's university campus. Candidates who do well at this first stage are invited to Livermore at the laboratory's expense. At Livermore they give a talk on their research, meet potential colleagues from laboratory programs, and are interviewed by a number of laboratory personnel. Hiring decisions follow a process in which prospective employees and laboratory divisions bargain for their first choices. I was told by Ted, a senior manager, that about one-half of the interviewees are offered jobs and about one-half of these accept.

Ted has been at the laboratory almost since its inception in 1952. He does not recall interviewees voicing qualms about nuclear weapons work until the time of the U.S.–Soviet nuclear testing moratorium from 1958 to 1961, which was immediately preceded by a vigorous national and international debate about the hazards of nuclear testing. During the Vietnam years, about 25 percent of the candidates refused to work on weapons, he said. This number fell off through the 1970s but rose again to about 25 percent in the mid-1980s thanks to the antinuclear movement. Ted told me that over the years he had learned to ask interviewees whether they would be willing to work on nuclear weapons in a way that made a "yes" more likely. This partly involved presenting them with a simple up-or-down choice rather than encouraging them to think in depth about where they would draw their own moral boundaries. He saw his own task as interviewer as, in part, one of "getting their [candidates'] interest in the physics to outweigh their natural repugnance at the task."

As recently as the 1960s and 1970s, many interviewers did not ask candidates if they would have difficulty working on nuclear weapons, often assuming that the interviewee would not be there if he or she did. One associate director also told me that in those days it was not unusual for scientists to accept a job at the laboratory without having a clear idea of what they would be working on: "We would just interview people in this big room with no windows and assure them they would be working on something interesting." More recently laboratory interviewers have tended to ensure that interviewees know what project they would work on and that they have given overt consent.

If candidates are not asked during the interview whether they would be willing to work on nuclear weapons, their moral consent is simply presumed by themselves and others once they begin such work. If they are asked this question, then at this point they must make a public proclamation of their moral identity in regard to nuclear weapons. Either way the interview is an important threshold in the social production of the novice's identity as a weapons scientist: this is the moment when, overtly or not, he or she consents to join the moral community of weapons scientists. Interviewees may feel, like a couple of younger weapons scientists I interviewed, that they have only given provisional consent, privately reserving for themselves the option of changing their minds about weapons work at a later date, but they are now embarked on a process of self-definition from which it is hard, though not impossible, to withdraw. They have begun a commitment.[22]

Clark vividly remembers his interview and the sense of taking a step toward a new and unfamiliar identity.

> I was invited out here and came out here and had the interview, and I was
> a little surprised. When I was invited out, you know, somehow I was still so
> wrapped up in what I was doing in the lab [in graduate school], I really

thought they were inviting me out somehow to use the skills I developed in graduate school, maybe on their fusion program or something. The first thing they told me when I came out was that I would be interviewed by the nuclear weapons program, as a potential nuclear weapons designer. My head started turning real fast on that one. I had given a little thought that I probably would talk to some people in the nuclear weapons program, but I thought I'd talk to people in other programs too, and somehow I had the choice or something. The way it was presented to me—in a very stark way—coupled with the fingerprinting and all that stuff was kind of a shock. . . . They used to fingerprint people when they brought them in for a job interview. They stopped doing that. I have no idea why they ever fingerprinted, but they did. . . . Now my only option at that point was to say "Fuck you guys" and walk out, or to go through with the process. And I heard that at least one person told them at that point, "Forget it. I'm getting out." . . . They had asked me something about nuclear weapons in the initial job interview. At that time I gave a guarded response that indicated I wasn't totally closed to it, but I was concerned and had to really think this through. . . . The fact that I expressed some ambivalence about it, that meant that everybody, all the interviewers out here, every single one of them would come in—they had read on the guy's interview report—and said, "Ah, it says here that you feel a little funny about nuclear weapons work. Tell me about that." Well I knew where my bread was buttered and so I said, "Oh, it feels a little weird, but I understand good people have to do it."

Laboratory employees have different rhythms for resolving or reaching a truce with the ethical dilemmas of weapons work. For some, the issue is never completely resolved. An engineer, for example, told me, "It [the ethical issue] always comes back—for me anyway. It's not pushed away for good. You read it in the paper all the time. Guys like you want to come along and talk about it. . . . There's no single turning point in a person's life I don't think—at least not in mine." Others told me they resolved the issue early on in their careers at the laboratory. One scientist put the issue to rest by taking a trip to the Soviet Union between accepting a job at the laboratory and beginning his work. He wanted to talk to Soviet citizens about the job offer and to make sure the work felt right after a trip to the Soviet Union. (It did.)[23] In the case of an engineer who worked at the laboratory, a close friend said, "He's like most of the guys at the lab. Maybe they thought once about whether it's OK to work on nuclear weapons or not, but it's not as if they're thinking about it all the time now. He said something like that the other night. He and his wife discussed it when they first got married, but now they don't discuss it anymore."

As weapons scientists mature, socially and ideologically, they develop a strong commitment to what we might call the "central axiom" of laboratory life: the laboratory designs nuclear weapons to ensure, in a world stabilized by nuclear deterrence, that nuclear weapons will never be used.[24] For example, the Livermore scientist John Futterman (1992: 7–8) writes, "I do what I can to make waging unlimited war dangerous, and preparation for it expensive. . . . I could say that if I didn't do it, someone else would, but that argument was rejected at Nuremberg. I support the nuclear weapons business . . . to hold up an unmistakable caution flag to humanity demanding we make peace."

To antinuclear activists and laboratory critics, this sort of thinking seems like a hollow and dangerous cliché, but then every group's most deeply held ideological beliefs appear to their opponents as inexplicable and meaningless clichés. Ideology naturalizes itself as common sense, and one group's common sense is another group's nonsense (Geertz 1983: 73–93). Part of the process of maturing as a weapons scientist, quite apart from learning the physics and engineering, is coming to see the laboratory's central axiom not as an empty cliché but as a simple truth. For Clark, struggling to make sense of his transition from physics graduate student protesting the Vietnam War to nuclear weapons designer, this took a little time.

> I had to wrestle with those differences [between the Vietnam War and nuclear weapons work] for a while, and I really did come to the conclusion— which I still feel—that there is quite a difference between kind of a stalemated nuclear deterrence and an active policy of dropping a bomb on friendly or moderate or neutral villages. Certainly one important difference to me was: in the one people were dying, in the other they weren't.

The important point here, and the one that was most difficult for me to grasp, is Clark's perception that it is *more* ethical to work on nuclear weapons than on conventional weapons. For many people, nuclear weapons are the more immoral because they can kill so many people, and kill them so indiscriminately: they are weapons of genocide. Clark sees things the other way round. It is the conventional weapons that he could never work on, precisely because they are less destructive and, consequently, are routinely used to kill people. For him, nuclear weapons, because they are so awful, are not so much a means of killing people as chips in a symbolic game.

To make the ethical issue still murkier, nuclear weapons scientists often point out that in a world where other countries can potentially attack the United States with nuclear weapons or where conventional wars happen, it may be as morally problematic not to work on nuclear weapons, thus exposing civilians to predatory attack, as to work on them. As Richard put it when I asked him whether his weapons work troubled his conscience, "No, your conscience should trouble you either way. If you don't work on weapons, think of all the people you may be endangering by leaving them undefended. The moral questions aren't simple." Phil, a warhead designer who came to work at the laboratory during Stalin's worst years, said he was reminded of

> some quote about what Cromwell said about war—you know, some of these things, if you had your choices, you wouldn't do it, but still it's something that has to be done. I think it's in this context that these were things that had to be done, and I still do think that I would not like to see the world today if the role in the atomic energy field between us and the USSR had been reversed.

Matthew, another designer, agreed: "The most likely road to war is the gradual encroachment on the weak by the strong."

In order for the scientists' central axiom—that nuclear weapons exist to save lives and prevent war—to be believable, nuclear weapons scientists must be convinced in their bones that deterrence will not break down; they must have internalized as an integral part of their feeling and thinking selves the conviction that the weapons really will not be used. As the veteran warhead designer Clark Groseclose put it in an interview with a local journalist,

> I gave a lot of thought to this before I started working on weapons. I still reexamine the issue as time passes. I've come to the conclusion that what I'm working on . . . will provide a deterrent capability that will prevent someone else from using explosives that would perhaps kill a million people. If I was working on an explosive with the thought it's going to be used to kill a million people, I wouldn't work under those circumstances. (Rogers 1980)

I heard the same point over and over again. For instance, Jack, a warhead designer, explaining why he accepted a job at the laboratory in the 1950s, said,

> We needed to get our military prestige back up to the place that we weren't going to have wars. We were attacked [at Pearl Harbor] because we were weak. . . . I think the first thing you do is you arm up, and I think that really

it's a matter of posturing. If you can arm yourself enough, then you don't get into those conflicts. . . . I think I must have had a faith that they wouldn't drop them unless it was a national survival issue. We weren't going to just go out and start dropping them on people just to flex our muscles and clout. . . . It's such a drastic step that you really can't think that somebody is going to do that willy-nilly.

In my interviews I made a point of asking weapons scientists whether they expected nuclear weapons to be used in their lifetimes, whether they had nightmares about nuclear war, and whether they themselves would ever use a nuclear weapon. Although some admitted to occasional concerns, none had had nightmares about nuclear war; with one exception,[25] none expected nuclear weapons to be used in his lifetime, unless it was by a Third World country;[26] and many said they could think of no circumstances in which they would themselves order the use of nuclear weapons. Michael, a warhead designer, said, "If I was president and we were under nuclear attack, would I order retaliation with nuclear weapons? No way. The things only exist to deter attack. Once you get to where they're being used, they've already failed, there's no use for them."

Besides the central axiomatic argument that nuclear weapons keep the peace by raising the price of war too high, I heard, less often, a few subsidiary rationales from laboratory employees. I heard it said, for example, that someone else would be doing the work if they were not, that people who design nuclear weapons are not responsible for the decisions of people who use them, and that in a world where nuclear weapons already exist, it is important that the best people work on them to make them as safe as possible.

Three warhead designers told me that it was illogical to hold weapons scientists directly responsible for what other people did with their designs. Barry told me, "It's not an ethical issue. You design them. Other people figure out what to do with them." Matthew said, "I help to provide these weapons. You ought not to use the weapons, but I don't connect that with whether I develop a particular warhead." And Harvey, one of the most experienced designers at the laboratory, retorted when I asked him if he worried about the weapons being used, "Is an automobile manufacturer responsible for the people killed by drunk drivers?"

A very different point of view was given by John, a nuclear chemist at the laboratory. In his interview with me he argued that in an imperfect world where the weapons already exist, it is important that highly competent scientists keep working on them. John is sometimes challenged about his work by people in his family, since some of them were bombed in Nagasaki in 1945. Unlike most of his colleagues, he does not accept that the bombing of Hiroshima and Nagasaki was justified, though he wonders why it was worse to drop an atomic bomb on these cities than to cause even greater civilian casualties with conventional bombing in Tokyo and Dresden. He had recently visited Hiroshima: "It was incredible to me that just being there would cause that much difference in my perception. It made me wonder if you've ever thought enough about what you do for a job." He points out how difficult it is for individuals to make a difference: "I can want for people not to go hungry, but how do I make that happen as an individual?" He did support a bilateral nuclear freeze in the 1980s, but the development of nuclear weapons continued. If individuals have so little power, he wonders how much responsibility they have, where the boundary lies that cannot be crossed with ethical integrity. "If you're a secretary or a custodian at the lab, you're not too close. You never have to confront it as fully as if you're a little closer. How close can you get before it bothers you? I could never be a button-presser at a missile silo."[27]

John has decided that he can contribute to the development of nuclear weapons because, even if he cannot stop the arms race, he can help ensure that American nuclear weapons are safer and less likely to pollute the environment, "that—this sounds really sick—that we have a better-quality product in the end." He added, "When I arrived at the laboratory the stockpile already existed. Guys were saying, 'How can we make bombs safer if they're dropped from a plane or hit by a bullet?' The things they worked on were very sensible. Here's this evil and, given the situation, how do you make it more stable?"[28]

THE CHURCHES AND NUCLEAR WEAPONS

Roughly two-thirds of the laboratory employees I came to know in Livermore identified themselves as members of a local church and went to church at least part of the time.[29] Of these, over one-third were Catholics. Thus the stance of the local churches, especially the two local Catholic churches, vis-à-vis the laboratory is important since many there and in the wider community look to local clergy for leadership.[30]

Many historians and sociologists of science have emphasized recently that laboratory science cannot be understood solely in terms of what scientists do in laboratories. They have stressed the importance of analyzing practical and ideological alliances between laboratory scientists and, for example, politicians, bankers, military leaders, and consumers.[31] Little has been said, however, about alliances between scientists and clergy—two groups too easily presumed since Galileo and Darwin to be in simple antipathy. In the case of many Livermore scientists, one cannot fully understand their moral development and ideological commitments without taking into account their membership in local churches. Furthermore, as the essayist Grace Mojtabai (1986) has pointed out in her fine portrait of nuclear culture in Amarillo, Texas, many Americans of all kinds reflexively reach for their Bibles when confronted with the dilemmas raised by nuclear weapons.

Churches in Livermore, in most of which laboratory employees play an important role as parishioners and officers, are institutions located outside the laboratory fence that act in concert with processes within the fence to socialize weapons scientists and to sustain the ideological identity of laboratory employees, although the relationships of individual churches with the laboratory may vary in subtle and interesting ways. While formally distinct from the laboratory, local churches are ideological apparatuses[32] enmeshed with the laboratory world in a way that is beautifully symbolized by the logo on the Livermore United Methodist Church's newsletter: a cross inside an atom.[33]

The synergistic relationship between church and laboratory in Livermore did come under pressure in the 1980s as a consequence of an unprecedented debate about U.S. defense policy in America's mainstream churches. In 1981, the National Council of Churches, the overarching organization of America's mainline Protestant denominations, issued a resolution urging the U.S. government to negotiate a nuclear freeze with the Soviets (Evan and Hilgartner 1987: 257). In the same year, the General Assembly of the American Presbyterian Church published its "Call to Halt the Arms Race," endorsing a nuclear freeze, deep cuts in nuclear weapons, and a transfer of resources from Western military spending to Third World aid (ibid., 254–255). In 1982, the United Methodist Council of Bishops released a pastoral letter exhorting the same remedies as the Presbyterians. (Four years later, they issued a book-length document making the same points.) In 1982, the Episcopal House of Bishops issued a pastoral letter condemning the arms race and excoriating the U.S. policy of striking first with nuclear weapons in certain circumstances (ibid., 255–256).[34] Even some Evangelicals were drawn into the groundswell of religious opposition to nuclear weapons: the National Association of Evangelicals issued a statement in 1982 calling for an end to the arms race, and Billy Graham began to speak out against the arms race, saying that, "if continued, [it] will inevitably lead to a conflagration so great that Auschwitz will look like a minor rehearsal" (Wallis 1983: 21). Finally, climactically, in 1983, the National Conference of Catholic Bishops (1983) published its controversial and widely publicized pastoral letter on war and peace, declaring that the use of nuclear weapons would be a sin, that the arms race should be ended, and that nuclear deterrence was morally acceptable "not as an end in itself but as a step toward a progressive disarmament." The bishops' pastoral letter, together with appeals by individual bishops to military personnel and defense workers to examine their consciences, received extensive national media coverage and even prompted some to leave the military (Broad 1992: 122).[35]

The national upheaval sent tremors through Livermore's ecclesiastical life, but none that caused structural damage. Whereas large sectors of the national ecclesiastical community moved in the 1980s toward public intervention in the nuclear weapons debate, churches in Livermore persisted for the most part in treating the ethics of the laboratory's work as an issue for individuals to grapple with in private. The biggest church in Livermore, the Catholic church, largely ignored its bishops' pastoral letter. The Episcopal church, dependent on the laboratory for about three-fourths of its congregation, likewise ignored its bishops. At one point in the 1980s, the Episcopal church had a young visiting minister who opposed the laboratory's work, but, I was told, he had a nervous breakdown and left. The United Methodist church in Livermore also downplayed its bishops' position, even though the regional Methodist bishop, Leontine Kelly, was arrested for civil disobedience at the laboratory gates in the 1980s. In 1983, the minister at the Methodist church in Pleasanton, the next town down the freeway from Livermore, also committed civil disobedience at the laboratory, but he was dismissed soon afterward (Butterfield 1983). The Livermore Presbyterian church has tended to support the laboratory's work in general while opposing the more extreme manifestations of cold war ideology. The Unitarian Fellowship hired a minister in 1981 who, along with some others at the Fellowship, was troubled by the laboratory's work, though, after a number of struggles, she drew back from confrontation with the laboratory employees in her congregation.[36]

The difference between mainline churches in Livermore and in surrounding communities was evident in 1988 and 1989 when an interdenominational group of religious antinuclear activists, brought together by Berkeley's Ecumenical Peace Institute, staged two peace pilgrimages from the Concord Naval Weapons Base to the Livermore laboratory forty miles away. The pilgrims walked ten miles a day for four days, stopping each evening for a public meeting on peace issues at a church along the way. The organizers were primarily Catholics, Methodists, Lutherans, and Baptists, though Anglicans, Jews, Buddhists, and a number of more loosely affiliated religious people joined in. The "pilgrimages" took place during Lent and culminated in prayer services and demonstrations (with civil disobedience) at the gates of the laboratory on Good Friday. Each day the walkers were fed and sheltered by different churches—Methodist, Catholic, Lutheran, Presbyterian, and Unitarian—in towns on the way to Livermore. In Livermore itself, they could find no church that would extend them such hospitality. The walkers' only interaction with Livermore congregations came when they scattered across town to various Maundy Thursday services, though in the case of the Episcopal church, the minister warned that he would have the police remove them if they attempted to proselytize or make trouble.[37]

When I asked local ministers what they saw as the principal concerns of their ministry, the presence of a nuclear weapons laboratory in their parish was usually not on the list. Instead they mentioned the breakdown of the family; marital counseling; the lack of community in a suburb full of commuters; maintaining church attendance, especially among younger people; and, in one case, Satanism. One local Catholic priest gave a not unusual answer when I asked, "I wonder whether being in a parish with a nuclear weapons laboratory creates any special issues or whether it's like being in any other parish." He replied,

> People have asked that kind of question many times. The fact that there's a lab out there has not really affected my ministry, how I deal with people and so on. . . . This has not been a big issue between the parish and the lab. . . . My main issues in Livermore would be the same I'd have anywhere I was

a priest—to try to help people spiritually primarily, but also materially. There are a lot of poor people in the parish who are in need, that sort of thing. Also psychological counseling, marital—either preparation for marriages or unhappy marriages. . . . Many of the people at the lab are people who work at the church in our various ministries. They perform some of the duties we have like reading the Scripture and so on. They sit on the parish council. They're involved in the Knights of Columbus. So you just think of them as other parishioners. I don't think, "This man's from the lab and this man's from K-Mart." They're just parishioners. . . . I find them basically very good family people, responsible people, raising some very good families. . . . They're very community-minded, proud of their community and what happens to it.

In this interview the same Catholic priest, explaining his dislike for antinuclear activists and Operation Rescue protestors, told me he did not see it as his job to condemn people for their actions, but to help them if they seek help. Some laboratory scientists came to him for counseling on their marital and child-raising problems, but they did not ask his advice on their work. "Sometimes I wonder why they don't talk about that. Maybe they discuss it with more senior theologians," he said. He personally considers the bombing of Hiroshima and Nagasaki to have been a sin but accepts the existence of nuclear weapons for purposes of deterrence. In what can only be described as a highly heterodox interpretation of the Catholic bishops' pastoral letter, he told me the bishops said it was permissible to use nuclear weapons "as a last resort against unlawful invasion" and as long as they were only used against military targets. In fact, the bishops' pastoral letter expressed skepticism about the distinction between military and civilian targets in the nuclear age and said, "We do not perceive any situation in which the deliberate initiation of nuclear warfare on however restricted a scale can be morally justified" (National Conference of Catholic Bishops 1983: 47). The priest concluded the interview by saying that, unlike some of the fundamentalist ministers in town, he believed that human beings would be rational enough not to use nuclear weapons. "I'm more optimistic. I don't see the end of the world. Christ came to the world to save it, not condemn it."

Four other interviews, three with mainline Protestant ministers and one with an Evangelical minister, paint a broadly similar picture of local clergy, often for quite different reasons endorsing, or at least not challenging, the work of the laboratory.[38] Although their reasoning and their politics are quite different, all four in their different ways lend their institutions' legitimating power to the laboratory's work.

The first Protestant minister told me he was not sure of his national church's stand on nuclear weapons—it had in fact come out in support of a nuclear freeze a few years earlier—but said that he personally supported the laboratory's work. He saw it as essential not only in preventing war but also, and here he gave the example of the Cuban missile crisis, in preventing "blackmail." He had occasionally preached on nuclear weapons, but not often, and nuclear weapons were not an issue in his personal counseling of laboratory employees. He referred to antinuclear activists as "idiots who come marching through town seeking confrontation" and wondered aloud if their protests were instigated by Communists.

The second Protestant minister with whom I spoke had very different politics. He was a pacifist and former conscientious objector who, like the Catholic priest, believed in treating people of all views with respect rather than confronting or condemning them, and he was anxious not to fracture his congregation with divisive political debates. He respected both those participating in the laboratory's work (about a third of his congregation) and those opposed to it (two whom he knew of in his congregation). He was heartened that the last two years had seen some opening of communication between the two sides in his congregation. The scientists in his congregation did not come to him with any struggles of conscience they might be having. They asked his advice only on their personal lives. He saw the essential ambiguity at the heart of the nuclear dilemma, saying, "'Blessed are the peacemakers' could apply to scientists at the laboratory, you know. That's certainly the way they see it." In the end, although he thinks a lot in private about the possible use of nuclear weapons, he retains his faith that the human capacity for love and creativity will triumph, that God's love will triumph, and that there will be no holocaust. "I don't expect the Second Coming to be cataclysmic," he says.

The third Protestant minister I interviewed has, over the course of some years in Livermore, come to know many senior scientists and administrators at the laboratory. He does preach about nuclear weapons policy from time to time, and he does quite often discuss the ethics and politics of the laboratory's work with individual scientists. Of all the pastors I spoke to, he was the only one who had a detailed knowledge of the laboratory's work and a rich understanding of the scientists' thinking—not to mention a passionate interest in laboratory gossip. He is guided in his attitude by a profound sense of the complexity and ambiguity of human affairs. "Good and evil both are ambiguous, and as human beings we try to steer between the rocks. It's an ambiguous course often, and we're not sure if we steer toward the light or toward its reflection." He sees ethics as a matter of "weighing evils" and assessing the consequences of different courses of action, each impure in its own way. This consequentialist approach provides provisional support, at least, for deterrence.

> I wish we could function without war. . . . [But] I don't want to be just a patsy. I respect the pacifists who say, "I'll live with what it takes. I'll sacrifice my children and your children for the sake of it." I respect their willingness to suffer like that. I do not agree with their willingness to let others suffer. And a good pacifist, I think, thinks about that, and that's their gut-ache. In the end none of us seems to have a morality that leaves us without a stomachache. . . . At least with the pacifists I share the view that you must try everything besides war. . . . But the pacifist has to accept the bodies that are caused by pacifism. And it's easy to create them now. I don't think pacifism has worked well in Latin America. The death squads love pacifists. They pick them up and bury them.

He believes that the only way to make these ambiguous judgments wisely is by integrating biblical understanding with knowledge of nuclear strategy and arms control so that ethical judgments can be made with technically informed knowledge of the likely consequences.

> If I just talk about ethics, apart from their machines, and, you know, the guy who went back to Washington said, "Let me tell you what I know they're developing on the other side. What do you think about that?" And I said, "Well, I don't know what to think about that, but I do know that in the Bible . . ." If I do that, they're going to just turn me off. I'd turn myself off. I don't see how you can talk ethics unless you know the nuts and bolts, to know what the effect is of what you say. And if you're saying "ban everything," just like that, it seems like you have a responsibility to know what the consequences are, and then it means you'd better learn about the machinery you're really talking about, and what happens if someone else does develop that little machine that shoots neutrons or high-particle beams.

It was on such grounds that he and most scientists in his congregation opposed the nuclear freeze, even though it was supported by his national church. "The feeling here was that it's just too simple. That was my view as well." Throughout the 1980s, he did, however, strongly urge arms control negotiations, and he preached about the danger of demonizing the Soviets.

> They [his congregation] know that I feel the Soviet Union is not the evil empire. They know that I feel it's full of some evil, but I know I feel we're full of evil. . . . If we as a congregation of the church believe that the spirit of God exists in all human beings, somewhere there is something to tap. . . . Doesn't it behoove us before we build weapons to first learn something about those who seem to be our opposition? So why is it we don't learn Russian in our local schools? Why is our sense of Russian history zero? . . . Why, if they're our enemy, don't we even learn their language, their culture, and their customs?

The Evangelical minister I interviewed presides over a smaller church that he describes as "Evangelical but noncharismatic with a strong missionary emphasis." The congregation is unanimous in opposing abortion. He does not see the laboratory as an issue in his ministry. The issues that concern him are the spiritual problems of suburban society: alcoholism, divorce, and family relationships. He has an alert sense of human sinfulness and mistrusts humanist beliefs that people can be redeemed by science—"What in the world does the space shuttle have to do with man's fallen nature? How does it solve the sin problem? How does it save us from Charles Manson? How does it keep man sexually satisfied?"—but at the same time he believes that

> God gave man authority over every creeping thing. God wants us to explore. He built that into our nature, and if I could, I'd love to be out there at that lab doing some of this stuff. . . . The weapons aren't so much of a moral issue to me because they're not here to be used; they're here to deter. . . . I sometimes wish we could take that money and spend it on the poor, not on missiles, but this is a dangerous world. My view of man is not quite so high. I'm pessimistic about man, optimistic about God.

When, in conclusion, I asked him about the third verse of the second book of Peter—the verse predicting that at the end of the world "the elements will be dissolved with fire and the earth and the works that are upon it shall be burned up"—he grew pensive.

> It's certainly a perfect description of a nuclear holocaust. Once I thought that was what it referred to. Now I don't know. That's really God's business, not mine. Maybe it means we'll kill ourselves with nuclear weapons, or maybe it means God will do it himself for some reason. I don't want to predict

anything. If you look at all the people who have tried to say who the anti-Christ was—first it was Hitler, then Mussolini, then Stalin—you see how pointless it is to try to predict exactly. . . . I see Peter as a warning, but it's hard to know what path this means we should take. Not building nuclear weapons might make Peter less likely, or it might make Peter more likely. . . . I'm optimistic about God. He has his reasons. If it happened, maybe it would be to spare unborn generations from the pain of man killing man. It's like Hiroshima; you know Hiroshima saved more lives in the long run.[39]

Four of these ministers do not treat the laboratory's work as an important issue in their ministry, reinforcing the laboratory's construction of the ethics of weapons work as a private rather than a public matter. The one minister who does take a keen interest in the laboratory's work endorses the popular belief at the laboratory that nuclear ethics should be approached consequentially rather than deontologically and that moral judgments of nuclear policy must be grounded in expert technical knowledge. Four of the ministers believe that the laboratory's work is an appropriate means of keeping the peace and defending important human values. The one who is inclined to disagree does not, however, press his disagreement because of his conviction that Christians should walk the world with an open heart. Four of these ministers are led by their theological instincts to believe that a nuclear holocaust is unlikely. The one who disagrees still sees no alternative to nuclear weapons in a world full of sin and danger, so his concerns about Armageddon lead him to a kind of fatalism rather than into opposing the laboratory's work. For him, the only solution to the conundrum of survival is a private one—receiving Christ into one's heart—rather than a collective project of political action.

No matter what their disagreements, the five ministers I interviewed are linked in an ecology of theologies that stabilizes the functioning of the laboratory and sustains new scientists in their voyage to maturity. Despite their differences, local churches in Livermore either endorse or decline to challenge the three main features of the laboratory's own approach to nuclear ethics: the privatization of moral thinking on nuclear weapons; the emphasis on consequentialism in that thinking; and the central axiom that, given the nature of the international system, nuclear weapons offer the best hope of preventing war and saving lives.

CHAPTER 4

Secrecy

To whom you tell your secrets
To him you resign your liberty.
SPANISH PROVERB

The practice of secrecy is an anvil on which the identity of new weapons scientists at the laboratory is forged. Having looked at the processes through which scientists are absorbed into the moral economy of the laboratory, here I turn to the ways in which the investigation of new scientists for security clearance and the insistent daily practice of secrecy help to reshape the identity of weapons scientists. The laboratory's rules of secrecy are applied quite unevenly, and individual scientists often differ widely in their interpretation and manipulation of these rules. Still, as we shall see, the laboratory's culture of secrecy does tend to produce certain effects in its scientists: it segregates laboratory scientists as a privileged but somewhat isolated elite; it inculcates a sense of group loyalty; and it thrusts on laboratory scientists an amorphous surveillance, which can become internalized.

A SECRET WORLD

The U.S. defense establishment has created an enormous secret world next to but separate from the everyday world inhabited by the rest of us.[1] In the 1980s it was occupied by four million Americans with security clearances (Miall 1987: 91). The Department of Energy (DOE), the agency responsible for nuclear weapons design, has classified over two and a half million documents and was adding about 130,000 more each year in the 1980s (DeVolpi et al. 1981: 142). During the same period, the U.S. government bureaucracy was creating new secret documents at a rate of about seven million a year (*Harper's* 1992). Some of these involve apparently quite trivial information; for many years, for example, the government classified as secret the number of toilet rolls bought by the Oak Ridge nuclear weapons facility—so that Soviet agents could not use this information to estimate the number of employees there (Davis 1990).

The secrets handled by nuclear weapons scientists are of a kind known as Restricted Data (RD). The Atomic Energy Act of 1954 defined RD as "all data concerning (1) design, manufacture, or utilization of atomic weapons; (2) the production of special nuclear material; or (3) the use of special nuclear material in the production of energy" (Atomic Energy Act 1954: Sec. 214). This means that any new ideas produced by weapons scientists concerning nuclear weapons design or nuclear materials production are automatically and immediately classified and continue to be considered classified until they are explicitly declassified. They are, as the government puts it, "classified at birth" or "born secret."

A laboratory scientist needs a Q clearance to see classified information, most of which is divided into categories according to its subject matter, and to see any particular category of information—for example, test results of X-ray laser experiments—an employee must, in addition to his or her Q clearance, have an officially certified "need to know." The need to know indicates that the scientist needs access to that category of information in order to do his or her assigned work (Hilgartner, Bell, and O'Connor 1982: 60–64; Phillips 1974). Each kind of need to know is called a "sigma," of which there are about a dozen. As one scientist, Ron, explained the system to me,

> If you have a sigma one clearance, that means that you have access to nuclear weapons design information of some kind or another. At sigma two you have some other information, and so on. They're not ranked,[2] it's just the more sigmas you have, the merrier, so to speak. Most people who would be in the weapons field would normally have sigmas one, two, and three. If they have anything to do with the X-ray laser, then they have another sigma. . . . It's complicated.

Q-cleared scientists at Livermore wear green badges. Employees without, or awaiting, Q clearance usually wear red badges, which, as one man with only a red badge sadly and with only slight exaggeration told me, "anyone can get." Employees who are allowed to see highly sensitive intelligence information about foreign countries' military capabilities wear blue badges. A small but growing number of laboratory employees have yellow badges, denoting L clearances, which afford access to areas of the laboratory where classified research is carried out but not to classified information. An L clearance is sought, for example, for the man who delivers bottled water throughout the laboratory or for those members of the laboratory's Environmental Protection Department who must monitor compliance with environmental regulations throughout the laboratory but have no need to know the details of research projects. L clearances, formerly very rare at Livermore, have become more common in the last few years: the government has become so backlogged in its Q clearance investigations that it is encouraging the laboratory to apply for L clearances wherever possible as they entail a less protracted and expensive vetting process.

This enormous and complex system for categorizing people and information structures the laboratory employee's experience of social and geographic space at work. The laboratory is an enormous grid of tabooed spaces and tabooed topics. These taboos become part of the everyday practical consciousness of all laboratory employees as the practice of secrecy is encoded in their daily routines in ways that soon come to be taken for granted. Every time employees move from one part of the laboratory to another, discuss their work with other employees, go to the bathroom, or take a coffee break, observance of the taboos is a part of their routine. It is, on a daily basis, engraved and reengraved into their practical consciousness.[3]

As a geographic space, the laboratory is divided into zones of greater or lesser exclusion that relate to the system for classifying information and clearing people. The laboratory is, as one employee put it, "a box within a box within a box" (quoted in Kiernan 1988b). A few areas on the perimeter of the laboratory are "white areas," to which even members of the public have free access. The white area contains, among other things, two cafeterias, some of the laboratory's athletic facilities, the public affairs department, the Visitors Center, and an employment office. Large parts of the laboratory are "red areas," where no classified work is done and where those with both red and green badges may wander freely.[4] Although no secret work is done in the red areas, they are off-limits to unescorted members of the public. Thus they act as a kind of buffer zone between the more sensitive areas of the laboratory and the outside world. As one employee put it, "The red zone controls who comes on site. It stops just any Tom, Dick, or Harry from coming in off the street looking for a bathroom right next to where classified research is done." The red zone is more than simply a buffer zone, however. It is also a place where laboratory scientists who lack clearances can carry out nonclassified research. It is essential to the laboratory's identity as more than just a weapons facility.

Classified research is done in "green areas," which encompassed roughly half of the laboratory in the 1980s. Only those with green or yellow badges may enter these areas unescorted. Within the green areas, there are "exclusion areas," set apart by barbed-wire fences with guard booths, where only those with special rights of access are allowed. To enter such areas, one must have special coding on one's green badge or special permission to enter (Kiernan 1988*b*). The most important exclusion area is the laboratory's plutonium facility. Here, in the words of a laboratory security manager, Lynn Cleland, "guards with automatic rifles, handguns and incripted [*sic*] radios patrol the area 24 hours a day. People who want to get into the building have to go through many layers of access and controls. Those who enter and leave the building, no matter what their access level, are subject to search and inspection by metal detectors and X-ray devices" (*Independent* 1989: 2).

There is also a "blue area," where highly sensitive intelligence information about foreign military capabilities is handled. Access to this area is allowed only to those with blue badges—a rare type of badge that I never saw because it cannot be removed from the blue area building itself. Employees collect their blue badges every day as they enter the green part of the building containing the blue area. The information handled in the blue badge area is considered particularly sensitive because, in the wrong hands, it might facilitate the identification of American spies in foreign countries.

Without a green badge, a scientist is not a full adult member of the laboratory. One official said life at the laboratory without a green badge was like being "in a leper colony" (Wald 1990). Scientists without green badges cannot visit their green-badged colleagues in their offices, unless chaperoned. They often hear their green-badged colleagues say, "We can't talk about that in front of so-and-so. He's not Q-cleared." And they must be "escorted" at all times when in green areas. One woman without a Q clearance told me about the time she was assigned with a group of four other people without green badges to consult in a green badge area. When one member of the group went to smoke a cigarette outside, the rest of the group and the escort had to go too. When one went to the bathroom, they all had to go. Once they reached the bathroom, the escort would go in and shout that an uncleared person was coming in, just in case classified material was being discussed over the washbasins. "That was really humiliating," she said. One particularly conscientious escort even stayed in the bathroom with her to keep her under surveillance. If an uncleared person enters certain buildings at the laboratory, for example, the director's building, sandwich boards may be put out in the corridor to warn of the outsider's presence, and a secretary may walk along the corridor announcing the outsider's arrival and shutting people's doors, to protect classified information they may be discussing or reading. To lack a green badge is to be continually set apart in ways that are routinely, if modestly, humiliating.[5]

INVESTIGATION

To obtain a red badge, employees fill out a short questionnaire and wait while the government does a rudimentary check to see if they have criminal records. They usually get their red badge within a couple of weeks. Yellow badges do not take much longer. To obtain a green badge, however, scientists must endure a more grueling process of investigation.

To acquire a Q clearance, to "turn green" as employees put it, scientists must submit to protracted investigation by the federal government. Although laboratory employees often talk about their "FBI investigations," in practice most investigations are handled by the Office of Personnel Management (OPM) rather than the FBI. Employees first fill out a lengthy questionnaire, on which they must indicate whether they are a member of the Communist party or have ever belonged to a group advocating the overthrow of the U.S. government, which organizations they belong to, whether they have been arrested, even if charges were dropped,[6] whether they have alcohol problems and whether, within the last five years, they have "used, possessed, supplied, or manufactured any illegal drugs."[7] And they must reveal any condition for which they sought the aid of a psychiatrist, psychotherapist, or psychologist (*Newsline* 1990a). They must also list relatives and all past employers, supervisors, and spouses as well as all the addresses at which they have lived. If an employee's job will involve handling "special nuclear material" such as plutonium, he or she must also submit to annual drug tests and psychological evaluations screening for drug or alcohol dependency (DOE 1989).

The government is quite strict about the level of detail it requires in filling out the application form. There are not supposed to be gaps of more than one month in applicants' home addresses and employment histories, and relatives are to be listed with middle initials and dates of birth. I know of one case in which government officials complained that a laboratory employee had not provided the birthdate of a stepbrother she had not seen in fifteen years.

The process of initial investigation for a Q clearance can take from six months to two years. During this time, the scientist under investigation must work in a red area and cannot do classified research. After the initial investigation, candidates may be reinvestigated every five years. In practice, however, the federal government lacks the agents to do so.

Edward Shils, writing in the 1950s, remarked on the speculative, open-ended quality of investigations for top-secret clearances. His observations are still applicable today.

> Since there is no adequate scientific indicator of the probability of infringement on security regulations, the quest is unbounded. Every aspect of the person's life is enquired into in the search for the indeterminate clues as to whether he might in the future do something he has never done before.
>
> The net must be cast widely because the investigator has no precise expectation regarding the predispositions of unreliability in the observance of security rules. Almost any quality is relevant and even the most narrowly delimited criterion such as political affiliations soon leads off into many highly ramified by-ways of personal friendship, relationship by marriage or blood, casual acquaintanceships, etc. (Shils 1956: 202)

In the course of their investigations, government agents search the files of schools, criminal justice agencies, employers, banks, credit bureaus, consumer reporting agencies, and hospitals for evidence of a criminal record, mental instability, financial unreliability, or a political history that might, in their opinion, disqualify the applicant from seeing secret information.[8] With the aid of the information given by the applicant, they track down and interview a miscellany of sources: family members, former roommates, employers, lovers, and neighbors. They ask what applicants say in public about their work, what their financial situation is, whether they entertain foreign visitors,[9] whether they use drugs or abuse alcohol, whether they have many overnight guests, and whether their sexual habits are monogamously heterosexual or otherwise. The purpose of these questions, so laboratory scientists told me, is to establish whether an applicant might have a loose tongue, poor judgment, an urgent need for money, or be susceptible to blackmail by a foreign agent.[10]

In some special cases, applicants for a security clearance are interviewed in person or sent to a psychiatrist for testing. Applicants with substance abuse problems, for example, may be required to see a psychiatrist for evaluation. I also know of two homosexuals at another weapons laboratory who, although they were eventually granted clearances, were interviewed in minute detail about their sexual histories and fantasies.

If, as it not infrequently does, an investigation drags into its second year, the applicant begins to feel increasingly anxious. On hearing fragmentary accounts from old friends around the country of the questions being asked, he or she begins to wonder why the investigation is still continuing and who else the government will question. Have the investigators found out about that one time he or she tried marijuana at a party? Or perhaps that drunk driving incident five years ago is the problem. Could that be it? Or even that trip to China two years ago. Has that made the investigators suspicious? Or is a malicious former neighbor telling lies?

In the end, however, the investigation process is not unlike oral examinations in many university departments: departments do not submit candidates for examination unless they think they have a good chance of succeeding, and, although they are subjected to a grueling inspection, it is unusual for them not to pass. Mary Douglas and David Gilmore observe that it is a common feature of initiation rituals, a part of their mystique, that people, especially the initiates themselves, believe there is a much greater danger of failure than is really the case (Douglas 1984: 96; Gilmore 1990). If we accept that investigation for a security clearance is a bureaucratized kind of initiation ritual, it seems that the rationale for the process is as much to unnerve, discipline, and transform as to evaluate candidates. For example, even if the government does find evidence of past drug use or current alcohol problems, it often grants clearance with the proviso that the applicant promise not to use drugs again, or that he or she go for counseling. I heard of very few cases in which people were denied Q clearance. In one case, a man had consistently declared bankruptcy every seven years and was thought to be too financially vulnerable. In another instance, a woman was refused clearance because colleagues reported they had smelled alcohol on her breath at work and because she had falsified time cards.[11]

THE DAILY PRACTICE OF SECRECY

Once laboratory employees receive their Q clearances, they become members of a new world with its own arcane daily practices of ritual secrecy. First they are given a laminated green badge bearing their photograph and special coding indicating the parts of the laboratory to which they have access. (The ritual significance of these badges in creating a new identity is nicely illustrated by a story told to me by an antinuclear activist: she was arguing with a scientist about the laboratory's environmental record when he suddenly took off his badge and said, "Now I'll tell you what I really think.") According to guidelines in the laboratory newsletter,

> When on site, your badge must remain under your immediate control and be worn so the view of the entire badge is unobstructed. Ideally the badge should be worn on the front portion of the body, somewhere below the neck but above the waist, on the outermost garment. Your badge should never be left unattended. For example, do not leave it on your desk, or hanging from the lock in your door, or unsecured in the swimming pool area. (*Newsline* 1990*b*)

The injunction to wear badges over the chest—which, along with the warning that badges should never be left unattended, is not infrequently ignored in practice—is for more than visual purposes: laboratory badges also have dosimeters that are supposed to be near an employee's heart and lungs so as to measure the exposure of vital organs to radiation.

To penetrate the laboratory each day, employees must present their badges to the armed guards at the outer perimeter. The guards, in theory at least, examine the photographs and touch the badges to make sure they have not been forged or tampered with. After this, to get into green areas within the laboratory, employees either pass through more guard gates or go through a mechanized passage point known as the "CAIN booth." When I first arrived in Livermore, these booths contained videocameras that enabled a guard in a remote location to see the coding on the badge and compare the photograph on it with the person in the booth. If everything was in order, the guard, who regulated several CAIN booths at once from one central location, would press a button and admit the employee to the secure area. While I was doing fieldwork, the laboratory replaced these booths with CAIN-II booths, which work like automated bank tellers: the employee puts his or her badge into a slot in the booth and enters a personal code. Meanwhile, scales in the booth measure the employee's weight and a computer compares it with that employee's recorded weight to ensure that two people are not sneaking through on one person's badge and that the person entering is the proper owner of the badge. The computer allows a few extra pounds of weight so that employees can bring in coats and briefcases. The booths also record the location in time and space of individual badge holders so that the laboratory knows who was where at what time in case this information should be useful later, for example, for an investigation into accidents or thefts.

There are also rules prohibiting certain items from being brought into the laboratory, and the perimeter guards conduct random searches of employees' cars to enforce these prohibitions. One prohibited item is alcohol, though I knew a couple of employees who became adept at incorporating alcohol into dishes they took into the laboratory for potlucks. Weapons are not allowed. Nor are tape recorders or cameras. Sometimes employees forget to take their cameras out of their cars at the end of the weekend; if the guards catch this, they either destroy the film or confiscate and develop it to make sure it contains no secrets or fragments from which secret information could be reconstructed.

The resources devoted to keeping secrets in their proper place can be considerable. In October 1988, for example, the laboratory mobilized its entire security apparatus to hunt down ten thousand copies of the laboratory newspaper in response to concerns that a snippet of classified information had inadvertently been included in the newspaper's summary of the director's annual "State of the Laboratory" speech. Security guards worked through much of the night, asking employees to return copies they had taken, emptying the newspaper boxes in the laboratory, and searching offices for additional copies. Later they decided that that issue did not contain classified information after all and rereleased it (Bodovitz 1988*b*).

In their daily routines, laboratory employees are supposed to observe certain rules to safeguard the secrets they work with. These rules are designed not only to prevent secrets from escaping the laboratory but also to ensure that no one employee knows too many secrets: the more secrets employees know, the more damage they can do if they are kidnapped or become spies. Thus, for example, employees are trained not to open folders marked Secret or Top Secret, despite their clearance, unless they have a certified need to know the contents of the folder. Nor do they show their documents to others unless they have a need to know. In the classified section of the laboratory's library, employees must demonstrate that they have the appropriate sigma before being allowed access to particular categories of information.

The laboratory takes special precautions to protect information in its computers. If computers are connected in a network, the communications between them are carried by special protected cable to prevent the interception of messages as they pass back and forth. Whenever employees leave their computers, even if they are just going for a cigarette break, they are supposed to make sure that others cannot read their computer files. Sometimes this means merely logging off the computer if no one else knows the password needed to log on again. Many computers have removable hard discs that are supposed to be locked in vaults whenever the person using the computer goes elsewhere. But some employees have to lock rollaway vaults around their computers each time they leave, or physically pick up their computers and put them in locked vaults. And the laboratory tells employees that even if they have erased secret information from floppy discs, they should still lock the empty discs in their vaults to protect the electromagnetic shadow of the erased information.

Employees in the blue area, the Secret Compartmentalized Information Facility (SCIF), where intelligence information is handled, work in a windowless environment. The absence of windows impedes spying and since work in the blue area partly involves working with secret radio frequencies, the walls are lined with copper mesh to prevent anyone outside from intercepting conversations and radiowaves inside. Some subjects are considered so secret that they can only be discussed within the SCIF, and even the laboratory director must come to the SCIF to discuss them. Access to this area is tightly controlled.

Secretaries also learn a special set of rules for using typewriters (though these are used less frequently than computers). If, for example, they have been typing a secret document, the typewriter ribbon must be locked in a vault so that no one can reconstruct the secret document by unraveling and reading the ribbon. Or if they are typing a secret document and someone goes to search for something in, say, the file cabinet behind them, they are supposed to remove the document from the typewriter and put it in their Secret folder until they can proceed with their typing unobserved.

Although the elite warhead designers each have their own offices, similar rules apply to them also. Their offices have locked filing cabinets and locked bookcases in which to store secret information, and the office doors themselves have special locks. During the daytime they are allowed to leave secret documents on their desks, as long as the office door is locked. But when they leave at the end of the day, they must make sure all secret documents are locked away and all secret calculations erased from the whiteboards in their offices. They cannot remove secret documents from the laboratory; it is a serious offense to do so, unless a laboratory security officer gives them an official "ticket to hand carry"— if, for example, they need to take secret documents on a business trip to Los Alamos or Washington. If they do hand-carry secret documents, they are expected to keep them with them at all times. And there are special procedures for disposing of secret documents. Confidential documents and secret drafts are thrown away in large locked trash cans scattered around the laboratory. Final drafts of secret documents, which are regarded as more important, each bear a unique serial number and are logged by a laboratory document custodian as being in the possession of a specific designer. After using them, the designer must return such documents to the document custodian for disposal. In some circumstances, secret documents can be sent to Q-cleared colleagues elsewhere in the country. In such cases the documents are placed inside a brown envelope bearing a warning that it contains classified documents that unauthorized people should not read. This envelope is itself placed inside a plain envelope and sent by registered mail.

Designers and other scientists must also exercise vigilance in their conversations within the laboratory. In theory at least, they are supposed to discuss with other scientists only what they have an officially certified need to know, and, in the words of a poster at the laboratory, Curiosity Is Not a Need to Know. Although scientists not infrequently exercise discretion in observing this restriction, the rule does set limits—however ambiguous—on discussion, and scientists know that in extreme circumstances infractions of this code can always be used against them, maybe even years later, in political struggles within the laboratory. One weapons scientist, articulating the situation with a vagueness that reflects the uneven enactment of many laboratory security regulations, told me about the effect of the need to know regulation on his conversations with a colleague who is a close friend.

> He and I talk a lot. But I have four sigmas and he has none. He just has a Q clearance. So that makes conversations with him tricky. I go to weapons talks, but he can't. There's a lot of stuff I can't talk about with him. Even with people who do have sigmas, it gets quite cognitively complicated to remember what information fits into which category and can or can't be shared. If you were very conscientious about it, the best procedure would be to contact the security people. Pick up the phone and say, "I'm about to talk to Joe Blow about something and I'd like to know what sigma categories he has." If the answer is "He hasn't got any," then you can't talk to him about quite a few things. Now people aren't that careful. If they were obeying the letter of the rule they should be, but I think usually what happens is, if a guy has a green badge, then you generally assume he can hear most everything. But you have to watch out because, again, if you're in a position where you would have reason to know that he didn't have that clearance, you couldn't just say, "Well, I didn't know that."

Thus the laboratory's system of secrecy appears to be more seamless and totalizing in theory, when stated as a set of rules, than in practice, when the rules may be enforced ambiguously and complied with erratically. Bill Perry,[12] a former head of public relations at the laboratory who went on to become an antinuclear activist, has written,

> The irony of all the security, at least during my time there, was that it didn't work very well. In 1982, for instance, a demonstrator climbed over the fence and entered the headquarters building unmolested before being apprehended on the seventh floor. The badging system was so loose an employee could quickly replace a lost badge (I did so three times) and then give it to anyone they wished. The "need to know" doctrine underlying the secrecy was regularly compromised by people using information to trade for information. . . . As Jack Saunders, one of my key staff people often observed, "This place leaks like a sieve." (1990: 25)

Such a comment, however hyperbolic, leads us to wonder what might be the other purposes of the secrecy regime than the keeping of secrets.

A SECRET SOCIETY

At the most obvious, functional level, the laboratory's colored badges, locked trash cans, exclusion areas, and conversational restrictions are part of a system that, however erratic, exists to ensure that foreign governments do not gain access to American military secrets. Looking at the laboratory's system of secrecy with a less literal eye, however, I argue that these regulations also have a role to play in the construction of a particular social order within the laboratory and a particular relationship between laboratory scientists and the outside world. As William Broad (1992: 70) has noted, "Upon acceptance into its [the laboratory's] ranks, one entered a culture that in many respects was separate from American society." Elaborating on this observation, my basic argument here is that the laboratory is a high-tech version of the secret societies that anthropologists have traditionally studied all over the world and that the process of investigation for clearance is a bureaucratic variant of classic initiation rituals found throughout the ethnographic record. In other words, its practices of secrecy should be analyzed not just as ways of preventing other countries from imitating America's weapons programs but also as, in their own right, symbolic practices with social, as well as military, functions and consequences.

Anthropologists and sociologists who have studied secret societies have emphasized that secrecy is a powerful means of making and breaking bonds. Practices of secrecy create loyalty and community among those they join together and, at the same time, a radical sense of separation from those they exclude. And by socially resituating initiates, secret societies remake their identities. Secret societies can also foster obedience and the expectation of special privilege.[13]

I have asked how the laboratory succeeds in bringing together people from different social, religious, and political backgrounds, remaking and melding them into a group that can work together in the development of nuclear weapons. The practice of secrecy itself is a large part of the answer to that question. This is because, as Sissela Bok has written about members of secret societies,

> what unites them is not any one purpose or belief. It is, rather, secrecy itself: secrecy of purpose, belief, methods, often membership. These are kept hidden from outsiders and only by gradual steps revealed to insiders, with

further secrets always beckoning, still to be penetrated. In this way the secret societies hold out the possibility of exclusive access to the forbidden roots of secrecy, and promise the brotherhood and community feeling that many lack in their daily life. [They] give insiders [a] stark sense of separation from outsiders. (1989: 46)

All secret societies are at least a little like what Erving Goffman, in his landmark study of prisons and mental hospitals, *Asylums*, calls "total institutions." These are institutions that are able to sever, control, or reduce the individual's contacts with the rest of society and regulate the minute details of his or her daily existence. Goffman defines a total institution as follows:

A total institution may be defined as a place . . . where a large number of like-situated individuals, cut off from the wider society for an appreciable period of time, together lead an enclosed, formally administered round of life. Prisons serve as a clear example, providing we appreciate that what is prison-like about prisons is found in institutions whose members have broken no laws. . . . Their [total institutions'] encompassing or total character is symbolized by the barrier to social intercourse with the outside and to departure that is often built right into the physical plant, such as locked doors, high walls, barbed wire, cliffs, water, forests, or moors. (1961: xiii, 4)

Goffman goes on to observe that entry to total institutions is usually mediated by a wide range of "admissions procedures" that socially reclassify and psychologically transform those admitted. Some of the examples he gives—undressing people, shaving their hair, replacing their clothes with uniforms—are extreme and do not apply to the laboratory. Others do, for example, "taking a life history, photographing, weighing, fingerprinting, assigning numbers, searching, . . . instructing as to rules, and assigning to quarters" (ibid., 16).

Total institutions have a powerful ability to "deself"[14] people: to alter their position in a field of social relationships and thus to peel away their old identities and create new ones. As Goffman himself puts it, "The recruit comes into the establishment with a conception of himself made possible by certain stable social relationships in his home world. Upon entrance, he is immediately stripped of the support provided by these arrangements. . . . His self is systematically, if often unintentionally, mortified" (ibid., 14).

The ability of the American security system to subordinate and deself individual scientists is vividly captured in Roland Joffe's film *Fat Man and*

If it Amer. sec. system that subordinates scientists how do they play any mol. role ???

Little Boy (1989), a fictionalized re-creation of the Manhattan Project. In one scene, General Groves, the military officer in charge of Los Alamos, greets the new scientists by telling them, "What you see, what you hear, what you read, what you dream about, whatever gives you heartburn or feeds your ulcers. Whatever gives you the sweats, keeps you up at night. Whatever. All of that belongs to the United States army. Or to me, if that makes you feel more comfortable" (quoted in Taylor 1993: 383).

I am not saying here that the laboratory is just like a prison or a Moonie camp. Obviously it is not. Its employees go home every night to their families, and they mix freely with people in Livermore and beyond who have nothing to do with the laboratory, who may even oppose its work. But thinking about the laboratory as a modest kind of total institution, a mild instance of a phenomenon whose characteristics are clearest when it is seen as an "ideal type,"[15] we can gain some analytic leverage on the question of how the laboratory transforms and resocializes its employees. Using the notion of a total institution as a backdrop against which to bring the laboratory into clearer focus, I examine below the part played by secrecy in the resocialization of laboratory scientists, in particular, the role of surveillance and segregation in this process.

SURVEILLANCE

At one point in my fieldwork, I took a young scientist from the laboratory to a large gathering in Berkeley hosted by some radical antinuclear activists, many of them self-described anarchists.[16] Dana had had the experience some months earlier, while being investigated for clearance, of entering her building at the laboratory just as a woman she did not know was leaving. She was puzzled that the strange woman smiled at her as if she knew her when she walked by. When Dana got to her office she heard she had just missed "her" Q clearance investigator, who had been asking questions about her. She was shaken by this direct experience of being known without knowing. Now, at the gathering in Berkeley, among so many political radicals, Dana assumed there must be an FBI agent there somewhere and that this agent could easily know who she was although she had told no one at the party her last name or place of work. "They have ways of finding out who you are," she said.

The gathering featured entertainment by local activists who sang, read poetry, and performed political skits. Out of routine politeness, I found myself applauding at the end of each performance, even if I did not much approve of it—as in the case of a presentation on different ways to defraud San Francisco's mass transit system. Dana, however, monitored her behavior continually, taking care only to applaud the politically inoffensive entertainment, for example, a brief classical guitar performance. "If there was an FBI agent there, he was taking note who was clapping at what, you can be sure of that," she said. The next week, when she told a colleague at work where she had gone, he joked that the FBI must now be following her.

Dana's story speaks powerfully to the potential, and mysterious, omnipresence of government surveillance in a Livermore scientist's life. Laboratory scientists gaze into the secrets of nature even as they themselves are subjected to the gaze of classification officers, FBI agents, cameras, and each other. (All employees receive a booklet instructing them how to detect spies among their colleagues [Smith 1990f].) In such a situation, Dana was learning not only that she might be under surveillance at any moment; she was also learning to internalize this surveillance, to keep a watchful eye on herself on the government's behalf.

The theorist who has written most systematically about this sort of surveillance is Michel Foucault. He argues in *Discipline and Punish* that the modern period in the West has seen the rise of surveillance as a privileged means of social discipline in a variety of disparate contexts: prisons, hospitals, asylums, schools, armies, and factories, for example. According to Foucault, the power to see and its corollary, the vulnerability to being seen, lie at the core of social discipline in modern society:

> Disciplinary power . . . is exercised through its invisibility; at the same time it imposes on those whom it subjects a principle of compulsory visibility. In discipline, it is the subjects who have to be seen. Their visibility assures the hold of the power that is exercised over them. It is the fact of being constantly seen, of being able always to be seen, that maintains the individual in his subjection. (1979: 187)

Foucault's analysis focuses on two techniques of surveillance in particular: the examination and the Panopticon. Both are essential components of the field of surveillance at Livermore.

The examination, Foucault says, is organized around a "normalizing gaze" that turns subjects into objects by making them into "cases." His examples include medical examinations, educational examinations, and criminal investigations. To turn people into cases, the examination "sit-uates them in a network of writing; it engages them in a whole network of documents that capture and fix them" (ibid., 189), and it defines them in relation to constructs of the normal and abnormal. As documented cases, subjects are fixed by the very process of investigation as unique individuals unlike any others; but they are also analyzed into component traits that can be mapped onto grids to enable normalizing comparison with others. In constituting each individual as a unique object of knowledge, Foucault says, the examination often focuses on his or her potential for deviance: "When one wishes to individualize the healthy, normal and law-abiding adult, it is always by asking how much of the child he has in him, what secret madness lies within him, what fundamental crime he has dreamt of com-mitting" (ibid., 193).

At Livermore the Q clearance investigation is clearly an example of the examination. It constitutes each employee of the laboratory as a unique individual known by the state in depth, down to his or her emotional struggles, sexual history, car payment difficulties, and substance use. By overtly collecting information on nuclear weapons scientists that the state is not allowed to collect on most of its citizens, the investigation also establishes the principle, essential in cultivating disciplinary compliance, that these individuals are legitimately special objects of the state's gaze and that, in regard to the state, their private lives are not private any longer (see Shils 1956: 201).[17] In the name of state secrecy, the membrane of personal secrecy around the individual self is stripped away. We have seen that social processes in Livermore often cast the ethical and political issues raised by weapons work as matters of private discretion. At the same time, the social processes of secrecy make traditional matters of private discre-tion into public affairs of state.

In opening the individual to the penetrating gaze of the state, the investigation thus prepares the subject for the second, panoptical tech-nique of power. Panopticism is a technique of power that, as Foucault describes it, is best understood by means of a concrete example: Jeremy Bentham's idea for prison design, the Panopticon. It consists of a tower surrounded by cells with windows. Individuals in these cells can be ob-served by whoever is in the tower, but they cannot see the observer. The isolation of individuals in their cells prevents them from communicating and collaborating with one another, and the arrangement of the tower in relation to the cells enables one person to keep a large number of subjects under continuous surveillance. But, as Foucault points out, the genius of the arrangement lies in the uncertainty at its heart: since inmates know they can always be seen but never know whether they are being observed at any given moment, the sense of surveillance becomes continuous and independent of the actual enactment of surveillance. This technique can enforce discipline even in the absence of actual observation as surveillance becomes internalized.

> Hence the major effect of the Panopticon: to induce in the inmate a state of conscious and permanent visibility that assures the automatic functioning of power. So to arrange things that the surveillance is permanent in its effects, even if it is discontinuous in its action; that the perfection of power should tend to render its actual exercise unnecessary. . . . [I]n short, that the inmates should be caught up in a power situation of which they are themselves the bearers. To achieve this . . . the inmate must never know whether he is being looked at at any one moment; but he must be sure that he may always be so. . . . Power should be visible and unverifiable. (Foucault 1979: 201)

I saw many instances of this kind of internalized surveillance while I was in Livermore. For example, one scientist told me that because of signs around the laboratory warning people not to discuss classified information on the telephone, she presumed, though she did not know for sure, that calls from within the laboratory were randomly monitored.[18] Consequently, she was always careful about what she said on the telephone.

The boundaries of such internalized surveillance often had an expansionary inertia since not only did people not know whether they were being watched at any particular moment but they also were not quite sure what behavior was permitted and what behavior might endanger their security clearances. Thus, even in the absence of overt warnings against political dissent, surveillance had expanded for many employees from a technique for finding breaches of classification into a more generalized mechanism for disciplining amorphous political deviance. In a situation in which the very boundaries of the permissible were blurred, many people, understandably, felt inclined to play it safe.[19] Thus when a laboratory employee with whom I shared a house was being reinvestigated for clearance and the investigation was taking a long time, he began to wonder why and joked a little nervously, "They've found out who I have living with me." "What's wrong with living with an anthropologist?" I asked. His reply, "Officially, nothing," tersely conveyed the uncertainty of the person under surveillance.

Internalized surveillance also had a chastening effect on laboratory employees thinking of signing petitions. An older scientist who tried to circulate a petition protesting new drug-testing rules found many younger scientists sympathetic but too nervous to sign. In the end the petition only got about one hundred signatures. Another petition, this one against the laboratory's plans for an incinerator and waste treatment facility, was similarly affected. Circulated by a local grassroots group, CAREs, the petition turned out to be popular with local residents, getting about ten thousand signatures. As I stood outside the Livermore Safeway with members of CAREs as they appealed for signatures, I was surprised by the number of people who said they would have liked to sign the petition but felt unable to because they worked for the laboratory. Although some laboratory managers insisted that employees were free to sign the petition—and, to be fair, there were numerous employees who did—the uncertainty had a disciplining effect on the behavior of some others. As Peter Carey (1990) has written, fear of losing a clearance "suppresses unorthodox political tendencies, keeping bomb builders in a sort of juvenile state where ideas must be weighed against possible judgment by a parental authority."[20]

The effects of surveillance can even persist after people leave the laboratory. I met a former employee who knew some details about the laboratory's attempts to conceal an accidental spill of plutonium into the city's sewer system, an incident he had been disturbed by. I asked if I could talk to him about it, stressing that I would not reveal his identity to anyone. Although he now had a new job and was not planning to return to the laboratory, he was very anxious about talking to me. "I don't want to get in trouble. You won't tell anyone who told you, will you?" he kept saying. Despite the fact that it was the laboratory that had something to hide in this instance, the culture of surveillance and the fear of being seen as a troublemaker in a small town still exerted a powerful pressure toward compliance in his life.

The fear of surveillance even spread, predictably perhaps, into my own life. Early on in my research one Livermore resident who had taken an interest in finding interviewees for me began to suspect that her telephone was tapped and that I might be the reason. From then on I found myself worrying about surveillance. I wondered what the FBI knew about me. The fact that they had never contacted me to ask about my research began, in the state of paranoia that surveillance can induce, to seem more sinister than reassuring: they did not need to ask me about my research because they already knew all about it; they had tapped my telephone; my room-mate was spying on me for them, telling them who I spoke to and breaking into my computer files when I was out; they were investigating their own scientists and gathering information on the antinuclear movement through me. I began to imagine that FBI agents would arrive at my door to interrogate me and what I would tell them. These are the fearful kinds of thoughts that surveillance produces.

SEGREGATION

To know a secret is to be important, even though many secrets seem more interesting to those who do not know them than to those who do. The secretary of energy, Hazel O'Leary, exclaimed when she read her first classified briefings, "What's so classified about this? . . . It was all the stuff I'd heard on CNN while I was getting dressed" (*Mirabella* 1994: 130). And many who have written about secret societies have observed that their forbidden secrets often turn out to be surprisingly mundane and unexciting once they are revealed (see Cohen 1971; Douglas 1984: 96; Kaiser 1980; Schaefer 1980: 163–165). Still, regardless of whether they are secret because they are important or important because they are secret, secrets are exciting. Secrecy is a means by which power constructs itself as power, and the knowledge of secrets is a perquisite of power. In the words of Bill Perry (1990: 25), former director of public relations at the laboratory, "At the lab, where information is tightly guarded, knowledge is power."

Barry used to be a warhead designer, but then quit. He says that in retrospect a lot of classified information is trivial, some of it known by people without clearances who do not realize it is classified.[21] When I asked him about the allure of weapons physics, he told me, "It seems like exciting physics because it's so secret. The excitement comes from the aura they put around it. You have this sense you're doing a kind of work no one else knows how to do, physics they don't even teach at universities."

To know these secrets, then, is to be transformed into a member of a privileged elite. As Henry Nash, a former intelligence analyst, put it,

> Being cleared had its rewards. These were personal and had to do with being confronted with a screening process, passing a test, and then enjoying final acceptance. Being cleared represented a flattering experience sharpened by the quality of selectivity, not unlike the feeling accompanying acceptance by a fraternity or country club. You knew you were chosen. Being included confirmed that you had been found worthy by those unseen and unnamed officials somewhere in the upper reaches of the bureaucracy who managed America's security needs. . . . Most analysts quietly savored the fact that someone had considered them fit to share vital national secrets in the cause of security. (1981: 154–155)

The rituals of secrecy lend an air of dramatic importance to all the work, no matter how mundane, carried out at the laboratory, and they give Livermore scientists a sense of their own distinctiveness. This sense of distinction and privilege is important for two reasons. First, it gives the laboratory a certain mystique, and it compensates laboratory scientists for the sacrifices they must make to work there. If their ability to publish freely is constrained, if their private lives are now a legitimate object of government interest, if their conversations with scientific colleagues, family members, and friends are henceforth bridled, they are nevertheless rewarded by membership in a privileged elite.

Second, given that the wisdom and morality of Livermore scientists' work has been increasingly contested by members of the public since the early 1980s, this sense of privilege gives scientists a confidence that they do after all know best. From Edward Teller's famously frequent retort to critics at public meetings—"If only you knew what I know, but I can't tell you: it's secret"—to the many scientists who told me that antinuclear protestors "just don't understand," the scientists' reflex is often to respond to criticism by claiming privilege. In constructing this sense of privileged status, the rituals of secrecy compound the effects of scientific training at elite universities, where scientists learn a robust confidence in scientific knowledge and a disdain for the superstitious views of the laity. Their standing as scientists who understand the secrets of nature is magnified by their status as scientists who know the secrets of state, so that there is a double sense in which protestors "just don't understand."

Meanwhile the practice of secrecy transforms scientists by reworking the web of relationships they inhabit and thus their sense of self. ("Secret information is part of your being. It's not something you put down and it's gone," said one scientist.) Their laboratory selves[22] become increasingly isolated. Laboratory scientists cannot discuss the details of secret work with friends, family, or even many scientific colleagues outside the fence: unable to publish their classified work in the open literature or to present it at the annual meetings of America's scientific societies, their relationships with the rest of their professional community may become increasingly tenuous. A University of California study reported, for example, that most weapons scientists at Los Alamos National Laboratory "stopped altogether attending national meetings in their specialties, and interacting with outside scientists, since they were never allowed to describe their work in any detail" (Senate Policy Committee 1984: 19). They become weapons scientists rather than, simply, scientists.[23]

Of course, laboratory scientists are not completely cut off from their professional colleagues elsewhere. Some do some unclassified work or find unclassified aspects of their classified work that they can publish or present, and Livermore scientists do go to open scientific meetings. Nevertheless, as one Los Alamos scientist put it, once one embarks on classified research, often "the scientific community loses sight of you" (Rosenthal 1990: 107). Debra Rosenthal even reports in her study of Los Alamos that some university scientists refused to send offprints of their articles and papers to scientists doing classified research (ibid., 105–106).

In a marvelously vivid recollection, Herb York, the first director of the Livermore laboratory, reveals how deeply the taboos around communication can reach into the inner reflexive life of the weapons scientist's self. He recalls working under Ernest Lawrence during the Second World War on a project to separate uranium. The word "uranium" was only mentioned to him once, when he arrived at the project, and from then on he was told to refer to uranium by the code name "tuballoy."

> To my recollection, following my first day I never again heard the word "uranium" either in a normal conversation or in a confidential aside. This custom—this way of living, working, and thinking with code words—became deeply ingrained in me and everyone I knew. As a result, after news of the bomb burst upon the public two and a half years later, it was deeply shocking for me to read that forbidden word in the headlines and to hear people utter it out loud—with a certain awe, to be sure, but nonetheless as if it were just another, normal word. Hearing it was one of those things that caused a sudden, queasy feeling in the pit of the stomach. Something was

badly awry. I clearly recall that for me, saying "uranium" out loud had become the equivalent to cursing one's mother—I could not possibly have done either. (York 1987: 14–15)

As York describes it, the taboos of secrecy penetrated his being so thoroughly that they even conditioned the reflexes of his body. In his final remark, York, groping to convey the meaning of secrecy in his life, metaphorically assimilates the prohibitions in his working group to the taboos of purity and defilement in the family.

In addition to restricting conversation across the laboratory fence, the rules of secrecy also dampen conversation within the laboratory itself. Since employees are not supposed, in theory at least, to tell one another anything secret that they do not have a need to know, the laboratory is also a community united, paradoxically, by what its members often cannot share with one another. Brian O'Connell (1980), Henry Nash (1981), and Elizabeth Brandt (1980) argue that within organizations practicing secrecy, compartmentalization of knowledge consolidates the power of senior members over their subordinates, who are less well informed. Secrecy also inhibits members from developing an overall picture of or sense of responsibility for an organization's work. In the words of Nash (1981: 155) who once selected Soviet targets for American nuclear weapons, "When I was denied access to special information I felt that I was not as fully informed as others and, because of this, I was not as fully a part of, or as responsible for, the ongoing work." In such situations compartmentalization of knowledge may have the effect of generating compliance within an organization.

Although managers and the laboratory's elite corps of warhead designers are allowed relatively unrestricted, free-ranging discussions, this is not the case for many lower-ranking scientists and engineers, who are often not allowed to know details about weapons they are not working on—or even details about particular aspects, held not to concern them, of the weapons they *are* working on. And, of course, few people at the laboratory are allowed to know much in detail about the basing and targeting of the weapons they develop, these matters being the province of other arms of the national security bureaucracy. Thus the compartmentalization of technical information discourages scientists from exploring in detail the connections between different components in the laboratory's or the defense bureaucracy's overall project. In a situation in which they often know the technical details of other people's work only vaguely, moral autarchy is reinforced and, except for the elite within the laboratory, employees may not be routinely exposed to facts about, say, design flaws in the Trident II[24] missile that might provoke questions about the central axiom of laboratory ideology—that the laboratory's work makes the world a safer place.

The X-ray laser affair at Livermore offers a classic example of the constricting effect secrecy can have on moral debate. In the early 1980s, some Livermore scientists suggested that it might be possible to create a weapon that would transform a nuclear explosion in space into X-rays capable of destroying Soviet missiles before they hit the United States. The idea was a source of considerable technical and political controversy: many scientists doubted that it was technically possible to develop such a weapon; others pointed out that should the weapon prove feasible, it would undermine nuclear deterrence and put immense pressure on the superpowers to rewrite existing arms control treaties that greatly restricted defensive weapons. In other words, the weapon raised substantial questions relating to the ethics of deterrence and of defensive versus offensive weapons. The X-ray laser was enthusiastically endorsed by Edward Teller and his protégé Lowell Wood at the laboratory and by a number of Reagan administration officials and space weapons supporters in Washington. The laboratory director, Roger Batzel, also threw his support behind it. When Roy Woodruff, Livermore's associate director for weapons development, insisted on writing to the White House to correct what he saw as misrepresentations of technical progress on the X-ray laser, particularly by Teller, he was forced to resign. However, at least until a dissident bureaucrat eventually leaked the story to the Southern California Federation of American Scientists, which in turn called a press conference, very few scientists at the laboratory knew much about the sharp disagreements among senior laboratory officials over the X-ray laser. In particular, they were not allowed to know why Woodruff had resigned. Nor, for that matter, did any but a tiny elite at the laboratory have access to the government's top secret Fletcher Report, which concluded that the probable technical characteristics of an X-ray laser would make it much more suitable for shooting down satellites than missiles, so that it would in all likelihood not be a defensive weapon at all. In such a situation most laboratory employees simply lacked access to information that would have enabled them to make technically informed moral judgments about the X-ray laser and their own participation in its development.[25]

Another example of the debilitating effect secrecy can have on moral judgment and independent thought is given by Sissela Bok. Arguing that secrecy creates for people an environment in which "neither their perception of a problem nor their reasoning about it then receives the benefit of challenge and exposure" (Bok 1989: 25), Bok is particularly interested in the original nuclear weapons scientists at Los Alamos, many of whom were persuaded to work on the bomb during World War II mainly out of fear that the Nazis would develop a nuclear weapon. Why did they continue to work on the bomb after Germany's surrender?[26]

> The secrecy that surrounded their efforts was at once necessary and debilitating. Isolated in New Mexico, most of the scientists were not told of the scope and aim of the research, though they often guessed. They were asked to disguise the nature of their work in letters to friends and relatives, or to talk in empty terms. Oppenheimer himself wrote in a letter in 1945: "For the last four years I have had only classified thoughts." . . . Without feedback and debate concerning their undertaking, and without day-to-day contact with the rest of the world, the scientists were an easy prey to complete absorption in their task, and to denying or rationalizing away any doubts about their own role. . . . In 1943, however, it became clear that the German effort to develop such bombs [atomic bombs] had failed. And in May 1945, when Germany finally surrendered, the original justification for continuing with the project had vanished altogether. A number of the scientists who took part in the Los Alamos project have looked back and asked themselves in amazement why they did not at that time reconsider, why they did not leave. Secrecy prevented feedback and criticism from the outside. . . . The inability to stop for which Oppenheimer adduced so many reasons . . . demonstrates the debilitating effects that secrecy can have on reasoning and moral judgment. The scientists at Los Alamos were in its power, and it had transformed them. (Ibid., 199–201)

Of course, Livermore today is not the same as Los Alamos in 1945. Livermore weapons scientists' families and neighbors know, at least in vague terms, what they do, and the town of Livermore is not so radically isolated from the outside world as was Los Alamos in 1945: Los Alamos was a town the scientists could not leave, even to go shopping, without permission; a town connected to the outside world by only three telephone lines, all of them monitored by government agents (Bartimus and McCartney 1991: 94–96). But this is part of the Livermore laboratory's problem today: the increasing difficulty of partitioning the laboratory from the outside world, of cocooning the scientists in the strictest secrecy, was dramatically illustrated by the huge protests at the laboratory gates in 1982 and 1983 and the ensuing public debate about its work. These protests partly ruptured the membrane of secrecy and discretion that kept laboratory scientists relatively isolated from potential challenges outside the laboratory world. The univocal experience of self that secrecy strives to cultivate was challenged.

THE NUCLEAR FAMILY

We could perhaps imagine a situation in which weapons scientists lived and worked in a setting similar to a monastery or an army barracks, forbidden to have spouses and permitted little contact with family members and friends outside the community. While such an arrangement would assure a high degree of segregation for the laboratory from the rest of the world, it is hard to imagine that many scientists would want to work at such a place. Scientists are not monks or soldiers. They are civilians with families, and for an institution based partly on segregation, secrecy, and rationalist masculinism, that creates a complex situation.

Ron, one of Livermore's most senior scientists, articulates the rub in that situation as follows:

> A person who works at the rad lab on nuclear weapons, and is surrounded by nuclear weapons people who are congenial in many of their opinions and ideas during the day, has got to go home. And . . . he's got a wife who, generally speaking, could care less about nuclear weapons and perhaps isn't too comfortable with the whole idea, . . . and he may have some kids who are old enough now to know about some of these things. . . . He's got a problem. While it's easy for him to justify to himself while he's at work the things he's doing, it's a different ball game when he gets home. . . . People in the nuclear weapons field for their own self-esteem have to develop arguments and justifications for what they're doing, not because they have to justify it to the guy working next door. He's got the same ideology as they do generally, but at home it's a different story. I mean the sixteen-year-old daughter or son is liable to come in and say, "Hey, dad, what do you do over there? You're building these nuclear weapons. Is that a good idea?"

Ron's depiction of the family as a potential locus of trouble for weapons scientists is worth exploring further. After all, the intimacy conventionally associated with family life is at odds with the secrecy and segregation required by laboratory life, and American society constructs the family as a repository for values of sentimentality that, potentially at least, conflict with the values undergirding the laboratory's scientific and military rationalism. Thus, although weapons scientists' families and the laboratory need and depend on one another, it is also true that each creates problems for the other.

At Los Alamos during World War II, scientists were permitted to live with their wives, but their wives were not supposed to know, or ask, about the nature of their work (Keller 1992: 44). In Livermore today, weapons scientists' families only know in broad terms that they work on nuclear weapons. Scientists are not supposed to discuss the details of their work with uncleared family members—or, for that matter, with cleared family members who do not have a need to know—and I even heard stories of husbands, especially older husbands, saying they could not tell their wives where they were going when they went on trips to Los Alamos, the Nevada Test Site, or the Rocky Flats production facility. I vividly remember my own surprise in one interview with a scientist when I asked him which division he worked for at the laboratory. When he answered, his wife, who was sitting in on the interview, suddenly interrupted: "I've been trying to get you to tell me that for years. How come you told him?"

Secret societies all over the world have often drawn a sharp line between the worlds of men and women by admitting only men and prohibiting the sharing of secrets with women (Brandt 1980; Herdt 1987; Hiatt 1979; Huyghe 1986). This is not really the case at the laboratory since women make up 26 percent of the workforce. Even if most of these women are concentrated in secretarial positions and the so-called softer sciences, others occupy important positions. Moreover, since secret documents at Livermore are often typed or filed by secretaries, many women who are not weapons scientists still have Q clearances. Thus instead of seeing the laboratory as a secret society that enforces a rigid demarcation between the worlds of men and women, we should see it as an institution that separates the (symbolically female) private domestic sphere of employees' families from the world of the laboratory, which, being concerned with science, politics, and international affairs, lies in the public sphere (even though it is, in its procedures, anything but public).

The putative separation between the public and private spheres is one of the core structural features of American culture (Ehrenreich 1984: 1–28;

Enloe 1990; Rapp 1978). This demarcation must, cross-culturally as well as in America, largely be understood in terms of the political symbolism of gender. In the domestic sphere, practices and cultural values identified with women and coded as female are held to prevail. The public sphere—even if some women play important roles in it as, for example, in the case of female corporate executives or university presidents—tends to be associated with practices and values coded as male (Collier and Yanagisako 1987b; Reiter 1975; Rosaldo 1974; Sanday 1974; Yanagisako 1987). Women who pursue careers in the public sphere may end up feeling that they must surrender some of their womanliness to do so, like one woman scientist at Livermore who told me, only half-jokingly, "I think there's something wrong with me. I think I've cut myself off from the feelings associated with women."

In her anthropological portrait of American society, Lucy Garretson explains the values conventionally associated with the public and domestic spheres:

> Relationships based on closeness and permanence and involving solace and tenderness—that is, love relationships—serve to differentiate the world of home and family from the world of work. In the outside world of public affairs Americans do not expect to find loving relationships. It is clear that the personality traits Turner[27] attributed to the frontier—coarseness and strength; acuteness and acquisitiveness; restlessness and nervous energy; and dominant individualism—have their place in the work world but not in the home. . . .
>
> Turner believed these qualities to be "uniquely American," yet if we look more closely at them we can see that qualities such as strength and coarseness are those Americans associate with men rather than with women. . . . Love is the symbol that stands for the home and family, while other qualities are brought into play in the world of work. (1976: 19)

In this gender-tinted universe of public and private spheres, military and scientific affairs clearly belong in the (symbolically masculine) public sphere.

Although the public and domestic spheres are symbolically distinct, a number of authors have pointed out that they are functionally interdependent and that their separateness is itself the product of an overarching ideological system that in producing them as separate betrays their unity.[28] Thus Rayna Rapp (1978), for example, has argued that in the West businesses rely on the family to produce and maintain, both economically and culturally, those who work in the public sphere, while the family relies on employment in the public sphere for its means of subsistence. She argues that the public and domestic spheres are best understood economically, politically, and ideologically if seen as separate but interrelated parts of a single system of production and reproduction.

Similarly, in her ethnographic study of the Stanford Linear Accelerator in California, Sharon Traweek (1988: 83) shows how vital this complementary separation of gender roles can be in the stable functioning of a physics laboratory. She argues that the predominantly male world of the laboratory requires as its complement a particular kind of family life (one in which wives are both self-sufficient and supportive of their hardworking husbands) and that senior physicists sometimes even acknowledge this overtly by discussing the character of junior scientists' wives in their letters of recommendation.[29]

Applying such ideas to military affairs, the feminist political scientist Cynthia Enloe (1983, 1990, 1993) points out that modern militaries rely on the family to produce and socialize the men who become soldiers and to supply the women who, as sweethearts, wives, daughters, prostitutes, and nurses, either provide support services for the fighting men or embody the sentimental ideals for which they are willing to fight. She presents the public and domestic spheres as, though not without points of contradiction, ideologically and functionally complementary.

> Thousands of women today tailor their marriages to fit the peculiar demands of states operating in a trust-starved international system. Some of these women are married to men who work as national-security advisors; others have husbands who work as civilian weapons-engineers; still others are married to foreign-service careerists. Most of these men would not be deemed trustworthy if they were not in "stable" marriages. . . . Marriages between elite men and patriotic wives are a building block holding up the international system. (Enloe 1990: 10–11)

The family in Livermore, then, occupies a position somewhat similar to that of the local churches: it is a separate institution located outside the laboratory fence, but it is inextricably enmeshed with the laboratory world. Although a few scientists, especially the younger ones, do not live in families, most depend on families for day-to-day attention to their physical and psychological needs and for the sense of belonging, identity, and respectability for which the family is considered the supreme vehicle in

America (Garretson 1976: 14–26; Schneider 1980). And many families in Livermore depend on the laboratory in return for their means of subsistence and for their sense of social location.

Yet there is in this interdependence of laboratory and family a potential contradiction, since the family, like the church, has custody over sentimental values with the potential to disrupt the masculine world of the public sphere. "Women," says Enloe (1983: 216), "may perform vital functions [for the military], but they present alternative values and competing values." It is, after all, in the domestic sphere that the sentimental values of tenderness, compassion, vulnerability, empathy, and nonaggression have historically been cultivated and confined. The public sphere is a space where, among other things, men protect national boundaries by using or threatening violence, while in the domestic sphere women are cast in the role of conflict resolvers. The gulf between the two spheres is symbolized by what opinion pollsters call the "gender gap" in attitudes toward war.[30]

Still, the gender gap is a gap, not an absolute divide, and the relations between the values I have schematically represented here as those of the public and private spheres cannot in real life be reduced to simple formulae of neat opposition. The formulae are more like a caricaturist's sketch than a true portrait of American life, and different couples at Livermore have different ways of organizing the relationship between male and female. Thus I found that many laboratory spouses wholeheartedly endorse their husbands' weapons work, and many more take the attitude of the wife who, when I asked her what she thought when her husband took a job as a warhead designer, said briskly, "If it was OK with him, it was OK with me." Some, however, have learned to keep their feelings to themselves. When one woman told me she did not like her husband working on nuclear weapons, I asked her if she pushed him to find another job. "No," she said. "People have a right to different opinions, don't they? You can't go around trying to change everything about someone just because you're married to them. I don't think we really discussed it. It was his job, that's all."

Another scientist's wife, Paula, recalled that her husband had only reluctantly agreed to work on nuclear weapons after the project he had been working on at the laboratory was canceled. She remembered how it had pained him when his cousin had once asked, "How can you do this, working on bombs to blow up the world?" Although she herself was not happy about his work, she did not challenge him. When I asked why, she paused and said, "That's a really good question, you know. I'm not sure really why I didn't ask him more about it, I mean push him more. I just didn't."

Another weapons scientist's wife told me she herself could never feel comfortable working on nuclear weapons and would have liked to have joined a peace group but did not do so out of respect for her husband: "People who are married never agree about everything. All marriages are about learning to live with someone different from you. This is just like any other marriage. We really hardly talk about it, to tell you the truth."[31] When I asked her what happens if she and her husband go to a party and meet someone who criticizes his work, she said, "Such people would be rude, wouldn't they? You treat them the way you treat all rude people. You certainly don't encourage them."

In her controversial book, *The Feminization of American Culture* (1977), Ann Douglas argues that the sentimentalism of women in the domestic sphere has always been subordinate to the values of public life and has functioned not so much as a source of resistance to developments in national and international politics but as a safety valve, allowing for the decorative articulation of foredoomed critiques of public life. Women, says Douglas, articulate sentimental values opposed to the harsh realities of life in the public sphere while accepting that they will always finally capitulate before the reasons of men. They will, as Jean Bethke Elshtain (1987) puts it, play "beautiful souls" to the "just warriors" of the male public sphere, accepting that they embody a critique more decorative than insurrectionary.

If these sentimental values have historically served as a subordinate worldview that complemented rather than undermined the values of the public sphere, they do, however, offer a potential critique or site of resistance against the work of the laboratory. Of fifteen Livermore scientists who recalled for me incidents in which they were challenged or criticized for working on weapons, it is no coincidence that eleven had been challenged by female members of their families.

Viewed in this context, we must partly understand laboratory practices of secrecy as a means of creating a disciplinary distance between weapons scientists and their families. Often working in concert with traditional American notions of appropriate roles in marriage, they open a space between the laboratory and the domestic sphere that, to some extent at least, insulates weapons scientists from questions and challenges about their work and maintains a seal between the values of the public and domestic spheres. As Joseph, an older weapons scientist, put it when I asked him how his classified work affected his family life,

> I think it really caused me to live in compartments. I lived one life at work, and when I was at home I lived another life. I knew I had to do that, and so I did it, and so did my wife, and so did everyone we were socializing with. . . . It was frustrating. . . . I really wanted to talk to her about my work. I couldn't. Not a bit of it. I think it causes a person to become—it caused me to become introspective.

The segregation of work and family is stark. Scientists' spouses and children cannot see where they work except once every two years on "family day," when the laboratory's secret places are opened to family members. Because scientists cannot bring classified work home, they often end up working long hours at the laboratory. Jack, a warhead designer, told me he bought a house near the laboratory so it would be easy to come in on weekends. "I've worked sixty hours a week minimum since I came to the laboratory. For about a seven-year period we were working eighty to a hundred hours." He added with a grin, "Almost had a divorce three times."

One scientist's former wife told me that she used to take an interest in the laboratory's projects, following them in the local press and in the laboratory newsletter, until this got her in trouble.

> We'd go to these parties with lab people and their families. Most of the other wives would talk to each other, but I liked to talk with the scientists. They were more interesting than the wives. I'd talk about these things I knew about, you know, like names of programs and things, and some of the scientists would look anxious because they'd read these things in classified documents and weren't sure if I was supposed to know them or where I'd found out about them. My husband told me to keep quiet in future, be more like the other wives.

Regardless of whether or not they approve personally of weapons work, many wives complain about the distance it so often creates in their marriages. This distance is not unique to Livermore: many people with spouses in business, politics, or science have similarly structured relationships. However, the experience of many Livermore spouses is, in the American spectrum of intimacy and distance in marriage, far from the statistical mean. Many local ministers and counselors told me that the most common problem in laboratory marriages was that scientists, however earnest they were about providing for their families, were often experienced by family members as painfully distant. (This was an observation not only on their physical absence from the home much of the time but also on their rationalist temperament and emotional distance when in the home.) A local minister called laboratory wives "science widows."

Robert Lifton and Erik Markusen (1990) tell the story of the progressive estrangement of the Los Alamos warhead designer Ted Taylor from his family as he was drawn deeper into the laboratory world.[32] "I felt more at home in the laboratory than at home," said Taylor. His wife and mother at first challenged him on his work but began to give up "because they didn't see how it had any effect on [him]." His family became less and less interested in hearing about his work and began referring to the laboratory as "daddy's workpen." The distance between Taylor's weapons world and his family world is most poignantly symbolized by his recollection of being in the Pentagon poring over intelligence data about nuclear targets in Moscow the night his wife was giving birth to one of their children. Years later, while visiting Moscow's Red Square, his memory of that night triggered a sudden outburst of uncontrollable weeping.[33]

One woman who had been married to a weapons scientist for many years described this sense of separation from the other side of the fence. Penny was politically supportive of her husband's work, but she also felt bereaved by it. She had married her husband when he was a graduate student in physics studying the characteristics of a particular particle. They first lived together in a cramped apartment where she would sit in the same room with him as he pored over his graphs. Her sense of their closeness when they first married is encapsulated in the memory of the time he looked up at her from his work and said, "Honey, you know, there are two things I love in life: you and my particle." When he or his group made a breakthrough, she would go to the celebratory party at their laboratory. This was a time when man and woman, science and love, public and private spheres, were aligned together. Now she knows little about his research, and when his group celebrates a triumph, the party is often on the other side of the fence she cannot cross. When his colleagues come to dinner, they talk about their families but never about their work. They have separate worlds.

CHAPTER 5

Bodies and Machines

*Knowledge which has not passed through the senses can produce none
but destructive truth.*
LEONARDO DA VINCI

Nuclear weapons scientists are mortally embodied people who work on machines that risk the annihilation of millions of human bodies, including their own. Here I explore that dilemma, asking how the human body is constructed and represented within laboratory culture and tracing the ways nuclear weapons work is simultaneously sustained and placed in jeopardy by the relationships Livermore scientists have developed with human bodies and with machines. These patterns of relationship are, in large part, the product of the culture of Western science itself, of which the world of nuclear weapons science offers a particularly striking subset.

It is by now a truism among historians and sociologists of science that Western science has grown up suspended in a web of intersecting dichotomies: objective and subjective, mind and matter, "man" and nature, thought and feeling, observation and experience. In Western cosmology the first category in each of these dichotomies is marked, in the context of its opposite, as a defining characteristic of science. None of these dichotomies can be reduced to any other, but they all reinforce and overlay one another, each strand keeping the entire web sturdy. And they converge in a grand polarity between the worlds of mind and body that dates back at least to René Descartes's famous equation of the self and the mind, which is only reinforced by the dualism of Pauline Christianity.[1] Within the terms of this mind/body dichotomy, the sensate, mortal body is marked as a centralizing symbol for the multiply unwanted phenomena of subjectivity, transience, vulnerability, and emotion. As the feminist critic Susan Griffin puts it,

> The dominant philosophies of this civilization have attempted to posit a different order of being over and against bodily knowledge. According to this order of being, we are separated from nature and hence above natural process. In the logic of this order, we are meant to dominate nature, control life, and in some sense felt largely unconsciously, avoid the natural event of death. Yet in order to maintain a belief in this hierarchy one must repress bodily knowledge. (1989: 77–78)

This separation of the worlds of mind and body is particularly extreme and piquant in the case of nuclear weapons scientists, since it is the essence of their work to use the products of the mind to hold the human body in jeopardy of pain and extinction. If scientists are to work on nuclear weapons, either they must believe strongly that the weapons will not be used or they must have a strong disidentification with the bodily suffering of the human beings on whom they will be used. Their task, even in comparison with other kinds of scientific research, demands and enforces a radical polarization between the worlds of mind and body—or, to put it a little differently, requires a particularly disciplined form of embodiment.

The literature on the culture of nuclear weapons professionals has largely ignored the body. Other studies ask the same basic question that animates my own research: How it is that ordinary men and women come to feel comfortable building, picking targets for, and training to use nuclear weapons? But since most other recent studies are indebted either to psychology or to theories that emphasize the importance of language in the social construction of reality, they look for the answer almost exclusively in the circuits of mind and language. They pay little attention to representations of the body or to bodily practices. Instead, they focus on the workings of euphemism and metaphor in language, on the tactical manipulation of discourse, and on phenomena of repression, denial, and disidentification that are described as psychological.[2]

I integrate and supplement the usual—and, it must be said, important—interest in ideology, discourse, and psychology with an attentiveness to what Foucault has called the "political technology of the body." In a now much-quoted passage, Foucault says,

> But the body is also directly involved in a political field; power relations have an immediate hold upon it; they invest it, mark it, train it, torture it, force

it to carry out tasks, to perform ceremonies, to emit signs. . . . The body becomes a useful force only if it is both a productive body and a subjected body. This subjection is not only obtained by the instruments of violence or ideology; it can also be direct, physical, pitting force against force, bearing on material elements, and yet without involving violence; it may be calculated, organized, technically thought out; it may be subtle, make use neither of weapons nor of terror yet remain of a physical order. That is to say, there may be a knowledge of the body that is not exactly the science of its functioning, and a mastery of its forces that is more than the ability to conquer them: this knowledge and this mastery constitute what might be called the technology of the body. (1979: 25-26)

Following the "interpretive turn"[3] in anthropology in the 1970s and 1980s, the body has, until recently, been too little evident in anthropology as well. Now anthropologists, especially the growing number interested in political violence and domination, are, thanks largely to the influence of Foucault, newly attentive to what Nancy Scheper-Hughes has called "the missing body" in anthropology and are struggling to escape the grip of bodies of theory that excessively reduce culture to symbolic or cognitive processes.[4]

INJURED BODIES

Michel Foucault (1979), Elaine Scarry (1985), and Talal Asad (1983) have argued, in regard to ritual torture and war, that mutilated bodies are points of exchange between power and knowledge. They suggest that the inscription of pain on the body produces effects of truth in society. It does this in a number of ways: for example, by producing confessions, by transforming bodies into gruesome texts engraved with the marks of power for all to see, or by transferring the undeniable reality of the body in pain to a contested political regime seeking pain's attributes of totality and unquestionable realism for itself.

Foucault (1979, 1980*a*, 1980*b*) argues that the spectacular mutilation of bodies as a display of power has been more characteristic of societies ruled by a sovereign individual than of modern bureaucratic societies. He makes the case that, partly out of sensitivity to the inflammatory effects of such displays on popular opinion at a time of increasing democratization, Western governments since the French Revolution have become more circumspect about displaying broken bodies in public. In modern bureaucratic societies, he argues, power tends to circulate and grow by means of a subtle disciplining of the movements and subjectivities of living bodies, turning them into what he calls "docile bodies," rather than through a graphic assault on their surfaces.

Foucault formulated this argument to describe the historical evolution of penal systems in the West, but his argument clearly applies also to the body in war. Whereas in the wars of "simple" societies, the killing and injuring of bodies has been one of the principal goals of fighting, in modern warfare it is now ancillary to the goals of capturing territory and destroying enemy infrastructure or arsenals. Although contemporary warfare often involves massive bloodshed, modern Western governments have become increasingly reticent about displaying the dead or injured as trophies of power. We saw during the Gulf War, when media coverage of the return of body bags to the United States and of the fighting itself was heavily controlled, that those in the West responsible for prosecuting the war were willing to go to extraordinary lengths to inhibit those displays that were once an integral part of war (Gusterson 1991*b*).

In a friendly amendment to Foucault's argument, Emily Martin (1987: 20–21) has suggested that practices of producing truth by mutilating or dismembering bodies are not completely extinct in our society: "Foucault is surely right in pointing to the different role of physical pain in the two eras, as epitomized by our use of drugs to prevent pain or anxiety during an execution. But dismemberment is with us still, and the 'hold on the body' has not so much slackened as it has moved from law to science."

Although Martin has in mind medical science rather than military science, her remarks are a useful place from which to begin a discussion of the complex and ambiguous relationship between nuclear weapons, nuclear weapons scientists, and the body. Nuclear weapons scientists have devised a spectacular and efficient new means of dismembering bodies in the service of power as well as elaborate techniques for decoding these dismemberings after the fact. Yet at the same time, they have undermined the exercise and display of this power by claiming that their weapons exist to prevent rather than to facilitate human dismemberment and by decoding nuclear dismemberings with a euphemistic discretion that effaces as much as it displays the power of the bomb (and, by extension, its owners). Nor have they, or the U.S. government, been keen on the dissemination of photographs showing the effects of the atomic bomb on Hiroshima and Nagasaki.[5] In other words, the practices of nuclear weapons scientists hover ambiguously between Foucault's two modalities of power over the body: they combine responsibility for a sensational new means of mutilating bodies with a reticence in regard to its exercise.[6]

Nuclear weapons first proved their power, and the power of their American owners, by destroying the bodies of at least 150,000 people in Hiroshima and Nagasaki while leaving marks on the surface and in the physical interior of countless thousands more living but wounded.[7] American nuclear scientists did not just create the bomb that made such a spectacular display of power possible; they also did the follow-up work that documented, codified, and formalized the effects of the bombing, distilling those effects into a body of knowledge that was simultaneously scientific and political. Almost as soon as the bombs had been dropped, they turned the dead and injured bodies of the Japanese into bodies of data, converting dismembered, charred, maimed, scarred, and atomized humans into equations. Immediately after the bombing, Manhattan Project scientists arrived in Hiroshima to make measurements: they used measurements of the shadows of people, burned into buildings and into the ground by the bomb's flash, to calculate the altitude at which the bomb had exploded (Else 1980); they used Japanese casualty figures, together with a mathematical formula called "the Standardized Casualty Rate," to calculate that Little Boy, the bomb dropped on Hiroshima, had killed and wounded people 6,500 times more efficiently per pound delivered than conventional high-explosive bombs would have done (Rhodes 1988: 734). American scientists spent subsequent years keeping careful track of Japanese casualties, trying to document the exact numbers killed and wounded by the initial flash, blast effects, the fireball, instantaneous radiation effects, and subsequent cancers.[8]

By carefully studying bodies inscribed by the bomb, American scientists were able to learn a great deal about the mysterious power they had created. At one point in my fieldwork, Henry, an older scientist who had worked on the Manhattan Project, showed me the photograph of a Hiroshima survivor (reproduced in fig. 6). He said, "You see the spotty burns on this woman's back. When the bomb went off, she was wearing a white dress with black flowers on it. Each burn on her arm and back is where there was a black flower. The black absorbs the heat and the white reflects it."

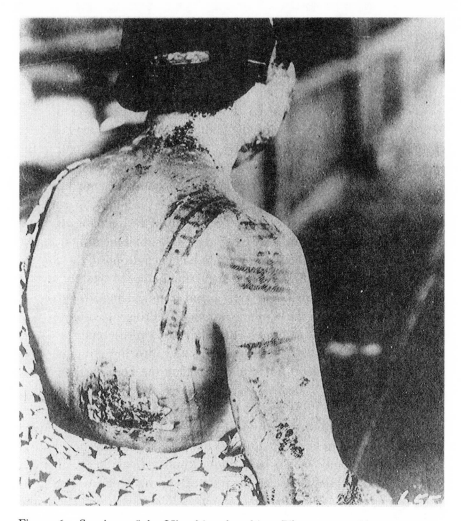

Figure 6.   Survivor of the Hiroshima bombing. The pattern of burns was produced by the black-and-white pattern of the dress the woman was wearing at the time of the blast: white areas reflected heat; black areas absorbed it. (Photo courtesy National Archives and Records Administration)

We now know that in addition to studying Japanese affected by the first two atomic bombs, American scientists also experimented after the war with radioactive substances on hundreds of Americans—usually sick, poor, incarcerated, or mentally retarded Americans. To give just a few examples: terminally ill people were injected with plutonium, uranium, and other radioactive compounds in many experiments around the country; mentally retarded children were fed radioactive breakfast cereal in Massachusetts; and prisoners' testicles were irradiated in Oregon and Washington states.[9]

Nuclear tests were used as opportunities for experiments too. In the 1950s, for example, many American soldiers were positioned close to atomic explosions at the Nevada Test Site and forced to march into the mushroom clouds to evaluate their physical and psychological reactions (Gallagher 1993: 55–108; Markle 1989; Rosenberg 1980).

Workers at nuclear weapons facilities have also been studied. Los Alamos National Laboratory has a tissue analysis group that performs postmortem analyses on the organs of some of those who work in America's nuclear weapons production complex. The government offers $500 to any of these workers who will pledge their organs to Los Alamos once they die. James McInroy, the director of the tissue analysis group at Los Alamos, described the workers' donations of their bodies as "one last donation to the body of scientific knowledge." So far, 275 Americans have been autopsied through this program, and 533 more have pledged their organs (Hamilton 1991).[10]

Nuclear accidents in which workers or scientists were exposed to radiation have been investigated with particular care. For example, Clifford Honicker (1989) describes a 1946 criticality experiment at Los Alamos that went wrong when two spheres of plutonium slipped, producing the infamous "blue flash" of radiation that nuclear workers so fear. Eight Los Alamos employees were exposed: one died, and the others became ill. Government scientists reenacted the accident using life-size dolls full of simulated blood, which they then compared with blood samples taken from the exposed employees.

Linda Roach Monroe (1990) describes a similar accident at the Hanford plutonium production plant in 1962, again involving a blue flash. In this accident, one worker, Harold Aardal, received 109 to 123 rems of whole-body radiation, 510 to 630 rems to the eyes, and 245 rems to the testicles. The accident sterilized him, made him seriously anemic for two years, and, according to his wife, scarred him psychologically for life. Two other workers were not so badly exposed. After the accident, government doctors "took blood samples hourly for days and continued regular blood tests for more than a year after that. . . . They tracked the radioactive decay in their bodies. They trimmed their fingernails close, shaved off all their radioactive body hair and considered pulling out their gold-filled teeth" (Monroe 1990: A1).

Needing more kinds of bodies to experiment on, scientists turned to animals. Scientists at the Nevada Test Site experimented with pigs—picked because their skin most closely resembles humans'. The pigs were strapped into position at precisely selected distances from a nuclear detonation and their skin carefully photographed as it was charred by the nuclear fireball and flash. Each pig wore a protective garment over about 80 percent of its body so that the protective capability of these garments and the effects of nuclear explosions on exposed flesh could be studied from the marks burned into its body.[11] Similar experiments were performed on monkeys: "Beginning in 1957, monkeys were placed at varying distances from ground zero during atomic bomb testing; those that didn't die immediately were encaged so that the 'progress' of their various cancers might be noted" (Elshtain 1990). And, in the 1950s, American scientists experimented with over eight hundred beagles, feeding them strontium-90, irradiating them with cobalt-60, or injecting them with radium. The dogs' deaths were carefully recorded and studied in an attempt to better understand the effects of radioactive fallout (Norris and Arkin 1990). Scientists even went to the extreme of implanting plastic portholes in the sides of cows that grazed on the Nevada Test Site, so the radioactive contents of the cows' stomachs could be monitored (McClatchy News Service 1994; Stewart 1995: 396).

The marked bodies of all these pigs, dogs, monkeys, cows, and people helped to produce a body of knowledge about the bomb. These mammalian bodies have served as texts from which to read the precise nature of the bomb's power and have thus been indispensable in constructing the regime of simulations that has grown up around nuclear weapons. Scientists have arduously metamorphosed the mutilated and suffering bodies of these people and animals into tidy bodies of data used in myriad strategic calculations. Such data are used to help calculate the efficiency of radiation and other nuclear weapons effects in killing and injuring enemy bodies and to devise measures aimed at protecting friendly populations against an enemy's nuclear weapons. Although nuclear war planners are principally interested in destroying enemy missiles, command and control facilities, and factories rather than in killing people per se, a nuclear war would inevitably involve enormous human casualties, and these casualties are integrated into the calculations.

Scarry argues that dead or injured bodies have a compelling realism that enables them to certify the authenticity of otherwise unanchored reality claims juxtaposed with them. Thus diviners often use animal entrails in proclaiming the unknown known, oaths are frequently solemnized across the dead bodies of animals, and wars seal national truth claims with the blood of the dead (Scarry 1985: 121–131). In a similar way, American (and other) scientists use human and nonhuman bodies, reincarnated as bodies of data, to help certify the realism of elaborate scenarios about hypothetical nuclear attacks—attacks that have not yet happened, and may never happen, but whose outcome is believed to be predictable despite strong historical evidence that the course of war is rarely predictable. These elaborate scenarios about the effects of "nuclear exchanges" form the basis for national arms procurement policies, arms control negotiation policies, civil defense policies, and national leaders' stratagems of threat and bluff in international crises. These scenarios are crucial in the regulation and replication of patterns of stability and hierarchies of dominance in the international power structure (Luke 1989).

DISAPPEARING BODIES

The discourse of scientists and other experts on the effects of nuclear weapons circulates across an ambiguous and dangerous terrain. The discourse needs injured bodies to make real the bomb's power and to construct stable regimes of truth around that power, and yet the mutilated bodies of atomic bomb victims have an incendiary, subversive potential that, at the same time, makes them dangerous. Thus the discourse on the effects of nuclear weapons is perched on a razor's edge between the bomb's need for bodies to display its power and society's need to conceal and transmogrify the bodies of victims and executioners if that power is to be stable. In the end, the relationship between bodies and weapons is such that the human body is simultaneously present and absent, so that even in its presence it is in the midst of a figurative disappearance that both presages and retrospectively erases its literal disappearance.

Take, for example, scientists' photographs of Hiroshima and Nagasaki survivors. These photographs feature close-ups of burns, mangled limbs, and exposed tissue that are often taken from the back or focus so closely on ravaged flesh that the race, age, and sex of the victim are unclear.[12] Human bodies are thus metamorphosed into body parts and pieces of human matter—fragments of bodies that have been fragmented by the weapons but also, in the act of documentation, by the photographers whose cameras separate limbs from bodies as definitively as the bomb itself did. The bodies are seen from so close up that they are objectified, impeding sympathetic identification with the people who inhabit(ed) them.

In laboratory culture the attention to detail is crucial. For example, one laboratory scientist told me he had recently watched a television docudrama about the bombing of Hiroshima. When I asked him how he felt about the program, expecting him to talk about the moral, emotional, or political issues it raised, his reply instead highlighted the importance of detailed precision in representing events: "It was poorly executed," he said. "They were quite accurate about the physical effects of the explosion, but the accents were all wrong. The actors spoke Japanese with American accents." In a similar vein, Henry, the same scientist who showed me the photograph presented here as figure 6, was annoyed with me when I showed him a paper in which I had written that many people in Hiroshima were "vaporized" by the bomb. At first I thought he must be annoyed because he felt "vaporized" implied that the bombing was an atrocity and its use signaled an alignment with the antinuclear camp on my part. In fact, he was concerned about its scientific imprecision, pointing out that the correct term was "carbonized." "That's the problem with nonscientists: you are so sloppy with detail," he added.

This scrupulously precise attention to detail is vital to the successful execution of scientific experiments and analysis, but it has collateral effects. When one's concern is focused on being precise about whether a body was vaporized or carbonized, when one's gaze is studying the pattern of the burns across the back, when the shadows on the wall become signatures of the bomb, then the body—the person in the body, the pain in the body, the subjectivity of the body—has begun to disappear. It is not impossible to combine these ways of seeing: to hold together in one's consciousness at the same time a dispassionate interest in the origins of the pattern of burns along the back and an awareness of the pain that radiates through another person's being from each of those marks. But, as any doctor will attest, it is not easy either. Indeed, that is part of the point of scientific training in medicine: to use a set of objectifying representations of the body to drive another person's pain from awareness so that the doctor can get on with his or her task of applying scientific rules and logic to the objectified signs of another person's pain without the pain itself getting in the way (Hafferty 1991; Konner 1987; Taussig 1980).

It is hard at the best of times to subjectively grasp another's pain. As Scarry (1985: 3) says, "When one hears about another person's physical pain, the events happening within the interior of that person's body . . . may seem as distant as the interstellar events referred to by scientists who speak to us mysteriously of not yet detectable intergalactic screams." Objectifying modes of representing bodily injury only make the pain harder to intuit.

The distancing and dismembering effects of such ways of representing the injured body are best illustrated by contrasting two texts that describe the effects of nuclear weapons on the human body, but in different voices and with different results. The first, from John Hersey's *Hiroshima*, was read into the *Congressional Record* by Sen. Mark Hatfield during a congressional debate on the defense budget.

> He found about 20 men and women on the sandpit. He drove the boat onto the bank and urged them to get aboard. They did not move and he realized they were too weak to lift themselves. He reached down and took a woman by the hands, but her skin slipped off in huge, glovelike pieces.
>
> Then he got into the water and, though a small man, lifted several of the men and women, who were naked, into his boat. Their backs and breasts were clammy, and he remembered uneasily what the great burns he had seen during the day had been like: yellow at first, then red and swollen, with the skin sloughed off, and finally, in the evening, suppurated and smelly.
>
> With the tide risen, his bamboo pole was now too short and he had to paddle most of the way across it. On the other side, at a higher spit, he lifted the slimy living bodies out and carried them up the slope away from the tide. He had to keep consciously repeating to himself: "these are human beings. These are human beings." (*Congressional Record*, 111st Cong., 1st sess., vol. 135, pt. 13, p. 17625)

The use of language in this passage not only transmits information to our minds but also produces unsettling feelings in our bodies. Although many weapons scientists would undoubtedly find it lacking in precision, this account, like scientific ones, does convey factual information about bodies that have been damaged by a nuclear weapon—they are fatigued, they are slimy and smelly, their skin falls off, their wounds turn yellow and red—but it foregrounds the subjective vulnerability and suffering of people with bodies and reminds us "these are human beings" as well as disintegrating bodies. It does this partly by individualizing the suffering of these people, presenting it as unique to them by locating it in a particular time and place rather than giving a generic account of what weapons in general do to bodies in general. Also, although this account is principally mediated through the observer's gaze, sight is not the only mediating sense: we learn not only what these people look like but that they feel clammy and smell bad. The multiplication of sensory contact with the victims undercuts some of the objectifying effects of the gaze and brings alive the reader's bodily rapport. Finally, the observer's gaze is itself contextualized: it is explicitly positioned within rather than outside the text and, in its use of vivid language, is emotional rather than objectifying and disembodied; it establishes a sense of relationship and compassion between reader and victim.

Contrast the following passage from *The Effects of Nuclear Weapons*, a Pentagon book widely used by nuclear weapons scientists and defense planners.

> The general interactions of a human body with a blast wave are somewhat similar to that of a structure as described in Chapter IV. Because of the relatively small size of the body, the diffraction process is quickly over, the body being rapidly engulfed and subjected to severe compression. . . . The sudden compression of the body and the inward motion of the thoracic and abdominal walls cause rapid pressure oscillations to occur in the air-containing organs. These effects, together with the transmission of the shock wave through the body, produce damage mainly at the junctions of air-containing organs and at areas between tissues of different density, such as where cartilage and bone join soft tissue. (Glasstone and Dolan 1977: 548)

In the same chapter of this book, the destroyed bodies of thousands of people are recomposed in the form of tables with such titles as "Average Distance for 50% Survival after 20 Days in Hiroshima" and "Tentative Criteria for Direct (Primary) Blast Effects in Man from Fast-rising, Long Duration Pressure Pulses." The latest edition of the book features a pouch at the back containing the "nuclear bomb effects computer"—a circular slide rule that enables the reader to calculate "1–99% probability of eardrum rupture," or the "probability of a glass fragment penetrating

1 cm of soft tissue," if they know the strength and distance of a nuclear explosion.

If Hersey's account of Hiroshima victims gave the suffering body vivid immediacy, this one makes it remote. This portrayal, abstracted from the experiences of Hiroshima and Nagasaki victims, has a generic quality: it is not about any particular body but about the body in general. The observer is not located anywhere and has no acknowledged relationship with the disassembled body; the observer is situated within what Haraway (1991: 183–202) calls "the conquering gaze from nowhere"—a place from which to see without being seen. And the body we see here is presented not as a locale for suffering or personhood but as a set of components that undergo mechanical interactions with blast waves and glass fragments. Instead of pain, slimy skin, and fatigue, we have compression, inward motion, and rapid pressure oscillations; instead of wounds, we have "damage," a word usually reserved for inanimate objects such as buildings and machines (Gusterson 1991*b*; Scarry 1985: 66–67).

Despite our common belief that formal language is more denotatively precise, this language is no less connotative than Hersey's. However, instead of using words that connote pain and vulnerability, it uses those that connote mechanical insentience. In our culture, such words are often marked as objective and precise, when in fact they have their own unseen connotative impact. If Hersey's words remind us that humans suffer, Samuel Glasstone and Philip Dolan's words tell us that human bodies can be thought of as systems of components. These are words that dismember, and they are integral to the laboratory's discourse on nuclear weaponry.

DISCIPLINED BODIES

It is not only the victims' bodies whose subjectivity is erased. Scientists' apprehension of mortality and vulnerability is also worked on so that their bodies become "docile" or disciplined. This bodily discipline is essential. To become a mature weapons scientist, one must not only know certain theorems, not only learn how to interact with colleagues, not only learn to observe the rules of secrecy, not only learn discursive legitimations of weapons work; one must also subject oneself to a discourse on and experience of the body within whose framework it subjectively feels appropriate to do the work. For the weapons scientist, the acquisition of this discipline is as important as the development of sexual discipline was for medieval monks, as important as the learning of physical courage was for warriors. It is a way of living in or through the body that makes their work feel right.

It is too easy to speak of this process of discipline as if it merely involves repression of the body. Discipline and repression are by no means the same (Foucault 1980*a*). To think solely in terms of repression implies that there is a "natural body" that is naturally afraid of nuclear weapons, when in fact antinuclear activists must work as hard to make bodies afraid of nuclear weapons as scientists must to make bodies unafraid of them. The human body is heterogeneous in its possibilities, and it is the work of culture to discipline that heterogeneity. In the culture of weapons scientists, that work involves learning to identify with the pleasures of the gaze and the power of the intellect; learning to think of bodies as machines and of machines as bodies; and learning to mistrust and reframe feelings of vulnerability or other bodily messages that conflict with normative beliefs.

This experience of the body is by no means unique to weapons scientists in our culture. Martin (1987), for example, has argued that a similar cluster of attitudes toward the body underlies the cultural world of American doctors. Still, this issue is freighted with a special significance in the case of weapons scientists because, unlike, say, particle physicists or botanists, it is the very essence of their work to use the products of the mind to threaten the body with extinction.

I caught a glimpse of the transmission and acquisition of this culture of the body when I sat in on a class on the physics of nuclear weapons at a major American research university. The two professors who taught the class themselves consulted on nuclear weapons for Livermore and Los Alamos, and a number of their students had gone on to work for the two laboratories. While the students struggled to master a difficult and complex body of unclassified knowledge about the physics of nuclear weapons, I noticed what Sharon Traweek (1988: 76–81) calls "the margins of physics." Traweek's margins are the place where students learn, not physics itself, but what it means to be a physicist. At the margins students learn "to live and feel physics" (ibid., 82). Here, embedded in the format of textbooks and lectures, concealed by its very obviousness, lies an implicit knowledge that, in their earnest attention to equations and particles, the students do not quite realize they are acquiring: the distinction between great and ordinary physicists, how to speak about experimental equipment, how to pose for photographs, how a physicist dresses, how a physicist gets married, how a graduate student behaves toward professors, and so on.

They also begin to learn what it means to a physicist to be embodied, or at least they did in the class I observed. One way they learned about this in the class I joined was through jokes, which can be an important way of inducting people into speech communities. For example, they convey a community's cultural expectations: particularly when teachers tell jokes, students learn what, or whom, to laugh at. Jokes are often also signals of conflict and anxiety. Following A. R. Radcliffe-Brown's (1965) pathbreaking work on joking relationships (relationships in which humor masks the presence of conflicting obligations), anthropologists have argued that jokes and joking relationships tend to grow up around the discomfiting and the taboo. This perspective is obviously heavily indebted to Freud's (1989) well-known argument that jokes are a way of dealing with psychological conflict and anxiety. Where there are jokes, so the theory goes, there is anxiety and conflict.[13]

A number of commentators have remarked on the black humor of nuclear weapons scientists. William Broad (1992: 71), for example, was struck by a poster at Livermore showing a nuclear warhead arcing toward the Soviet Union. The caption on the poster, parodying the cards of a well-known greeting company, reads "When you care enough to send the very best." In a similar vein, Josephine Stein (1988: 6), an outsider who was a friend to some young Livermore scientists, mentions that the scientists of Livermore's O Group "joked that they should be certain never to take Teller . . . to see the movie *Star Wars* because Teller might become enamored of the Death Star, a contraption that destroys planets with a single deadly burst of energy."

In the case of the class I joined, it was remarkable that almost all the jokes I heard had to do with the vulnerability of the human body and the ignorant fears of nonscientists. For example, one of the professors told the story of going for a bone scan and being injected with radioactive magnesium, which has a half-life of six hours.[14] For six hours he was "hellishly radioactive," he said.

> I was so radioactive I registered nothing on the department's radiation detection equipment; I sent it off the scale. I calculated that anyone talking to me for five minutes would have got the equivalent of six chest X-rays.

Now, if I'd stayed that radioactive for months, I'd have died without any doubt. But magnesium only has a half-life of six hours, so I was fine.

The professor and the students laughed uproariously.

The other professor began class the same day with an experiment to demonstrate that "heavy water" (D_2O) is indeed heavier than ordinary water (H_2O). He brought into class a lead container, supposedly containing the heavy water, and leaned against it a Danger, Radiation sign. He solemnly told us we had to treat this substance very carefully. "You shouldn't take the top off this container in an unprotected space," he said gravely and then, to our bemusement, removed the top right in front of us. "This is dangerous. You should only handle the bottle of heavy water inside with tongs," he said. Then he pressed his face into the top of the "dangerous" container, exclaiming theatrically, "There's nothing there! Oh, here it is in my pocket!" With a flourish, he removed a small bottle of clear liquid from his pocket, then told us to relax: heavy water is a harmless, stable isotope. It was just a practical joke.

In another session one of the professors told the class about a region in Africa that was so rich in uranium centuries ago that a spontaneous nuclear reaction, as in a nuclear power reactor, is now thought to have sustained itself there.[15] The professor shared with the class his surreal fantasy that cavemen could have invented nuclear energy before they discovered fire. "They could have noticed that if you put these green rocks together and poured water on them, then you cooked your meat very quickly." Pausing briefly, he then deadpanned, "Of course, they'd have died an hour later." The class roared with laughter. When the laughter had subsided, he added, elaborating his fantasy, that the cavemen could have developed channels for guiding water to the rocks from a distance so they would not be killed by sudden fierce bursts of radiation.

> If this had happened, there'd be higher levels of radioactivity, of course, but we'd have got used to them. We'd accept the risks of radioactivity the way we accept the risks of fire. Lots of people have been killed by fire, but we accept that.

These jokes would not be funny if, for example, they were about a danger such as AIDS, before which we feel helpless. The radiation jokes are funny, at least for physicists, because although radiation is dangerous, physicists feel confident that they understand radioactivity and know how to deal with it—though the jokes have an extra edge because they nag anxiously at this confidence. The jokes play with the body's vulnerability to radioactivity, teaching students to laugh both at the danger and at those who, not understanding that heavy water is not radioactive, for example, have an exaggerated fear of it. The coda to the last joke, the idea that in different historical circumstances we might think of nuclear energy as no more dangerous than fire, is a reminder that popular fears of nuclear energy are arbitrary in a way that physicists are uniquely privileged to understand. Thus these are jokes that make an elite community. Not everyone would find them funny, and, a little like racist or sexist jokes, they draw lines: if you do not find these jokes funny, maybe you take the wrong things too seriously, maybe you do not belong in this class. As Traweek (1992: 448) says in her own discussion of physicists' jokes, "Every laugh is a warning to students about exactly which borders are never to be crossed."

Other jokes told in the class were less complex. They simply encouraged students to laugh at death and bodily suffering whenever the subject came up. There were plane crash jokes, briefcase bomb jokes, and earthquake jokes. We laughed to hear that you measure radiation levels after a nuclear attack at a height of three feet from the ground "because that's the average height of a human being after a nuclear war." And we laughed when we were told, "This formula tells you how long you will live after a nuclear war, but this isn't very useful because it won't be very long."

All in all, in this class—taught, I want to emphasize, by two very likable and friendly professors—we learned an attitude of dark or absurdist humor toward death and bodily suffering, and we learned a certain disidentification with our own bodily subjectivity that is best conveyed by one professor's comment to the class: "What is life? You may think this is a philosophical question, but it's actually very simple. We're all just bags of chemistry. Life is ($C_5 H_4 O O_8 N$). Radiation is bad for chemistry, so it's bad for life."

At the Livermore laboratory, where I noticed many physicists knew surprisingly little about the interaction of radiation with the body,[16] I saw a great deal of this kind of dissociation from the subjectivity of the body. For example, bodily vulnerability is usually discussed by laboratory scientists, in informal as well as formal contexts, in terms of statistical constructs that, whatever their descriptive and predictive utility, distance speakers and listeners from the subjective experience of embodiment. For example, at one public hearing I attended Livermore scientists told local residents that a planned new waste treatment facility would increase the "average" resident's chances of getting cancer by a factor of three in one million, which, they explained, was the equivalent of smoking eight cigarettes over seventy years.[17] The linguistic conventions that codify and distance the vulnerable body are deeply internalized by laboratory scientists as they become disciplined members of their community. This became most vividly clear during a hike I took with Sharon, a Livermore resident, and Bernie, a retired weapons scientist who was reminiscing about an aboveground nuclear test he had seen in his youth. Sharon and I were trying with little success to get him to talk about his feelings during the test. Finally Sharon asked him if he hadn't felt afraid of the radioactivity, accenting the word "felt." Bernie answered, "I was exposed to about 3.5 rems during the test. They monitored us. If you get 100 rems you're dead, 50 rems and you have a 50-50 chance of dying. I only got 3.5 rems." This statistical mode of discourse helps laboratory scientists to think dispassionately and scientifically about the interactions between the human body and its environment, but it can also distance scientists from more emotionally laden questions such as How would I feel if I or my spouse was the one extra person who got cancer?

Laboratory culture encourages a stance of suspicion toward the body and its inward messages. Rosenthal (1990: 205) describes a Los Alamos scientist who dismissed his occasional fears of nuclear war in these terms: "Every once in a while, if my blood sugar's real low, I'll think, 'My God, my daughter's at home. If there was a nuclear war, how would I ever get to her?'" This anecdote beautifully illustrates the workings of bodily discipline in nuclear weapons work. The scientist's primary commitment is to the ideology of deterrence, and, at a moment when he doubts the ideology, he attributes this to a malfunction of his body rather than to the possibility of a malfunction in the system of deterrence. Instead of being a guide, the body is a trickster who may deceive.[18]

At its most extreme, this sensibility finds expression in the fantasy that Susan Bordo (1990: 653) identifies as a central yearning of postmodern American society: the "imagination of human freedom from bodily determination . . . defying the historicity, the mortality, and indeed the very materiality of the body." Thus one weapons designer, Barry, his imagination liberated by a large number of beers, once told me apropos of "Star Trek" that he believed it might one day be possible to "beam people up." In terms reminiscent of the professor who saw human life as nothing more than chemistry, he said,

> After all, what makes each of us unique is simply the configuration of our electrons. If you could map that for each person, then you could transmit electrons at the speed of light. So it might one day be possible to transmit memory and consciousness over vast distances very quickly. We might also be able to crack immortality. It should eventually be possible to replace people's entire bodies as they age, giving their minds a new lease on life and allowing people to get older and wiser.

This is a fantasy of using the power of the mind to escape the prison of embodiment.

CYBORG BODIES

Laboratory culture celebrates what Yaron Ezrahi (1990: 139–143) calls the "poetic view of the machine." Within the laboratory, even the most casual observer cannot help but notice the ubiquitous iconography of the machine and the constant aestheticization of technology. At the entrance to many buildings—for example, the Nova laser and the free electron laser facilities—one finds glass cases featuring enormous intricately constructed and brightly colored models of the machine within the building. These models inform all who enter of the aesthetic virtue, engineering complexity, and scientific importance of that building's machine. In the case of the laboratory's National Magnetic Fusion Energy Computer Center (NMFECC), instead of models of machines, the visitor encounters a large glass wall behind which four supercomputers (worth over $10 million each) are displayed as if they were works of art. Fact sheets about each laser, supercomputer, giant magnet, or whatever, give vital statistics that emphasize the machine's awesome ability to transgress previously known limits of size, power, and speed.

Then there are the photographs. The interior walls of laboratory buildings are frequently decorated with photographs of laboratory machines or parts of them. If there are people in the photographs, they are often shown peripheralized and dwarfed by the machines they maintain. Even laboratory postcards, on sale at the Visitors Center until recently, foreground the machines. They are the fetishized objects of the collective human gaze at the laboratory, constantly positioned at the aesthetic, thematic, and visual center of the laboratory stage. And they function like the totemic animals of many "simple" societies as defining symbols of group identity: for those who have worked on the Nova laser, the free electron laser, the laser isotope separation facility, and so on, the machines become totemic emblems of group identity and solidarity. In terms of social classification, people take on the identity of the machine they work on. These machines may also become vehicles for the identity of their originators, after whom they are named. Thus Edward Teller will be immortalized as the "father of the H-bomb"; and E. O. Lawrence, the founder of the laboratory, will always be associated in scientific memory with the synchrotron he ran.[19]

It is hard for a nonscientist to appreciate the beauty scientists see in machines that appear to differently trained eyes to be disfigured by welds and gauges and protruding wires. However, Livermore scientists repeatedly describe their machines as beautiful. For example, Lester, a weapons designer, once told me, "You go out to the test site, and there's this huge 200-foot canister filled with all this *beautiful* equipment, and they're about to put it down [the test shaft]. That's a real gut-wrencher. . . . To a physicist to see a really nicely put together set of measuring apparatuses is beautiful. How do I explain that? To me, a spectrometer is a very pretty thing. And you feel badly that it's going to be destroyed. And, if you see a shoddy thing, it's like looking at a garbage dump." Another scientist, taking the aestheticization of technology even further, had photographs of a missile test and an aboveground nuclear test in Nevada on the walls of his living room. They were quite beautiful, even to my eye, but they were by most people's standards an odd choice for living room decor.

I only fully realized the poetry weapons scientists see in technology when I went flying in a small plane with Jim, a senior weapons scientist. He was piloting the plane and I was watching the landscape below, marveling at the panoramic overview of gulleys, hills, and craters. Although far from the ground, I felt strangely at one with it. Jim broke into my reverie, saying, "This is so Zen, you know." I thought he must have read my mind, sensing my meditative response to the scenery, until he explained, "Both hands on the plane. Both feet working the plane. It's like a complete man-machine continuum." For him, it was the human relationship to technology, not to nature, that was Zen.

Sherry Turkle (1984) has written that people who work extensively with machines, especially very sophisticated machines, start to use them as mirrors with which to examine their own identity. Machines are, as Turkle puts it, "good to think with," and the more people think with them, the more they come to exchange and fuse the characteristics of people and machines: they attribute human characteristics to machines and find mechanical attributes within themselves. The machine becomes a metaphor in which they discover new human possibilities.[20] They develop what Haraway (1991: 149–181) has called "cyborg identities," becoming "a hybrid of machine and organism." Haraway argues that the cyborg is a key image of our time: as the Terminator and Robocop, it is taking popular culture by storm, and, thanks to artificial body prostheses from implants to pacemakers, humans are literally becoming cyborgs. But ultimately the figure of the cyborg does not so much describe a literal phenomenon as provide a metaphor for the increasing technicization of daily life and interdependence of humans and machines. This interdependence is very highly developed at the laboratory.

I pointed out earlier that laboratory scientists often speak of their own and other human bodies in language more appropriate to machinery. They often refer to people as "human resources" or "components" in systems, to communication as "interfacing," and to miscommunications between people as "disconnects." But the reverse also happens: they use the language of the human body in describing machines. Weapons are, as prosthetic extensions of human reach, called arms, and, as embodiments of human intelligence, they have heads—warheads. The best weapons are "smart weapons." If ever used, it is hoped that they will successfully destroy the enemy's command and control facilities—an attack known as a "decapitating strike." When combined, America's strategic nuclear weapons are said to constitute the three "legs" (air-based, sea-based, and land-based) of a triad. The legs of the triad are coordinated by space-based satellites sometimes referred to as "our eyes and ears." Missiles have "skins"; bombers store fuel in "rubber bladders." The laboratory's Brilliant Pebbles, if they are ever built, will orbit in "life jackets" (Stober and Klein 1992). Meanwhile, the worrisome part of the nuclear body is the torso: a recent laboratory study into the possibility that American warheads might be susceptible to accidental detonation found that they are most vulnerable "around the waist" (Drell 1991). Weapons can also, according to one scientist, "grow whiskers" as they age, and these whiskers can interfere with their proper functioning or, as he puts it, their "health" (Rosenthal 1990: 21). Another scientist told me he had to perform a "lobotomy" on a weapon that had turned out wrong. The insides of weapons, what one designer described to me as "the guts," contain, like human bodies, plasmas and discs. A weapon, when used, "couples" with the ground. The ensuing explosion produces, among other things, "daughter fission products." Even the term "fission" here is a refraction of the human body and its processes: it was deliberately named after the process of human cellular division by the physicist Otto Frisch, who saw the splitting of atoms as analogous to the splitting of cells in human growth and development (Easlea 1983: 67).[21]

Clearly there is a well-established circuit of metaphors here within which the attributes of humans and machines are exchanged.[22] Some of the particular metaphors that facilitate this exchange—the notion of "warheads" and "legs of a triad," for example—are fixed in the official and widely shared discourse on nuclear weapons; others are spontaneously invented by scientists as they go about their work. In either case, they are part of the same basic family of metaphors, part of a single broad phenomenon.

What is the significance of these metaphors? While it may seem that their existence is a trivial fact, of interest only to cultural critics in dogged pursuit of obscure hidden meanings, the system they represent is an important and revealing part of laboratory life. Metaphors matter because, a little like Freudian slips, they offer hints about emotional and ideological connections in the individual unconscious or in collective cultural consciousness. As Chris Gray (1997: 125) puts it in his discussion of metaphors in scientific discourse, "Tropes . . . represent a swerve from the literal that often marks a point of emotional importance. . . . In the case of scientific and government texts, uses of rhetoric are all the more significant because the style of the genre is itself the style of non-style." As well as reflecting emotion, metaphors also function more constitutively as linguistic molds that shape the collective consciousness of speakers for whom, in Evelyn Fox Keller's words (1985: 78), "language and metaphor can become hardened into a kind of reality." As speakers repeat old metaphors and coin new ones, they learn over and over, in a systematically patterned way, to construe one thing in terms of another. Whereas literal language is more denotative, metaphors, as they "swerve from the literal," construct the connotative meanings of things. They make symbolic connections. It is through metaphors, though not only through metaphors, that we make sense of the world, establishing relationships of similarity and difference that orient our behavior and beliefs, and it says something important about a group if its discourse repeatedly likens people and machines, finding the characteristics of each in the other. As Jane Caputi (1991: 490) puts it in her own discussion of body-machine metaphors in nuclear discourse, "Under the influence of such metaphors, humans and machines slur/blur ever into one another, the humans becoming more cold, the machines acquiring soul."

Obviously nuclear weapons scientists are far from being the only people in contemporary American society to use metaphors that fuse the characteristics of humans and machines. Other scientists, indeed many ordinary citizens, also use such metaphors, and the metaphors say as much about postmodern, postindustrial consciousness in general as they do about nuclear weapons scientists in particular. Nuclear weapons scientists are not unique in using such metaphors then. However, insofar as the general use of these metaphors reflects a widespread and profound reconceptualization of the relationship between human beings and technology in our contemporary social imaginary, the cultural world of nuclear weapons scientists is a good place to examine its workings in vivid relief. Metaphors that dehumanize people while humanizing machines may be freighted with additional importance for scientists whose work it is to develop extraordinarily powerful machines with the potential to kill millions of human beings. Working in concert with the discipline of the body and the iconography of the machine at the laboratory, the metaphors help legitimate nuclear weapons work, shaping minds and bodies that feel comfortable with and excited by the work. They do this in two ways.

First, as Elaine Scarry (1985) and Carol Cohn (1987) note, metaphors that imbue humans with the characteristics of machines make it easier to do work that entails the risk of injuring humans. If instead of being "hurt" they are "damaged," if instead of being "killed" they are "disassembled," then they have been changed, in the world of language at least, from sentient to insentient. They are no longer sites of fear, pain, and feeling. As Cohn (1987: 704) puts it in her discussion of the subjective transformation she experienced as she learned the discourse of nuclear professionals, "The more conversations I participated in using this language, the less frightened I was of nuclear war. How can learning to speak a language have such a powerful effect? One answer, I believe, is that the *process* of learning the language is itself part of what removes you from the reality of nuclear war."

Second, the metaphorical mixing of humans and machines also works in the opposite direction, expanding rather than contracting the human experience of embodiment. These metaphors, at the same time that they deny the sentient physicality of human embodiment in one way, extend the scope of that embodiment in another. The linguistic construction of machines in terms of human body parts signifies a claim of human affinity and identity with the machines, a will for self-extension through them. In the metaphors, in Barry's drunken fantasy that the road to immortality might be paved with mechanical body parts, there is a dream, a cyborg dream, of extended life and power, of reembodiment or reproduction even, through technology.[23]

REVOLTING BODIES

The anthropologist Michael Taussig (1980: 4) says that "in modern capitalist culture the body acquires a dualistic phenomenology as both a thing and my being. . . . Things like my body organs are at one instant mere things, and at another instant question me insistently with all too human a voice regarding the social significance of their dis-ease." The laboratory's discipline of the body is always incomplete, and bodies can sometimes become sites of resistance to its cyborg culture. Since the discipline of the body is a crucial part of the socialization of weapons scientists, certain experiences or apprehensions of bodily subjectivity can have profoundly subversive potential.

Such moments in which an alternative reality erupts through the body may be disregarded or repressed, but they may also become the basis for a reorganization of the self. Many antinuclear activists say they first became aware of their fear of nuclear weapons because of bodily sensations of nausea, sleeplessness, heart palpitations, and tingling in response to films, speeches, or newspaper articles about nuclear war. One Buddhist antinuclear activist told me of her feelings of dis-ease after a conversation in which I had profoundly shocked her by mentioning that I knew a Buddhist weapons scientist: "I hung up the phone and my pulse started to race, my face flushed, my limbs felt weak, and I felt sick to my stomach. I felt quite ill for an hour." I mentioned earlier a nuclear weapons scientist who had learned to attribute his occasional fears of nuclear disaster to low blood-sugar levels, seeing his body as an entity that occasionally obstructs or contaminates the judgments of his mind. But such a bodily signal might be read differently. It is possible to reverse the Christian and Cartesian hierarchy of mind and body and treat the body, in Merleau-Ponty's phrase, as a "nascent logos," as a source of insistent and critical questions. Citing Merleau-Ponty, Hubert Dreyfus and Paul Rabinow (1983: 167) say, "If the lived body is more than the result of the disciplinary technologies that have been brought to bear upon it, it would perhaps provide a position from which to criticize these practices."

And indeed it does. One Livermore scientist who refused to work on nuclear weapons explained her decision to me in these terms, touching her stomach as she spoke: "There's this thing in my stomach. My head understands the reasons to work on the weapons, for deterrence and so on, but when I think about doing this work, I feel this thing in my stomach." Just as warheads are most vulnerable to accidents around their waists, so it is in their stomachs that weapons scientists are most vulnerable to second thoughts. In the documentary film *The Day After Trinity*, the physicist Robert Wilson, who worked on the Manhattan Project, remembers a sudden attack of trembling and vomiting when he heard about the bombing of Hiroshima (Else 1980). In the same film, the physicist I. I. Rabi recalls his reaction to seeing the first nuclear test: "It took a few minutes until I realized what had happened. I had gooseflesh when I thought of the consequences for the world." Both refused ever to work on nuclear weapons again.

We can best appreciate the contours of the relationship between bodily discipline and nuclear weapons work at Livermore by comparing the accounts three different scientists gave of nuclear tests. The three scientists, Jack, Joseph, and George, had all seen aboveground tests, but their accounts evince three quite different attitudes toward the relationship between the body and nuclear weapons work. These three scientists are spread across the spectrum of attitudes toward continuing weapons work. Jack has continued to work on warhead design with dedication and enthusiasm. Joseph feels uneasy, "sad" he says, about weapons work but has continued to be involved in it. George decided some years ago that he could no longer work on nuclear weapons.

Here are Jack's reflections on an aboveground nuclear test. They are structured around a contrast between lay people's exaggerated fears of nuclear weapons and his own expert knowledge. In reading his words, I hear echoes of a physics professor making jokes about the radioactive magnesium in his bones and cavemen cooking their meat with uranium rocks.

> People tend to think of a nuclear weapon as some system of very mass destruction. I saw some tests in the Pacific. I saw half a megaton at ten miles. I had on black glasses and I faced the blast, and all I got was a little bit of sunburn from it. It was a little closer than it was supposed to have been. I got a little. . . . It's very impressive how hot it gets and how fast it is, but it's also impressive how fast it goes out, and at ten miles away from a very large blast—this was a very large blast, not the largest, but. . . . It's interesting to think that you drop one on Pleasanton [the town next to Livermore] and, if you weren't looking at it and you didn't get killed by flying glass, you would survive very nicely. And of course you'd have fallout. It's a small amount of energy put into a very, very small mass, and so it has a very spectacular result when you do that, but it is not very much energy, and in terms of the energy release, a small rainstorm over the Livermore Valley puts out many, many times what our largest nuclear devices do. And so in terms of total energy under your control, you can't use them to trigger earthquakes, you can't do all these catastrophic things that nature can do. You can black out a city because you can set it on fire and blast it down, but cities tend to be fairly small areas.

Jack finishes by saying that although "if we lost ten of our largest cities we would know that for a long time," a limited nuclear war would be survivable.

In this account Jack briefly mentions his bodily experience of the nuclear test in terms of "impressive" heat and minor sunburn, but he downplays his physical experience of the explosion and soon switches the narrative so as to subordinate this level of experience to a set of cognitive comparisons that transform a personal reminiscence into a set of abstract musings about the relative energy output of bombs and storms. In the end these musings seem more concrete, and more confidently articulated, than his own physical experience of a nuclear blast.

Joseph remembers the nuclear test he saw as "just stunning." "I was simply unprepared for the vastness of the display and the aurora that persisted—the colors, the power was stunning. There are just no words to adequately describe it." At the time he tried to connect what he was seeing with what had happened to the bodies of Hiroshima's inhabitants but was unable to make the connection real. "Making that connection with what they had seen just a second before it happened to them was really, really kind of a split."

Joseph is an unusual man who over the years has come to see his weapons work as a source of spiritual pain in his life. He has even gone so far as to seek out antinuclear activists to discuss his feelings and their own actions with them. He said that in the course of changing, he came to realize that "pain to a scientist or an engineer is just not very relevant." "I think we really work hard to prevent ourselves from feeling pain and we're able to do that." In his interview with me he recalled the beginning of his disenchantment, connecting it with a bodily feeling of heaviness.

> I remember shortly after I joined [the laboratory], sitting at a meeting, a large meeting, and I can't remember what the topic was, but it was some kind of topic—nuclear effects or nuclear deterrence or something—and finding myself with a very heavy feeling, a very foreboding feeling, and I simply couldn't shake it. I could go to work and it would go away, but it would come back. And I, for some time I put that down to—however you want to call it—moral, ethical concerns or superego concerns or something, you know. And I am concluding now that it could have some of those overtones, but really it's a feeling of sorrow. I mean it's sadness that we live in a situation right now where we, some of us, feel as if we have to stay where we are, to make the best of what we've got in the short term and hopefully try to bridge to this long-term goal of either partial or complete disarmament. . . . And that is very sorrowful to me. I feel a very heavy sense of sadness at having to do that.

As Joseph explored these feelings of sadness and heaviness in the interview, they had a nebulous, muffled character. They were suspended in an ambiguous space between bodily and emotional feelings, and although Joseph's thoughts had only a few days earlier been interrupted by "an odd musing" about a bomb being dropped on San Francisco, he said he had never personally felt in danger from nuclear weapons. Whereas Jack's account subordinates the sensations of the body to the calculations of the mind, Joseph has started to explore feelings of pain and doubt grounded amorphously in his body, but he is still in the process of deciding on the meaning of these feelings. By noticing the feeling of heaviness in his body, he has come to question the work he has been doing, but his questions are still in search of answers.

George is a scientist who decided he had to stop working on nuclear weapons. His account of two nuclear tests has an astonishing physical immediacy that is utterly unique in all the test narratives I collected at the laboratory. I asked him if he remembered the first test he saw.

> Well, you will always remember. . . . It was a balloon shot, pretty high up, and it was a few kilotons, and I was probably eight or nine miles away from it. And to protect our eyes we were given goggles, high-density goggles—high-density in the sense that you could look at the sun with these goggles and at times had a hard time figuring out where the sun was. You essentially put them over your eyes, and strapped around them they had big foam so that no light could leak in. . . . And there is this incredible flash of light, and you always go back to thinking how Oppenheimer describes this incredible flash of light. He described it as brighter than a thousand suns. Just incredibly intense. And it's very frightening. Just terrifying. Just absolutely terrifying. I was crouched over. I'm sure that I urinated in my pants at the time as a result. . . . And then while you're watching you see the difference in the index of refraction. You could actually see the shock wave traveling toward you. You know, there's a difference in the index of refraction. And so you prepare yourself to keep from being blown over by this blast, because it's a phenomenon. You just see this thing coming, and it just takes forever to come, and so you're sort of crouched, and finally the thing gets to you, and the wind whips past you, and there's a lot of dust and, yeah, your heart's beating a lot faster and you just, you just never forget it.

Some years later, George witnessed the explosion of a hydrogen bomb from a Pacific atoll.

> They gave you white coveralls to put on, and they gave you blast goggles. What they did is they faced you, you essentially sat down, assumed the fetal

position with your back to ground zero. So you were looking away from the event. You don't get to see the flash. And it goes: three, two, one, zero, and with your head buried in your arms with these goggles on, facing away from it, you see a flash. So something, some radiation particles, went through enough to stimulate your eyes. And then you feel this tremendous burst of thermal energy, and it decays away pretty good, and you're feeling pretty good about that time, and then it starts to get hot, gets hotter, and about that time the ground wave comes through and the whole—you're moving up and down maybe 12 to 18 inches, and in the back of your mind you're thinking about what is a coral atoll. It's a volcano—comes up, and there's the reef that's around it. What happens if you start rocking enough? Is it possible you can just break the coral, you know, if you're firing the bomb on one edge? Is it possible that the whole coral reef could just break off and you could just slide off into 12,000 feet of water? And you're thinking about that, and it continues to get hotter and hotter and hotter, and pretty soon you know you haven't reached the peak, and you're beginning to worry. You're convinced that your overalls are going to catch on fire. What are you going to do? Are you going to just roll over in the sand and put it out, or are you going to try to run down to the beach and put it out? . . . And about that time the blast wave comes through. And it literally, I mean here you are, you're still kind of buried and you're pretty terrified by the whole business, and it's taken a long time, and the blast wave comes through. . . . And you're literally picked up, you know, a few inches, so that when it goes by, you know, you've sat down again.

It is hard to believe that George and Jack are describing the same kind of event. If we compare their accounts—the test Jack describes was much larger than the first test George saw—it is not difficult to guess which of the two men still works on nuclear weapons and which decided to quit. George's account is saturated with feelings of terror that he consistently connects to and reads from his body as he urinates in his pants, as his heart races, as his skin temperature rises, and as his body is involuntarily lifted off the ground. George has a scientist's understanding of the event, as is evident from his discussion of the index of refraction from the shock wave and the stimulation of his retina by a few radiation particles, but instead of using this understanding to distance his direct bodily experience of the explosion, he integrates the two modes of description in his narrative so that the two complement one another. Finally his narrative is about the terror of embodiment in a world of nuclear weapons. George's experience of bodily terror here is a particularly grand example of the kind of experience of fear, subjectivity, and vulnerability that the scientists' culture of bodily discipline, objectifying gazes, and cyborg fantasies usually contains and inhibits. Surely it is obvious from George's narrative—an example of what happens when those inhibitions fail—why the laboratory's culture of the body is so important in maintaining the stability of laboratory life and the felt legitimacy of nuclear weapons work.

CHAPTER 6

Testing, Testing, Testing

*Nuclear weapons are both symbols and pieces of hardware. Their role as symbols
is what matters to most people, including scientists, most of the time.*
MICHAEL MAY, DIRECTOR OF LAWRENCE LIVERMORE
NATIONAL LABORATORY, 1965–1971

The testing of nuclear weapons was a focal concern of both the Livermore laboratory and the antinuclear movement in the 1980s. The laboratory organized itself around the production of nuclear tests; the antinuclear movement organized itself to end them. Carrying out or ending nuclear tests has been, for each, the mission that facilitated its integration as a community and connected it in contentious antipathy with the opposed community.

The birth of the nuclear age, and of the nuclear weapons community, is conventionally described in terms of the preparation and execution of a nuclear test: as most participants and observers tell the story, the climactic moment of triumph in the history of the Manhattan Project came with the July 16 Trinity test in the New Mexico desert, the first ever nuclear explosion on earth, not the bombings of Hiroshima and Nagasaki on August 6 and August 9, 1945.[1]

At Livermore, nuclear weapons testing has structured much of the organizational and symbolic life of the laboratory community. Diverse everyday tasks, throughout the laboratory and at the Nevada Test Site five hundred miles away, have taken on organizational purpose and symbolic meaning because of their contributions to programs converging in the production of nuclear tests. In a test—an "event" in the parlance of weapons designers—a "device"[2] with about five thousand components must work perfectly in the fraction of an instant before the components are destroyed by the explosion they create.[3] The preparation for such an experiment generates fantastically complex interactions over a period of years among thousands of physicists, engineers, computer scientists, chemists, administrators, technicians, secretaries, and security personnel. A single nuclear test is a kind of busy intersection where individual lives, bureaucratic organizations, scientific ideas, complex machines, national policies, international rivalries, historical narratives, psychological conflicts, and symbolic meanings all come together. Although the government's secrecy laws leave large parts of this intersection concealed in shadow, here I explore, as far as possible, the organizational production of nuclear tests and the political and symbolic meanings these events have for the scientists who have created them. It is my contention that these tests are important for their cultural and psychological as well as for their technical significance and that they have been vital not only in the production of nuclear weapons but also in the production of weapons scientists and in the social reproduction of the ideology of nuclear deterrence.

HOW TO DESIGN AND TEST A NUCLEAR WEAPON

Nuclear tests have been done for a variety of purposes: to explore the basic physics of nuclear explosions; to test a new warhead design approach; to recertify the reliability of an old warhead; to test the effects of nuclear explosions on military hardware; to adapt an old warhead design to a new delivery vehicle; or to validate the finished version of a new design. Any individual test may serve more than one of these purposes. Ambitious young designers know that they can make a reputation for themselves by finding new ways to calculate the basic physics of a nuclear explosion and by thinking of new design ideas.[4]

The nuclear weapons design, testing, and production process consists of six phases (Broad 1992: 128). In phase 1, concept study, designers review the results of earlier tests, thinking about how to push the limits of the basic physics. Meanwhile they consult with officials from the Department of Energy and the Pentagon to learn what capabilities the military seeks in its new nuclear weapons. In Harvey's words,

> Much of the time the laboratory develops (and tests) designs to satisfy needs independent of the DOD, or needs that the DOD has not yet appreciated. Some represent ideas whose time has come (and gone)—and may yet return. The DOD tends only to ask for capabilities that they know exist. Perhaps sometimes also for capabilities that don't exist but have been heavily advertised by the labs' "sales departments." . . . Many features develop into

DOD requirements after being provided, without request, by DOE or as a result of DOE initiative. We can anticipate DOD requirements.[5]

Matthew put it a little differently:

> Word will come down about certain needs and specifications—whether it's [the new warhead] to be tactical or strategic, how heavy it should be, how powerful, and so on. I start to think how I might design a weapon that would fit those general specifications. Meanwhile I'm thinking what the tests might show about basic physics. I'm asking what the tests tell us about our computer codes. I'm asking day by day, What don't we understand? How could we design a test to make that clear?

Much of this work involves conceptual thinking about first principles and hours spent comparing diagnostic data from old tests with the massive supercomputer calculations that simulate nuclear explosions.

In phase 2, scientific feasibility, weapons designers turn their ideas into specific design proposals that are evaluated by the bureaucracies within the laboratories, in the Department of Defense, and in the Department of Energy. This evaluation process may involve some nuclear testing. It also involves review meetings, often lasting as long as three hours, in which reviewing scientists try to pick holes in the proposals. "These are not nice reviews," said Lester.

> They're very critical. I've seen men all in tears. The big reward in our division is to do an experiment, to get your idea tested. It's highly competitive. For every twenty things people propose, maybe one is going to make it onto that shot schedule. So you do lots and lots of computer calculations. You try to anticipate every question that somebody's gonna ask you about the physics. And you prepare computer graphs that will answer those things as best you can. You try and identify what are the weak parts of it. Usually there's physics in it that we don't know, otherwise we wouldn't be doing the experiment. . . . There's even a culture about the review, and people learn it by osmosis. You start out by presenting what's been done in the past that's relevant, and then you present your idea, everything you know about the physics, and what you think the pitfalls are. . . . You can have a really bloody review and have the people who were practically yelling at each other, see them an hour later standing in the hall talking to one another like old friends.

An older designer, Barry, remembers how he used to dread the presence of Edward Teller at design review meetings.

> He would usually shuffle into these meetings about a third of the way through the talk and sit at the back. He'd listen for a while as other physicists

made objections or asked questions. Eventually he'd say in that gravelly voice of his, "Excuse me, but . . ." Those were the words I always dreaded hearing. When any designer heard that, their heart would sink, because Teller is a very profound thinker. He had the ability to get right to the heart of a problem. It was as if he was looking at a house of cards and always knew how to find the card right at the bottom, the one that would make it all fall down if you pulled it out.

Review committees try to strike a balance in their selections, approving some tests mainly for what they reveal about basic physics and some for their immediate contribution to a finished weapon. The division leader or associate director tries to find a basic consensus in the meetings, but often rival group and division leaders will disagree about the merits of their subgroups' ideas, and sometimes the director of the laboratory must intervene. Designers frequently complain about their vulnerability to managerial interference.

For phase 3, engineering development, one of the two weapons laboratories is selected by the Washington bureaucracy to develop a finished prototype device.[6] This might involve slightly adapting an old warhead to a new delivery vehicle, then testing its performance, or it might require the development of a new warhead design. The two laboratories often compete quite intensely for the phase 3 assignment. In deciding which weapons laboratory will be assigned particular design projects, Washington decision makers consider the merits of the two laboratories' proposals, but they also try to divide the spoils fairly evenly.

In developing phase 3 designs, the weapons laboratories are guided by a ranked list of target characteristics for nuclear weapons. These priorities are fixed by the Department of Defense and the Department of Energy. The requirements, in order of priority, are

1. High confidence that there can be no accidental nuclear explosion.
2. Compatibility in size, shape, and weight with the bomb's delivery system.
3. High confidence that plutonium will not be dispersed in an accident.
4. High likelihood of giving a full explosive yield when used.
5. Yield within the limits specified by its contractors.
6. Conservative uses of expensive materials such as plutonium and tritium.

7. Minimum maintenance required.

8. Simple operational features. (Craig 1988: 27)

Groups of physicists, chemists, electrical engineers, mechanical engineers, and technicians are assembled from divisions throughout the laboratory to turn abstract ideas and calculations into actual devices and packages of diagnostic equipment. These groups typically contain designers and code developers from both weapons design divisions at Livermore. A Division assigns its own lead designer for the secondary (fusion) component of the test, while B Division assigns a lead designer for the primary (fission) component.[7] One of them serves as the overall design physicist, or project manager, for the experiment—the position of greatest power and responsibility. "There are very few places in the country where the physicists are the top dogs, but Livermore is one of them," says Lester. Toward the end of the process, after the major physics decisions have been made, an engineer sometimes takes over as project manager.

In the engineering development phase, designers work long hours—often sixty to eighty hours a week. Broad (1992: 196) quotes one Livermore designer who described the climax of the engineering development phase by saying, "I have never seen people work so hard. They would sleep in assembly rooms for days, not seeing their families. Many times I saw people with tears running down their face because they had worked so hard." The designers are under constant pressure because other members of the team are waiting for their calculations so they can decide how to make parts of the bomb as well as the diagnostic equipment needed to measure its performance.

The designers consult with engineers on the choice of materials for the bomb, with chemists on choosing how to fit the bomb with tracer elements for diagnostic purposes, and with technicians, who, often working with highly toxic materials in glove boxes, must machine the device's components with extraordinary precision. Since parts of the device are machined at Rocky Flats in Colorado and the device is assembled at the Nevada Test Site rather than at the laboratory, this phase of the project can involve a lot of travel. Barry recalls traveling to Rocky Flats to watch the technicians machine the plutonium "pit" for his device.

> I looked at the plutonium in its glass case. It was black, with an oxide skin. It's like coal, except that it's hot to the touch because it's constantly emitting

radiation. You know plutonium is pyrophoric. The technician scraped the skin off with his gloves, and white sparks flew out. I remember thinking, "Holy shit! This lump of rock is going to go in *my* bomb. *That's* going to be that powerful."

Gradually the test date approaches. Clark remembers his test nearing completion.

Here was an experiment I had been working on for three years with a cast of hundreds, and [I was] watching this thing as it got all put together laboriously at a couple different places around the country. . . . So you see this whole thing coming together, gee, it's almost like having a baby or something. It's a comparable length of time and many more people are involved in the process. . . . One of my big fears was that pieces would get misplaced somehow and the wrong end would be facing forward. It was a complex thing. It had lots of parts. And so here this whole process comes down, and by the time you're done this is at least a $5 million deal, and yet I'm thinking this whole thing rests on a few of my late-night computer calculations.

As the device and the diagnostic equipment are being assembled, the test site workers are busy drilling the shaft into which the device and its diagnostic canister will be emplaced. The cylindrical canister, crammed full of sensitive diagnostic instruments and cables, can weigh hundreds of tons. When the canister is ready for final assembly, the nuclear device is transported with an escort of armored vehicles to its rendezvous with the diagnostic equipment (Nuclear Notebook 1990). There the device and canister are bolted together ("married" or "mated" in the parlance of weapons scientists) within a portable building, known as a bogey tower, which sits astride the test shaft to shield it from both the weather and the gaze of enemy satellites. Once the device and canister have been lowered into the shaft, they are connected to nearby trailers on the desert surface by thick cable wires that will transmit a chorus of measurements from the exploding bomb underground to the scientists above ground.

Different kinds of shafts are drilled for weapons development and weapons effect tests. For the former, conducted to verify the performance of a particular weapons design, the shaft is vertical, 7 to 12 feet in diameter, and 600 to 2,100 feet deep (above the Pahute Mesa water table). For the latter, conducted to investigate the effects of a nuclear explosion on military artifacts, a horizontal tunnel, located closer to the surface, is drilled out from the device's underground test chamber, and military equipment and diagnostic devices are positioned in the tunnel. The tunnel and shaft take months to excavate, and they are eventually destroyed in a fraction of a second (Soble 1984). Over the last three decades, as tests have become more complex, underground nuclear tests have grown more expensive in constant dollars. By the late 1980s, a weapons development test could easily cost $30 million; and a weapons effects test, $50 million to $60 million.[8]

Lester remembers finally seeing his device ready to be lowered into its shaft and covered with hundreds of feet of sand and gravel as well as coal tar epoxy plugs designed to keep all the radiation below ground.

> You go out to the test site, and there's this huge 200-foot canister filled with all this beautiful equipment and they're about to put it down. That's a real gut-wrencher [laughs loudly]. As you go out there . . . you have to sign at the time that they bring the device out and marry it to the canister.

Before dawn the arming party goes out to arm the device. Broad describes one instance of this process:

> A small group of scientists and security guards . . . drove out to a trailer known as the red shack to electronically arm the weapon, which had earlier been placed at the bottom of a 1,050-foot-deep hole and covered with dirt. At the red shack, security was tight as usual. Two of the scientists carried a special briefcase and a bag of tiny cubes that had numbers painted on their sides. They alternately took cubes out of the bag and punched the numbers into an "arm enable" device in the briefcase, generating a random code that was sent to the buried weapon on a special electrical cable. The scientists then drove across the desert to the control point in a mountain pass overlooking the test site. . . . There, in a high-technology complex surrounded by armed guards and barbed wire, they again opened their briefcase and sent the same random code to the weapon. It was now armed. (1992: 87)

Now a small group gathers in the control room to direct the shot. The group generally includes the design physicist, the test director (a test site official who is now formally in charge), the chief experimentalist (an L Division scientist responsible for the diagnostic equipment), and some technicians. The test director has the privilege of naming tests, a privilege held jealously from the designers. Each series of tests is named around a particular theme, the names usually connoting rarity and obscure knowledge. Livermore has named its tests for San Francisco street names, California wildflowers, California and Nevada ghost towns, and rare cheeses. When Livermore was naming its tests for cheeses, Los Alamos named a series after wines, and the scientists used to joke that the two laboratories could hold a wine-and-cheese party together.

On the day of the test the test director works closely with a test controller from the Nevada Operations Office, who has the right to postpone the test if his advisory panel (containing a meteorologist and an Environmental Protection Agency official) advises him that the weather conditions are wrong. Even though the tests take place underground, it is official policy not to test a device if the wind is blowing toward Los Angeles, Las Vegas, or other densely inhabited areas—in case radioactivity is accidentally released.[9] When the shot does go forward, the scientists see the detonation in two ways: first, on video monitors that relay the picture from a helicopter hovering over the test shaft and, second, as a set of flickering needles on seismographs and oscilloscopes registering in the control room what the diagnostic equipment has picked up from the transitory flare of a small star beneath the surface of the earth just miles away.

Clark described his test as follows:

> We got up at 3:30 or 4:00 in the morning. Drive out. Stars are out. Go out to this remote outpost. Standing around going through the what-ifs. "God, what if this happens, what are you going to do then?"
>
> And everything went smooth, and it went off and they show a picture on the TV screens there of a helicopter hovering above the site and you could actually see dust rising. I mean it's not like you're watching the old atmospheric tests. I mean it's pretty benign really. You can see a shock wave ripple through the earth. It's a couple thousand feet under the ground. Nevertheless you see a ripple, and under the ground there's still a fireball and that material gets molten. I mean it vaporizes and then eventually it condenses, gets molten, and there's a little puddle and there's a cavity left, because now the molten stuff there is higher density than the initial rock was. So here's this big cavity and the earth above it is pressing down on it and eventually it collapses the cavity and that leads to the formation of the crater at the top. And so you're not allowed out to the site until the crater is actually formed, and that can happen in 30 seconds, it can happen in 10 hours. Turned out with mine that it happened in about an hour, and so then we could drive out to the site. And that was really awesome, standing there with this thing that was at least 100 yards across, and see what I had been looking at on my computer screen for years all of a sudden show up in this gigantic movement of the earth. It was as close as I've been to personal contact with what the

force of the nuclear weapon is like, because I've never been present at an atmospheric burst, nor has anybody else in my generation, since the last atmospheric burst was in 1963. . . . And then eventually some of the data starts to come in and by the end of the day it was clear that it was going to be a success. It was a very complicated shot, so I knew that would be good for my career.

As the day progresses, the data through which the bomb's performance will be interpreted are retrieved from the diagnostic devices. "We bury these things half a mile underground and you get some electricity out of a wire and some melted glass that's radioactive and go out and analyze those, and you can tell somebody all about what happened," said Jack, marveling at the almost magical nature of the diagnostic technology.

In what Lester describes as "show-and-tell," the scientists gather to share the data after it arrives: "Sometimes they'll flash up *beautiful* data, and then there's sort of euphoria. A typical experiment will have dozens of pieces of data, and that goes on one at a time [laughs]. Everybody sees it together." Next the lead scientists hurriedly write the "six-hour report," a preliminary evaluation of the test, so called because it goes to the laboratory and to top military officials about six hours after the test. Then the scientists, feeling despondent or elated by the test's results, catch the daily plane from the test site to Livermore.

Once a design has been validated by the underground tests of phase 3, it moves through three production phases: phase 4, production engineering; phase 5, first production; and phase 6, quantity production. Laboratory scientists continue to be involved with the weapon throughout these phases, but not so extensively as in phases 1, 2, and 3. It is the testing process, not the production process, that is climactic for Livermore's weapons designers.

Many weapons designers told me about the exhilaration and satisfaction they experienced at the conclusion of a successful nuclear test. Clark said he felt "proud" when his test worked. Michael said that when a test is over, he usually feels "a sense of accomplishment, an inner elation." Rick told me, "Sometimes in my work I get this feeling that no one else ever figured this out before, and I figured it out, and it made the earth move over there. It's a neat feeling." Barry said he felt "euphoria" when his tests worked. He once even brought his wife a piece of macadam blasted by his device, telling her, "My bomb did this."

NUCLEAR TESTING AS A CONTESTED PRACTICE

Not everyone has been so enthusiastic about nuclear testing. Over the last forty years there have been repeated attempts to ban or restrict it. These attempts date back to at least the mid-1950s, when the American public became increasingly concerned about the possible health consequences of atmospheric testing.[10] The campaign against atmospheric testing was spearheaded by the Nobel Prize-winning scientist Linus Pauling, who announced his calculations that nuclear tests already conducted would kill ten thousand civilians and that continued testing would probably kill a million people. Arguing that unchecked atmospheric testing would lead to an international epidemic of genetic mutations, cancers, and leukemias, he gathered the signatures of more than ten thousand scientists in support of a campaign to end nuclear tests. The scientific community was, however, quite divided over this issue, and many scientists sided with Edward Teller and Ernest Lawrence, the co-founders of the Livermore laboratory, who publicly accused Pauling of scaremongering and insisted that radioactive fallout was essentially harmless. During these years, as he roamed the country making speeches, Teller became identified as the foremost public champion of continued nuclear testing (Divine 1978: 104–124; Gilpin 1962; Greb and Heckrotte 1983; Holgate 1991).

As the scientists debated the safety of atmospheric testing, a mass movement against testing, drawing most of its support from the educated middle class, crystallized in the United States. Focusing on the dangers posed by radiation for the food chain, this was more an environmental movement than a movement against the arms race per se. Nuclear testing became an important issue in the 1956 presidential campaign, with Adlai Stevenson opposing it and Dwight Eisenhower defending it. Then in 1957, the Committee for a Sane Nuclear Policy (SANE) was founded to lobby for an end to nuclear testing. With Norman Cousins and Dr. Benjamin Spock, two popular public personalities, as its spokesmen, SANE grew rapidly to 130 chapters and 25,000 members nationwide.[11]

By mid-1957, Eisenhower was leaning toward a moratorium on nuclear testing. At this point, Teller and Lawrence had a forty-minute meeting with Eisenhower to put the case for continued testing. They told him that the most recent nuclear tests were producing 90 percent less fallout than earlier ones and projected that the Livermore laboratory was perhaps seven years away from perfecting a "clean bomb" that would be a safe engineering tool for digging canals and harbors and a more humane weapon in war. It would be a "crime against humanity," they said, to prevent the development of such a device. They also warned Eisenhower that a testing moratorium would not be completely verifiable (Blum 1987*b*; Broad 1992: 46–47; Divine 1978: 147–150; Gilpin 1962: 168–169).

Eisenhower was not persuaded, and in November 1958, after a flurry of thirteen American nuclear tests in seven days at the end of October, he initiated a moratorium on nuclear testing with the Soviets. While the moratorium was in place, the Americans and Soviets tried to negotiate a verification regime for a permanent ban on nuclear tests, both above and below ground.

As these negotiations proceeded, there was continued opposition to a test ban from what Eisenhower, in his 1961 farewell speech to the nation, was to christen the "military-industrial complex." The Joint Chiefs of Staff and the two weapons laboratories were particularly strongly opposed to a ban. Teller and Lawrence from Livermore continued to lobby against it, but with new arguments. They now argued that nuclear tests very high in the atmosphere and "decoupled" tests (in which the explosion's seismological signature is muffled by a large underground cavity) could escape detection, thus allowing the Soviets to cheat on a test ban. They also suggested that the Soviets might secretly test nuclear weapons behind the sun or the moon and that a test ban would freeze in place a Soviet lead in multimegaton weapons (Blum 1987*b*; Bundy 1988: 333–334; Daalder 1987: 22–27; Divine 1978: 253–255; Ruina 1991).

In the end the test ban negotiations bogged down and collapsed. The Soviet and American negotiators could not agree on the number of on-site inspections needed to verify a treaty. Meanwhile Soviet-American relations grew increasingly tense after the Soviets shot down Gary Powers's spy plane in 1960 and, once John F. Kennedy became president, as the Berlin crisis unfolded in 1961. Shortly after the French ended the worldwide pause in nuclear testing by testing their first nuclear weapon in 1961, the Soviets announced their intention to resume their own testing program. In just three months they exploded fifty nuclear devices with a cumulative yield exceeding the total yield of all previous tests by all nations. The American weapons laboratories, which had been worried that they would lose many of their brightest weapons designers if the moratorium continued much longer, were not far behind: in 1962, the United States tested ninety-six nuclear devices (Norris and Arkin 1991: 57).[12]

Ironically, it was at this point, after the moratorium collapsed and nuclear testing resumed with a vengeance, that the Soviets and Americans finally agreed to ban atmospheric nuclear testing. Although the popular movement against nuclear testing had by now abated, the near-disaster of the Cuban missile crisis in 1962 provided the impetus for Kennedy and Khrushchev to negotiate the Limited Test Ban Treaty the following year. Remarkably, the two superpowers negotiated the treaty in only two weeks. However, as McGeorge Bundy (1988: 460) puts it, "The Limited Test Ban Treaty was indeed limited." David Morrison (1985: 35) calls the treaty "more an atomic 'clean air' act than the restrictive arms control measure once envisioned." It forbade nuclear explosions above ground and underwater, but not underground, and the average annual number of nuclear tests continued to rise in the years immediately following the Limited Test Ban Treaty. The Kennedy administration had attempted to negotiate an end to *all* nuclear tests but gave up in the face of opposition in Congress, disagreement with the Soviets over the number of annual inspections needed to verify compliance, and arguments from the weapons laboratories that it might not be possible to detect low-yield underground explosions, especially if they were decoupled (Bundy 1988: 460–461; Daalder 1987; Evernden 1986; Greb and Heckrotte 1983; Holgate 1991: 18; Seaborg 1981).

Teller's opposition notwithstanding, the Limited Test Ban Treaty was a treaty the Livermore and Los Alamos laboratories could live with. They had already moved much of their testing underground anyway[13] and were planning to conduct many underground tests even if they were still allowed to test in the atmosphere since there were advantages to underground testing: diagnostic measurements were more easily carried out underground; underground test series could proceed more quickly, being less vulnerable to weather conditions than aboveground tests; and testing in Nevada was more convenient than testing in the Pacific (AEC Meeting 1377, 1958).

After the signing of the Limited Test Ban Treaty, nuclear testing largely disappeared from the public agenda as a topic of controversy until the late 1970s. In these years the weapons designers of Livermore and Los Alamos were, on the whole, left in peace to manipulate the basic principles of atomic and hydrogen bomb design in ever more subtle ways and to continue testing their new ideas. They learned to design "cleaner" bombs that produced less radioactive fallout. Conversely, they succeeded in designing an "enhanced radiation bomb," popularly referred to as the "neutron bomb," which produced a violent burst of radiation but a comparatively low explosive yield. They learned to make bombs that used up less precious uranium and plutonium, bombs that were more portable, and bombs of different shapes. They developed "dial-a-yield" weapons whose explosive power could be selected immediately before use.[14] And they developed permissive action links (PALs)—electromechanical locks that had to be opened before nuclear weapons could be armed and that therefore made unauthorized use of nuclear weapons less likely (Bracken 1983: 168–169; Hansen 1988: 225, 227).[15]

Most important, at the beginning of the 1970s, the United States introduced MIRVed weapons, missiles with multiple independently targetable warheads that enabled a single missile to destroy several targets at once. This breakthrough was the result of Livermore and Los Alamos scientists' skill in designing lighter, more compact thermonuclear warheads at the same time that missile engineers developed new kinds of guidance technologies (MacKenzie 1990). By giving an attacker the potential capability to destroy several enemy missiles with each missile used, MIRV technology profoundly transformed the U.S.–Soviet balance of terror, giving a new hypothetical advantage to the attacker.

The arms control treaties that were signed in these years did not greatly impede the laboratories' work. The Non-Proliferation Treaty of 1970 focused more on blocking the spread of nuclear weapons to new countries than on ending the arms race.[16] The ABM Treaty of 1972 restricted the deployment of antimissile technology but not the development of nuclear weapons. The SALT I Accords of 1972 placed numerical limits, slightly in excess of existing levels, on the number of missiles each superpower was allowed to acquire, but, since the treaty did not restrict the development of new weapons, both sides were able to retire old weapons and replace them with new ones. Also, since the treaty, signed just as MIRVed weapons were being developed, limited the number of missiles but not the number of warheads, the superpowers were able to double the number of warheads they deployed over the next decade (Harvard Nuclear Study Group 1983: 74).[17]

It was not until 1977 that nuclear testing itself returned to the political agenda, putting the discreet industriousness of the laboratories in jeopardy once more. In 1977, President Jimmy Carter decided to make the nego- tiation of a comprehensive test ban treaty (CTBT) one of the main goals of his administration. Toward this end, he sent a team of negotiators to Geneva under the leadership of Herb York, a former director of the Livermore laboratory who had subsequently become a critic of the arms race (York 1970, 1987). The negotiations themselves soon became bogged down in wrangling about verification, with the Americans pushing for more intrusive verification agreements than the Soviets wanted. However, according to York (1987: 316–317), these problems were far from insu- perable, and the Soviets were making unprecedented concessions in regard to on-site inspection.

The negotiations, unsurprisingly, ran into opposition from the domes- tic nuclear establishment. The Department of Energy, the Joint Chiefs of Staff, and the two nuclear weapons laboratories were all strongly opposed to a complete test ban, and they had strong allies in Congress (Greb and Heckrotte 1983). The opposition from the laboratories centered on a new argument to the effect that under a total test ban, the continued reliability of old stockpiled weapons (or of slightly modified versions of old designs) could no longer be guaranteed since it would not be possible to test these weapons to resolve any suspected problems that might have arisen. As one leading Livermore scientist, Milo Nordyke, later put it: under a test ban treaty "not only would the stockpile turn to green cheese, but our ability to correct the situation would turn to green cheese" (Rogers 1982).

Harold Agnew, the director of Los Alamos National Laboratory, mak- ing a claim that has subsequently become highly controversial,[18] said later that Carter abandoned the idea of a CTBT because of a two-hour con- versation he had at the White House with Agnew and Roger Batzel, the director of Livermore. Agnew claimed that Carter was strongly committed to a treaty banning nuclear tests for at least five years but that he and Batzel persuaded him to drop the test ban primarily because of the weapons reliability issue. York disagrees that Agnew and Batzel had any particular influence on Carter, saying that the negotiations mainly failed because the Carter administration put them to one side after the Soviet invasion of Afghanistan and the Iranian hostage crisis in 1979. York insists that Carter discounted the laboratory directors' opinion in the face of a strong countervailing endorsement of a test ban by his White House scientific advisory panel. Whatever the reason, no treaty was signed (Agnew 1981; Blum 1987*b;* Evernden 1986; York 1987: 285–287).

Throughout the 1980s, the Reagan and Bush administrations strenuously resisted suggestions that the comprehensive test ban negotiations should be reopened, saying that important verification problems remained to be solved and that it was, in any case, vital to continue nuclear testing so as to assure the reliability of existing nuclear weapons. The Reagan administration suggested that instead of opening negotiations for a CTBT, the United States and the Soviet Union should cooperate on a series of experiments using a new technology developed at Livermore, CORRTEX, to compare their measurements of the explosive yields of nuclear tests. The purpose of these joint verification experiments was partly to provide a technical basis for resolving American allegations that the Soviets had been breaching the Threshold Test Ban Treaty of 1974, which had set an upper limit of 150 kilotons (about ten times the strength of the Hiroshima bomb) for nuclear tests.

By the 1980s, the fundamental principles of nuclear warhead physics and engineering were well established, and, with regard to new warheads, the main design task was to push their yield-to-weight efficiency ratios to the limit. Some nuclear scientists were also developing weapons incorporating new materials or kinds of conventional explosive designed to reduce the risk of accidental nuclear explosions.[19] Others were working on highly speculative concepts for third-generation nuclear weapons such as the nuclear bomb-pumped X-ray laser, which was widely advertised in the 1980s as one of the more promising of the SDI weapons.

Throughout the 1980s, the United States came under intense pressure to end nuclear testing completely. Domestically the pressure came from the nuclear freeze movement, which made a bilateral ban on nuclear testing one of its principal demands. But the most unexpected and dramatic pressure in favor of a nuclear test ban came from the Soviet Union itself. On August 6, 1985, the fortieth anniversary of Hiroshima, Mikhail Gorbachev initiated a unilateral Soviet testing moratorium that lasted for eighteen months, even though the United States did not join in. On October 19, 1989, just before the fall of the Berlin wall, Gorbachev again unilaterally suspended Soviet nuclear testing, this time for a year. He also announced, on March 10, 1990, that the Soviet Union intended by 1993 to close its main nuclear test site at Semipalatinsk, partly in response to the protests of local Kazakh citizens.[20] On October 5, 1991, Gorbachev initiated yet another one-year moratorium. Boris Yeltsin's government turned this into an indefinite suspension of nuclear testing, later joined by the U.S. government, which, under Bill Clinton, resumed negotiations for a comprehensive test ban treaty despite the initial opposition of the Livermore and Los Alamos laboratories.

THE LABORATORY AND THE TEST BAN

Antinuclear stereotypes notwithstanding, Livermore scientists have not been incorrigibly opposed to all arms control measures. As Clark, a warhead designer, put it when I interviewed him in 1988, "Almost everybody I talk to at the lab is in favor of reduced numbers of strategic warheads. Most people, I think, are in favor of continuing to support at least some form of the ABM Treaty. . . . I think most people at the lab went along with SALT I." Moreover, some scientists at Livermore helped the Democratic party write its platform in favor of constraining SDI (Dearborn 1990).[21] Some Livermore scientists argued for the elimination of intermediate-range nuclear missiles in Europe before the Intermediate Nuclear Forces (INF) Treaty achieved that in 1987 (Immele 1984). Other scientists and managers at the laboratory played an important role in devising scenarios for a 50 percent cut in the strategic arsenals of the two superpowers. For example, Michael May, director emeritus of the laboratory, suggested a scenario of substantial cuts in strategic nuclear weapons together with the elimination of the MX missile and a ban on SDI deployment long before the idea of a 50 percent cut was taken up by the Bush administration in the START II talks (Heller 1989; May et al. 1988).[22] Also, Roger Batzel, then the laboratory director, and three senior scientists at the laboratory—Milo Nordyke, Roy Woodruff, and Bill Scanlin—publicly contradicted the Reagan administration when it accused the Soviets of cheating on the Threshold Test Ban Treaty.[23] Batzel and Nordyke made their views known in testimony to the Senate Armed Services Committee, while Woodruff and Scanlin defended the treaty and expressed skepticism about charges of Soviet cheating in a 1983 interview with the *Washington Post*. Woodruff, who was at the time director of Livermore's weapons programs, was reprimanded for this by the secretary of energy in a 5:30 A.M. telephone call to his home, though he reportedly stood by his position (Brown 1989; DeWitt 1990: 4–5; Marsh 1983*b:* 4).

A ban on nuclear testing is the only arms control proposal that has provoked almost unanimous hostility at Livermore. Why is this?

If you ask critics of the laboratory, they say it is simply a matter of self-interest. In the words of Hugh DeWitt (1986: 104), an internal critic at Livermore, "The laboratories oppose a comprehensive test ban because they want to continue nuclear weapons development—to refine existing designs and do research in exciting new areas such as the X-ray laser." Such critics argue that it is easy for Livermore scientists to support arms reduction treaties since, whether there are one hundred MX missiles or fifty, Livermore scientists still design and test the warhead. Under a test ban, however, there would be nothing for weapons scientists to do but run simulations of nuclear explosions on their supercomputers, perform nonnuclear tests on stockpiled warheads, rake over old data from dead tests, and supervise the reproduction of old warhead designs at weapons manufacturing plants. They would be unable to test any new theories and ideas. They would be experimentalists without experiments.[24]

Livermore scientists themselves have explained their opposition to a test ban differently. In the 1980s, they told me it was important to keep testing in order to "modernize" the arsenal, to investigate potential new Star Wars defensive weapons, to train new weapons designers, to make safety improvements, and to keep abreast of possible breakthroughs in weapons technology by other countries. But, throughout the 1980s, the main rationale for continued testing given by laboratory officials and by many warhead designers concerned the reliability of the nuclear stockpile. Many Livermore scientists insisted throughout the decade that the reliability of the arsenal could not be assured without continued nuclear testing and that it was therefore vital that no test ban treaty be signed.[25] Bill Zagotta, a longtime warhead designer, put it this way in an op-ed piece in one of Livermore's local newspapers:

> Why is testing necessary? There is a common sense answer to this question. All man-made hardware can deteriorate. Testing is a way to help discover deterioration. Nuclear weapons are tested to make sure that they have not deteriorated. It's as simple as that!

Testing is necessary for stockpile reliability. There are other purposes for tests but reliability is the reason why testing is necessary. (1990)

Another experienced warhead designer, Jack, put it in similar terms in an interview with me.

I think a lot of people think a bomb is a bomb; build it once and it's there forever. It's not true. If you bought a Cadillac, you wouldn't just stick it in your garage and stake your life that you could start it ten years later if you didn't do anything other than put air in the tires and charge the battery. I wouldn't bet on it. And so, in that sense, as long as we have a requirement for deterrence, I think we're going to want to have evaluation of the systems that we have. . . . If they're something you depend on, you can't afford to have somebody suspect that they're not credible. That could mean an invitation to a conflict that you might not want to get into.

Jack added that in addition to assuring the reliability of weapons, tests assure the reliability of the scientists who must ultimately make judgments about weapons reliability. Tests are the only means, according to him, of training the scientists on whose expertise the reliability of the arsenal ultimately depends: "I am a unique asset to the country, not because I'm good, just because of the opportunity, because of what I've seen. Much of the information about a test is not written down. It's in the memory of people."

Put this way, the issue sounds simple enough. However, as one probes more deeply, one has a vertiginous sense of standing on shifting ground as the distinction between political and technical judgments—a distinction anchoring the expert case both for and against a comprehensive test ban treaty—melts into air.

DECONSTRUCTING RELIABILITY

When the directors of Livermore and Los Alamos advised Jimmy Carter against a comprehensive test ban in 1978, they warned him that, over a number of years, the materials inside a nuclear weapon corrode and interact in unpredictable ways that could necessitate remanufacture of the warhead. This, in turn, might require a retest, especially if some of the materials used in the original warhead design were no longer available and had to be replaced with new materials not previously used in that warhead. The directors also argued that Soviet warhead designs were more robust and enduring than American models, so that a test ban might leave the

Soviets more assured than the Americans of the reliability of their weapons. Finally, they pointed out that without testing, many American weapons designers would leave the weapons laboratories so that in the event that a test ban ended it would be hard to reassemble design groups, whereas, given the nature of Soviet society, the Soviets might be able to coerce their scientists into remaining "on call" for an eventual resumption of nuclear testing (York 1987: 285–287; Zuckerman 1983: 122–125). The memory of 1961, when the Soviets ended a testing moratorium with a vigorous hail of tests, was not forgotten.

At the same time Carter received a two-page letter from Norris Bradbury, a former director of Los Alamos; Carson Mark, former head of the theoretical physics division at Los Alamos; and Richard Garwin, a nationally known consultant on nuclear weapons physics who played a major role in developing the hydrogen bomb.[26] Bradbury, Mark, and Garwin assured Carter that in their technical judgment the laboratory directors were mistaken and that the continued reliability of the U.S. nuclear stockpile could be assured without any further nuclear tests. York (1987: 286), Carter's lead negotiator, says in his memoirs that "the nuclear establishment's fears were exaggerated. . . . We concluded that regular inspections and nonnuclear tests of stockpiled bombs would uncover most such problems and provide solutions to them. Moreover the laboratories could, if they tried, find ways around those that might remain." Hans Bethe, another former head of the Los Alamos theoretical division who was now a test ban supporter, also disagreed with the laboratories' position. In 1985, he wrote to Dante Fascell, Chair of the House Committee on Foreign Affairs, advising him that "weapons can . . . be detonated without their nuclear components in order to ensure that their complete assembly operates correctly. Nonexplosive tests are also available for determining whether the nuclear components have deteriorated during storage" (quoted in Rogers 1985).

Scientists at the laboratories largely disagreed, and Livermore's director, Roger Batzel, continued to cite the weapons reliability issue in testimony to Congress. On February 26, 1987, he told the Senate Armed Services Committee,

> Approximately one-third of all modern weapon designs placed in the U.S. stockpile have required and received postdeployment nuclear tests for resolution of problems. In three-fourths of these cases, the problems were

discovered only because of the ongoing nuclear testing. (Cited in Kidder 1987: 4)

Later in 1987, the Livermore laboratory provided the U.S. Congress with a report on weapons reliability prepared by three of its leading weapons designers (Miller, Brown, and Alonso 1987). The report gave details of fourteen warhead designs that had needed postdeployment retesting to detect and rectify flaws. In the case of the Polaris missile, the problem was serious enough that, some years after deployment, about one-half of the warheads were found to be "lemons" (Craig 1988: 29; Wilson 1983: 199).

The same year, Rep. Les Aspin, Chair of the House Armed Services Committee, made a highly unusual move by asking Ray Kidder, a well-regarded Livermore scientist known to sympathize with the test ban cause, to reanalyze the information in the Livermore report. Kidder was allowed full access to all the relevant classified information. In his own report, which appeared in both classified and unclassified versions, Kidder argued that the laboratory's position was unconvincing. He pointed out that nine of the fourteen problematic designs were rushed into the stockpile without full testing because of the 1958–1961 testing moratorium. The other five problems concerned weapons constructed in the 1980s. Kidder claimed that they were all inadequately tested in the design process and that the subsequent tests that revealed problems after these weapons had entered the stockpile should more properly be thought of as deferred design tests than as postdeployment reliability tests. He also argued that it is possible to remanufacture warheads in proven ways that render reliability testing redundant, saying that if the laboratories were concerned about reliability, it would be easy for them to design more robust and reliable warheads (Kidder 1987).[27]

I might note in passing here that the number of tests assigned to verification of stockpile reliability has been a small fraction of the total number of tests. My own best guess, on the basis of hints dropped to me, is that no more than one test a year was dedicated to reliability assurance in the 1980s.[28]

What are we to make of this arcane but hardly trivial dispute?[29] Physicists who support a test ban have tended to side with Kidder, but most weapons scientists at the laboratory, whether speaking on or off the record, have vehemently disagreed with him. We could plausibly argue that the technical judgment of the weapons scientists has been compromised by their vested interests; or we could just as plausibly argue that weapons scientists are uniquely placed to know about the mechanical reliability of nuclear weapons and that their opponents are technically less informed or have allowed their own politics to color their technical judgments. Laboratory Director Batzel used the latter argument when he pointed out to Representative Aspin that although Kidder had had a distinguished career in laser physics, he "has not had recent, direct responsibility or experience as a nuclear weapons designer" (Miller, Brown, and Alonso 1987: 45).

My goal here is neither to judge the honesty of the participants in this debate nor to provide a definitive judgment of the technical concerns at issue—a task that would clearly be beyond my competence in any case. Instead I would like to follow the lead of a young physicist at Livermore who, having read some of the literature in the sociology of science, reminded me that I was an anthropologist, not a physicist, and advised me to stop thinking of these technical judgments as right or wrong answers to a question and start thinking of them as interpretations of highly complex and ambiguous information. Instead of seeking a definitive technical judgment, then, we should ask about the processes by which judgments come to be considered definitive and their authors authoritative. After all, part of the argument made by the designers is that Kidder was not in a position, despite his knowledge of thermonuclear physics, to make the technical judgments he made. By means of what processes, then, social as well as technical, does one acquire the authority to make such judgments?[30]

Furthermore, what is reliability? How much weapons reliability is enough, and why is reliability so important? We have been incited to a discourse[31] here in which weapons reliability is taken for granted as an indispensable asset. The proponents of testing argue that your enemies are less likely to attack you if they are sure, and you are sure, that you have reliable nuclear weapons. Some opponents of testing have argued, on the contrary, that if neither side is particularly sure that its nuclear weapons work, then neither side will have the confidence to attack or pressure the other, so that a test ban might result in low confidence in weapons reliability, which, in turn, would enhance deterrence (Chomsky 1988: 196; Forsyth 1990). We must ask, then, how a social world comes to be constructed such that deterrence depends on the hyperreliability, not on the questionable reliability, of nuclear weapons. Given that one could imagine a world where the unknown reliability of weapons acted as a bulwark against aggression, how is it that in the collective consciousness of weapons scientists the experimental demonstration of the exact reliability of nuclear weapons has become associated with the safety and reliability of nuclear deterrence itself?

A RITUAL ANALYSIS

As should by now be clear, to be a weapons scientist is not just to have mastered a body of knowledge about physics but also to have submitted to an array of practices and discourses in regard to ethics, secrecy, the body, and machines. It is also—and this is the importance of nuclear testing in this context—to have participated in and been produced by a series of processes involving the design and testing of new nuclear weapons. In the remainder of this chapter, I examine nuclear tests as cultural processes that re-produce weapons scientists as persons and that enable weapons scientists to play with, maybe even resolve, core issues in their ideological world. In doing a processual analysis of nuclear testing, it is heuristically helpful to think of nuclear tests as sharing some of the characteristics of rituals. Many anthropologists have argued that the myths and rituals of nonliterate peoples often contain what we might call, in our own terms, "scientific knowledge" about the world (Evans-Pritchard 1937; Horton 1967; Lévi-Strauss 1966). I argue the complementary converse, that some of our most expensive scientific experiments are saturated with elements of myth and ritual. This is not to say that they are not really scientific experiments. It is to say that there is more to scientific experiments than meets the eye.

Since my comparison of nuclear tests with rituals may seem improbable, even offensive, to some, particularly the scientists who carry them out, it bears a word of explanation. My intention in making the analogy is not to be cute; nor is it to satirize nuclear weapons scientists by comparing them to tribal "savages," nor yet to deny that nuclear tests are rigorously executed scientific experiments. At a time when many anthropologists are struggling to apply anthropological theory to contemporary Western societies without descending into the realms of either triteness or grotesque caricature, I make the guarded analogy between ritual and nuclear testing because it seems to me to genuinely illuminate the significance of testing for Livermore scientists in a way that affords a new vantage point not only on the vexed debate over nuclear testing but also, more broadly, on the cultural and psychological significance of scientific experimentation in general. After all, it is not for nothing that when I asked Barry who he considered a real weapons designer, he replied, "Anyone who's been through the ritual all the way." Obviously there are many ways in which nuclear tests are not at all like, say, church services or adolescent circumcision rituals. Still, as S. F. Moore and Barbara Myerhoff (1977) argue in their book on "secular rituals," while we should avoid the temptation to mechanically label almost every social process a ritual, ritual analysis can profitably be applied to many events that are not, formally speaking, religious or sacred. In the case of nuclear weapons testing, if we bracket the obvious differences between a scientific experiment and a sacred ceremony, the comparison with ritual processes brings into focus certain kinds of intense symbolic meaning nuclear tests carry for scientists that might otherwise go unnoticed.[32]

Anthropologists have theorized ritual in a number of different ways. Emile Durkheim and his intellectual descendants have stressed the power of ritual to heal social conflicts. They argue that ritual allows the symbolic expression and transcendence of conflicts, facilitating the intersubjective production of a sense of community (Durkheim 1915; Gluckman 1954; V. Turner 1967, 1969, 1974). This sense of community may be experienced most deeply within ritual in moments of mystical transport that Durkheim labeled "collective effervescence" and Victor Turner called "communitas." Another school of thought in anthropology, articulating a more psychological function for ritual, has presented ritual as a means of allaying anxiety by simulating human control over that which ultimately cannot be controlled—death, disease, crop failure, and so on (Evans-Pritchard 1937; Homans 1941; Malinowski 1932, 1948). Still others have focused on the ability of certain kinds of rituals, "rites of passage," to transform those who participate in them. In "rites of passage" (tribal initiation ceremonies, for example), the social status of initiates is irrevocably changed as they are indoctrinated with the special, or even secret, knowledge of the initiatory group (Moffatt 1988; V. Turner 1967, 1969; Van Gennep 1909). Finally, some American anthropologists have portrayed ritual as a text—as a means of celebrating, performing, displaying, and transmitting the ethos, symbols, and norms of the particular cultural community that uses ritual to clarify and speak to itself about its values and identity (Benedict 1934; Geertz 1973: 412–453; 1980). In the analysis that follows, I draw eclectically on all these traditions in ritual theory to illuminate the significance of nuclear testing for Livermore scientists.

Prohibited by national security regulations from participating in or observing tests directly, I investigated the meaning of nuclear tests in the cultural world of nuclear weapons scientists by collecting nuclear test narratives. I asked the scientists to tell me the story of tests they had worked on and what was important about them. The first thing one notices about these narratives is that, unlike official laboratory statements about the importance of nuclear testing, they say nothing about reliability testing of old weapons. In fact, Clark went so far as to preface his test narrative with the statement, "Stockpile maintenance is boring, so I don't do that." The main themes in these narratives have to do with the fulfillment of personal ambition, the struggle to master a challenging new technology, the scientific drama of bringing something fundamentally new into the world, and the experience of community and communitas in a deeply competitive world.

Nevertheless, although the reliability testing of old weapons is absent from this narrative world, that world is still saturated with a more broadly and diffusely expressed anxiety about the reliability of the weapons. The narratives are largely about reliability, but they frame that concern very differently than the laboratory's official policy statements do.

Overtly, these narratives are about a purely technical process and have nothing to say about the broader political purposes of the weapons or about the system of international relations and international meanings into which the weapons are inserted. It is, however, my contention that these physics experiments as they are narrated do embody a kind of politics, that the technopolitical worldview of the weapons scientists is embedded in, experienced through, and simulated by these experiments—that it is in the design and testing of a nuclear device that the abstract clichés that comprise the ideology of deterrence become experientially real to the scientists who must live deterrence as a truth.

INITIATION

Nuclear weapons tests are not only a means of testing weapons designs. They are also a means of testing and producing weapons designers—the elite within the laboratory (cf. Pinch 1993). (A disproportionate number of the laboratory's senior managers were recruited from the weapons design divisions.) To become a full-fledged member of the weapons design community, new scientists must master an arduous, esoteric knowledge, subject themselves to tests of intelligence and endurance, and finally prove themselves in a display of the secret knowledge's power.[33]

If a test goes well, and it is a designer's first, his or her social status is changed. In the words of Seymour Sack, a senior designer, testing is a way of "punching your ticket by having your name associated with a particular test" (quoted in Stober 1990*b*). Martin remembers the day after his first test, a particularly challenging one: "It was extraordinary. I was walking around the lab and people were coming up to me, I mean just all over the place, people I didn't even know were coming up to me and shaking my hand, congratulating me on this tremendous achievement."

Tests are also the socially legitimated means of producing knowledge about nuclear weapons. This knowledge takes the form both of a socially attributed knack for judgment and, more concretely, the view graphs summarizing the results of tests that scientists display in briefings after tests. Thus participation in nuclear tests confers a kind of symbolic capital that can be traded as power or as knowledge.[34] The more tests scientists participate in, the more authority they acquire as they move toward the status of senior scientists whose judgment about nuclear weapons is particularly respected and sought after. It is these elder designers, men such as Dan Patterson and Seymour Sack, whose judgment is most trusted when they promise that a weapon will continue to work if an old part is slightly redesigned or the interior a little reorganized.

It is partly in this context that we should understand the debate about weapons reliability. This debate is as much about the authorization of knowledge and the hierarchical authority of knowers as it is about the reliability of weapons. The laboratory argues that there is only one way to know for sure whether a weapon will work, only one way to train people to know this, and only a very select group who can certify the continuing reliability of old weapons whose parts are decaying, weapons that have had a piece replaced, weapons that have been slightly redesigned without another test. That select group is the group of senior scientists who have experienced many nuclear tests and who therefore "really understand" how the weapons work. Other scientists speak of these men as irreplaceable, because so much of their knowledge is tacit knowledge that is not, and probably cannot be, written down. They stress the mysterious uniqueness of knowledge about nuclear weapons—knowledge that cannot be learned entirely from textbooks or briefings, knowledge whose uniqueness is marked by its very nontransferability and ultimate nontradeability. The senior warhead designers themselves worry that the younger designers have too much confidence in the predictive ability of their computer codes and the basic principles of physics.

This throws new light on the significance of Ray Kidder's intervention in the weapons reliability debate. He was not only attacking the central mission of the laboratory in saying that the reliability of nuclear weapons could be assured without continued testing and assenting to the prohibition of the ritual by which membership in the laboratory community is regulated. He was a physicist intimately acquainted with thermonuclear physics who attacked the whole system of power/knowledge that organizes the status hierarchies and cosmology of the laboratory. This system is based on nuclear testing as the means of production of both knowledge and power. By suggesting that knowledge could be separated from its local production in nuclear tests, Kidder threatened to tear the social and political fabric of the laboratory world.

We can bring the power/knowledge stakes in the conflict between Kidder and the weapons establishment into still sharper focus if we consider the conflict in the context of Kidder's scientific biography. Earlier in his career, Kidder had weapons experience and served on a number of weapons design review committees. From there he went on to start the laboratory's inertial confinement fusion program, which created microscopic thermonuclear explosions by firing enormously powerful lasers at pellets smaller than a pinhead. In so doing he developed a different technology, one that did not involve the nuclear weapons design process or the use of the Nevada Test Site, to simulate within the laboratory itself the basic product of the weapons designers. More recently it has been suggested that if there were a nuclear test ban, the laboratory should rely much more heavily on laser fusion to explore the physics of thermonuclear explosions. Seen in this light, Kidder was not just a very intelligent physicist with some weapons experience and heterodox views on a nuclear test ban (though he was all of that). He was also an author of a different social-technological system for producing thermonuclear power/knowledge, and his intervention in the debate on reliability represented a deep challenge to the power/ knowledge system of the laboratory's weapons community.

MASTERY

Robert Lifton (1982*a*) points out that the very existence of nuclear weapons inevitably raises the question of whether the weapons are under our control or whether we are at their mercy. The issue here is not only whether humans can be relied on not to use the weapons deliberately but also whether people are capable of devising fail-safe systems to prevent the weapons from exploding accidentally. Lest the latter be thought a far-fetched concern, there have been a number of unfortunate accidents involving American nuclear weapons. In one incident, in 1961, a B-52 accidentally dropped two multimegaton hydrogen bombs on a farm in North Carolina and, in the case of one of the two bombs, almost all of the safety devices designed to prevent an unintended nuclear explosion failed (Barasch 1983: 41; Drell 1991). Nuclear weapons were again lost in accidents involving B-52s in 1966 and 1968, in Spain and Greenland, respectively. In both cases the conventional explosive in the weapons detonated, and, although there was no nuclear explosion, plutonium, possibly the deadliest substance in existence, was dispersed over wide areas (Barasch 1983: 42; Drell 1991; Ruina 1991). In 1955, a B-47 with nuclear weapons onboard caught fire as it was landing at Kirtland Air Force Base, and in North Dakota in 1980, a B-52 with nuclear weapons onboard caught fire (*Albuquerque Journal* 1989; Bartimus and McCartney 1991: 59–60). Recent computer simulations of the latter incident have suggested that if the wind had blown the fire in a different direction, there might have been at least a conventional explosion dispersing plutonium as widely as at Chernobyl. Other simulations have suggested that the W-79 nuclear artillery shell, formerly deployed in Europe, might, in certain circumstances, have detonated if accidentally struck by a bullet (Drell 1991; Drell, Townes, and Foster 1991; J. Smith 1990*a*).

Despite these mishaps, nuclear weapons scientists, unlike many antinuclear activists, have been reasonably confident that nuclear weapons would not explode due to human or mechanical error. Many cultural commentators have been struck by the confidence of nuclear weapons scientists and other nuclear professionals that nuclear weapons are well under human control. In explaining this, most commentators have emphasized the importance of nuclear discourse—a discourse that aligns its speakers with the owners rather than the victims of nuclear weapons while using euphemisms to mask the horrendous disasters the weapons might cause (see Chilton 1985; Cohn 1987; Hook 1985a). Carol Cohn, for example, argues that

> much of the reduced anxiety about nuclear war commonly experienced by both new speakers of the language and long-time experts comes from the characteristics of the language itself. . . . In learning the language, one goes from being the passive, powerless victim to the competent, wily, powerful purveyor of nuclear threats and nuclear explosive power. The enormous destructive effects of nuclear weapons systems become extensions of the self, rather than threats to it. (1987: 706–707)

While nuclear discourse is undoubtedly important in creating a sense of mastery over nuclear weapons, for scientists at Livermore, I suggest, a lived experience is as important as their collective discourse in fostering that sense of mastery and that lived experience is the experience of participation in nuclear testing. Just as, according to classical anthropological theory, the performance of rituals can alleviate anxiety and create a sense of power over, say, crops and diseases, so nuclear tests can in an analogous way create a space where participants are able to play with the issue of human mastery over weapons of mass destruction and symbolically resolve it. Since the stability that nuclear weapons are supposed to ensure—nuclear deterrence—exists so much in the realm of simulations, and since the reliability of deterrence involves the absence of a catastrophe more than the active, direct, positive experience of reliability, nuclear tests play a vital role in making the abstract real in scientists' lives. Nuclear tests give scientists a direct experience of what can only otherwise be known as an absence, bridging the gulf between a regime of simulations and the realm of personal, direct experience.

When working on nuclear tests, weapons scientists find themselves committed to meet onerous deadlines and dependent on the reliability of colleagues and the machines they work with. The anxiety this can induce is beautifully illustrated by a dream a senior designer told me he had the night before a nuclear test. In the dream, he and a colleague were told they had to transport the device they had designed to the Nevada Test Site themselves. The device was fitted with a timer to make it explode at a particular time, whether they had reached the test site or not. They were given an old pickup truck to transport the bomb, and, predictably, the truck broke down on the way, causing them to lose time repairing it. Eventually they reached the test site—fifteen minutes before the bomb was due to explode. Usually the test site is well guarded, but it was now deserted, presumably because their bomb was about to go off. They thought the guards would have taped the deactivating key to the guard post, but they had not. He and his colleague decided to drive on to Ground Zero to look for the key there. Ground Zero was also deserted, and they could find no key there either. They now had one minute left and were panicking because they knew they could not get far enough away from the bomb in one minute. Now they found a chainsaw, with which they planned to cut the bomb in half. Just as they were about to start the chainsaw, the designer's alarm clock went off to awaken him for the real test!

The issue of human control over nuclear technology is a recurrent theme in nuclear test narratives. Many involve a sequence of events in which scientists fear that their machines will not behave as predicted but, after a period of painful anxiety, learn that humans can predict and control the behavior of technology. The most exciting narratives are those, as in any story, in which the outcome seems in doubt for a while. Eric told me this story when I asked which tests stood out in his mind as the most memorable:

> The most exciting tests were the ones where we had enormous difficulties, and through some enormous heroic development of solutions to problems, we were able to save the test. . . . And the sense of reward then is just enormous, just fantastic.
>
> There was one test in which we finally solved the problem, and it was an electrical problem, by deciding to do what I should call a lobotomy. We had to destroy a component. And so we finally decided that by sending a powerful pulse of electricity down a pair of wires we could burn that component out into the condition that it would allow the rest of the system to function. And so then finally we talked this out and we rehearsed it and we practiced it with cables of the right length and components of the right sort and so forth. And, if it had failed, the experiment would have been completely lost, buried. We couldn't have pulled it back to the surface. It would have been just a piece of garbage at the bottom of the hole.
>
> I came home from the test site the day after the test. We were all feeling really satisfied. I drove home and within five minutes the head of the nuclear design division drove up in front of my house to thank me for the effort of

saving that test. And that particular test, I felt we had to do something to commemorate it, and so within a few weeks I had invited all of the principals here, and we had a party and set up pictures in the backyard of all of the trials and tribulations we had gone through.[35]

Many of the narratives have complex emotional rhythms wherein control over the technology and helplessness before it alternate with one another. If the final point of the story is that humans can control nuclear technology, the scientists often learn on the way that they must also trust the technology and let go of their concerns. This happens particularly in the period between the emplacement of the device in the test shaft and the actual test. "This is a hard period for the designer, especially the younger designers," says Lester. "You go through a period where you have a lot of doubts because the computer codes don't cover everything." As Clark put it, "You're kind of helpless after a time. You've got to just take your hands away and hope everything works out alright." This confidence that we can make the weapons do our bidding mixed with a trusting helplessness before them is, of course, the basic psychology required by deterrence.

Whereas many of us worry that a nuclear explosion will occur at some point in our lives, Livermore scientists worry that one won't. Over and over again scientists have the experience of fearing that something will go wrong with the bomb, only to learn—in most instances—that it does not. By means of this lived journey from anxiety to confidence, structured by the rhythms of the testing process itself, scientists learn that the weapons behave, more or less, predictably, and they learn to associate safety and well-being with the performed proof of technical predictability. Then, like Lester, they can say, "When you're a device physicist, it [the bomb] is no more strange than a vacuum cleaner. You don't feel a fear for it at all, and it's not an alien thing. And I understand that for the people who don't do it, it is an alien thing. I felt the same way before I went to the lab."

This remark, which implicitly equates safety from nuclear annihilation with technical mastery over the bomb, only makes sense in the context of the practical consciousness embodied in and engendered by nuclear testing. Participation in the practices of nuclear weapons design and testing has restructured Lester's subjective world so that he now feels in his bones that nuclear weapons are as benign as vacuum cleaners. For many of us, understanding the engineering of an H-bomb will not allay our fear that a mad president, general, or colonel will misuse it. If anything, it may magnify that fear. This scientist's world, however, has been constructed in such a way that the experience of technical mastery has provided him with an internalized simulation of the reliability of the system of deterrence itself.

To put it a little differently: in addition to assuring the technical reliability of nuclear weapons, nuclear tests provide in an elusive way a symbolic simulation of the reliability of the system of deterrence itself. Each time a nuclear test is successfully carried off, the scientists' faith in human control over nuclear technology is further reinforced. Seen in this light, the "reliability" the tests demonstrate has an expandable meaning, extending out from the reliability of the particular device being tested to the entire regime of nuclear deterrence. It is this extension of the connotation of reliability that enables Lester to say that he has learned from nuclear tests not to fear being killed by a nuclear weapon.

LIFE AND DEATH

Rituals in general are often marked by particular kinds of language: an abundance of birth and death metaphors, allusions to mythic or divine entities, and so on. American nuclear weapons culture, as we might expect, is full of mythical allusions. Thus, for example, we have the Polaris and Poseidon missiles. Los Alamos scientists have also named some of their experimental chambers "kivas," the name given to sacred ceremonial spaces by the Pueblo Indians who live around Los Alamos.[36]

But more striking than the use of explicitly sacred language in American nuclear weapons culture is the absence of metaphors of death and the superabundance of birth metaphors. It is hard for an anthropologist not to notice the fertility images and metaphors strewn about the business of nuclear weapons design and testing. The physicists themselves, when I pointed it out to them, laughed at my observation as entertainingly inconsequential—the strange kind of remark one might expect from an anthropologist. They either insisted that I had found a fact without significance or pointed out that scientists other than weapons scientists also use birth metaphors quite liberally.

Still, the pattern is startling, and it goes back to the beginning of the nuclear age, when scientists at Los Alamos, where the nuclear reactor was named "Lady Godiva," wondered aloud whether the bomb they were about to test would be a "boy" or a "girl" (i.e., a dud).[37] They called the prototype tested in New Mexico Robert's [Oppenheimer's] baby and the bomb dropped on Hiroshima Little Boy. Teller cabled Los Alamos the message "It's a boy" after the first successful H-bomb test (Easlea 1983: 103, 130). In subsequent years there were debates about whether Edward Teller was really the "father" of the H-bomb or had in fact been "inseminated" with the breakthrough idea by the mathematician Stanislam Ulam and had merely "carried" it.[38]

And now we have bombs constructed around fissile "pits." The production of these pits may involve the use of "breeding blankets" and "breeder reactors" to produce plutonium—an artificial substance that does not exist in nature. After the bomb has been "married" to the diagnostic canister, it "couples" with the ground, producing "daughter fission products" that go through "generations." Clark referred to the process of bringing this about as "like having a baby" and talked about the tense decision at the moment of the test as being whether to "push" or not. Another designer told me he has "postpartum depression" after his tests. When the first nuclear weapon was tested, the Manhattan Project scientists referred to the apparatus from which it was suspended as a "cradle." Subsequently, the steel shells in which ICBMs sit in their silos became known as "cribs," and missile officers referred to the ICBMs as being connected to control panels by "umbilical cords" (Bartimus and McCartney 1991: 257; Gerzon 1982: 79).

What is going on here? Brian Easlea (1983) has suggested that nuclear scientists are men who are impelled to their work by womb envy: an overpowering jealousy that women can create life and a determination, inflamed by the distance from women and from birth enforced on men in modern society, to themselves do something as awesome as birth. Easlea uses Mary Shelley's *Frankenstein* as a revelatory text to argue that modern (masculine) science is grounded in a tragic impulse to match and transcend female reproductivity.[39]

There are problems with Easlea's interpretation. The first is that since birth imagery is applied to so many activities in our society (from writing term papers to growing gardens), we would, following Easlea's logic, have to argue that all these activities are animated by womb envy. The second problem is that a few of the weapons scientists I knew—including at least one who used these birth metaphors quite inventively—are women.

Where most cultural feminist theories can fairly easily account for a few women who behave like stereotypical men, Easlea's theory is so closely tied to female reproductivity as an absolute index of difference that this is more problematic for him. More seriously, as I argued in chapter 4, weapons scientists bring a diverse array of motivations to their work. This creates great problems for any theory that attempts to reduce the reasons behind their work to a single, unconscious group-motivational structure. As Carol Cohn (1987: 693) has written in a slightly different context, "If . . . imagery is transparent, its significance may be less so. . . . Individual motivations cannot necessarily be read directly from imagery; the imagery itself does not originate in these particular individuals but in a broader cultural context." While there can be no doubt that the culture of nuclear testing is a scientific celebration of the values of masculinism, rather than use a broadly Freudian strategy of reading these birth metaphors as clues or "slips" that enable the determined investigator to uncover preexisting unconscious motives at the individual level, I prefer to see a shared language as a means of giving ambiguous actions pointed meanings and of shaping individual subjectivities so that people can work together to get things done.[40]

Still, it is surely more remarkable to find birth metaphors applied to the process of creating weapons that can end the lives of millions of people than to find them used to describe the process of, say, writing a book or a computer program. All metaphors achieve their effect because of the gulf between the literal and the figurative, but in the case of birth metaphors used to describe nuclear weapons development, the gulf between the literal and the figurative is great enough that the metaphor is as dissonant as it is evocative. But this is the point. Thus I take the recurrence of images of fertility and birth in weapons scientists' discourse about weapons of destruction as an attempt to cast the meaning of this technology in an affirmative key. In metaphorically assimilating weapons and components of weapons to a world of babies, births, and breeding, weapons scientists use the connotative power of words to produce—and be produced by—a cosmological world where nuclear weapons tests symbolize not despair, destruction, and death but hope, renewal, and life. In this semantic world the underground transformation of a mass of metals and chemicals into a transient star under the surface of the earth is phrased in images of life and birth. And, after all, in the context of these scientists' practices and beliefs about deterrence, we can see how each nuclear explosion might symbolize for them the fertility of the scientific imagination, the birth of community, and the guarantee of further life. A weapon is destroyed and a community is born. A nuclear test is, in the words of the caption in a laboratory publication accompanying a picture of dawn at the Nevada Test Site, "a time of renewed vigor."

The scientists' use of such images should also be seen in the context of the argument, in the previous chapter, that the laboratory discourse systematically exchanges and mingles the attributes of humans and machines. This way of speaking in general and the birth images in particular create a discursive world where nuclear weapons appear to be "natural." This happens because the discourse fuses, or confuses, the spheres of production and reproduction, depicting machines made by humans as fruits or babies, as if they grew on trees or inside human bodies instead of being assembled in laboratories and factories.

It is the hallmark of ideology that it seeks to legitimate the contested products of human labor and human political systems by presenting them as somehow inherent in nature (Giddens 1979; Habermas 1981). Karl Marx (1972) argued over a century ago that in presenting interest and profit as something that naturally accrues to invested capital, as if by breeding, capitalist ideology obscures the way profit is produced in social relationships that extract some of the value of a worker's labor and convert it into the investor's profit. In the same vein, we might argue that the scientists' metaphorical cosmology, by assimilating the world of mechanical production to the world of natural reproduction, obscures the social relationships and political choices underlying the design of new nuclear weapons. This semantic system constructs nuclear weapons by metaphorical implication as part of the natural order, and it gives metaphorical vigor to the "realist" assumption that the arms race and the development of new nuclear weapons have a momentum of their own, that "you can't stop technology."

CHAPTER 7

Crisis

Crisis: (1) an unstable condition in political, international, or economic affairs in which an abrupt or decisive change is impending . . . (2) the point in a story or drama at which hostile forces are in the most tense state of opposition.

AMERICAN HERITAGE DICTIONARY

The 1980s and early 1990s were not good years for the laboratory. Between the end of the 1950s and the beginning of the 1980s, there had been little public opposition to the arms race. Most people, nationwide and in the San Francisco Bay Area, did not even know what kind of work was done at the Livermore Laboratory, let alone oppose it.[1] All this changed dramatically. The early 1980s were years when the collapse of détente between the superpowers, plans to deploy new weapons systems, and loose talk about limited and survivable nuclear war by Reagan administration officials, intended to frighten the Soviets, instead frightened many Europeans and Americans.[2] In Western Europe, NATO's plans to deploy the ground-launched Cruise missile, the warhead for which was designed at Livermore, provoked massive demonstrations; in the United States, the nuclear freeze movement began to stage large rallies and win popular referenda across the country in response to Pentagon plans for a new generation of nuclear weapons. Antinuclear sentiment, both in Europe and the United States, was exacerbated by the careless remarks of Reagan administration officials. Vice President George Bush and Defense Secretary Caspar Weinberger, for example, both spoke about the importance of new weapons systems that would enable the United States to "prevail" in a nuclear war, and T. K. Jones, a deputy undersecretary of defense, made the widely quoted remark that to survive a nuclear war, Americans needed only to "dig a hole, cover it with a couple of doors, and throw three feet of dirt on top" (Waller 1987: 17–19). Meanwhile Secretary of State Al Haig said that he could imagine firing a "nuclear warning shot" over Europe to deter Soviet expansion, thus, in the words of the political sociologists Frances McCrea and Gerald Markle (1989: 105), "recruiting thousands of Europeans to the disarmament movement with a single phrase."

The peace movement of the early 1980s was massive, even by comparison with the mass movement against the Vietnam War that had left such a large imprint on the politics of the preceding two decades. In June 1982, at the time of the UN Special Session on Disarmament, one million people marched against the arms race in the streets of New York. It was the largest demonstration in American history, and it came at a time when opinion polls showed about three-fourths of the American people supporting an end to the arms race. Meanwhile, at its height in the early 1980s, the European antinuclear movement generated protest crowds of 200,000 in Athens, 300,000 in Bonn, 350,000 in Amsterdam, 400,000 in Madrid, and 750,000 in London and Brussels (Mehan, Nathanson, and Skelly 1990). Opinion polls showed that the majority of British, Dutch, German, and Italian citizens supported the movement in opposing the deployment of Cruise missiles in their countries (Wilson 1983: 296; Young 1987).

The nuclear arms race was suddenly being challenged by an enormous grassroots movement on two continents. In the United States, the traditionally liberal San Francisco Bay Area was, along with Boston, the main regional center of this movement, and that could only mean trouble for the laboratory.

Many of the laboratory's problems in the 1980s are symbolized by the story of Karen Hogan. Karen grew up in Livermore, where both her parents worked at the laboratory, her father as an electrician and her mother as a secretary. When she was growing up, neither of her parents talked much about their work, about nuclear weapons, or about the cold war. "It just never came up. Things were innocent then," said Karen. As a teenager in suburban America in the 1960s, Karen said, "I mainly worried about whether I would get out of high school without getting pregnant, whether I would get invited to the prom. That's the stuff that dominates your life in high school." When she was a teenager, Karen occasionally had nightmares about dying in a nuclear war, and sometimes when she heard a loud plane overhead, she would imagine that the war was beginning. She discussed these fears with no one, however, not even her close friends.

Karen's fears went away until the early 1980s when, in her thirties and now living an hour away from Livermore, she had two vivid nightmares about nuclear war. In one of them, everything everywhere was on fire. In the other, she was being ordered to press the button to launch the nuclear missiles that would end everything and was panic-stricken to find no way out. The nightmares came at a time when many other people were having similar nightmares and, in the context of a burgeoning antinuclear movement, were discussing them with one another. Karen, who was now a writer, joined the movement and also began volunteering at a hospice to make herself confront the issue of death. Now she began to tell her friends and family that she felt the laboratory should not be working on nuclear weapons.

Finally, in 1989, Karen came back to Livermore to speak out publicly. She was in the audience at a meeting about the laboratory's planned radioactive waste incinerator. The meeting, which took place on a Saturday at Livermore's high school, was organized by the Sierra Club, and Karen was in the front row listening to laboratory and opposition experts make their presentations. The laboratory's Susi Jackson was in the middle of a presentation about the low statistical risk of cancer associated with the planned incinerator when Karen interrupted. Momentarily rendering the speaker speechless in a way that was savored by antinuclear activists for days after the meeting, Karen called out from the front row, "This is what makes people angry, the way you use numbers like this to say nothing. What does this *mean?* Have you ever *seen* anyone die of cancer?" Recalling that moment later, she said, "I was numbed. I felt I couldn't absorb one more meaningless number. How does one-tenth of a person get cancer? They were saying, 'We're not going to get emotional here. Use your mind; don't use your emotions.'"

A few months later Karen spoke out in Livermore again. At an antinuclear rally on the anniversary of the bombing of Hiroshima, she read a poem called "Acceptable Risks" that she had written about the laboratory's planned incinerator, and she told the assembled crowd of about 150 people, "I do not believe we can make nuclear weapons without jeopardizing my life or the lives of living beings for generations to come. I don't know who made the decision about acceptable risk, but it's not acceptable to me."

Karen's is the story of a woman who lived unobtrusively on the laboratory's margins until she decided to take fears she had hitherto considered idiosyncratic, embarrassing even, and redefine them as social rather than individual: as urgent omens of an impending disaster and as the basis for membership in a mass movement against nuclear weapons. When she finally spoke out it was with the emotional voice of a woman refusing to defer any longer to the laboratory's masculine culture of expert rationality and with the angry voice of a local citizen refusing to defer to the community's principal employer. She also embodied a bridge between two movements: an established national movement opposed to the arms race and an incipient local movement of citizens troubled by the laboratory's environmental record.

THE FIRST REAGAN ADMINISTRATION, 1980–1984

In 1980, Randall Forsberg, a longtime peace researcher who was at that time a Ph.D. student in political science at MIT, tossed out the spark for a nationwide movement against nuclear weapons when she issued her four-page document entitled "Call to Halt the Nuclear Arms Race" (McCrea and Markle 1989: 97–101).[3] In discussions within the East Coast peace and justice community, this document became the basis for the nuclear freeze movement, which had as its goal a bilateral (U.S. and Soviet) halt to the testing, production, and deployment of nuclear weapons.

The nuclear freeze movement was successful in changing the terms of the national debate on nuclear weapons policy. It took the weapons establishment's global narrative of an unending bilateral process of weapons development producing a perpetually shifting uneasy equilibrium between the superpowers and publicly reframed it as in Herb York's (1970) memorable phrase, a "race to oblivion."[4] It offered the public an alternative global scenario of a nuclear freeze followed by bilateral weapons reductions: "end the race or end the race," as a popular bumper sticker put it, framing the choice as one between the arms race and the human race.

The freeze idea was simple enough to catch the imagination of large numbers of Americans, even though most arms control experts were more or less critical of it. It was also a sufficiently moderate and pragmatic proposal that it appealed to a broad cross section of citizens, and by 1982, opinion polls were consistently showing that three-fourths of Americans supported a bilateral freeze (Kazin 1983).[5] Since the Soviets were offering to negotiate such a freeze, this put the American government in an awkward position.

Freeze organizers increased the pressure on the government by using the 1982 elections to develop a nationwide campaign that, in Pam Solo's (1988: 98) words, was "the closest thing to a national referendum in the history of the country." Around the country freeze resolutions were approved on the ballots of 9 states, 43 towns, cities, and counties, and 446 New England town meetings. Freeze resolutions were also passed by 370 city councils and 23 state legislatures. Six months later, in May 1983, the U.S. House of Representatives, by a margin of 287 to 149, passed its own freeze resolution (McCrea and Markle 1989: 105–107, 137; Solo 1988: 84–98).

In the process of winning these victories, the Nuclear Freeze Campaign became a powerful national movement. It developed its own organizational infrastructure in forty-seven states, and its sympathizers created a national mosaic of middle-class guild organizations broadly in support of a freeze: Educators for Social Responsibility, Computer Professionals for Social Responsibility, the Lawyers Alliance for Nuclear Arms Control, Business Executives for National Security, and many more. The medical profession was particularly active in opposing the government's nuclear weapons policies: in 1981, the American Medical Association passed a resolution urging doctors to educate their patients about the danger of nuclear war, and groups such as Physicians for Social Responsibility (PSR) and International Physicians for the Prevention of Nuclear War (IPPNW) were among the most prominent in the new movement. PSR grew in three years from a group with a few hundred members mainly concentrated in Boston to one with 18,000 members spread across forty-five chapters nationwide. Of these forty-five chapters, those in the San Francisco Bay Area, the laboratory's regional base, were among the strongest.

The national movement against nuclear weapons hit California in a big way in 1982, when Proposition 12, the Nuclear Freeze Initiative, appeared on the electoral ballot. Bankrolled by Harold Willens, a southern California millionaire, freeze volunteers gathered twice the number of signatures they needed to qualify the issue for the ballot, and, despite heavy opposition from California's defense industry, the resolution passed with 52 percent of the vote. In the San Francisco Bay Area, where the measure was supported by the Catholic archbishop and by San Francisco's mayor and Board of Supervisors, over 70 percent of the electorate voted for a nuclear freeze (McCrea and Markle 1989: 106; Solo 1988: 98). Proposition 12 not only demonstrated a public will in California to end the arms race; the struggle to pass it created a massive geography of new peace groups. Within a year, by 1983, there were sixty different peace groups in the San Francisco Bay Area alone.

The early 1980s also saw the meteoric, and enigmatic, nationwide rise of the Beyond War movement, which, by 1984, had a national office in the San Francisco Bay Area with about forty staff members and an annual budget of over $1 million (Faludi 1987; Schiffman 1991). Beyond War mixed the basic message of the peace movement with the tone of the New Age and the technology of Silicon Valley to create a stylishly high-tech group with a discreetly messianic edge. Beyond War had tremendous appeal to upper-middle-class suburbanites, especially those in the corporate world who usually ignore or revile peace movements. Using high production quality videos, carefully choreographed workshops mixing corporate and New Age support group techniques, and a unique networking system based on friendship between upper-middle-class couples, Beyond War in the Bay Area built an influential and powerful suburban community committed to its message that "war is now obsolete" and that the time for a "new way of thinking" had arrived. Beyond War did not take a position on particular electoral races, legislation, or even weapons systems, and it kept its distance from other, more déclassé peace groups, which, in turn, regarded it with some suspicion. Still Beyond War had an important impact, especially in California. It helped legitimize the peace movement's basic message that the planet had to find a new way of dealing with conflict, and it found a constituency of mainly middle-level corporate managers who would not have joined the conventional peace movement but who were willing to identify themselves with Beyond War and its message.[6]

At the opposite end of the spectrum was the direct action[7] movement, which, bypassing the formal political machinery of ballot initiatives and legislative campaigns, made the laboratory itself the target of massive, rowdy protests in the early 1980s. According to the laboratory's own statistics, it was the object of forty-four separate protests in 1982 and another twenty-seven in 1983. Many of these protests were staged by church-based peace groups from around the Bay Area. Fourteen of them, including the largest ones, were organized by the Livermore Action Group

(LAG), an eclectic organization formed in the fall of 1981 around a core amalgam of anarchists, pagans, feminists, radical Christians, environmentalists, former anti-Vietnam activists, and antinuclear energy activists.[8] In 1982, about two weeks after one million people marched in New York in support of the UN Special Session on Disarmament, LAG organized a demonstration of between 4,000 and 5,000 people at the laboratory early on a Monday morning. In the course of the protest, around 1,300 people were arrested for attempting to block the roads into the laboratory. This protest was one of the largest civil disobedience actions in American history (Diehl 1988; Epstein 1985: 35).[9] The following year, on June 20, LAG staged a protest at the laboratory that drew about 4,000 people, over 1,000 of whom were arrested for civil disobedience.[10] Four days later, a coalition of religious groups attempted to entirely encircle the laboratory, although the 3,500 protestors who took part were not quite sufficient to complete the circle.

Numbers alone do not begin to tell this story, however. One must imagine how these protests were experienced by a community of scientists accustomed to laboring over their weapons in anonymous and disciplined isolation in a small town hitherto largely ignored by the rest of the Bay Area, only to find their lives suddenly invaded by thousands of people from nearby towns—singing, shouting, weeping, praying people, many dressed as skeletons, grim reapers, or clowns, one even on stilts, some in wheelchairs, clasping mock missiles, waving banners calling the laboratory the new Auschwitz; some spilling their own blood on the road; some, nuns and priests, being led away in handcuffs; others, women and teenage children, screaming and crying as they are dragged by burly policemen into paddy wagons (figs. 7 and 8). Two participants described the June 20, 1983, protest as follows:

> A jubilant mood prevailed . . . as thousands of demonstrators filled the streets and intersections around the Livermore Laboratory, with their banners and balloons aloft. A large contingent of elders and juveniles led a procession that included a marching band, nuns, punks, and doctors. Hundreds of "affinity groups" participated in the attempt to shut down the Lab, using a variety of means. One group erected a windmill in the middle of the road, and a small forest of tree people came dressed in branches. Blockaders joined hands and stretched out across the roadways to block incoming cars. Some sang and danced, others meditated or prayed. Support people took possession of backpacks and other personal belongings; watched, cried, and called out

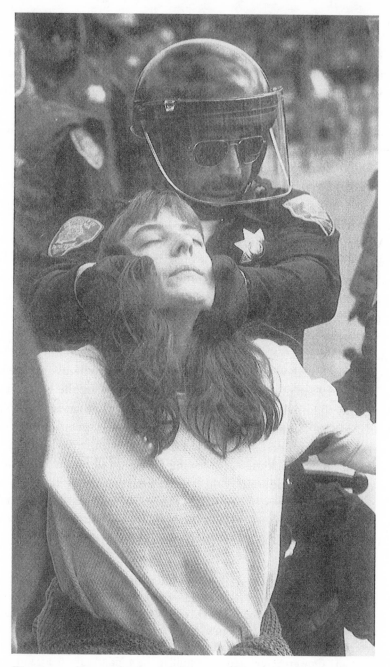

Figure 7. Arrest of a demonstrator at the 1982 protest at Lawrence Livermore Laboratory. (Photo by Doug Jorgensen, courtesy *The Independent Newspaper*, Livermore, California)

Figure 8.　Demonstrators at the 1982 protest at Lawrence Livermore Laboratory. (Photo by Doug Jorgensen, courtesy *The Independent Newspaper*, Livermore, California)

words of encouragement as their friends were arrested, handcuffed, and loaded onto waiting buses. (Cabasso and Moon 1985: 3)

The local judicial system responded sternly to this disruption but ended up making matters worse. In 1982, those arrested for civil disobedience had been given a choice of three days in jail or an equivalent fine. They had considered this reasonable. In 1983, Judge Al Lewis decided not only to punish the protestors more forcefully but also to impede their future return. He announced that protestors would be given two days in jail, a $250 fine, and two years probation (Cabasso and Moon 1985: 8). Explaining the probation, Judge Lewis told the protestors,

> There are 7,000 men and women who work there [at the laboratory], and who have had their lives disrupted this past week. All of them are of high moral character and for the most part they've suffered your accusations in silence. The situation has created a great chasm in the community. Court probation was a symbolic method of securing a promise not to return to this community for rearrest. (Green 1983)

The plan backfired. When they were summoned for arraignment, over 80 percent of the protestors refused to leave the enormous circus tents in which they were confined (in lieu of sufficient jail cells), saying they considered the probation an unfair restriction on their right to protest. For ten days there was a standoff between judge and protestors, with the judge refusing to change his sentence and about a thousand protestors refusing to be arraigned. In the course of this standoff, the media increasingly portrayed the protestors as martyrs suffering for their principles and the judge as an obstinate and partial man who was bending the judicial process improperly since during these ten days it emerged that Judge Lewis was a member of the Valley Study Group, a local organization with strong links to the laboratory, and that he had solicited the advice of local leaders in determining a sentence for the protestors (O'Connor 1983). Meanwhile the case was constantly on the front page of San Francisco newspapers—as I well recall, since it was the news coverage of this case that finally drew me, a young man living in Berkeley at the time, to join the Nuclear Freeze Campaign in July 1983, a few days after Judge Lewis finally backed down from his insistence on probation.

This sudden eruption of protest, at the laboratory gates and beyond, left the laboratory in an embattled position. As the authors of the laboratory's 1983–1988 Five-Year Plan put it, "The following factors are having an adverse effect upon recruiting: nuclear-freeze ballot initiatives, an increasing number of public demonstrations, resurgence of anti-weapons groups on college campuses, the media accounts of litigation arising out of early weapons-test programs, and the general public concern over radiation effects" (quoted in Senate Policy Committee 1984: 23). The same year George Dacey, president of Sandia National Laboratories, wrote,

> I am concerned about the Nuclear Freeze movement, more concerned than I would be if it were not coming from a central segment of our society. . . . In the early "peacenik" movements, we were dealing with people who were on the fringes of society. Today, however, the debate features Catholic Bishops, members of the American Bar Association, American Medical Association—people whose views cannot be dismissed as not representative. That is one reason, I think, that it is an important movement. But I regard it as dangerous. (Ibid.)

THE SECOND REAGAN ADMINISTRATION, 1984–1988

As the historian E. P. Thompson (1986: 11), himself a leading figure in the European antinuclear movement, has written, "Historians of social movements know that they do not often attain their goals at their first moment of assertion. What they do, more often, is transform the climate of expectations and redefine the limits of what is possible." American nuclear politics in the 1980s certainly conformed to this dictum, and the laboratory together with the rest of the nation's nuclear complex, battered but not yet beaten, weathered the immediate storm, only to find that the ground was shifting beneath it.

In the 1984 election, Ronald Reagan, a hawk, defeated Walter Mondale, a freeze supporter, despite the momentum of the freeze movement and despite the apparatus of antinuclear political action committees and precinct volunteers working against Reagan's reelection.[11] Meanwhile, as many members of Congress who had voted in favor of the freeze resolution then voted funding for new weapons such as the MX, many peace activists grew demoralized when it became clear how difficult it would be, especially given the extent of defense industry lobbying in Washington, to translate abstract support for a freeze into a real change in government behavior. Now the organizational vital signs of many antinuclear groups began to decline as exhaustion set in, as new issues such as Central America and South Africa drew away core activists, and as the Reagan administration started to parry the movement's rhetorical thrust by arguing that the weapons laboratories themselves had the antidote to the arms race in the Strategic Defense Initiative (Kazin 1984; Kurtz 1988: 158–179; Linenthal 1989; Mehan, Nathanson, and Skelly 1990; Solo 1988).

Thus by 1986, the national and local Nuclear Freeze Campaigns were in dire financial straits, and many local chapters of the freeze and other mainstream antinuclear groups saw their membership fall by about one-half between 1984 and 1988. Meanwhile LAG's largest protests at the laboratory in 1985 and 1986 drew only six hundred people. In 1986, having reached a point where it was several thousand dollars in debt and many of its former members were now more drawn to other issues, LAG finally closed its doors (Diehl 1988; Frankel 1990; McCrea and Markle 1989: 16, 133).

The laboratory's problems were far from over, however. In fact, its crisis was moving into a second, possibly more damaging phase marked less by dramatic confrontations with the massed armies of protest and more by deep structural erosion of the laboratory's local, national, and international foundations. To begin with, the international system that had provided such a hospitable environment for the laboratory throughout the cold war began to undergo dramatic transformations after Gorbachev took over leadership of the Soviet Union in 1985. Confronted with impending structural collapse brought on by the costs of the cold war, the Soviet Union sought to capitalize on the momentum created by the Western peace movements and was, by the mid-1980s, trying to disengage itself first from the arms race and then from the cold war itself. For example, on August 6, 1985, on the fortieth anniversary of the bombing of Hiroshima, Gorbachev initiated a unilateral Soviet moratorium on nuclear weapons testing that continued for eighteen months. Then the Soviets startled American arms control negotiators by accepting the American terms for the 1987 INF Treaty, banning intermediate nuclear missiles in Europe.[12] The INF Treaty, the first ever to mandate the destruction of an entire class of weapons that had just been built, dramatically deescalated the cold war and showed that it was indeed possible to negotiate treaties that actually rolled back the arms race.

Moreover, in the domestic arena, the antinuclear movement in the late 1980s did not so much disappear as mutate. Some parts of the movement atrophied while others evolved and continued to press the laboratory, often in new ways and from new angles. The dominant narrative in the media that the antinuclear movement was a monolithic entity that had enjoyed a meteoric rise followed by an equally rapid decline, that it was a fad whose time had passed, glossed a situation that was, in reality, more complex and more interesting. Many of the short-term activists—the citizens who only join protest movements in unusual circumstances and who were brought into the antinuclear movement by the extraordinary atmosphere of crisis in the early 1980s—did indeed return to their ordinary lives in the mid-1980s. This particularly hurt mainstream groups such as the Nuclear Freeze Campaign, Beyond War, and Physicians for Social Responsibility, which relied on an atmosphere of emergency to recruit busy middle-class citizens who are rarely available to social change movements. But it did not mean the end of the movement. Many of the mainstream groups reorganized themselves so they could survive the hemorrhage of support at the grassroots level, while the direct action movement experienced a rebirth that was almost entirely missed by the American media. Meanwhile new kinds of peace and environmental groups sprung up to press the case against the laboratory, which was, in any case, increasingly damaged and demoralized by a slew of internal scandals that were aggressively reported by the media.

In the late 1980s, the Nuclear Freeze Campaign and PSR, the organizations that had been at the forefront of the first wave of antinuclear unrest during the first Reagan administration, now dropped back and pushed from behind. PSR moved on, albeit without much of its membership, from its old campaign about the dangers of nuclear war to a new one about the health and environmental hazards of nuclear weapons production in the United States. Meanwhile, the Nuclear Freeze Campaign merged in 1987 with SANE and compensated for its loss of volunteers by developing a professional door-to-door canvass operation. It adjusted to its new circumstances by converting itself organizationally from a wildfire grassroots movement into a group modeled after the Sierra Club that largely relied on the methodical work of paid canvassers to sustain membership and legislative campaigns over the long term. San Francisco SANE/Freeze, for example, hired about twenty professional door-to-door canvassers who raised roughly $300,000 in 1989, enabling the organization to maintain a stable, if diminished, membership base (Gusterson 1989). SANE/Freeze continued to be a presence, even if its attempted statewide ballot initiative on defense industry conversion fizzled in 1990.

As for the direct action movement, regular protests still took place at the laboratory gates, although they were much smaller than the mass mobilizations of 1982 and 1983. The largest of these took place on Good Friday when about four hundred people would converge early in the morning for a religious service at the laboratory gates, after which about fifty people would commit civil disobedience.

But the declining number of protestors and arrests for civil disobedience at the laboratory in these years is misleading since the direct action wing of the antinuclear movement had now shifted its focus from Livermore, where nuclear weapons were designed, to the Nevada Test Site, where the weapons were tested. At almost the same time that LAG had collapsed in financial disarray, the American Peace Test (APT) had appeared to take its place at the vanguard of the direct action movement. Founded by a group of activists on the left of the nuclear freeze movement who were disgruntled when the annual freeze conference passed a resolution against civil disobedience in 1984, the APT began to attract large numbers of activists from all over the country to epic weeklong protests in the middle of the Nevada desert. The pattern of these protests was as follows: those protestors (in 1988 and 1989, they numbered several hundred) whose schedules enabled them to spend an entire week away from home would establish a peace camp in the desert and build momentum by staging protests that grew each day. On the weekend those protestors whose jobs or family commitments prevented them from spending a whole week in protest would come in from all over the country by plane, car, or bus, attend the big Saturday rally, and then, if they chose to, get arrested, knowing that they would be back home by Monday. The staging of these events in the middle of the desert, seventy miles from Las Vegas and without the benefit of easy local supply lines, was a major logistical triumph since it involved the transportation, housing, and feeding of thousands, the recruitment of speakers and participants from all over the country, and the establishment of a workable political structure to integrate scattered national groups who had not worked together before.

The main procedure for arrest during these protests was oddly ritualized and choreographed. Protestors would stand patiently in line in front of the cattle guard separating the test site from the public highway and, when their turn came, step across the cattle guard, usually in groups of about four, so the police could arrest them. The police, told ahead of time by APT organizers roughly how many protestors would be arrested and when they wanted the arrests to begin, would put a board across the cattle guard to make sure no one twisted an ankle crossing it. The more daring protestors crossed the flimsy barbed-wire fence marking the test site boundary and started walking into the test site with DOE security police, often in dune buggies, in pursuit. Few got more than a hundred yards. The most hard-core protestors, many of them anarchists from the Bay Area, arrived early on weekday mornings to block traffic into the test site. The police took a dim view of this, especially if they locked arms or went limp, and often treated them quite roughly, twisting their arms, pulling their hair, or dragging them through desert scrub.

In March 1988, about four years after the antinuclear movement had, according to the media, largely withered away, the APT "Reclaim the Test Site" action attracted about eight thousand participants, and produced 2,065 arrests. This meant that despite the inaccessibility of the Nevada Test Site, it was bigger than any protest that had ever taken place at Livermore. In fact, it was at the time the largest civil disobedience action to have taken place in American history (though it was later surpassed by the antiabortion movement). Still, it remained almost unknown to most Americans since television stations tend not to be interested in stories in the middle of the desert, and the print media outside Nevada almost entirely ignored it. The 1989 "Reclaim the Test Site II" action produced 1,551 arrests, and the 1990 "Decade to Disarm" protest generated 1,112 arrests (Levy 1990; *Test Banner* 1989: 8).[13]

Faced with such enormous protests, the local judicial system was stretched almost to breaking point. The sheriff of Nye County, where the test site is located, had to bring in police officers from all over the county and deputize some people especially for the protests. Meanwhile, the district attorney, Phil Dunleavy, who had campaigned for office on a promise to prosecute protestors vigorously, found himself in a situation in which he had no financial assistance from the federal government and thousands of protestors to prosecute, some of them celebrities such as Carl Sagan, Kris Kristofferson, and Martin Sheen whose trials promised to invite potentially embarrassing national media attention. At one point the protests were consuming a quarter of the district attorney's budget (Jenkins 1988). In 1987 he adopted a policy of prosecuting only the few who trespassed deep into the test site, such as the group of women calling themselves the Princesses Against Plutonium who in 1988 hiked under cover of darkness into the small town of Mercury inside the test site and, dressed in radiation protection suits, began putting up antinuclear posters all over town. The vast majority of protestors, however, were arrested, driven in buses to the town of Tonopah, 140 miles north, then released without charges. The leniency of this procedure only encouraged more people to get arrested, thus increasing the burden on the local law enforcement system.

The revivifying effect of the American Peace Test on the direct action movement was soon felt far beyond Nevada. By 1989, there was a Bay Area Peace Test, many of its members veterans of LAG, which recruited protestors for the Nevada actions and also for occasional actions at the Livermore laboratory and at the Lockheed facility in nearby Santa Cruz. Also, although most Americans never heard about the large Nevada protests, they were (ironically) widely reported in the Soviet Union, where they helped to inspire the rise of a counterpart movement around the main Soviet nuclear test site at Semipalatinsk. This movement called itself the Nevada-Semipalatinsk movement in honor of its American cousin. By 1990, leaders of the American and Soviet movements were visiting one another's protests and organizing synchronized U.S.–Soviet demonstrations. In December 1990, Bay Area antinuclear activists brought the leader of the Soviet movement, Olzhas Suleimenov, to Livermore. Suleimenov, a charismatic poet and engineer who had by now been elected to the Supreme Soviet, gave a press conference and was allowed inside the laboratory to make the case for a nuclear test ban, which was coolly received by Livermore's scientists (Several 1990). One weapons designer joked to Suleimenov afterward, "We used to tell our protestors to go and protest in the Soviet Union. Now that you're here, I guess you've taken that away from us."

TROUBLE WITH THE NEIGHBORS

The laboratory soon found that it was no more popular with the emergent environmental movement than it had been with the antinuclear movement, and the environmental movement—less easily tainted as unpatriotic—had a potentially broader appeal, especially within the town of Livermore where local citizens increasingly came to see themselves as living on the environmental front line.[14]

In Livermore, the late 1980s saw the rise of Tri-Valley Citizens Against a Radioactive Environment (CAREs), a group of local citizens who took on the role of laboratory watchdog under the leadership of Marylia Kelley, an indefatigable single mother from Livermore who spent hours every week combing through the laboratory's enormous, and enormously dull, environmental impact reports. When I arrived in Livermore in 1987, CAREs was widely perceived as a small group of malcontents out of step with the local community and looking for any excuse to bash the laboratory. This perception changed dramatically in only two years. Those two years, 1988 and 1989, saw a plague, national and local, of media revelations of widespread health and environmental problems at nuclear weapons facilities all over the country. By the end of the decade, the government was estimating costs for a nationwide cleanup of the weapons complex at between $100 billion and $200 billion (Chen 1989; K. Schneider 1990). The Livermore laboratory, which a 1988 DOE report ranked as having the third most contaminated groundwater of any nuclear weapons facility in the country, had its own problems that the local media now began to publicize relentlessly.[15]

The laboratory's environmental crisis began in earnest in 1987 when the EPA declared the laboratory a federal Superfund site because the groundwater beneath it contained carcinogenic solvents up to 120 times and benzene up to 9,000 times the allowed federal limit.[16] The contaminated groundwater was slowly seeping toward local drinking water supplies, and its westward migration had already forced the sealing of private wells owned by nearby residents. The DOE estimated at the time that it would cost $26.4 million to clean the groundwater. Once the laboratory was declared a federal Superfund site, Tri-Valley CAREs was able to win a grant of $49,951 from the EPA so that it could hire consultants and monitor the cleanup. This grant greatly expanded the profile and organizational capability of Tri-Valley CAREs, which until then had largely lived off small change and had been unable to pay for any staff time (Bodovitz 1989*d*).

The laboratory's environmental and public relations problems only got worse from here. In 1989, the DOE announced that it would cost over

$300 million to clean up the laboratory and $1.2 billion to bring it into full compliance with environmental standards (Rogers 1989*e*; E. Roth 1989). Then in 1990, the EPA announced that the laboratory's Site 300, about fifty miles from the main facility, would also be put on the federal Superfund list. This made the laboratory a Superfund site twice over (Smith 1990*d*). Meanwhile the local media was aggressively reporting a string of environmental infractions from the laboratory's past. These included the release of 21,000 curies of tritium into the air over fifteen years, the release of plutonium, chromium, americium, and sulfuric acid into the city sewer system, leakage of PCBs, the accidental transportation of americium to the county dump site, and an explosion at the laboratory's waste yard (De Wolk 1989; Rogers 1987*b*, 1989*d*; Smith 1990*g*).

But the laboratory's worst public relations problems and CAREs' greatest triumph followed the laboratory's announcement of plans to build a new $41 million waste treatment facility, including an incinerator to burn hazardous and radioactive waste. In retrospect, this announcement can only be seen as a gesture marked by hubris of near-suicidal proportions given the gathering atmosphere of environmental scandal at the time. The laboratory's environmental scientists said in a series of public meetings that the incinerator would use state-of-the-art technology that would destroy hazardous and radioactive waste with 99.99 percent efficiency and that the increased risk of cancer to the local community would only be 0.006 cases over seventy years. Many members of the local community were skeptical, and their skepticism only increased with time, especially when Marion Fulk, for many years a respected nuclear chemist at the laboratory, announced his opinion that the filters for the proposed facility would allow plutonium particles to escape. At public hearings laboratory officials soon found themselves facing questions not only about the incinerator but also, no matter how hard they tried to set rules to restrict broader discussion, about the laboratory's entire environmental record, including past mishaps regarding which the laboratory had been less than candid with the community. The constant juxtaposition in these discussions of promises that the future incinerator would work safely and allegations of untold past accidents was not a happy one for the laboratory. Meanwhile many hitherto agnostic members of the community grew increasingly skeptical of the laboratory as they encountered what was widely perceived as the haughty attitude of its officials toward members of the public. CAREs member

Roman Morkowski was not being completely hyperbolic when he blurted out at one of these meetings, "The Rad Lab used to be God around here; now it has zero credibility."

The laboratory's credibility decayed further when its existing incinerator, in use since 1979, failed two trial burns administered by the Department of Health Services (DHS) and the EPA in late 1988 and early 1989 and was ordered permanently closed (Rogers 1990*a*). The laboratory had insisted the old incinerator was safe.

By 1990, the laboratory found itself in a situation in which ten thousand local residents had signed a petition against the new incinerator (Smith 1990*b*); the nearby town of Pleasanton's environmental monitoring committee had appealed to it to redo its environmental study of the incinerator (*Oakland Tribune* 1989); the Livermore City Council had voted unanimously to recommend closing its old incinerator and to censure the DOE for its high-handed management of the public hearing process (Dillon 1989*b*); the local *Valley Herald* had run a front-page story about people in Livermore who were considering selling their homes if the new incinerator was built (Bodovitz 1989*e*); and Livermore's Congressman Pete Stark had threatened to sue it if it proceeded to build the incinerator without further study (Brewer 1989). At this point, Laboratory Director John Nuckolls announced, in February 1990, that the incinerator project was canceled.

Livermore's congressman, Pete Stark, had always been critical of the laboratory, but he became considerably more forthright in his opposition during and after the struggle over the incinerator. A liberal Democrat who enjoys speaking bluntly, he infuriated laboratory scientists when, invited to speak at a public meeting on the incinerator in Livermore in March 1989, he accused the laboratory of having a "father knows best attitude" and said "the Lawrence Livermore Laboratory has a long history of misrepresenting the truth, particularly in dealing with the Livermore public." He encouraged Livermore citizens to take the laboratory to court "as soon and as often as possible" and declared that "the lab should move . . . elsewhere, where it is not so densely populated" (Bodovitz 1989*f*; 1989*g*; A. Miller 1989). He also lobbied his colleagues in Congress to vote against funding the laboratory's new plutonium research facility, saying "when safety should be foremost, both in and out of the lab, management acts like plutonium is no more dangerous than paint thinner" (Rogers 1990*g*). If he had any friends left at the laboratory, he surely lost them when he told a local journalist that "4,000 of the 6,000 Livermore folks have Ph.D.'s, so presumably they can read without moving their lips, and 99% of them know in their heart of hearts that Star Wars or this Bright Pebbles or whatever the hell it is is . . . Alice in Wonderland stuff" (Haddock 1990*a*).[17]

The struggle between the laboratory and the local community over the incinerator and other issues was symptomatic of a broader transformation that had overtaken the town of Livermore. Although there had, since the 1950s, been a social divide between laboratory employees and other Livermore residents, the effects of the divide had been contained by the stable dominance of the laboratory within the community. Between 1960 and 1990, however, the population of Livermore tripled, from 16,000 to 56,000, as San Francisco pushed outward, as developers discovered relatively cheap land in Livermore, and as young families moved there to live, often commuting to work elsewhere in the Bay Area on the two new freeways that passed by Livermore. Also in the 1980s, companies such as Triad, Intel, and Hexcel started to move to Livermore's new industrial park. By the late 1980s, the number of Livermore residents not connected to the laboratory had grown enormously. As one observer put it,

> Livermore is not the same city as it was ten years ago. . . . Housing developments have replaced cows on the dry hills surrounding old Livermore. Young and upscale, the new residents—who likely as not commute to San Francisco each day—have no ties to Livermore's past. In 1987 the city council voted to consider cutting the whirling electrons symbolizing atomic energy from the city's insignia. . . . Nothing was done, but the debate itself was significant. (Tompkins 1990)

Many of the new residents looked to the developers and new businesses more than to the laboratory for Livermore's future, and Livermore's local politics in the late 1980s featured a series of struggles over a range of issues between the laboratory community and the newer interests.

In his senior thesis on civic life in Livermore from the 1950s to the 1970s, David Kang (1987) presents the town as divided between "old-timers" and "labbers." By the time I arrived in Livermore in 1987, the principal schism was, to simplify a little, between "labbers" and "newcomers." An analysis of donations to candidates in the 1989 election shows that Livermore was clearly divided into two patronage communities: laboratory centered and developer centered (Dillon 1989*a*; Jeffers 1989). At first these two factions struggled mainly over local growth issues, but over time the laboratory itself became an increasing source of conflict. The council, dominated throughout the period of my fieldwork by the developers and led by a mayor who was a banker, wanted to increase the pace of development in Livermore, while the slow-growth movement—with the laboratory community at its core—sponsored a local ballot initiative to try to block some of the new development. Meanwhile the developer-oriented city council took some unprecedented measures in regard to the laboratory: the mayor publicly complained about the laboratory's leaks into the city sewer system (Bodovitz 1988c); the council insisted that the laboratory, which is tax-exempt, pay $7.8 million for road improvements near the laboratory (Bodovitz 1989b); the council complained that the DOE was mishandling the public hearing process on the incinerator, and they sought to block the laboratory's attempt to close a public road next to the laboratory for security reasons (*Independent* 1988b). Eventually, in an extraordinary move, the city council hired a lobbyist to lobby against the laboratory in Washington (*Independent* 1988c). In 1989, Dale Turner, the mayor, was quoted in the local *Valley Times* as saying, "The Lab's got some serious problems. I'd hate like the devil to see it go away. But you do things wrong for a long enough time and nobody wants to see you around" (Dillon 1989b).

TROUBLE WITH THE UNIVERSITY OF CALIFORNIA

Finally, by 1991, the laboratory was also having increasing difficulties in its relationship with the University of California, which manages both the Livermore and the Los Alamos laboratories in exchange for an annual fee from the Department of Energy. Livermore scientists are for the most part enthusiastic about this arrangement: they would much rather be managed by the University of California than, like other parts of the nuclear weapons complex, by a corporation such as Rockwell or AT&T. In fact, when in 1991 the University of California threatened not to seek a renewal of its contract, many Livermore scientists circulated a petition to insist that the UC contract be renewed. They argued that the university affiliation assured them better retirement benefits, gave more protection to whistle-blowers than industry management would, and insulated the laboratory's research from the profit-minded priorities of the corporate world (Stern

1991). A 1984 University of California study reported that "[laboratory] staff members . . . take pride in their freedom to disagree with their bosses, and often insist that the atmosphere and decision-making at their lab—thanks to the University of California management?—are far closer to the open-minded, semi-collegial academic style than to the hierarchical style prevalent at most government and industrial laboratories" (Senate Policy Committee 1984: 22).

Many UC faculty, however, have for some years been unhappy about their affiliation with the two nuclear weapons laboratories. They argue that the university has no business managing research that might have the direct consequence of killing millions of people and that cannot, as academic norms require, be openly discussed. Moreover, throughout the 1980s, a series of scandals at the Livermore laboratory, reported in the Bay Area's major regional newspapers and sometimes by the *New York Times* and *Washington Post* as well, embarrassed the University of California and aggravated opposition by faculty and students to the association with the laboratory.

To begin with, in 1987, the local media ran a series of articles revealing that Livermore laboratory officials had given about $600,000 of public money to the model shop at the Rocky Flats nuclear weapons plant to produce personal gifts including plaques, medallions, foot massagers, phallus-shaped monks, a winepress, and a spiral staircase. The gifts went to laboratory officials or their favored suppliers (Doyle 1989). In 1991, the scandal would sour relations between the University of California and the Department of Energy when the latter withheld $595,000 from the university's management fee to penalize it for allowing such misuse of public funds and the university threatened to sue the DOE in retaliation (McKenzie 1991a).

In 1987, it was also alleged in the press that Livermore and Los Alamos managers had, under the guise of giving technical briefings to members of Congress, organized an illegal lobbying campaign against a motion in the House of Representatives to end nuclear testing. Although laboratory managers and scientists are allowed to give technical advice to Congress when requested, they are not supposed to actively seek out opportunities to brief members of Congress, since this would involve the entrepreneurial use of public money to influence the outcome of a congressional vote. In such a situation the line between licit and illicit briefings can be a fine one.

In 1987, the laboratories were accused of crossing the line by drawing up a hit list of congressional swing votes on the test ban and setting out to offer them "technical briefings" (Rogers 1987*a*; J. Smith 1987). Media charges of impropriety resulted in an official investigation by the General Accounting Office (GAO). The GAO report,[18] which noted the ambiguity of official regulations governing such conduct, exonerated the laboratories and the DOE, but many people remembered the allegations more than the exoneration and the University of California was embarrassed by the controversy.

The following year, 1988, the press published a number of stories alleging drug abuse at the laboratory. These proved particularly controversial because of the dangerous materials handled by laboratory employees and because of the possibility that employees with access to secret documents might be susceptible to blackmail. The stories began when Rep. John Dingell's House Committee on Oversight and Investigations held hearings on "Operation Snowstorm," a 1986 undercover operation to investigate drug abuse at the laboratory. The investigation was carried out by one undercover police officer, Robert Buda, who posed as a truck driver at the laboratory and had an L clearance (a yellow badge), which gave him limited access to classified areas. In eight months the undercover operation led to the arrests, mostly for selling and using methamphetamine ("speed"), of six people (four of whom were contractors rather than direct laboratory employees) and the resignations of another ten. Although the Drug Enforcement Agency wanted to continue the operation, laboratory managers terminated it after eight months—just three days before the undercover agent was to get the Q clearance that would have allowed him much freer access to classified areas and personnel within the laboratory. Representative Dingell charged that the undercover agent had many more leads to follow up and that, armed finally with a Q clearance, he was on the verge of finding serious drug abuse at higher levels in the laboratory, among scientists and engineers. Dingell said that the laboratory's decision to end the investigation amounted to a coverup. Laboratory managers, however, said that they had already extended the investigation twice, they had no idea the undercover agent was about to get his Q clearance, and they finally stopped the operation when they did because it seemed to have run out of steam and they wanted to make arrests rather than allow drug dealing to go on while the undercover operation continued. Robert

Godwin, the laboratory's senior security official, accused Dingell of using the laboratory as a "whipping boy" in his own long-standing feud with the DOE.[19]

After the Snowstorm controversy, there were additional media reports of drug abuse at the laboratory and even allegations that some laboratory employees were stealing and selling equipment to finance their drug purchases (Iwata 1988*b;* Meyer 1988). The latter suspicion was lent credibility by the highly publicized case of Ronald Stump, a laboratory chemist who disappeared in 1987 following allegations that he was involved with drugs, had stolen $11,000 worth of precious metals, and had taken a $125,000 kickback fee for a defective spectrometer he bought on the laboratory's behalf. Stump fled to Mexico but was later arrested in Arizona (Meyer 1988). Soon after this, almost two grams of marijuana seeds and stems were discovered in the plutonium facility, and $1,500 worth of methamphetamine and cocaine used to train the laboratory's drug-sniffing dogs were discovered missing from the safe where they were usually kept (Stober 1989*b*).[20]

But the most damaging allegations of managerial incompetence and impropriety concerned not drugs but the laboratory's controversial X-ray laser program. Between 1983 and 1985, Roy Woodruff, then director of all nuclear weapons research at Livermore, became increasingly concerned that Edward Teller and his protégé Lowell Wood were, in his view, using their influence in Washington to mislead senior White House officials and arms control negotiators about the laboratory's progress in developing such a laser. For example, although laboratory scientists disagreed as to whether they had even measured X-ray laser tests accurately, in December 1984, on the eve of the Geneva arms talks, Teller wrote to Paul Nitze, the lead negotiator for the United States, "We expect to be able to realize this advance [the x-ray laser] in this decade." He added: "A single X-ray laser module the size of an executive desk . . . could potentially shoot down the entire Soviet land-based missile force" (Broad 1992: 166–167). Teller also wrote to George Keyworth, the White House science adviser, "We are now entering the engineering phase of X-ray lasers" and "We have . . . developed the diagnostics by which to judge every step of engineering progress" (ibid., 151–152). (Within five years of these statements, the X-ray laser had been abandoned as infeasible.) Woodruff was concerned that the Reagan administration's arms control policies and budget allocations were being distorted by such communiqués from Teller and Wood. Forbidden by the laboratory's director, Roger Batzel, from correcting such statements on laboratory letterhead, he resigned in 1985. He appealed to the university to investigate what he considered to be gross misconduct by the laboratory's management, but the university refused to get involved and UC President David Gardner refused to meet with Woodruff. Later, when the affair became public after an anonymous UC official leaked the details to the Southern California Federation of Scientists, the affair received widespread media coverage both nationally and locally and was even reported on the national CBS show "Sixty Minutes." It would be difficult to exaggerate the damage this incident inflicted on the laboratory's credibility in Washington (Blum 1988; Broad 1988*b*, 1992; Perlman 1988; "Sixty Minutes" 1988).[21]

By the 1990s such developments produced a situation in which most UC faculty opposed continuing UC management of the laboratory. In 1989, a UC Academic Senate Committee, which took three years to complete its report, concluded that the classified work done at Livermore and Los Alamos was "inherently inconsistent with the university's essential commitment to freedom of expression" and that continued management of the laboratories was "contrary to the fundamental nature of the university." The committee recommended that the university "should, in a timely and orderly manner, phase out its responsibility for operating the laboratories" (Jendreson et al. 1989). In June 1990, 64 percent of the faculty who voted in a referendum at all nine UC campuses recommended that the university sever its forty-year relationship with the Los Alamos and Livermore laboratories (Gordon 1990). And on June 4, 1991, the UC Academic Senate voted 50 to 2 to end the relationship (Irving 1991). At its hearings in September 1990, the UC Board of Regents was urged to discontinue the university's relationship with the two weapons laboratories by a former State Supreme Court justice, by a Nobel laureate in physics, by fourteen state legislators, and by a string of faculty, one of whom, Charles Schwartz, was arrested for refusing to leave the university president's office. University officials, however, maintained that the university was performing a valuable public service by managing the weapons laboratories and that it had a special contribution to make in acting as a buffer between the laboratories and the government (De Wolk 1990; Jeffers 1990*b*; Link 1990; Newman 1990).[22] In the end, the regents voted to continue managing the laboratory in 1990, and in 1992, after what were by all accounts the most difficult contract renewal negotiations ever between the university and the Department of Energy, the university did renew its management contract for another five years.

The campaign against the laboratory within the university was, in terms of its immediate outcome at least, as unsuccessful as the broader regional and national movement against the laboratory's work—and, compared to that movement, it was of less concern to laboratory managers. Nevertheless, along with a decade of Soviet reform, riotous protests, hostile ballot initiatives, internal scandals, and burgeoning criticism in Livermore itself, it constituted one more problem for the burdened and embattled laboratory to deal with.

The laboratory's intensifying problems with the university also served as a barometric reading of its deteriorating public reputation and of the widening gulf between it and its local environment. By the end of the 1980s, laboratory employees were complaining that morale was the lowest anyone could remember, and an $85,000 public opinion survey commissioned by the laboratory in 1990 showed that most residents of the San Francisco Bay Area wished the laboratory did not do weapons work and most laboratory employees felt that the general public was hostile or indifferent to the laboratory (Armantrout 1990; Rogers 1990b). The laboratory's legitimacy as a public institution had been seriously called into question.

CHAPTER 8

A Different Reality

*There are no longer problems of the spirit. There is only the question:
when will I be blown up?*
WILLIAM FAULKNER

MAKING SENSE OF THE CRISIS

So far I have discussed the antinuclear movement largely in terms of its impact on the laboratory. But who were the people in this movement? Where did they come from, and why were they so effective? Besides its stated goal of ending and reversing the arms race, what did the antinuclear movement represent as a cultural phenomenon, and what does it tell us about postindustrial American society? The answers to such questions became clearer to me after I left the movement, made my journey into Livermore, and began to write about nuclear culture from the other side. My repositioning as a consequence of that journey enabled me to see more clearly the means by which the antinuclear movement itself functions as a system, disciplinary as well as emancipatory, that transforms the identities of its members. It also afforded me a more panoramic perspective from which to survey not only the obvious differences between nuclear scientists and antinuclear activists but also the less immediately obvious commonalities.

Like Livermore scientists, the great majority of those who were active in the antinuclear movement of the 1980s were white middle-class Americans. Although the movement did enjoy considerable armchair support from minority and low-income communities, it was white middle-class Americans who provided the money and the volunteer time that propelled the movement into national politics (Epstein 1985, 1988, 1991; Kazin 1984). Most antinuclear activists already had, or were in the process of earning, college degrees; and, with its copious output of earnest books, films, and lectures, its predilection for interminably long committee meetings, and its continual talk of the need to "educate" those outside the movement, the antinuclear movement clearly stands in that long tradition of middle-class social reformism that once caused Pauline Kael to remark that every educated American is a social worker at heart. Antinuclear activists are what Frank Parkin (1968) in his study of the British antinuclear movement calls "middle-class radicals."[1] They exhibit what Fredric Solomon and Jacob Fishman (1970) call "rebellion within a framework of identification": their radicalism impels them to oppose their own government, often by dramatic means; meanwhile, their middle-class sense of privilege gives them the confidence of social ownership, the sense that they are entitled to speak and that those who disagree with them need to think more clearly—a characteristic many outside the movement find irksome.

There is, then, a sense in which the scientists and engineers at the laboratory and the activists who have opposed them are strikingly similar: they are mostly white, middle class, well educated, and confident in their social and intellectual authority. Seen in this light it should not surprise us that some scientists and protestors, opposed to one another on this issue, have at other times participated in the same largely white middle-class movements, for example, against the Vietnam War and on behalf of the environment and civil rights. However, there is an important distinction—concealed by gross categories such as "white," "middle class," and "college educated"—between the social profiles of the weapons scientist and antinuclear activist populations: whereas the weapons scientists have been, by definition, trained in technical fields, antinuclear activists tend to have been trained in the humanities and social sciences and, as Parkin (1968: 180) phrases it, to work in "the welfare and creative professions." They are part of what Michael Harrington calls "the constituency of conscience"[2] in the middle class. Of course, scientists and engineers have participated in the antinuclear movement, but they have been more the exception than the rule. More commonly those in the antinuclear movement have tended to work, if they are socially successful, as doctors, teachers, psychotherapists, nurses, social workers, and ministers. The less financially secure, and these have tended to be more drawn toward the direct action wing of the movement, have worked, often episodically, as artists, students, paralegals, substitute teachers, word processors, natural food workers, house painters, and so on (see Epstein 1991: 5). The latter are part of, or on the edge of, that sizable counterculture in the San Francisco Bay Area that constitutes an alternative middle-class community.

Thus the struggle over the laboratory can be seen in part as a struggle between what the British intellectual C. P. Snow (1959) called "the two cultures": scientists and humanists. To put it with a little more sociological precision, we might say that the struggle was between the technocratic and humanistic wings of what has come to be known by sociologists as "the new class"—that subset of the middle class that relies on its cultural capital[3] (in the form of technical or humanistic knowledge) rather than financial capital (factories, stocks and bonds, real estate) for its income.[4] Alvin Gouldner (1979), the sociologist most closely identified with the notion of a "new class," argues that the conditions of late capitalism, a form of economy based as much on the circulation of information and images as commodities and raw materials, has swollen the ranks of this new class and given it a central importance in contemporary political life. Gouldner explains the availability of the humanistic wing of the new class to radical political movements in terms of its members' resentment at the discrepancy between their high cultural status as an educated elite and their lower status, compared to technocrats and those in business, when it comes to income and social power. McCrea and Markle (1989: 28) suggest that the "overproduction of university graduates" relative to jobs over the last three decades has exacerbated the political volatility of the humanistic new class. For those who, like myself, are wary of theories that connect ideological positions and socioeconomic status too reductively, we might add that the humanistic fraction of the middle class has other reasons, more illuminated by Weberian than Marxist thinking, for participating in the antinuclear movement: Lisa Peattie, quoting Parkin, argues that the liberal education and occupational practices of the humanistic middle class are grounded in "the notion of service to the community, human betterment or welfare and the like, or upon self-expression and creativity." She points out that there is a resonance between such cultural values and the internationalist, reformist ideals of the antinuclear movement, so that in joining the movement "such persons were not so much rebelling or breaking away from normal practice, as extending it, building on it, carrying it forward" (Peattie 1986: 4).

It is easy to understand why the humanistic middle class might have produced a mass movement against nuclear weapons in the early 1980s. To begin with, they were restive because their vision of society was assaulted by the nationalist-populist materialism that became identified with the Reagan years and because their own economic position in society had begun to deteriorate at the end of the Carter administration and continued to deteriorate through the Reagan and Bush administrations. After the Soviet invasion of Afghanistan and the commencement of the Iranian hostage crisis, Jimmy Carter started to shift the allocation of national resources to military programs, away from the social and educational programs that support and are supported by the humanistic middle class. Reagan amplified this shift in priorities, increasing the military budget from $150 billion a year in 1980 to $300 billion a year by 1988—a level of military mobilization that, in constant dollars, exceeded that during the Korean and Vietnam wars (Sivard 1987: 36–39). Thus in the early 1980s, the humanistic middle class saw a shift of national resources toward military programs they found ideologically abhorrent and away from social and educational programs that embodied their values and from which they, to some extent at least, benefited as a group.

But nuclear weapons were not merely a cipher for other concerns. To understand why middle-class dissatisfaction found expression in a movement against nuclear weapons rather than a movement against, say, Reagan's social spending policies, we must look at the politics and technology of nuclear weapons themselves in the early 1980s. These were years when the arms control negotiation process with the Soviets all but broke down for the first time since the 1960s, while high government officials talked loosely and publicly of limited and winnable nuclear wars. Since arms control policies and the changing technical characteristics of nuclear weapons are complex and dull matters, most citizens leave them to the experts. But within the humanistic middle class there are people who do follow arms control issues with a reasonable degree of expertise and attention, and this group of people grew in size in the early 1980s thanks to the proliferation of popular literature on nuclear weapons.[5] This burgeoning literature made it easier to follow, and harder to ignore, changes in nuclear weapons technology and in the official rhetoric of deterrence that alarmed some people considerably. They were upset to hear Weinberger, Haig, and other high government officials talk about firing "nuclear warning shots" over the Soviet bow and fighting limited and winnable nuclear wars. They were also alarmed to learn that the latest nuclear weapons seemed to be designed to fight nuclear wars rather than simply to deter them. The Trident II, MX, and Pershing II missiles, designed to drop warheads within 400, 300, and 100 feet of their targets, respectively, could, in theory at least, destroy Soviet command and control centers and Soviet missiles in their silos (Kaku and Axelrod 1987: 200–202). The Trident II was capable of reaching Soviet targets in ten to fifteen minutes (Aldridge 1983: 74), and the Pershing II, slated for deployment in Germany, was capable of reaching Soviet targets within about ten minutes—quickly enough that the Soviets might not have time to launch under attack. To weapons scientists these weapons were part of the natural rhythm, the alternation of technical measure and countermeasure, that provided the dynamic equilibrium in the relationship between the superpowers. To many others they were ominous, even terrifying, developments that showed the final bankruptcy of nuclear deterrence as a system for organizing global security.[6] The new weapons technologies, together with the loose statements by senior government officials, created a contagious nervousness that became the basis for a mass movement.

This movement was comparatively easy to build in northern California because the humanistic middle class in the San Francisco Bay Area had, by dint of its participation in a number of recent political struggles, accumulated an organizational infrastructure, a collective memory, and organizing experience that provided the kindling for a new mass movement. The civil rights movement, the movement against the Vietnam War, the women's movement, and the movement against nuclear power had all enjoyed considerable support in the Bay Area. They left behind a reservoir of seasoned organizers, grassroots political networks, nostalgic memories of protest, and critical feminist, ecological, and peace-oriented ideas that were easily assembled as the basis for a new movement.

That movement was, despite its inability to recruit many minorities[7] and low-income citizens as more than well-wishers from the sidelines, complex and multifaceted—much more so than the previous, considerably smaller movement against nuclear weapons in the 1950s.[8] The movement knitted together at least six different constituencies. First, there were the professionals' groups such as Physicians for Social Responsibility and Computer Professionals for Social Responsibility, which deployed their cultural authority and their vocational expertise as resources against the expert authority of the nuclear weapons complex. Second, there were the electorally oriented pressure groups such as SANE and the Nuclear Freeze Campaign, which sought to influence the outcome of elections and to pressure national and local legislators into taking measures against the arms race. Third, there were women's groups such as Women's Action for Nuclear Disarmament (WAND), Women's Strike for Peace, and the Women's International League for Peace and Freedom (WILPF), the oldest peace group in the country. These were organized around the notion that, in a patriarchal society where, in Diana Russell's (1989a: 74) words, "the nuclear mentality and the masculine mentality are one and the same," women have a special role to play in making peace.[9] Fourth, there were New Age groups, the best known of which was Beyond War. Beyond War eschewed protests and direct involvement in political campaigns but produced lavishly made videos, books, pamphlets, conferences, and retreats to spread the idea that it was time for the planet as a whole to move to a new stage of civilization in which war would be obsolete. Fifth, there were religious peace groups such as the Ecumenical Peace Institute in Berkeley and the Nevada Desert Witness, and there were peace-oriented sections within many major churches in the Bay Area, especially the Catholic, Methodist, and Unitarian churches. In the early 1980s, as the theological tide turned against the consequentialist logic that had been used to legitimate the arms race, Christians and Jews brought a strong ethical critique of deterrence into the movement and, often, a fierce concern about the detrimental effects of weapons spending on the poor in the United States and in the Third World. Some Christians worked within their churches or in the Christian segment of the peace movement. Some took their perspective to mainstream peace groups.[10] Many joined direct action groups, the sixth segment within the movement. This grouping was itself a potpourri of diverse countercultural constituencies. In her studies of the Livermore Action Group, Barbara Epstein (1985, 1988, 1991) characterizes it as a coalition of anarchists, radical Christians, radical feminists, environmentalists, and pagans. (The pagan community was enjoying tremendous growth in the Bay Area in the 1980s as many looked to paganism for a spirituality that would express their concern for the well-being of the earth and their disillusion with the spiritual politics of masculinity.)

The polycentricity of the antinuclear movement created immense problems of coordination and integration, but it was also one of its greatest strengths. The movement was able to work against the political culture of the nuclear weapons establishment in complex, cross-cutting, albeit not infrequently contradictory, ways. Because it operated on so many fronts at once, the movement was able to mobilize a variety of incommensurable discourses—moderate and radical, rational and emotional, pragmatic and ethical—to keep the nuclear weapons establishment perpetually off balance. In the process the movement created a heterogeneous set of narratives, values, symbols, and emotional reflexes that constituted an alternative nuclear culture to that offered by the laboratory and the nuclear weapons establishment. It also targeted and eroded some of the central cultural pillars of the established ideological order, whittling away at the authority of experts, the fearless confidence in technical predictability, the privatization of ethics, the denigration of emotion, the rationalist masculinism, and the training of the body that sustained the laboratory's nuclear culture.

FEAR AND LOATHING IN THE NUCLEAR AGE

When I am invited to speak publicly, I often make a point of asking how many people have had nightmares about nuclear war. If I poll members of peace groups, often about two-thirds of the audience raise their hands. In a group of about twenty citizens at a church in Livermore, no hands were raised. When I once asked a group of about seventy laboratory employees, two raised their hands. One scientist once told me, "It's not rational to have nightmares about nuclear weapons. There's nothing you can do about them."[11]

Nuclear weapons scientists learn not to fear nuclear weapons. They learn, even to the point that their dream lives and bodily reflexes are affected, to see nuclear weapons as machines that, although they need to be handled with more care than other machines, extend the powers of their owners. In the 1980s, the antinuclear movement set out to challenge the dominant portrayal of nuclear weapons as instruments of security and to reconstruct them as unpredictable tools of death and mayhem, as foul things to be feared. This involved the development of a culture of terror.

Antinuclear activists felt that the dominant construction of nuclear weapons as instruments of security was sustained by a pervasive denial, at the laboratory and throughout society, of the truth about the weapons' awesome capacity to kill and destroy. Thus protests at the laboratory have been full of visual and verbal images of death.[12] Some protestors dress as skeletons or grim reapers (see fig. 8). Others carry pictures of mushroom clouds or of the dead and wounded from Hiroshima, or signs such as Livermore: America's Auschwitz, and Close Livermore's Death Factory. Many antinuclear protests feature "die-ins"—moments when everyone falls down as if dead. At one Nevada Test Site action, protestors marched to the entrance and planted crosses in the ground while the women wailed in mourning as loud as they could—a hideous, piercing, relentless wailing that lasted for about fifteen minutes. At a Hiroshima Day protest at the laboratory in 1989, a group of women went to the front gate and reenacted the bombing of Hiroshima, writhing and screaming so loudly that scientists came out onto the balcony of the main building to see what was happening.

Imagery of Hiroshima and Nagasaki has been particularly important in antinuclear protests. As the only occasions when nuclear weapons have been used to kill people in large numbers, the bombings provide a storehouse of images of atomic death from the past whose concreteness the protestors have sought to project into the present so as to lend realism to their prophecies of the future. Thus on Hiroshima Day in 1989, one peace group, the American Friends Service Committee, staged a one-day exhibition in Livermore of photographs and eyewitness accounts from Hiroshima immediately after the bombing. And in 1985, on the fortieth anniversary of Hiroshima, protestors painted shadows on the sidewalks of Livermore and all over the San Francisco Bay Area: after the bombing of Hiroshima all that remained of some people were their shadows, burned into buildings and sidewalks by the extraordinary heat of the bomb. The shadows were symbols, arrested somewhere between a presence and an absence, designed to make real the already destroyed but no longer visible bodies of the bomb's first victims to memorialize and rescue the still undestroyed bodies, not yet visible, of the bomb's presumed future victims. By bringing the shadows to Livermore, protestors sought to confront weapons scientists and the members of their community with a unique image of death in the nuclear age.

In purveying these images of death and terror, protestors have been trying to make real to others what is real to so many of them—a visualized experience of the all-too-possible extinction of self and society in a nuclear war. Protestors have developed a number of devices to help those who are "psychically numb" or "in denial" about nuclear weapons to, in Lifton's (1982*a*) words, "imagine the real." Some of these devices, such as weekend workshops and books of exercises, help deepen the involvement of those who are already in some way committed to the movement;[13] but many other devices were developed as recruitment tools. One, formerly in widespread use by the Nuclear Freeze Campaign, is the dot chart presented in figure 9. One dot symbolizes all the explosive power, including the Hiroshima and Nagasaki bombs, used in World War II. The other five thousand or so dots symbolize the firepower of all the nuclear weapons in the world in the 1980s. An even more effective technique, widely used by Beyond War, takes the information in the dot chart and thrusts it into the individual's consciousness through the ears rather than the eyes: while members of the audience sit with their eyes closed, a single BB is dropped into a metal bucket to represent the explosive power of World War II; then more than five thousand BBs representing an all-out nuclear war are poured slowly and loudly into the bucket. The experience for those listening to the cacophonous noise of the BBs against metal can be excruciating since the relentless stream continues, like hammer blows to the senses, far beyond the point where most people expect it to stop until the mind starts to say, "Surely now is enough, surely now is enough." I have seen this technique bring people to tears.[14]

Another technique was used widely by Physicians for Social Responsibility in the early 1980s. They called it "the bombing run." Here an authoritative figure, usually a doctor, talks in horrifying and relentless detail about the consequences of a nuclear explosion in the city inhabited by the audience. Similar in some ways to fire-and-brimstone preachers' evocations of hell, the aim is to terrify the audience and make them seek salvation, in this case through political action.[15] Here are excerpts from a bombing run by one of the virtuosos of the genre, Helen Caldicott:

> Six miles from the epicenter, every building will be flattened and every person killed. Because the human body is composed mostly of water, when it is exposed to thousands of degrees Celsius, it turns into gas and disappears. . . .
> Twenty miles from the epicenter, all people will be killed or lethally injured, and most buildings will be destroyed. People just beyond the 6-mile,

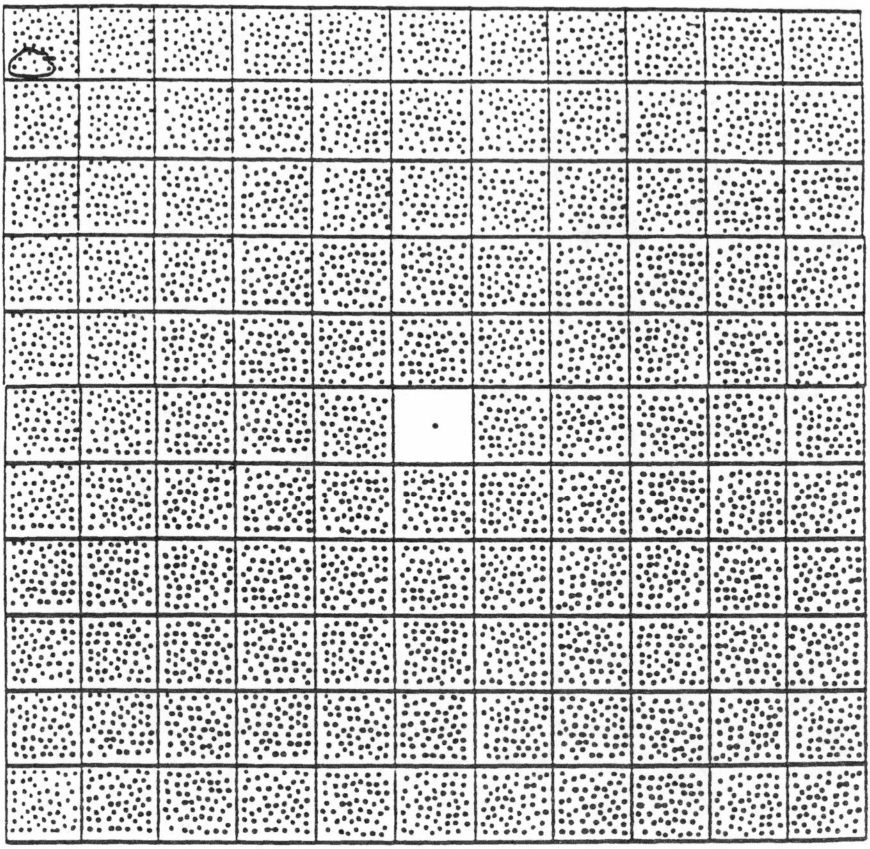

Figure 9. Chart, titled "The World's Nuclear Weapons Stockpile," which appeared in a flyer distributed by the Nuclear Freeze Campaign. The dot in the center represents all the explosive power used in World War II, 3 megatons; the other dots represent the power of the global nuclear arsenal in the 1980s, 16,000 megatons. The dots circled in the upper left-hand corner represent the explosive force of twenty-four Trident II missiles, 24 megatons.

100-percent lethal range who happen to glance at the flash could have their eyes melted. . . . Other people will be charcoalized from the heat.

Enormous overpressures will create winds of up to 500 miles per hour, causing hundreds of thousands of injuries. . . . These winds will literally pick people up off the pavement and suck them out of reinforced-concrete buildings, together with the furniture, converting them into missiles traveling at 100 miles per hour. When they hit the nearest wall or solid object, they will be killed instantly from fractured skulls, brain trauma, fractured long bones, and internal-organ injuries. . . .

Twenty-six miles from the epicenter, the heat from the explosion will be so intense that dry objects such as clothes, curtains, upholstery, and dry wood will spontaneously ignite. People could become walking, flaming torches. . . .

Forty miles from the flash, people who glance reflexively at the incredible light will be instantly blinded by burns to the retina or back of the eyes. . . .

The resultant fires, fanned by prevailing winds, could spread to cover an area of up to 3,000 square miles. . . . Within this area, of course, fallout shelters would be useless because the fires would suck all the oxygen out of them. They would fill with noxious gases, carbon dioxide, and carbon monoxide, asphyxiating the occupants. The intense blast and heat would convert most shelters into crematoria. (1986: 10–12)[16]

Physicians for Social Responsibility packaged this message in documentary films such as *The Last Epidemic* and *If You Love This Planet*—films that were shown at high schools, colleges, churches, union meetings, neighborhood meetings, and so on, as part of the antinuclear movement's outreach drive. The thematic content of the bombing run even reverberated through Hollywood, which, in 1984, produced the ABC television movie *The Day After* and the general release film *Testament*, both of which dramatized the aftermath of a nuclear war for a popular audience.

Many of the activists I interviewed, especially women, reported being permanently transformed by such films and by the visualized experience of extinction they produced. For example, Elaine, who was a teacher at the time, had had no interest in the antinuclear movement until, for some reason she still cannot explain, she went to see *The Last Epidemic* at a local church.

I still don't know why I did it. I'd never been to this church down the hill. I must have read somewhere that they were showing it and I walked in. There were about forty people there. I saw the film and afterwards . . . I walked out, got in my car, and I drove for about an hour around the hills, and I was married at the time, and I came home and I couldn't talk about it. I couldn't sleep that night. I slept a couple of hours, but I really hardly slept that night. And I woke up in the morning thinking, right, I'm changing all my priorities. This is it . . . , I think I went through the stages overnight a lot of people go through over a period of time. I remember distinctly feeling straight after seeing the film very angry. . . . And then I felt very depressed. . . . Very sad. "Oh God! What on earth are we going to do?" It seemed so inevitable. And [I was] just really grief-stricken. And then gradually there just comes an acceptance, not of the situation, but of the fact that you know about it, you can't get away from it, and you have to do something about it, and if you don't make it the highest priority in your life, what the hell does your life mean? Once you've really owned up to the situation, there's no other way to go. There was no decision, you know. That's the funny thing. A lot of people say to me, "Well, what made you decide to be an activist?" I didn't decide. There was no other course once you'd really owned up to it. I mean, if you are not making this the highest priority . . . then you haven't really seen it as it is.

Another woman, Norah, a psychotherapist, remembers seeing *The War Game*, a dramatization of nuclear war made in the mid-1970s by the BBC but never shown on British television because it was thought to be too disturbing.

> It made nuclear war real for me. I have this very strong image of a small nuclear weapon lying on the ground, gleaming. Even in its concrete presence like that, it looked very abstract. Then they cut to the explosion of that weapon, and a woman and children running screaming with blood all over them. It was this juxtaposition of this sort of gleaming male rationality and the terrible experience of the bomb going off that got me. Nuclear war had been abstract for me until I saw the film. Seeing that in the film changed something in me forever.

After seeing the film, Norah became an antinuclear activist.

These transformative moments, which clearly have the intensity of conversion experiences for some core activists, could lead people to dramatically reorganize their priorities. Paradoxically, the sense that extinction might come at any moment led some to an exquisitely heightened awareness of each moment and a complete existential aliveness. Gwyneth, a psychotherapist whose own transformation was triggered by an antinuclear rally she attended immediately after seeing *The China Syndrome*, said, "I lived about a year after that like I was totally in touch with that reality, just living and breathing it, and just walking around feeling the plutonium in the air, and reading everything I could read. . . . It was really like being in touch with life, the flow of life, the energy." Shirley, a doctor who had undergone a similar transformation, would sometimes find herself in the middle of treating patients thinking, "In milliseconds this stuff is going to be reduced to its component atoms. . . . All these patients are going to be as nothing when somebody just decides it's time." Explaining the impact of this sensibility on her life, she said, "It [the arms race] is the reason, probably the main reason, I've decided not to have kids, because I need time to do this [be an activist] and kids would take away from that. On my deathbed I would rather say that I did some little thing to prevent nuclear war than have a piece of my genome walking around."

Such attitudes can isolate activists from friends, relatives, and colleagues. Elaine remembers that her friends stopped inviting her to parties for about a year after her transformation: "I'd never talk about anything else, and my friends really got depressed about inviting me to any parties." The same happened to Gwyneth. Shirley's husband called her activism "the albatross" in their marriage.

These stories are extreme. Many people joined the antinuclear movement without experiencing this kind of terror or transformation. Nevertheless, a large proportion of people in the movement, especially its leaders, were transformed by terror in some form. The cultivation of terror was a crucial part of the movement's strategy and, in a country that had always expected its citizens to trust their leaders' management of nuclear weapons, the sudden eruption of this public culture of fear had profoundly subversive potential.

How did this culture of fear arise? Many activists saw it as a natural, and healthy, response to the existence of nuclear weapons: not to be afraid of nuclear war was to be dead to oneself.[17] As one who once had an experience very similar to Norah's when I also saw *The War Game*, which I left in tears, and as one who also used to experience insurgent bursts of excruciating awareness that everything around me could be destroyed at any moment, it is tempting to see the culture of fear as a "natural" response to the arms race and to say, along with many activists, that only repression or fear of fear itself prevents more people from experiencing terror. In fact, however, these experiences of terror were, for many people, specific to a particular historical moment in the early 1980s. At the peak of this moment, in 1983, according to Lawrence Wright (1989: 158), "a poll taken in California . . . found that eighty-five percent of the respondents expected a nuclear war in their lifetime." These experiences were systematically produced by an elaborate social technology of films, lectures, leaflets, and workshops designed to manufacture or rescue fleeting moments of fear that might otherwise have been lost or written off as meaningless and to use them as the basis for a reorganization of the self and the solidification of a mass movement. Just as the cultural world of the laboratory tends toward producing a certain structure of feeling and a particular relationship of the self to others, so the cultural world of the antinuclear movement has tended to produce—even if it by no means always succeeded in doing so—a community of the afflicted with their own culturally constituted experience of self.

Movement culture enabled the inner spaces of the self to be penetrated and disciplined by the image of the bomb. It encouraged activists to confess their fear of the bomb and to feel liberated by their urge to confess it. The public confession, even celebration, of fears hitherto considered private, embarrassing, maybe even deviant, was a means—not so dissimilar in effect from the FBI investigations undergone by weapons scientists—of redrawing the relationship between individual and community, of rendering the private open for inspection, thus establishing the claim of the group on the individual. In other words, it was, somewhat like techniques of surveillance and segregation within the weapons scientists' world, part of a normalizing process for the reengineering of identity, though this process was subjectively perceived as liberating rather than disciplining. Gwyneth, observing the loss of individuality inherent in this phenomenon but marking it as emancipatory, described the process in these words: "There's a connection that's made. If you're in a room with twenty people and everybody's going through the same pain, you realize how connected you are. . . . In this society we're so individualized and cut off from one another that that connection is rare."[18]

ASK THE EXPERTS?

The laboratory's culture is one of expert rationalism. From the beginning of their scientific training, weapons scientists, like most other scientists, learn that emotions obstruct clear logical thought and problem solving (see Keller 1983, 1985; Merton 1973; Weber 1946). One of the things scientists most revile about protestors is their frequent emotionalism. (Lester, for example, characterized the protestors as having "a lot of hysteria but not a lot of solid thinking behind them.")

Scientists also learn that every problem has its proprietary experts, and weapons scientists learn that scientists, especially physicists, have a special privilege as experts on nuclear policy. This sense of privilege—encapsulated in the remark one scientist made to me that "if you don't understand the technology and physical effects of the weapons, then in my view you don't have a right to an opinion on nuclear policy"—has been encoded in the practices of government since the very beginning of the nuclear age: in 1945, nuclear weapons scientists helped to pick the Japanese targets for the first nuclear weapons, and since then they have played an important role in picking Soviet targets, deciding which new weapons to build, and consulting on arms control policies.

In other words, nuclear weapons scientists have, in regard to nuclear policy, been important agents in the creation of what Foucault (1980b) calls a "regime of truth." Foucault argues that we live in the age of the expert wherein the past cultural hegemony of "general intellectuals"—men like Voltaire—has been supplanted by that of experts or "specific intellectuals," Foucault's prototype of which is Oppenheimer, the scientist behind the first atomic bomb (ibid., 127–129). These new specific intellectuals, "strategists of life and death" as Foucault calls them, police the exchanges of power and knowledge that pulse through the circuits of contemporary technocratic societies. Whatever they say is presumed to carry a special authority, and they set the standard in general for determining which kinds of statements count as true and which kinds of speakers count as truthful.

Applying such notions specifically to the nuclear situation, Carol Cohn (1987) suggests that nuclear normality has been sustained by the hegemony of what she calls "technostrategic discourse." She argues that nuclear weapons scientists have, along with defense intellectuals and military officials, developed such a discourse about nuclear weapons and that it has acquired privileged status as the way one must speak about nuclear weapons to be taken seriously. Technostrategic discourse is characterized by its lack of emotion, its game-theoretic models of human motivation, its fondness for abstraction and for passive sentence constructions, its focus on hardware rather than people, and its fundamental, unquestioned and unquestionable, assumption that weapons development must continue. Cohn points out that the word "peace" has no place in technostrategic discourse, a discursive regime in which terms such as "stability" and "security" are the closest synonyms.

The antinuclear movement of the 1980s led an assault both within and against technostrategic discourse. Some in the movement pressed their attack by recruiting esteemed but now oppositional technostrategic speakers to speak on their behalf, simultaneously subverting the nuclear state and reinforcing the authority of expert discourse. Meanwhile others sought to enlarge the range of expertise that qualified people to speak with authority on the issue. Still others sought to abolish the notion of expertise itself. Thus the laboratory found itself under attack on several fronts at once.

The movement's most conservative tactic was simply to match laboratory experts with equivalent experts who held opposite views. For every Edward Teller they deployed a Carl Sagan.[19] Thus Livermore scientists found themselves arguing about the need to keep testing nuclear weapons with retired weapons scientists such as Hans Bethe, Norris Bradbury, Carson Mark, Richard Garwin, Glenn Seaborg, Herb York, and their own Ray Kidder.[20] When they said it would be difficult, if not impossible, to verify a nuclear test ban, they found themselves opposed by respected seismologists such as Jack Evernden.[21] If they argued about the survivability of nuclear war, they found themselves in an argument about nuclear winter with Carl Sagan and the atmospheric scientist Richard Turco.[22] If they argued that new weapons would make the country more secure, they found themselves arguing with such unlikely freeze supporters as William Colby, former head of the CIA, Robert McNamara, former secretary of defense during the Vietnam War, and George Kennan, former ambassador to the Soviet Union and leading architect of containment.[23]

Even at the local level, within Livermore itself, there was some bifurcation among the experts. When the laboratory was attempting to press ahead with its new incinerator, for example, it found itself being publicly criticized by Marion Fulk, a retired laboratory expert on airborne radioactivity who was now working with Tri-Valley CAREs. Fulk argued that the design of the incinerator might spread plutonium particles in the air over the Livermore Valley. The laboratory was also opposed by experts such as Perry Cole, an environmental science professor from San Francisco who argued that there were safer and more efficient ways of dealing with laboratory waste than incineration.

When experts disagree, the consensus-building effects of expert discourse are undermined. In an article on popular perceptions of risk, Harvey Sapolsky (1990) argues that whenever both sides in a debate succeed in mobilizing experts, the public begins to lose faith in experts as a group and to think more independently. This clearly happened in the 1950s when public clashes between experts over the safety of fallout from atmospheric nuclear testing damaged the credibility of all experts, but especially the government's (Divine 1978: 106, 195, 321–322). Something similar began to happen in the 1980s. As Joseph, a Livermore scientist, put it to me, "The fact that the establishment is questioning the establishment—people like Bundy and McNamara—I think makes people feel more able to wonder now than they did for a while."

Meanwhile entire new categories of experts were attempting to establish their authority to speak on nuclear weapons policy. These were, above all, clergy, lawyers, doctors, and psychotherapists—the humanistic wing of the new class challenging the authority of the technocratic wing.

In the early 1980s, the arms race was condemned by the Catholic and Anglican bishops, by Methodist and Presbyterian clerics, and by many other important ecclesiastical figures. These clerics sought to undo the technicization of moral judgments that is a consequence of consequentialist moral thinking and to reframe the nuclear issue as a matter on which moral as well as technical experts had to be heard.

Some lawyers also attempted to interject their expertise into the nuclear debate. They argued as speakers at rallies and as expert witnesses in court that, as potential instruments of genocide, nuclear weapons violated the Nuremburg laws under which Nazis were tried.[24] Antinuclear lawyers tried, without success, to use this argument in defense of those arrested for civil disobedience, saying that the laboratory, not the protestors, was in violation of the law. In the late 1980s, lawyers from Oakland's Western States Legal Foundation also argued that the laboratory's Environmental Impact Statement did not comply with minimum legal standards and took the laboratory and the University of California to court.

But it was the doctors' insistence on the relevance of their expertise that was most damaging. As Bernard Lown, one of the leaders of International Physicians for the Prevention of Nuclear War put it, "If you have a serious problem, where do you go? In a secular age, the doctor has become priest, rabbi, counselor. Then, too, the doctor brings all the credentials of a scientist" (quoted in McCrea and Markle 1989: 96).[25]

Members of the physicians' movement against nuclear weapons, trading on their scientific credentials, used their status to advance claims that had little or nothing to do with their expertise in medicine: claims as to why SDI would not work, how to negotiate with the Soviets, how the military would fight a nuclear war, and so on. (Of course, in claiming to speak authoritatively about matters strictly outside their expertise, they were only doing what laboratory scientists had been doing for years.) But they were particularly effective when they carved out areas where their expertise as doctors made them seem more qualified to speak to the policy issues than the defense experts who had hitherto dominated the debate. In the early 1980s, for example, when Physicians for Social Responsibility argued that the government was underestimating the vulnerability of the human body to nuclear attack and therefore underestimating the casualties that would result from a nuclear war, it was easy for them to claim to know best. Then, in the late 1980s, when PSR began a national campaign around the local health hazards associated with nuclear weapons facilities, again they were able to claim a special privilege to speak with authority. Thus one of the speakers at a 1989 rally in Livermore who was among the most effective was a PSR oncologist, Jan Kirsch, who assured the crowd that the laboratory's planned incinerator would definitely cause additional cancers in the community. Emphasizing her authority as a doctor, she said, "I'd like to invite any laboratory employees in the crowd to come on my ward rounds with me and see what else you're producing besides nuclear weapons."

Kirsch was quoted a number of times by the Livermore press. In 1991, she was quoted in a local newspaper article discussing the mysterious case of a lone pine tree at the laboratory that registered 250 times the legal limit of tritium per liter. A laboratory spokesman said that anyone standing next to the tree "would get the same amount of radiation as if they ate one-tenth of a banana" and, in any case, the tree was a freak occurrence. Dr. Kirsch was quoted at length in the article, saying, "This is not innocuous. . . . If this is an aberration, then Livermore has had an epidemic of aberrations. . . . Human beings living in Livermore drinking water and breathing air are themselves becoming that tree" (Haun 1991).

One more expert community that mobilized against the arms race was the psychotherapeutic community, which is particularly powerful in California. Antinuclear psychotherapists worked on two different discursive fronts. On the one hand, they used their status as mental health professionals to legitimate their claim that the laboratory's work was poisoning the minds of the nation's children—that, even if nuclear deterrence worked, it did so at the cost of the psychological suffering of the millions of teenagers and children growing up with the fear of extinction. Some psychologists connected everything from teenage pregnancy to low school achievement with this suffering.[26]

On the other hand, they used their status as experts to undermine, at least in part, the whole idea of expert rationalism itself: if laboratory scientists had for years purveyed a normalizing discourse based on the premise that it was only appropriate to be "rational" about the nuclear dilemma, psychologists now spearheaded the development of a new normalizing counterdiscourse in which it was claimed that it was inappropriate, maybe a sign of personal inadequacy or numbness, not to be emotional about nuclear weapons. In concert with the women's sector of the peace movement, psychologists developed a discourse presenting rationalism, often construed as male rationalism, as part of the problem. This discourse validated emotional states of fear, anger, and grief as more appropriate responses to the nuclear predicament. There is a fine example of this alternative normalizing discourse in *If You Love This Planet*, one of the most successful antinuclear documentaries of the 1980s. At the end of the film, Helen Caldicott tells the viewer that if, as a doctor, she encounters parents who appear not to be upset that their child has cancer, she sends them to a psychiatrist. She then says that the existence of nuclear weapons means that the whole planet has cancer, so to speak, and anyone who is not distressed by that has an "inappropriate" response.

WOMEN AND CHILDREN TALK BACK

I have argued that nuclear weapons scientists operate in a gendered world in which the mission of the laboratory is coded as masculine, rational, and superordinate while the subordinate sentimental and emotional values associated with women and children are ghettoized in the domestic sphere. In this world the sentimental values of the domestic sphere have the status of what Foucault (1980b: 82) calls "subjugated knowledges"—"naive knowledges, located low down on the hierarchy, beneath the required level of cognition or scientificity." The antinuclear movement of the 1980s disrupted this order by mobilizing the values, as well as the personnel, of the domestic sphere and using them to confront the masculine world of the laboratory. Thus we cannot properly understand the antinuclear movement of the 1980s without looking at the role of women, and of values constructed as women's values, in that movement. Women were as important in building the movement as scaffolding is to a building under construction.

To begin with, women were vital in providing membership and leadership in the movement. Nationally, the two most important leaders of the movement were Helen Caldicott and Randall Forsberg. Caldicott, a pediatrician at the Harvard Medical School, was, for a long time, president of Physicians for Social Responsibility. She was also one of the founders of Women's Action for Disarmament. Her book, *Missile Envy*, is among the most widely read in the movement. She developed an extraordinarily effective speaking style that combined the authority of a doctor with the passionate warmth of a mother and the charismatic energy of an Old Testament prophet. She was the Billy Graham of the peace movement, and many of the activists I interviewed said their lives were permanently changed by hearing her. As one woman I interviewed put it,

> Nobody has moved more people than Helen. . . . Just like people remember where they were the day Kennedy was shot, they remember so distinctly that day she touched them. . . . I really felt the love for people she was talking about. She could show her emotions, and I remember crying when she finished speaking. She ended up her talk that day with describing how beautifully a baby moves, one baby. Very corny shit if it wasn't done the right way, but she meant it. And then I realized, all my life, this is what I'd been after—to try to do what she does.

Forsberg, another woman who played a vital leadership role in the antinuclear movement, had a very different persona. Where Caldicott thought prophetically, Forsberg thought strategically. A longtime peace researcher with training in political science, it was Forsberg who formulated the idea of a nuclear freeze. In the early 1980s she founded her own think tank, the Institute for Defense and Disarmament Studies, in Boston. She rubbed shoulders with arms control experts but, at the same time, sought to democratize the arms control debate, touring the country to talk to ordinary people about her proposal for a nuclear freeze. While Caldicott spoke inspirationally but had a reputation for being a little careless on matters of detail, Forsberg combined an encyclopedic knowledge of weapons systems with a knack for proposing simple, readily understandable solutions to complex problems.[27]

Other important national leaders—Jane Gruenebaum and Carolyn Cottom of the Freeze, and Jesse Cocks, the founder of the American Peace Test—were also women. In the San Francisco Bay Area in the 1980s, most of the staff of the Nuclear Freeze Campaign were women; the director of

Alameda County Physicians for Social Responsibility was Joan Ali; the founder of Beyond War (most of whose members were women) was Emilia Rathbun; the founder of Tri-Valley CAREs was Marylia Kelley; and many of the leaders of the Livermore Action Group and the Ecumenical Peace Institute were women. There were also all-women peace groups, such as Women's Strike for Peace, Women's Action for Disarmament, and the Women's International League for Peace and Freedom. The volunteer rosters of local antinuclear groups were also packed with women.

But women gave the movement much more than their time and leadership. Much of the movement's stock of images, symbols, values, and metaphors was drawn from the domestic sphere of women and children, and the movement must be seen in part as an insurrectionary assertion of the culture of the domestic sphere against a masculine public culture of science and war.[28] Consider, for example, the nature of protests at the laboratory in the 1980s. At these protests the barbed-wire fence around the laboratory separated two worlds from one another. On one side a group of people lived the commitment that the appropriate way to deal with nuclear weapons was to give seminar talks and write bureaucratic memoranda about them, to model their characteristics on computers, to represent the weapons in terms of numbers and graphs and diagrams, and always to be dispassionate and analytical in discussing a predicament invariably constructed in terms of "policy options" and "mission operationalizations." On the other side people responded to the weapons by publicly singing and shouting and weeping and hugging one another while clutching balloons and posters of rainbows and children's handprints. Some people decorated the barbed-wire fence with brightly colored yarn, homemade "peace quilts," and their children's paintings of a world at peace. Grandmothers wearing photographs of their grandchildren around their necks were dragged from the road and handcuffed by police officers as their friends called out "We love you" and "Don't hurt her." Speakers at the microphone insisted that international relations are properly not about "deterrence" or "stability" or "alliances" but about "love" and "reaching out," or about creating a "family of nations." Men, women, and children stood holding banners and signs saying Love Your Mother (with a picture of the earth); Childcare Not Warfare; Nuclear War Is Bad for Children and Other Living Things; You Can't Hug Children with Nuclear Arms; Another Family for Peace; Another Grandma for Peace;

Pay Mothers, Not the Pentagon; Take the Toys Away from the Boys; and I Want to Grow Up. At one protest a young man, the son of a weapons scientist, stood with tears staining his cheeks as he held a sign that said, simply, Convert Dad. Meanwhile some protests were deliberately scheduled for Mother's Day, and many of the "affinity groups"[29] into which people were organized for protests bore names that symbolized the world of women: Ovary Action, Princesses Against Plutonium, Spiderwomyn, Kin of Ata,[30] Gaia,[31] and Moms Against Bombs.

In addition to this pool of images and symbols, the domestic sphere provided the position from which a formal intellectual critique of the arms race could be mounted. Building on two decades of intellectual and political momentum in the women's movement, antinuclear women (and, to some extent, men) developed feminist standpoints on the arms race that formally codified the "subjugated knowledges" of the domestic sphere. Three main positions in the feminist critique of the arms race emerged in the 1980s, although it is better to think of these three positions as ideal types than as watertight categories for classifying individuals. The three positions are androgynous, maternal, and separatist.[32]

According to the androgynous position, both militarism and contemporary gender roles are the intertwined products of a patriarchal culture that has been historically produced and can, through debate and struggle, be changed. Such a perspective was in tune with broader developments in middle-class America in the 1980s—a decade that saw substantial (if incomplete) renegotiation of traditional gender roles in the family and in the workplace—and it diffusely informed much of the antinuclear movement's sensibility: a large number of men as well as women accepted, in the abstract at least, the notion that gender roles can change and that traditional male thinking, with its competitiveness, "missile envy," and inattention to feelings of vulnerability and connectedness, is part of the nuclear problem. Thus Barbara Epstein (1985: 42) concluded in her study of LAG that "virtually everyone in LAG had been shaped" by the feminist movement and that "the kinds of assumptions about men's and women's abilities that went more or less unchallenged in the new left are at least considerably rarer in LAG." One woman who attended a meeting of Tri-Valley CAREs remarked to me that it was the first group she had seen where the women discussed facts and numbers with one another while the men talked about their fears that their children might not grow up.[33]

The maternal position mobilizes archetypal woman against archetypal man, accepting the roles of the traditional gender system but inverting the values attached to them. Here women are valorized as mothers who give birth, nurture life, and resolve conflicts within the family. This traditional construction of women's identity is then used as a point from which to criticize the uncaring masculine world of war and weaponry.[34] The most articulate exponent of this approach is Helen Caldicott, who has insistently used maternal thinking to interrogate the nuclear state. Take this example in which she attempts to establish a maternal vision of womanhood as the basis for peace activism:

> A typical woman is very much in touch with her feelings. . . . Women are nurturers. Their bodies are built anatomically and physiologically to nurture life. . . . Mothers or not, most women care deeply about the preservation of life. Women are also capable of capitulation and can move into conflict resolution if they make a conscious decision. It is almost always the woman who makes the initial move to seek marriage or partner guidance counseling if there are problems in a relationship. (1986: 236)

The separatist position, like the maternal, is based on an essentialist conception of woman, but its politics are different. This position is most commonly found in the lesbian-separatist wing of the direct action movement. It takes as its central issue male violence in all its manifestations, from rape to war. Here the root problem is construed as an inherently pathological masculinity, and the solution lies in the development of a separate community of women. Proponents of this perspective established the women-only peace camps that were such an important part of the antinuclear movement in the 1980s, though not all the women who joined these camps were separatists or espoused essentialist views of gender identity.[35]

In sum, in its symbolism, in its recruitment of large numbers of women and children, in its recruitment of many men interested in changing traditional gender roles, and in its development of self-consciously feminist critiques of the arms race, the antinuclear movement reflected the sea change in middle-class gender politics under way in the 1980s and represented a heterogeneous insurrection of the domestic sphere against the prevailing gender system that had stabilized American military institutions for many decades. For weapons scientists, the sense of a world turned upside down, of order unraveling, in the course of this mobilization is nicely encapsulated in a story told to me by one laboratory scientist's wife: after feeling uneasy about her husband's work for many years, she decided in the 1980s to attend a protest at the laboratory gates, where she was clearly visible to many of her husband's colleagues as they arrived for work. Inside the laboratory her husband was apprehensively watching the protest with his supervisor on closed-circuit television when the cameras showed his wife at the front of the crowd. His supervisor turned to him and asked, "Isn't that your wife? Can't you keep her under control?" In the 1980s, many women who opposed the arms race refused to be kept under control.

BODIES OF RESISTANCE

I argued in chapter 5 that laboratory culture involves dissociation from the vulnerability and subjectivity of the body and symbolic identification with the power of the machine. The antinuclear movement of the 1980s set about reconstructing the nuclear body. Here the doctors of Physicians for Social Responsibility and International Physicians for the Prevention of Nuclear War played a crucial role. By insisting that their expertise qualified them to speak on nuclear weapons policy, they helped shift the focus of the debate on nuclear weapons back to their area of expertise: the human body. Until the doctors intervened, the terms in which nuclear weapons had been discussed were constrained by the parameters of technostrategic discourse. As Carol Cohn (1987) has observed, the central referents of technostrategic discourse are not people but the weapons themselves: their detectability, their accuracies, their vulnerabilities, and the stability of their configurations. Under the influence of technostrategic discourse, politicians and experts discussing nuclear policy invariably talked about nuclear weapons in terms of their ability to deter or strike other weapons and their contribution to an overall pattern of stability or instability in the rivalry between the superpowers. In the early 1980s, by making the lethality of nuclear war their main issue and the "bombing run" their main pedagogical tactic, the physicians scattered human bodies among the missiles. They reminded people that nuclear weapons do not just take one another like pieces in a board game; they also kill people and hurt human bodies. And, in a deliberate attempt to make people squirm, they described the precise effects of nuclear explosions on the human body in great detail, often with the aid of photographs of Hiroshima and Nagasaki victims.

Then there was civil disobedience—another way of dramatizing the body and using the power of the body to contest the power of machines. The direct action movement developed its own vision of the human body as a symbolically potent instrument of resistance whose very vulnerability at the moment of confrontation and arrest could be mobilized, paradoxically, as a source of power to challenge the state and the world of machines.

Civil disobedience, like science, requires bodily discipline, but this discipline takes different forms than the bodily discipline practiced at the laboratory. Protestors often rehearse and train, mentally and physically, for their arrests by attending nonviolence training sessions. They prepare to have their wrists cuffed and their bodies confined. They role-play with one another the art of going limp and staying limp while being dragged or carried and the art of locking arms and legs while police try to tear them apart. Civil disobedience not infrequently involves bodily pain and fear: I have seen police use pain holds—pulling back fingers and jerking arms high behind people's backs—to try to persuade protestors to stand up when they are limp. I know two protestors whose wrists were broken this way. I have seen protestors who refuse to stand up get pulled by their hair or dragged through scrub in the desert. I interviewed one man, his face still bruised, who hiked several miles into the Nevada Test Site, then lay still while guards kicked and stamped on him. I interviewed a woman who used a cryptonite lock to chain her neck to a pole deep inside the Nevada Test Site, then refused to tell the guards where the key was hidden even as they took a saw to the lock on her neck. To keep the body limp in such circumstances, to resist the bodily urge to strike back at the police, to master the fear of pain felt in the speeding of the heart and the trembling of the hands—all of this requires discipline.

The practice of civil disobedience is crucial in the re-production of citizens as activists and in the production of commitment to the antinuclear movement's alternative regime of truth. It uses fear, pain, and ritualized transgression to produce an often transcendent moment in which activists experience themselves as a community of truth separate from other communities. People who commit civil disobedience talk about being changed forever by the experience, and some activists joke that the act of civil

disobedience can produce an altered state, a "rush," that can turn protestors into "CD junkies." The experience of civil disobedience is particularly powerful and transformative the first time. Here are two protestors—Jim, a minister, and Shirley, a doctor—remembering their first
such experience. Jim was arrested at the Nevada Test Site.

> You're challenging all your fears about going to jail and what that means:
> encountering the legal system, dealing with police. I had feelings of "I'm
> betraying my country, I'm a traitor, my parents aren't going to like it." And
> it was a moment in my life that I think was significant, in which I stopped
> sort of being a good boy and I started to tell the truth, the truth being that
> nuclear weapons testing is wrong. And I've known that for years. . . . The
> sense of knowing that what I was doing was right and challenging fears and
> being connected with a community and a group—it made the hair stand up
> on my arms. Yeah, as I walked over the cattle guard, I was terrified. I was
> frightened. I was crying. It was really scary, but there came a moment of
> liberation when I felt free for the first time: when they put the little plastic
> handcuffs on, when I had essentially entered another world. It was like, it
> really felt like I was walking through some sort of door that I could never
> return to.

Shirley was arrested at the laboratory.

> It was a wonderful feeling to feel those handcuffs go on. . . . Well, I'm not
> really into bondage. [Laughs] It was more the words: "You're under arrest."
> The handcuffs themselves were sort of boring, they kind of hurt a little. But
> it was that "You're under arrest." All right! Your law sucks and I'm under
> arrest! Hallelujah! That's just such a good feeling. . . . Oh, just the feeling
> of saying to national law that is wrong, saying "Fuck you!" is such a good,
> good feeling.

In the practice of civil disobedience an acute sense of the body's vulnerability is parlayed into a transitory but overwhelming experience of the
individual's or movement's power. The greater the involvement and suffering of the body in civil disobedience, the more empowering the experience can be. Tim is a protestor I met at Livermore who recounted for
me one of the most exciting moments of his life when he was one of about
eighty people who blocked the famous "white train" that carries nuclear
warheads around the country.

> About eighty of us were on the tracks in kind of a human clump, in the
> middle of the ties; and some were sitting on the rails and some were sitting
> right in the cradle of the tracks. So here comes the train, and it looks like

it's not going to stop! These big, huge bullies, I mean men, huge dudes, were sitting all over the train. There must have been forty of them or so all over that train. They must have known we were coming. So they started coming down on us, and they grab us like this [puts his hand around his throat] by the collar up round your neck and try to choke you, and they started tossing us off the tracks. And we were bouncing off of there like rubble [laughs], like a nuclear shakedown. So we bounce off and we choke, and it was like potato sacks being thrown off. And they were just huge guys, and they were just pulling us off and throwing us, like bouncing us, four feet. Bodies flying all over the place [laughs], you wouldn't believe it, bodies flying. They just kept doing that, and we'd run right back on the tracks. I got thrown too [chuckles]. We'd go right back on the tracks, and then they'd throw us off, then back on the tracks and they'd throw us off—kind of like a piston effect. . . . This lasted for a good twenty minutes, and then all of a sudden these human arms that were running a piston of a combustion engine were just starting to run out of gas, slow down, and we'd run back on the tracks and they'd be dragging us slower and slower, and finally their poor big—muscular—arms—just—stopped [his voice drags for effect]. [Laughs] They couldn't pull us off anymore, and that's when the train stopped. They just pooped out after all that work, and they sat there huffing and puffing, huffing and puffing [laughs]. We all just cheered and cheered: "We stopped this white train! We stopped this nuclear train!" And we were crying tears, and the women were running around taking pictures of the license numbers on the train.

Tim's description of that day vividly communicates the ecstatic feelings of empowerment civil disobedience can induce, and his use of mechanical metaphors to describe the guards who confronted him dramatizes the ultimate meaning of this confrontation for him—the triumph of a community of determined human bodies over the world of machines.

This is one more example, then, of ways in which the antinuclear movement was able to invert the culture of the nuclear state. Where Livermore scientists celebrated the human ability to control technology, activists mourned the dangers of technology out of control; where the laboratory deployed scientific experts in its defense, the antinuclear movement captured some of these experts for itself and added others such as psychotherapists, doctors, and lawyers; and where the laboratory relied on the compulsive privatization of nuclear politics, activists created a moment where people felt compelled to confess the bomb and make it a matter of public debate. This, finally, was one of the most subversive, and at the same time disciplining, achievements of the movement. The comfort of scientists in Livermore, and of their neighbors and family, had always in some sense been premised on a collective understanding that nuclear weapons work was—a little like sex in the Victorian Era—something that everyone knew about, something that everyone recognized as a necessary part of life, but something that was largely to be struggled with alone and was only to be discussed delicately in public. The antinuclear movement brought the bomb out of the closet and made it a matter of rude debate.

CHAPTER 9

Conclusion:
The End of an Era?

It was an incredible feeling the morning I opened the paper and saw the Berlin Wall coming down. I wept for joy. Yet all the things I've operated on in my whole professional life are coming to an end.

CAL WOOD, LIVERMORE WEAPONS DESIGNER

And now, without the Barbarians, what is to become of us? After all, those people were a kind of solution.

CONSTANTINE CAVAFY

I have sought in this book to interpret two opposed visions of America in the nuclear age. These opposed visions, which are ultimately different visions of modernity itself, clashed at a particular moment in the 1980s that was defined by the intersection of the Reagan-Bush military buildup, the rise of a mass antinuclear movement in the United States, Soviet attempts to end the cold war, and the daily lives of the weapons scientists and antinuclear activists on the local frontlines of the struggle over nuclear weapons. In this transitional historical moment the Livermore laboratory, which had traditionally enjoyed a secure position within the nuclear weapons complex and the national archipelago of scientific laboratories, found its legitimacy as an institution increasingly contested.

We can make a few crude sociological generalizations about the weapons scientists and antinuclear activists. Weapons scientists, for example, tend to be white men of rationalist temperament with degrees in science or engineering who, more often than not, are active churchgoers, usually in mainline denominations. Despite widespread media framing of the nuclear debates of the 1980s in terms of a left-right divide, weapons scientists are as likely to be liberal as conservative: many of them opposed U.S. intervention in Vietnam and Central America and have supported an array of liberal causes from the Sierra Club to women's rights. Antinuclear activists are also mainly white and are often active churchgoers, mostly in mainline denominations. They are, however, more likely to be female or feminist-identified men, are often students or employees in the "welfare and creative professions," and are almost uniformly liberal or more radically to the left.

These ensembles of demographic types were melded into communities within particular constellations of discourse and practice. In the 1980s almost no weapons scientists at Livermore shared the sense of impending nuclear catastrophe common among activists. Instead, Livermore scientists believed that nuclear weapons had a stabilizing effect on the cold war rivalry between the superpowers, deterring each side from attacking the vital interests of the other. The laboratory is organized ideologically around a central axiom, accepted by liberal and conservative weapons scientists alike, that nuclear weapons are weapons so terrible that their only function is to deter wars, not to fight them, and that it is therefore ethical to work on them. This line of moral reasoning eschews moral absolutes in favor of a pragmatic consequentialism—a moral stance that has generally been sustained by either the silence or active endorsement of local church ministers in Livermore despite the fact that, at the national level, most mainline Christian denominations turned against the arms race in the 1980s. The ideological force of the central axiom has been reinforced by an informal norm at the laboratory that the ethics of weapons work is more a matter for private reflection than public debate, and by a set of practices in regard to secrecy that can cultivate attitudes of compliance. These practices, starting with the investigation for security clearance that regulates admission to the laboratory for weapons scientists, encourage employees to internalize their own surveillance by the government while compartmentalizing the flow of information within the laboratory and partly segregating weapons scientists from their families and the sentimental values they embody. In addition, the discourse of weapons science makes it hard for scientists to identify with the vulnerability of the human body in the nuclear age because this discourse, eschewing references to pain and suffering, euphemistically figures damaged bodies as numbers or in the imagery of broken machinery, while encouraging a romantic identification with the fetishized power of high technology machines.

The weapons scientists' sense of mastery over nuclear weapons is reinforced by participation in nuclear tests. Through nuclear testing the elite cadre of weapons designers experiences as a lived reality the human ability to predict and control nuclear weapons that nuclear deterrence requires. I characterize nuclear testing as sharing some of the qualities of ritual because of its importance in alleviating weapons scientists' anxiety about the safety and predictability of nuclear weapons and because nuclear tests play a vital role in regulating status hierarchies among senior scientists at the laboratory.

The antinuclear movement of the 1980s created an alternative regime of truth within which nuclear weapons were engines of imminent genocide, the stability of nuclear deterrence was precariously fragile, and the weapons establishment was dangerously in denial about the risks of life on the edge of the nuclear precipice. This movement, unwittingly abetted by the first Reagan Administration's reintensification of the cold war, recruited new members and consolidated its claims on existing members by developing a cult of terror around nuclear weapons that used antinuclear films, books, brochures, and speeches as well as, in some parts of the movement, the practice of mass civil disobedience to inculcate an apocalyptic sense of fear and urgency. The antinuclear movement built authority for its counter-discourse by recruiting dissident arms control experts (such as Robert McNamara) and deploying such new kinds of expert speakers, in the context of the arms race, as psychologists and physicians. The psychologists and physicians shifted the focus of the debate away from the stability or instability of interlocking configurations of weapons to the mental health of nuclear decision-makers and the vulnerability of the human body. Meanwhile, drawing on the imagery, infrastructure, and intellectual capital of the women's movement, the antinuclear movement also attacked the rationalist masculinism of the nuclear state, portraying it as more masculine than rational.

Although these contending ideologies, nuclear and antinuclear, were diametrically opposed, it is important to remember that they were also both expressions of the political culture of the American middle class and thus subtly linked. Whereas Livermore scientists are members of the technocratic wing of the middle class, the antinuclear movement was largely peopled and led from the humanistic wing, which is less closely tied to business and military elites in American society and has a different vision of the good society. The nuclear debates of the 1980s, triggered by the escalation of the arms race and the Reagan Administration's reallocation of resources away from the Great Society programs, and enabled by a partial reconfiguration of the middle-class gender system, can be read as a struggle between these two wings of the middle class over the meaning of modernity in the years when the militarization of the superpower relationship was intensifying and the collapse of Fordist liberalism was becoming evident.

The analysis of this historical moment offered here departs from most recent writing on nuclear weapons issues in that it does not adopt a stance of what one might call "policy positivism." In fact it seeks to problematize such a stance. Policy positivism is the doctrine that there is a single best, or most "realistic," set of policies in regard to nuclear weapons and that it is the purpose of public debate and expert discourse on nuclear weapons, through the power of reason, to finally determine what those policies are. There are antinuclearist as well as nuclearist versions of policy positivism since most of the antinuclear activists described in this book, also invoking the rhetoric of rationality and realism, share with the weapons scientists they otherwise oppose the belief that reasonable people, unblinded by emotion or self-interest, will agree upon the best set of policies. Antinuclearists in the 1980s claimed it was irrational to continue the arms race while nuclearists insisted it was unrealistic not to. Policy positivism obscures what is hopefully by now quite obvious about the nuclear debates of the 1980s: that differently positioned communities with different sets of values may find diametrically opposed policies compellingly realistic.

Instead of asking which community was more rational or realistic, I have aimed here, in a more relativist vein, to uncover the cultural construction and legitimation of different rationalities and realisms in the nuclear age. Rather than trying to adjudicate which one is true, the position of the weapons scientists or the antinuclear activists, I have drawn on Michel Foucault's notion of "regimes of truth" and asked how "effects of truth are created within discourses which in themselves are neither true nor false" (Foucault 1980b: 60). Rather than ask whose position is more "realistic," the weapons scientists' or the activists', I have asked how, in Roland Barthes's (1972) striking phrase, "the effect of the real" is created within separate ideological worlds.

Such an approach involves rethinking the role of the expert. The arms control specialists, political scientists, and political psychologists in universities and think tanks who have played such an important role in recent debates over nuclear policy sometimes speak as if they had knowledge while other people have ideology—as if they could speak from outside politics, looking into political struggles with what Donna Haraway (1991: 188) calls "a conquering gaze from nowhere." I have tried to suggest that, far from standing outside politics, experts are inextricably enmeshed within it, their knowlege and authority being vital in the construction and maintenance of regimes of truth. Thus the (neo)realists played an important role in legitimating institutions such as the Livermore laboratory by arguing that the arms race was the inevitable, and potentially stabilizing, product of an anarchic international system dominated by the rivalry of two superpowers, while the antinuclear psychologists, with a success that reflected the increasing diffusion and authority of psychological concepts in American popular culture in the 1980s, partly undermined the legitimacy of institutions such as Livermore by portraying the arms race as a dangerous compulsion enabled by collective psychological dysfunction.

As well as offering a constructivist alternative to the policy positivism that has informed much writing on both sides of the nuclear debate, this book has also, allying anthropology with recent neoliberal critiques in international relations theory, broken with the radical separation of the domestic and international levels of analysis that has been a defining feature of dominant thinking in international security studies, especially (neo)realism. (Neo)realists often speak as if the international system were a space of pure power politics inhabited by actors maximizing interests and responding to structural imperatives originating entirely within that space or, insofar as domestic politics does impinge on the international arena, responding to bureaucratic rivalries within the state apparatus. Throughout this book I have sought to make the international and domestic arenas much more porous to each other. Refracting the global processes of the cold war through an ethnographic lens, I have sought to understand the contestation of the arms race that erupted in multiple sites around the globe in the 1980s by means of a fine-grained study of one key site in the American nuclear weapons complex. I have shown, tracing the downward pressures on domestic life from the international sphere, how for people in this book the cold war reshaped careers, marriages, church life, even their dream lives and the decision whether to have children. But I have also traced the upward pressures on the international system from below, exploring the interaction of local capillary changes with the arterial processes of international politics. Here, discussing the emergence of grassroots opposition to the laboratory, I showed that the stable continuity of the arms race and of a key site in the U.S. nuclear weapons complex was affected by the rise of new knowledge systems such as feminism and popular psychotherapy, by church politics, by the shifting dynamics of relations within the middle class and within the family, and even by changes in the local real estate market. These developments affected the local environment within which the Livermore laboratory operated, and also the meanings people attached to its work.

If this book has attempted to open a space for a cultural turn in security studies and international relations, it has also sought to model some new directions for American anthropology, particularly the anthropology of science that is currently in the process of crystallizing. At a moment when there is considerable talk of "repatriated anthropology" and "anthropology as cultural critique," I have attempted to demonstrate the potential of a repatriated anthropology that, instead of focusing on the marginal and powerless populations that have traditionally magnetized the anthropological gaze, adapts traditional techniques of participant observation to the study of key sites of power in contemporary society—an anthropology that "studies up" in Laura Nader's (1974) celebrated phrase. But, instead of simply studying the weapons scientists at Livermore, I have analyzed them in the context of their relationship with local institutions and their conflict with an array of local and national oppositional movements. This wide-angled view is a way of adapting for a new context the tradition of holistic analysis in anthropology, while the juxtaposition of opposed cultural communities, each throwing the assumptions of the other into relief, is a way of achieving the denaturalizing effect that Marcus and Fischer (1986) identify as the essence of anthropology as cultural critique.

Rather than breaking with traditional anthropological approaches, this study extends and reworks them in the context of a critical repatriated anthropology. Thus, for example, the discussion of nuclear testing in this book draws on an old body of theory about ritual in anthropology (associated with Malinowski, Evans-Pritchard, Van Gennep, and Turner), to suggest that nuclear tests, although scientific experiments, can also be thought of as sharing some of the features of ritual. In a context where the rituals that originally inspired such anthropological theories have either died out, hybridized into new forms, or decayed into folkloric performances for the global tourist, such an analysis remakes the relevance of an older, but deeply insightful, body of anthropoligical theory by applying it to new, more contemporary, contexts while denaturalizing and reframing a particularly important form of scientific experimentation in our society.

Anthropologists have a long tradition of studying knowledge production in "traditional" societies, but have only recently begun to study the culture of science in the United States. The new literature in the anthropology of science is strongly influenced by, and is merging into, a more established literature in the sociology of science. The dominant tradition in the sociology of science has been constructivist, but this constructivism has focused on the ways in which scientific knowledge itself is constructed in agonistic struggles between rival networks of scientists. Once startlingly fresh, this approach is now in danger of becoming mechanical as small platoons of scholars fan out across the territory of science to hunt down the social construction of everything from the virus to the gravity wave. Although my perspective here has also been constructivist, it has been more concerned with the laboratory as a node of ideological production and conflict than with the microsociology of laboratory life. Thus I have focused on the ways in which the meaning of nuclear weapons technology is constructed by different communities as the technology is incorporated into society, and the ways in which nuclear deterrence is made real and unreal in the nervous system of global society, not on the social construction of the physics underlying weapons design or of the engineering of the weapons themselves. Indeed, it would seem to me to be almost grotesquely irrelevant and scholastic to argue that the scientific principles of weapons design are social constructions, no matter how true this may be in some formal academic sense, when the weapons' ability to wipe out entire nations has already been experimentally demonstrated on two cities and rehearsed hundreds of times over on Pacific islands and in desert wastelands. So, rather than dissect social and epistemic microprocesses within the laboratory in the tradition of classic laboratory studies in science and technology studies, I have focused here, as does much other work in the emergent anthropology of science, on the ways in which scientists remake society as they go about their scientific work, on the identities and ideologies of the scientists who now exercize such power in our society, and on the processes by which their projects may be appropriated, contested, and undermined by other social groups. In an era when our understanding of what it means to be human is increasingly being transformed by the men and women in white lab coats who splice genes and split atoms, in an era when the practice of daily life is increasingly mediated by such technologies as the internet, Prozac, and television, we need more anthropologists to explore the complex articulations and disjunctures between science and society.

THE END OF AN ERA?

Since I left the field, the terms of the confrontations explored in this book have been reconfigured by historical developments whose gathering force was already discernible when I was doing research. By the end of the 1980s, an era was drawing to a close. Ronald Reagan was gone, soon to be followed by George Bush. They took with them the forty-year-old cold war they had at first prosecuted so vigorously, only to negotiate its termination. Gone also, except for a few determined remnants, was the massive antinuclear movement Reagan and Bush unintentionally did so much to produce.

Since I began my fieldwork in 1987, the United States and the Soviet Union have signed the INF Treaty, banning all intermediate nuclear weapons. They have signed two START treaties, implementing deep cuts in their remaining nuclear arsenals, and have agreed not to target their weapons against each other. And, following a series of unilateral moratoria on nuclear testing by the Soviet Union and the closure of the Soviet Union's principal test site,[1] the United States has frozen its own nuclear testing program and announced its intention to sign a comprehensive test ban treaty. Now the Soviet Union no longer exists, having disintegrated in the wake of glasnost and perestroika into its constituent states, all of which now seem more interested in capturing Western economic aid than in capturing territory from the Western alliance. The Warsaw Pact has likewise fallen apart, and many of its former members have applied to join NATO. Meanwhile the U.S. government has also closed down a number of facilities in its nuclear weapons complex, including the Nevada Test Site, saying they are either no longer needed or are unsafe to operate.[2]

By the 1990s, then, the Livermore laboratory, already weakened by a decade of scandals and protests, was deprived of the international struggle between the superpowers that had given it its defining purpose for almost four decades and was situated in the midst of a rapidly shrinking nuclear weapons complex. This, combined with a deepening federal budget crisis in the United States, made the laboratory's managers understandably nervous about the future. In 1989, the U.S. government gutted Livermore's free electron laser program, stripping $37 million from the laboratory's budget, and began a series of sharp cuts in its X-ray laser program as well. In 1990 the lab was forced to close down R Program, its X-ray laser design division. In 1991, George Bush canceled the SRAM II—the last remaining weapons system for which the laboratory had been commissioned to design and develop a nuclear warhead.[3] Then, in 1992, as the laboratory's planned nuclear tests were put on indefinite hold and its weapons budget sank back to the levels of the Carter administration, Rep. George Brown, chair of the House Science Committee, floated a much-publicized suggestion that all nuclear weapons work should be consolidated at Los Alamos, the laboratory that designed three-fourths of the weapons remaining in the post–cold war nuclear stockpile. In 1995 this suggestion was reaffirmed by the DOE's own blue-ribbon panel on the future of the national laboratories (Galvin 1995).

It is too early to write the laboratory's obituary, however. Livermore has tremendous bureaucratic and ideological resources at its disposal with which to defend itself, and, even if the cold war is definitely over, it may prove possible to adapt to a new situation the culture and ideology that anchored the laboratory for forty years. Thus, at the time of writing, even as some scientists and managers at the laboratory talk about emphasizing new missions such as industrial technology research and environmental cleanup, others talk about maintaining Livermore's primary focus on nuclear weapons work—even under a test ban treaty. The weaponeers who used to thrive on designing new weapons in the rivalry with the Soviets are now emphasizing the need to maintain a substantial cadre of weapons scientists in order to deal with threats from emergent nuclear nations and terrorist groups in the Third World, in case a new cold war develops, or in case safety and reliability problems appear in America's remaining nuclear arsenal. They argue that in the absence of nuclear testing, the laboratory should be given new resources for weapons work—an improved supercomputer capability and a more powerful laser fusion facility to mimic some aspects of nuclear testing, for example.[4] They rebut arguments that, in an era of downsizing, America now needs only one nuclear weapons laboratory by saying that weapons scientists at Los Alamos need peer review from colleagues at Livermore.

A FORK IN THE ROAD

America's weapons scientists now stand at a fork in the road. This is particularly so since maybe a third of them are nearing retirement age, and the rest of the community is wondering not only whether they will be able to keep practicing their craft but also whether their dwindling numbers will be replenished.

At stake here is not just the future of this particular esoteric community but also the future shape of American society and of the international system it partly dominates. We cannot ask about the future of nuclear weapons scientists without also calling into question the meaning of America—what it will stand for and how it will seek to project its authority. We cannot ask about the future of nuclear weapons scientists without also calling into question the meaning of modernity—what its science will be used for and whether its dreams of security and power will continue to be based on technocratic militarism. And we cannot ask about the future of nuclear weapons scientists without also calling into question the nature of humanity itself—whether it is capable of finding another way to organize its international affairs than around acts and symbols of mass destruction.

In the post–cold war debate about the future of the weapons laboratories, there have been three broad positions. The first, staked out by the left wing of the antinuclear movement, is that the United States should be working toward the prompt and complete abolition of nuclear weapons by all nations (Cabasso and Burroughs 1995a). In April 1995 a coalition of 198 NGOs, saying that "a world free of nuclear weapons is a shared aspiration of humanity," issued this statement:

> A nuclear weapons-free world must be achieved carefully and in a step-by-step manner. We are convinced of its technological feasibility. Lack of political will, especially on the part of the nuclear weapons states, is the only true barrier. As chemical and biological weapons were prohibited, so must nuclear weapons be prohibited. (NGO Abolition Caucus 1995: 1)

According to this vision, the weapons laboratories would verify and supervise the dismantling of existing nuclear weapons, then convert to other missions. Needless to say, this scenario does not enjoy much support either at Livermore or within the defense bureaucracy of the U.S. government.

The second position, espoused by top managers of the weapons laboratories and within the defense bureaucracy, is that the United States should maintain a substantial community of weapons scientists who would continue to do weapons work but within a virtual world of simulations. In the words of Dick Fortner, former director of the laboratory's nuclear testing program,

> One of the things we are looking at is the development of new facilities that will not involve nuclear testing, but will give us some ability to continue our job. . . . The way I look at it, stopping nuclear testing is sort of like amputating one of our legs. What we need is a prosthesis that allows us to keep hobbling along. (Quoted in Saltonstall 1992)

Thus, rather than practicing weapons science by building actual weapons and testing them underground at the Nevada Test Site, Livermore and Los Alamos scientists are now planning to use supercomputer programs, giant lasers, pulsed power, and high-explosive experiments to simulate and integrate different aspects of nuclear tests.[5] Laboratory managers argue that such technologies are important both to maintain an expert community of weapons scientists as a hedge against future national security emergencies and to assure the continued safety and reliability of the remaining nuclear stockpile. Critics have argued that, with such technologies at their disposal, weapons scientists will continue to work on new weapons in a sort of virtual arms race (Cabasso and Burroughs 1995b). Furthermore, some factions of the defense bureaucracy have lobbied for a nuclear test ban treaty that would permit very low-yield nuclear tests of one hundred to five hundred tons. Such tests would permit some weapons design work to continue with final experimental validation of new designs. This would be particularly useful in the development of a "micronuke" or "mininuke," a new weapon advocated by some defense experts for use against an enemy leader's underground bunker (Ramos 1991).

The third position is an intermediate one that has been proposed by the laboratory's own Ray Kidder. Kidder has suggested that the community of weapons scientists could shrink to a small group who would play a minimal custodial role as guardians of the arsenal, checking old weapons for signs of deterioration and supervising the remanufacture of identical copies when necessary. Where laboratory managers anticipate a community of weapons scientists actively improving its understanding of weapons physics even in the absence of underground tests to validate new designs, Kidder's envisaged residual community would not engage in extensive nonnuclear experiments aimed at improving their understanding of the physics underlying nuclear weapons design or at refining the supercomputer codes used by weapons scientists to aid in the design of new weapons (Medalia 1994: 52–56). Livermore's veteran warhead designer, Tom Thomson, articulated this sort of vision of the future:

> The good old days of lots of money and big missile projects all around are over. . . . [Nuclear weapons] will eventually wind up stashed in a bunker somewhere. There will be a few of us old bomb designers hanging around, but mostly we'll be looking at proliferation issues, safety and security issues—all the fancy locks and switches that keep these things safe. That's the way this business is going to wind up. We're going to have a bomb designers' reserve. We're going to come in once a month, in case we're ever needed. (Quoted in Stober 1991)

Such an evolution in the work of the weapons scientists might occur in tandem with a successful conversion of the Livermore laboratory to primarily nonmilitary purposes or as part of a painful attrition of the laboratory's resource base. It could also take place within the current framework of two competing moieties of weapons scientists at Livermore and Los Alamos, or in the context of the consolidation of all weapons work at Los Alamos.

We stand at a fork in the road separating contending visions of the future. The antinuclear movement has sought to persuade us that nations are capable of negotiating their differences and living together in peace and that American science should be largely demilitarized. They envision a different kind of modernity than that which now reigns, believing with the poet Denise Levertov (1988) that

> A line of peace might appear
> If we restructured the sentence our lives are making
> Revoked its reaffirmation of profit and power.

The cold warriors had, and still do have, a different vision of the possibilities of this world. It has been starkly articulated by Robert Budwine, a Livermore weapons designer, in an op-ed piece entitled "Weapons Research Must Continue" that was published in Livermore's *Tri-Valley Herald* in 1990. Citing Iraq's invasion of Kuwait in 1990, he asks, "What more do we need to bring us back to reality?" He quotes General Charles de Gaulle:

> Hope though we may, what reason have we for thinking that passion and self-interest, the root cause of armed conflict in men and nations, will cease to operate; that anyone will willingly surrender what he has or not try to get what he wants; in short that human nature will ever become something other than it is? . . . In whatever direction the world may move, it will never be able to do without the final arbitrament of arms.

However, he follows up this apparently pessimistic evaluation of a universal human fallenness with these words:

> The United States, for all our manifest faults, is without a doubt the best hope for a future world of peace and prosperity. . . . Weapons research and development simply must continue at a determined and intensive level for our nation to have the opportunity to lead humankind toward some future utopian world order.

Budwine's article is at once utopian and despairing about human nature, and it mixes a faith in the redemptive power of technology with an American sense of unique mission. This militarist utopianism is the laboratory's vision of the future whose own future now hangs in the balance.

Postscript

When I give talks on my research I am often asked how, as a former antinuclear activist, my own views on nuclear weapons have been changed by my extended stay among the weapons scientists. This is the question I have come to dread, and during my fieldwork, I often found myself trying to bracket the question in my own mind as my research took me backward and forward across the border separating nuclear weapons scientists from antinuclear activists—a recurrent border crossing that punctuated a personal voyage deeper into uncertainty and double vision. Still, it is a question that deserves a serious answer.

When I was an antinuclear activist, it seemed incontrovertible to me that if the arms race continued we would destroy ourselves. The new weapons of the 1980s and the belligerent rhetoric of leaders on both sides of the cold war persuaded me that we were in grave danger, and I had great difficulty understanding why many other people did not share my sense of living on the edge of a precipice. There were times when I felt the imminence of this destruction so keenly that I found my day-to-day life interrupted by nightmares or waking visions of holocaust. It is ironic—though, given the analysis in chapter 8, quite understandable—that I felt most anxious about the arms race in those years when, as an antinuclear activist, I was doing the most to stop it.

During my sojourn among the weapons scientists my unconscious life was restructured in ways that reflected my acculturation to the world of the laboratory. Although I now lived less than two miles away from a nuclear weapons laboratory, with all the risks one might expect that to entail, and although I spent most of my days focused on nuclear weapons issues, I lost my anxiety about the weapons and progressively absorbed the sense of ease I found among the scientists with whom I now spent most of my time. The apocalyptic rhetoric of antinuclear activists came to seem increasingly quaint and even tiresome. This is not to say that I decided antinuclear activists were wrong after all. It is to say that I had been socially (and hence emotionally as well) repositioned.

My new vantage point afforded fresh perspectives on old questions. Where I had formerly been preoccupied with contradictions in the weapons scientists' ideology, I now found myself increasingly struck by contradictions and puzzles in the activists' program. If I started my fieldwork puzzled that weapons scientists could believe that the more rigorous the plans we make to use nuclear weapons, the less likely it is they will be used, the dialogic nature of my fieldwork confronted me with other questions too: How could activists who were so skeptical about the safety of one kind of technology, nuclear weapons technology, then put so much faith in the technology needed to verify arms control measures? And why had activists seized on a ban on nuclear warhead tests as the single most important arms control measure when it was breakthroughs in missile guidance technology, not nuclear warhead design, that had made the new weapons of the 1980s so threatening? Could it be that, blinded by the symbolism of nuclear tests, the activists had become as obsessed with ending these tests as the scientists were with continuing them, despite their relative unimportance in the development of new weaponry?

While living in New Mexico as I rewrote this book, two events made me realize how much I had been changed by my fieldwork. First, when a friend came to visit and we were driving by Los Alamos National Laboratory, I suggested we eat lunch at the laboratory's cafeteria, which has tolerable food and a very fine view of the mountains of northern New Mexico. Nuclear weapons scientists had long since ceased to seem strange to me, and I felt as much at ease there as in any university cafeteria. I was well into my burrito when I realized that my friend was barely eating and was, in fact, looking faintly nauseated. She felt deeply troubled by the pervasive air of normality in a place dedicated to the design of weapons of mass destruction. Unable not to think of Auschwitz, she found it difficult just to be there. I remembered that, long ago, this was how I too had felt when I first ate lunch at the Livermore laboratory cafeteria, looking around with disbelief at the people who designed weapons that could kill millions as they chattered over lunch about their children and their church groups. But somehow, long ago, I had lost this sense of unreality; nuclear weapons laboratories had become banal, everyday places for me.

The second shock came when I decided to, intermittently at least, attend the meetings of the local peace group in Santa Fe. I attended not so much for ethnographic purposes as to see what it would feel like to return to my former community. It felt strange. The world of antinuclear activists, which had once felt so natural, now seemed profoundly cultural. I felt like a lapsed Catholic at mass: everything was familiar, but I was, in T. S. Eliot's words, "no longer at ease in the old dispensation." I found myself feeling simultaneously a wistful sense of belonging and a perverse sense of alienation and distance. This became dramatically apparent to me one week when the New Mexico activists announced a march of mourning to protest yet another nuclear test at the Nevada Test Site. The announcement that another nuclear test had taken place stirred contradictory reflexes in me. On the one hand, I felt the same indignation I would have felt ten years earlier; on the other, I was curious as to whether it was a friend from Livermore who had designed the device, and I found myself hoping the test had gone well for them. I no longer knew whether to celebrate or mourn. Nuclear tests seemed to me, as before, a sad misuse of scarce resources and scientific talent, but I also knew that they could be ways of improving the safety of a technology that will not just go away, and I had come to see nuclear tests not just as dark rehearsals for extinction but also as powerful rituals celebrating human command over the secrets of life and death. When I tried to imagine attending the protest against the test, I now saw it, in part at least, in personal terms: I would perhaps be protesting the work of someone I knew, even someone I had come to like. The political had become personal for me in a most ironic way.

I came to Livermore in search of "the truth" about nuclear weapons but left with two truths, one for each of the communities I had come to know through the strange practice we anthropologists call fieldwork. Although my earlier sense of terror about nuclear weapons has dissipated, I still believe that, based on probability theory if nothing else, human beings and nuclear weapons cannot coexist indefinitely without calamity and that the cold war might easily, more easily than weapons scientists like to acknowledge, have ended in the incineration of Western civilization rather than the liberation of the Eastern bloc. I also believe that the billions of dollars spent every year on the military would create a more immediate sense of security and well-being in the daily lives of millions of Americans if they were spent on schools, hospitals, homeless shelters, mass transit, and renewable energy—and I would prefer to live in a society that cared more about the daily well-being of its citizens and less about what we call national security. However, I have also come to accept the plausibility of the weapons scientists' view that nuclear deterrence played a key role in averting the genocidal bloodshed of a third world war and that if a world full of nuclear weapons is a dangerous place, so in a different way is a world without the terrible discipline enforced by nuclear weapons. So let us say that both the weapons scientists and the antinuclear activists were in some sense right, each side holding tenaciously to their corner of a larger truth. But now that the cold war is over, we have a new opportunity to rethink our relationship with nuclear weapons and our use of science unencumbered by the ossified animosities of cold war domestic politics. I hope this book will make a modest contribution to such an enterprise.

Comments on the Text

In 1992, while I was writing this book, I asked a number of the people who figure in it to respond to the text. Several agreed to do so, and their responses follow. The titles and affiliations listed for the respondents may not be current.

DAVID S. P. DEARBORN

Weapons Designer, Lawrence Livermore National Laboratory

First of all, if we won the cold war, where is my parade? I am not greedy; Caldicott can march too. Frightening people was the idea behind deterrence, and her dramatic but inaccurate fantasies worked better than a Bram Stoker novel in a kindergarten. If we merely wished to mutilate bodies and burn the flesh from helpless children, conventional weapons and napalm work fine, and with the reduction in nuclear forces around the world, we should have more opportunities to exercise those options. But enough pleasantries. Hugh has offered me an opportunity to vent my devalued emotions over his study, and his readers a chance to look directly at the face of the Gorgon.

This attempt to define and describe weapons designers provided me with a mirror that few people outside of New Guinea will ever have, and I will never again think of the quantum mechanics term "coupling" in the same way. Reading the words "ritual" and "shaman" applied to people engaged in modern physics research seemed a bit odd, but no more derogatory than the terms my physics colleagues (at universities) apply to members of the social sciences.

Hugh recognized weapons designers as individuals with a broad range of interests and motivations, avoiding the simplistic stereotypes that show the limitations of the "researcher." Among the characteristics identified to unify and distinguish this group was training against trusting senses or emotions. If physicists devalue emotions, they are certainly not so dehumanized as to ignore them, and even in the weapons community, very few physicists are known to eat their own children. A failure to temper emotion with quantitative assessment is perhaps the greatest danger that exists to world peace.

In the absence of quantitative assessment, sincere people are manipulated for political motives. Failing to obtain a national consensus banning nuclear weapons, antinuclear groups took on environmental colors and forced a "cleanup" of the groundwater at the lab estimated to cost $30 billion per cancer prevented. A legitimate concern over carcinogenic materials in the environment would be better and less expensively served by a campaign to reduce the consumption of fried hamburgers.

Having seen the end of the cold war, and watched Pete Stark (not the lab) get out of town, I have to wonder what will happen next. The direct threat to the United States has been greatly reduced, resulting in a decrease in strategic nuclear forces. Still, defense continues to be a legitimate issue, with questions to be studied. First among these will be how to maintain the remaining weapons systems in the absence of testing. Even more exciting is the potential research on the border areas of nuclear weapons. As always, we cannot permit a mine shaft gap.

ALEX FORMAN

Activist, Nuclear Weapons Freeze Campaign

As a co-founder of the Nuclear Weapons Freeze Campaign in northern California, I saw that movement grow from four people sitting around an old wooden table in San Francisco in April 1981 to a massive grassroots campaign that was able to influence the debate on nuclear weapons on the national and international level. Hugh Gusterson's book captures the spirit of rage that drove much of the antinuclear movement. His moving account of Karen Hogan, standing up at a meeting about a planned radioactive and toxic waste incinerator and shouting, "Have you ever seen anyone die of cancer?" exemplifies that righteous anger precisely and with the necessary passion.

What is not clear from Hugh's account is the depth of despair and anger that drove so many people like Karen, Hugh, and myself to alter the course of our lives and join the antinuclear movement. Looking back from this post–cold war era, it is difficult to understand that millions of people believed that unless enough of us made halting the arms race our top priority, the world would soon be destroyed in a nuclear war. We were driven to this frightening conclusion by the statements of officials in the first Reagan administration. They spoke of "winning a nuclear war," "fighting a limited nuclear war," and of course "surviving one if only there are enough shovels to go around." They advocated no negotiations on nuclear weapons for at least ten years to allow the United States time to "catch up with the Russians." Whenever these statements appeared in the media, our office would be flooded with phone calls, contributions, and new volunteers. The administration's extremist rhetoric of fighting a nuclear war literally called forth a "peace army" of women and men to place their bodies on the line and demand that this madness stop. For the first time in history a social movement developed whose sole mission was preserving the very existence of life on earth.

Caught between the militant antinuclear movement and the escalating rhetoric of the early Reagan years were many scientists at the Livermore laboratory. As one who often debated with these scientists, I can verify Hugh's findings on the diversity within that group. However, whether my debate opponent was a fundamentalist Christian, who accepted nuclear Armageddon, or a liberal secularist, who defended nuclear deterrence as a rational way to maintain peace, these men consistently refused to challenge the basic assumptions of the Reagan administration. Their commitment to perpetuating their jobs seemed to overshadow any willingness to question the horror of an endless arms race. I encountered no one with the humanistic sensitivity of an Oppenheimer or a Szilard in those publicly representing Livermore.

Our modest proposal for a verifiable, bilateral halt to the nuclear arms race was viewed more as a direct threat to the power of these scientists than as a reasonable plan to end the arms race. Hugh's insight on the socialization process of the nuclear laboratories helps to explain much of the hostility we encountered in those years. It was the clash of alternative truths that made honest communications so difficult between some of the scientists and members of the antinuclear movement. Yet throughout this period there were always leading nuclear scientists—not usually affiliated with Livermore—who stood with us against the extremists of the early Reagan years.

By 1983, in the face of massive worldwide protests, the Reagan rhetoric changed and negotiations were begun. Later, thanks largely to the wisdom of Gorbachev, new treaties succeeded in slowing the arms race and leading us to the possibility of an era of nuclear disarmament. Nonetheless, even in 1992 the nuclear warriors at Livermore and in the Bush administration still resisted the call for an end to nuclear testing.

It is unlikely that either negotiations or new arms reduction treaties would have occurred without the pressure of the antinuclear protests. Hugh's book provides a rich blend of information and insight to help us understand the motivations of both sides during that crucial time. His enlightening narrative helps to preserve the heroic legacy of those who continue to struggle to ensure that the rhetoric of the nuclear war planners never becomes the reality of a nuclear holocaust.

RAY E. KIDDER

Weapons Scientist, Lawrence Livermore National Laboratory

Professor Gusterson has referred to my intervention in the weapons reliability debate and the challenge it represented to the power/knowledge system of the Laboratory's weapons community. I believe it might interest the reader to know something of the background and motivation of that intervention.

My first intervention in a nuclear weapons controversy in which I publicly took a position contrary to that of the Laboratory and the Department of Energy occurred in 1979. The Government sought a temporary restraining order, to be followed by a permanent injunction, to prevent publication of an article by Howard Morland in the *Progressive* magazine[1] that, it claimed, threatened national security by disclosing

1. A. DeVolpi, G. E. Marsh, T. A. Postol, G. S. Stanford, *Born Secret: The H-Bomb, the Progressive Case, and National Security* (New York: Pergamon Press, 1981).

secrets of the H-bomb. I concluded that it did not. The article contained errors that were more likely to mislead than aid a potential H-bomb builder, and the information alleged to be secret could all be found in the open literature. I filed both classified and unclassified affidavits pointing this out with specific examples. Affidavits were filed by many distinguished people in opposition to or in support of the Government's position, the latter group including the Secretaries of Defense, Energy, and State. The Government ultimately abandoned its case and the offending article was published in its entirety.

In the *Progressive* case, secret technical information was needed in order to decide the issue. Unless one knew the secrets of how an H-bomb worked, one would not know whether Morland had got them right. Unless one knew what had already been published about H-bombs and H-bomb physics, one would not know whether Morland's article contained any information that could be considered secret. Virtually all those filing affidavits on either side of the issue lacked sufficient knowledge of one or both of these relevant areas of information to make an informed judgment. As it happened, I had knowledge of both, although secrecy prevented me from openly identifying those publications that had preceded Morland in "letting the cat out of the bag."

My participation in the *Progressive* case brought me to the attention of the public as a nuclear weapons physicist with long experience (now 36 years) at the Lawrence Livermore National Laboratory who was not afraid to provide, within the limits of classification, factual information about nuclear weapons not necessarily supportive of official positions taken by the Laboratory or the DOE. As a result, I began to be consulted by members of the Congress on matters concerning nuclear weapons where they felt they were not being told the whole story, and in March of 1987 I received a letter endorsed by six members of Congress, including the Chairman of the House Armed Services Committee, asking me to undertake an independent evaluation of the question of nuclear weapons reliability referred to by Professor Gusterson.

More recently I was asked by several members of Congress to carry out an independent evaluation of the safety of the nuclear weapons stockpile and its relation to a possible test ban. In the letter to the Laboratory requesting my services I was pleased to learn that "Dr. Kidder has earned a reputation for incisive empirical analysis of these issues that is free of the ideological spin imparted by other participants in the test ban debate."

I'm doing my best to live up to this "spin-free" reputation.

ELIZABETH SELLE JONES
Minister, Unitarian Universalist Church, Livermore

On page 358, Gusterson states, "The laboratory has for forty years been a part of, and has helped to reproduce, a nuclear regime of truth whose power to compel has been sustained not only by its own plausibility but also by the resources of the state, the sanctifying halo of expert science, *and the endorsement—or at least compliant inattention—of the church.*"* It is the line that I have italicized on which I focus.

As background to my statement the reader needs to know that at a General Assembly several years ago, our denomination passed a resolution condemning the development and the use of nuclear weapons and recommended that such research and use cease.

Before I was called to this church in Livermore, I made it clear to everyone associated with the church that I was opposed to the development and/or use of nuclear weapons as well as nuclear power. Not surprisingly, this statement was met with the same discounting responses as Gusterson reports. In spite of my position, I was unanimously called to be their minister.

In a congregation such as ours in which ten years ago nearly 75 percent of the member families were associated with the laboratories, and even now almost 50 percent have that association, the question of how to deal with the ethics and morality of nuclear weapons is a complicated one. People who work at the laboratories and their families are valued members, leaders, and in some cases founders of this church.

Starting early in my ministry in Livermore I tried many processes, simplistic and sophisticated, to get conversations started about the nuclear weapons issue. For example, we engaged in an exercise to compare the stated values of those members who supported, even engaged in the research on nuclear weapons, and those who opposed them. The lists were almost identical, although we neglected to ask each group to list their

*The quoted sentence is from the Ph.D. dissertation on which this book is based.

values by priority. This might have been informative. I invited a colleague to share my pulpit. We had guest speakers, other ministers, and public forums, but none of these generated the dialogue that might have helped us understand each other's points of view. One Lent we had a foot-washing ceremony for the peace walkers, at their request, but many restrictions were put on this gathering by the board.

The issue of nuclear weapons is both ethical and moral in nature, and the church is the place for examining these dilemmas. However, these divided church communities may not be the place for this highly charged conversation to take place, for there are other considerations.

A church is a covenantal community. It *should* be a safe place in which people are free to express their beliefs and opinions without fear of rejection. A church *should* be a community in which to explore the meaning of life and its sacredness, but real community cannot happen when some people are condemned for their beliefs or where they work. And there are limits to what the church community can and should condone with their silence in an effort to be a religious home. However, for a church community to publicly condemn *or* support the legal activities of some of its own members seems to me to break the trust and damage the covenant within that very institution.

For a church to find the appropriate response to divisive and deeply controversial issues such as the building and use of nuclear weapons is just one of the conflicts between the pastoral role (caring for) and the prophetic role (calling to account) of the church's ministry. Ministers who lean toward the prophetic often lose their congregations and congregations lose their members for being too radical; those who lean toward the pastoral can be seen as weak, self-focused, or *compliant.* Such is the conflict in our souls and tension in our lives within our congregation in Livermore.

ROGER W. MINICH
Weapons Designer, Lawrence Livermore National Laboratory

I am a physicist at LLNL and for eleven years have been engaged in nuclear weapons research. I am also a Christian. As a Christian, I am particularly drawn to the moral issues raised throughout Dr. Gusterson's book. All such debates lose their meaning for a Christian outside the context of God and His intended purpose for mankind. This purpose is not hidden from man, but is revealed in His Law established prior to the foundation of the cosmos. This is the starting point for my response to Dr. Gusterson's book.

I was not a Christian when I arrived at the laboratory. It is not possible to become a Christian by any willful act of man. I did not one day declare myself to be a Christian. It is an act of creation by a sovereign God. Christians are born of the Spirit of God according to His good pleasure. As a Christian I have an absolute reference frame—the Word of God. It is the immutable Law by which all work is judged. It is appointed for man once to die, then the judgment. It is not possible for man to justify himself by keeping the law of God. This poses a dilemma for all men, whether they be those outside the laboratory fence who seek to show their good works by protesting nuclear weapons research or those inside the classified fence who seek to justify the work of their hands, whatever the rationale. I was guilty under the Law before entering the laboratory. Yet I was justified by Jesus Christ, while yet employed at the laboratory. The justification of a sinful man (breaker of God's Law), such as myself, points to the incomprehensible mercy of God, made manifest in the person of Christ in this world for our benefit. Incomprehensible, because the price paid to redeem His people is infinitely greater than His physical suffering while suspended on the cross. And all this in accordance with the Law.

Also, under the Law the universe is temporary, and wears out like a garment. There is a specific day appointed by God when the world will end. In fact, the history of man and universe proceeds according to a precise timetable under the Law, which no man or civilization can alter. Thus even if it were possible for mankind to destroy themselves in a nuclear holocaust, that event would pale in comparison to the end of time and the known universe.

It is quite evident I am writing as a Christian and have sought to direct the moral debate suggested in Dr. Gusterson's book to be cast in the light of the Word of God. It is common for men to formulate their own law or moral code by which their work might be justified. Of course, once the declaration is made by any man that there is no Word of God and that the Bible is but the moral code or doctrine of men and not of God—then one source of authority is as good as another and all men become right in their own eyes. The purpose of God for this world is the salvation of a people condemned to eternal death under the Law so that they may have eternal life. It is not possible for mankind to frustrate this plan (by, for example, a nuclear holocaust), for God has said in His Word that He would bring it to pass.

WILLIAM E. NEBO

Minister, First Presbyterian Church, Livermore

When Hugh Gusterson came to Livermore to scrutinize the people of our laboratory community, he came as an outsider with a decidedly different approach to national security than that which prevails among the people of Lawrence Livermore National Laboratory. I believe that he leaves our town with the same different approach to national security, but not as an outsider. He has taken the time and put forth the effort to look deeply into what we of this town think and feel about nuclear weapons and has done so with both a scientific mind and a human heart. Whether we of this laboratory world agree or disagree with his descriptions of our motivations, we are richer for his having viewed us as a part of our community.

I believe that Hugh has directed a very intense beam of scrutiny at nuclear scientists through the lens of current anthropological thought in order to decipher "truth." I also believe that for some reason this same critical beam of scrutiny was not charged with equal intensity when it was aimed at the motivations of those who oppose nuclear weapons work. This leads to the impression that underlying Hugh's research was a subterranean question: "What makes scientists and technical people, normally good people, sin by making nuclear weapons while others choose salvation and oppose making nuclear weapons?"

If indeed this was an undercurrent in Hugh's work, then it may explain why what I have known of the darker side of the motivation of activists referred to in the book was not discussed, even without their identities revealed. If it was not an underlying question of the work, then I would simply say that for some reason the dark side of activist motivation was not illuminated in this look at the controversy over nuclear weapons in the mid- and late 1980s.

Having read Hugh's viewpoint on a reduction in the nuclear arsenal rather than its total destruction (a view expressed before the events that so changed Europe), I am inclined to believe that his work concentrated more on Livermore scientists only because he was working hard to penetrate their culture, whereas he already had access and positive familiarity with activists and their culture. I believe that this more accurately explains the weakness of the scrutiny of the forces opposing the moral positions taken by supporters of deterrence.

As a pastor who was involved in many very heated exchanges regarding national nuclear policy that involved both the lab community and people from outside of the community, I am sad that Hugh was not on hand for these exchanges in the early 1980s. Much of the Presbyterian and Catholic steam over this issue was expended in those discussions. Possibly this would have given his "complicit" judgment a different outcome.

Then again, realizing that most of us in Livermore were called to a community of faith by people who would not be keen on pastors haranguing them Sunday after Sunday about the "sin" of their chosen occupation it is clear that our faith communities tend to have pastors like myself who cannot in good conscience advocate unilateral nuclear disarmament. This also explains why many pastors in Livermore are not activists against nuclear deterrence.

Hugh's comment about the secrecy of the laboratory has been, like much of what he writes, a great concern to many of us. It has helped create the insulated environment that has made it difficult for churches to have a dialogue with the laboratory officially, a fact made clear in the laboratory's refusal to participate in the excellent forum on nuclear weapons held annually in our area by the Archdiocese of Oakland (a forum originated by the efforts of the Catholics and Presbyterians of Livermore).

LLNL has undergone many changes since the changes in Central Europe. Still, Hugh's work makes many of us reflect on what we have believed and what might be true. For this we will be ever grateful for his efforts.

THOMAS F. RAMOS

Weapons Designer, Lawrence Livermore National Laboratory

Hugh drew my interest immediately in the very beginning of his book, when he mentioned the incident that motivated him to research the nuclear weapons community, namely, the debate with a nuclear weapons designer in a high school. That nuclear weapons designer was me. I also vividly remember that day, because the group of students were especially hostile to me. My feelings, though, were quite different from those that Hugh said he felt. After an initial feeling of bewilderment, I felt anger growing within me. I was not angry at the students, rather I was angry at their teacher. The students were continually interrupting, asking pointed questions, and citing clichés about the role of nuclear weapons in the country and in the world community. It was clear to me their teacher had filled them with his personal philosophy on the matter, and had done little else.

I have met many persons, young and old, who are afraid of the destruction that can be wrought by nuclear weapons and who are, therefore, skeptical of arguments that they are needed. I could feel their frustration, and I felt I sometimes learned from them. But the high school teacher of the students mentioned above infuriated me with his one-sided approach to teaching. Certainly, there are risks to possessing large numbers of nuclear weapons, but there are risks to disarming too. Were our "nuclear age" presidents, from Truman through Reagan, each bloodthirsty maniacs, or did they each believe they were doing what was best for our society? If the answer is the latter, then why did these presidents form the policies they did? Are nuclear weapons issues really simple? The teacher did not truly train his students how to think for themselves.

The second section concerned Hugh's description of conducting a nuclear test in terms of being a ritual. At first, I was taken aback by the comparison, and I am certain most nuclear weapon designers would find the choice of the word "ritual" as being offensive. After reading the entire section, however, I began to understand why Hugh would choose to view a nuclear test in this way. I also felt many of the emotions he stated were felt by the physicists. I also believe Hugh was correct in stating that many physicists who had never been through an entire nuclear weapon design cycle, that is, performing calculations on a computer, creating a design based on those calculations, observing engineers build a device based on the designs, and then having the device actually tested at the Nevada Test Site, felt somewhat inferior to those who had been through the process many times. Then Hugh went on to describe the experience of going through a nuclear test for the first time as an initiation rite. His words were something like, "joining the club." I think it is not that simple.

As I can best recollect the first time I participated in a nuclear test, my feelings were much more complicated than feelings I might have had for going through an initiation ritual. For one thing, I already felt like a welcomed member of the design group long before we traveled to Nevada. My biggest concerns were whether or not I would hold up my part of the group's efforts, that is, that I had done my calculations correctly. I recall having a definite fear of failing before my colleagues. Once the nuclear test was conducted, I first felt exhilaration that I had not failed, then I quickly became deeply absorbed by the anomalies that inevitably occur in the test data. There was no backslapping and going off for beers, as one might have done after an initiation rite of passage into a club. As I recall, we all sat around until fairly late at night poring over the data.

As I look back on it now, there were later nuclear tests in which I was more nervous, and went through greater emotional ups and downs, than I did with my first test. This was because, as I gained experience, I was given more responsibility. These nuclear tests were the culmination of at least a year's effort, and the future of one's work necessarily depended on maintaining a degree of success in predicting one's results. As a result, a nuclear test certainly was a unique experience, and it was natural to feel that anyone who had not been involved in one, had not gone through the full range of experiences of a nuclear weapons designer. So, although I can see how Hugh could visualize nuclear tests as rituals, I would not have used "ritual" to describe how I felt about the experience.

Let me finish by saying that I found Hugh's manuscript fascinating to read. His observations rang true to me, even though they occasionally stung my sensitivities. I believe his book will be a valuable aid to anyone wanting to learn about the people who design nuclear weapons and the people who oppose them.

SEYMOUR SACK

Weapons Designer, Lawrence Livermore National Laboratory

This work had the potential to provide a useful, if unexciting, presentation of diversity within the Livermore nuclear weapons establishment, along the lines of Debra Rosenthal's study of the New Mexican weapons community. It has not realized that potential. The author seems to have chosen a mild sensationalism, quoting dreamy, naive, ignorant and/or irresponsible sources, with a penchant for self-dramatization (or appealing to the interviewer's interests, à la the Margaret Mead syndrome).

Embedding these interviews in academic sociological jargon intermixed with classical anthropological techniques for analysis of primitive cultures (Bronowski et al.) does not compensate for omission of the banal realities. Most laboratory people are simply doing their best at what have been important and responsible, if sometimes unpopular, tasks—an illustration of the "Protestant ethic" regardless of their religious background. Perhaps less commendably others have chosen the laboratory jobs for good pay and excellent benefits with considerably more freedom and a more attractive work environment than either the commercial world or the academic jungle. Of course, there are careerists and a bureaucratic reluctance to recognize the declining importance and relevance of nuclear weapons work. But the functional output of the laboratory has been entirely independent of the individuals and/or "views" of most of the quoted interviewees. The "ritualization" of nuclear testing is one example of the overdramatization of an activity that is quite analogous to test flights of an airplane, missile system, tests of an automotive engine, or tests of the efficacy and safety of a new drug. It is fortunate that the childish anecdotes quoted are not a reliable measure of the responsibility with which new weapons are developed. The section on secrecy shows similar dramatic exaggeration creating a mystical hierarchy of access to magical knowledge out of practices that are little different from conventional industrial security and safety procedures. There is at least as much rationale to preventing wide-scale dissemination of nuclear weapon design technology as details of an improved microchip. Of course there have been many specious arguments for the necessity of continued nuclear testing, founded on the reluctance of a bureaucratic institution to contract in size and responsibility; "secrecy" has been used in nuclear weapons areas as in conventional political areas to prevent potential embarrassment. But these facts are obviously less impressive than a description of a "shamanistic" culture. Dull reality be damned. Some of the work's nonsense might have been excused on grounds of the author's naïveté; but he has been amply exposed to sober, mature (if dull) views of laboratory reality. Finally I imagine that the solid, sober, often critical analysts of the nuclear weapons establishment (Bethe, Drell, et al.) might take similar umbrage at the presentation of the emotional extremes of the antinuclear movement.

DAVID SOLNIT
Activist, American Peace Test

I first remember reading part of your dissertation in 1991 when I was in Las Vegas organizing against nuclear testing for the American Peace Test. We found interesting your idea that nuclear weapons scientists desperately desired to continue nuclear testing because it served as a community ritual and rite of passage for them.

We were both involved in the direct action campaign to stop nuclear testing at the Nevada Test Site. You were involved as an anthropologist and I as an organizer. It was never quite clear if you were involved because you were studying the antinuclear movement or because you wanted to prevent nuclear war. Academics usually hide their assumptions and interests behind a facade of objectivity, so it seemed that the two were at odds. The University of California, which is publishing your book, is a prime example: while posing as an institution committed to education they have lent the legitimizing academic facade—"management"—to the Livermore and Los Alamos labs. Did you think your best contribution to the antinuclear struggle was to provide some insight and analysis into the nuclear weapons establishment that has been such a driving force behind nuclear weapons development, production, and deployment, as well as into the antinuclear movement itself? While I think your dissertation has given some valuable insight and stimulated some debate (hopefully more will happen when UC finally publishes it), I can't help thinking that, if your goal was to stop the arms race or to abolish nuclear weapons, then your time would have been better spent doing grassroots organizing.

I would like to give some of my own views on the direct action part of the antinuclear movement. I became active in high school against registration for the military draft, during the Carter Administration. A couple of years later I was introduced to the direct action wing of the antinuclear movement when I was arrested at the Livermore Labs in the huge 1982 action. Many in the direct action movement had a deep critique of society and saw nuclear weapons as one manifestation of a sick hierarchical system—though perhaps the most blatant manifestation. The direct action movement also had a different vision of how society could be run, which it attempted to practice in its organization and decision making. Directly democratic affinity groups and spokescouncils were modeled on the Spanish anarchist workers movement in the Spanish civil war. They involved tens of thousands of people through affinity groups and through regional and national councils directly representing these affinity groups. In Spain this movement and the experience of this organizational structure contributed to a widespread social revolution that reorganized much of society—six million people—along decentralized, directly democratic, and cooperative lines. The direct action movement's deep critique of society and its positive vision, which it acted out in its own organization, made sense to me and has inspired me to organize direct action since then.

After I moved to Las Vegas to work with the American Peace Test the human cost of the arms race became particularly clear to me. Now I have met atomic veterans who were marched into mushroom clouds, downwinders in Utah who were in the path of radiation from the tests, and the Western Shoshone Indians whose land was stolen from them by the government for nuclear weapons testing. The struggle will continue until we have peace and justice for all!

NOTES

PREFACE

1. Notable examples of this genre include Bellah et al. 1985; Cohen 1980; Ginsburg 1989; Kunda 1992; Marcus 1992; Martin 1987; Moffatt 1988; Rose 1989; Weatherford 1981; Willis 1981; Zonabend 1993.

2. For recent contributions to the anthropology of science, see Bijker, Hughes, and Pinch 1990; Davis-Floyd 1992; Haraway 1991; Kunda 1992; Latour 1987; Latour and Woolgar 1979; Lynch 1988; MacKenzie 1990; Martin 1987, 1994; Pickering 1984, 1992; and Traweek 1988.

3. The scientist in this story later became one of my principal interviewees and a generous source of advice and guidance during my fieldwork.

CHAPTER 1. INTRODUCTION

1. Not much has been written about nuclear weapons issues by anthropologists. For three edited collections of essays, largely by anthropologists, on nuclear weapons, see Rubinstein and Foster 1988, 1989; and Turner and Pitt 1989. Anthropological writings on nuclear weapons largely fall into three categories. First, there are evolutionists, who see the problem in terms of adaptation: human culture, especially as it relates to war, is lagging behind the situation created by technology and we must adapt (Barash and Lipton 1985; Brasset 1989). Second, others argue that the arms race or foreign policy can be explained in terms of an essential American or Western cultural "zeitgeist" whose unfolding constancy can be seen over periods of decades or even centuries (Beeman 1989; Franklin 1988; Smith 1989). Third, recent years have seen a number of ethnographic studies of antinuclear movements (Krasniewicz 1992; Neale 1988; Peattie 1986, 1988; Simich 1987; Wilson 1988). For a critical discussion of general trends in nuclear ethnography, see Gusterson 1993a.

2. This is not the place for an extended discussion of the social construction of reality. Interested readers are referred to Berger and Luckmann 1967; Foucault 1973, 1980*b;* Laclau and Mouffe 1985; Latour 1987; Latour and Woolgar 1979; and Lyotard 1984.

3. For discussions of the paradoxical nature of nuclear strategy, see Glaser 1991; Jervis 1984; Kavka 1987; Prins 1984, 1988; and Schelling 1966.

4. MIRVs stands for multiple independently targeted reentry vehicles. A MIRVed missile is one with several warheads each capable of striking different targets.

5. ICBMs are intercontinental ballistic missiles.

6. ABM stands for anti-ballistic missile.

7. See, e.g., Derrida 1978; Lyotard 1984; Laclau and Mouffe 1985.

8. For the classic enunciation of practice theory, see Bourdieu 1977*a*. I have found the following texts explaining or implementing practice theory to be particularly helpful: Comaroff 1985; de Certeau 1984; Foucault 1979, 1980*a*, 1980*b*; Giddens 1984; Ortner 1984; and Ruddick 1989.

9. The best introduction to neorealist thought on international relations, apart from Waltz himself, is Keohane's (1986) edited volume containing essays by leading neorealists and their critics. See also Gilpin 1981; Mearsheimer 1993; and Waltz 1959. For more classically realist perspectives, see Bull 1977; Carr 1964; Hoffman 1978; and Morgenthau 1948.

On nuclear weapons issues, the Harvard Nuclear Study Group's *Living With Nuclear Weapons* (1983) is one of the best, and most popular, introductions to nuclear realist thinking. I draw strongly on it here. The Harvard nuclear realist perspective on deterrence has also been articulated in Allison, Carnesale, and Nye 1985; Carnesale and Hass 1987; and Nye 1986. For broadly similar views on the stabilizing benefits of nuclear deterrence, see Brodie 1946; Gaddis 1986; Jervis 1984, 1989; Mandelbaum 1981; and Schelling 1960, 1966.

See Vasquez 1983 for an overview of realist thought and Gusterson 1993*b* for a more extended critique of realist thought.

10. On the difference between "peace" and "stability," see Smoke 1984 and Cohn 1987.

11. For a strong articulation of the proposition that bipolar systems are more stable, see Gaddis 1986 and Mearsheimer 1993. Mearsheimer argues that the end of the cold war, far from being good news, has dissolved a stable bipolar security system and threatens to make actual war more likely. Deutsch and Singer (1964) make the classic argument for the greater stability of multipolar systems.

12. I am indebted to Carol Cohn (pers. comm.) for clarifying the realist perspective on arms control.

13. Some of the best-known articulations of regime theory include Keohane 1984 and the set of essays in Krasner 1983*b*. For critiques of conventional notions of anarchy, see also Kolodziej 1992; Rosencrance 1986; and Wendt 1992. Some anthropologists—likening the current international system to political systems in

precolonial Africa, where political and cultural regimes existed in the absence of integrative political authorities—have articulated a position broadly similar to that of the regime theorists in political science: see, for example, Pitt 1989; and Worsley 1989.

14. The bureaucratic politics approach is most closely identified with the work of Graham Allison: see Allison and Halperin 1972 for a general statement of the perspective, Allison 1971 for a bureaucratic politics interpretation of the Cuban missile crisis, and Allison 1977 for an argument that the nuclear arms race is the product of bureaucratic rivalries within the United States as well as international rivalries between the United States and the USSR. For a broadly similar perspective on nuclear weapons acquisition, see Sapolsky 1972. For a different kind of domestic politics argument—namely, that democracies do not fight one another—see Doyle 1983.

15. The most systematic, elaborate, and elegant attempt to understand the arms race within the broad framework of Marxist categories is E. P. Thompson's (1982a) essay arguing that the two superpowers are characterized by "exterminist" social formations. Other Marxist analyses of the arms race, many inspired by or reacting against Thompson's framework, are gathered together in New Left Review (1982). See also Melman 1974.

16. On this point, see Cohn 1987; Enloe 1983, 1990, 1993; Reardon 1983; Sylvester 1994; Tickner 1992; and the special issue of Millennium (1988) on women and international relations.

17. The best introductions to the poststructuralist critique of international relations theory are Campbell 1992 and Der Derian and Shapiro 1989. Two articles by Ashley (1986, 1987) are also good introductions. See also Der Derian 1987; Keeley 1990; Klein 1988; Shapiro 1988; and Walker 1986.

18. The comparison between nuclear weapons professionals and Nazis runs throughout Lifton's work, finding its most explicit and systematic formulation in Lifton and Markusen 1990. The same comparison is made in different ways by Mack (1989); Schell (1982: 194–195); and Staub (1989).

19. For broadly similar arguments about psychic numbing or denial, see Glendinning 1987; Kull 1986, 1988; Mack 1984, 1985; Macy 1983; Peavey 1986; Rowe 1985; Rubin 1988; Taketomo 1988; and Woodward 1986. The notion that weapons scientists are characterized by psychodynamic rigidity, influenced by Adorno's (1950) and Fromm's (1942) Nazi-directed theories of "the authoritarian personality," is articulated in different ways by Kull (1988), Mack (1985), and Steiner (1989). One psychotherapist was so convinced I would find nuclear weapons scientists had authoritarian personalities and antinuclear activists did not, that she gave me an authoritarian personality testing kit to take into the field with me. The kit consists of a series of pictures of a dog that gradually changes into a cat, becoming more catlike with each successive picture. The subject is shown the pictures in order and, with each new picture, is asked, "What is this?" According to theory, authoritarian personalities, unable to tolerate the ambiguity of an animal

that appears to be both dog and cat, make a sudden leap from dog to cat at some point, whereas others talk about catlike dogs and doglike cats when shown some of the intermediate pictures. I administered this test to a few weapons scientists and activists and was unable to find any "authoritarian personalities" on either side.

20. On this point see Mack 1983, 1985, 1988 and, above all, Volkan 1988. For less elaborately psychodynamic models, see Frank 1982; Keen 1986; Kovel 1983; and Zur 1987.

21. My critique of the psychological paradigm draws to some degree on Blight 1987 and Hoffmann 1986, as well as Gusterson 1993a.

22. To be fair to Kull, in an earlier, brilliant article (Kull 1985) he does this. In his more widely read book (Kull 1988), however, he gives what, from this vantage point, must be seen as a less complex account of the strategists' psychology.

23. I mention Teller in this context because Lifton repeatedly uses him as a prototypical exemplar of nuclearist psychology (even though many of Teller's colleagues at Livermore strongly disagree with his views, which they see as extreme). See, e.g., Lifton 1982a: 20–21, 91–92, and Lifton and Markusen 1990: 42, 71–72, 81, 83–87, 92, 114, 124–125, 154. For a more sympathetic portrait of Teller, see Blumberg and Panos 1990.

24. To say this is, of course, to recapitulate the critique within anthropology of the culture and personality school. For a good statement of this critique, see Wallace 1970.

CHAPTER 2. BEGINNINGS

1. The car belonged to a Livermore Laboratory employee but was parked in the parking lot of the adjacent Sandia Laboratory. The bomb blast, which took place at 1 A.M., destroyed one car, made a two-foot crater in the ground, and blew out the windows of buildings seventy-five feet away. The next day the Associated Press in San Francisco received a phone call claiming responsibility on behalf of the "Oppenheimer Brigade" of the Nuclear Liberation Front, an organization formerly unknown either to the FBI or to local peace groups. In April 1988, the FBI arrested a forty-year-old miner named Stephen Michael Dwyer for the bombing.

For news coverage of the bombing incident, see Rogers 1988a and Tri-Valley Herald 1988.

2. See Owen 1973 for a photographic portrait of Livermore in the 1970s that contrives to make Livermore appear both mind-numbingly dull and offbeat at the same time.

3. This figure comes from the Livermore Chamber of Commerce's economic profile for 1988–1989, p. 5.

4. This term comes from the baseball caps with little multicolored plastic propellers on top that some of Livermore's residents imagine as appropriate headwear for laboratory scientists. As one woman from Livermore put it to me,

"the physicists are not like other people. You see them all, always on their bikes, and they're just not like the rest of us in Livermore." For a detailed exploration of the tensions between laboratory employees and other residents of Livermore, see Kang 1987.

5. The smaller Sandia National Laboratory has a lower profile in Livermore. Reporters rarely write about it, and protestors literally turn their backs on it while they blockade the larger Livermore laboratory across the road.

The Sandia laboratory in Livermore is an outpost of the larger Sandia laboratory in Albuquerque, New Mexico. Sandia has mainly worked on weapons, though it is also known for its industrial and energy research. Where the Livermore laboratory is dominated by physicists, Sandia is mainly an engineering laboratory. In contrast to the Livermore laboratory, which is managed by the University of California, Sandia was managed by AT&T until 1993, when it was taken over by Martin Marietta. Sandia-Livermore has an annual budget of about $140 million compared to the Livermore laboratory's $1 billion annual budget (Bodovitz 1989a). For histories of Sandia, see Alexander 1963 and Furman 1990.

In my research I mainly interviewed scientists from the Lawrence Livermore Laboratory, though I occasionally interacted with people from Sandia as well.

6. In 1990, the Livermore laboratory was by far the biggest employer in town, with a workforce of 8,000. Next came Sandia-Livermore, which employed 1,000. After that, the next biggest employer was Triad, with 700 employees (*Tri-Valley Herald* 1990).

7. According to the laboratory's own figures, in 1988 54% of its employees lived in the Livermore Valley, and 19% lived farther east in the Central Valley (Tracy, Stockton, etc.). The proportion of laboratory employees living in the Central Valley increased 7 percent in the five years between 1983 and 1988. As house prices became increasingly stratospheric in the rest of the Bay Area, laboratory employees seeking to own homes, especially technicians, were pushed out to the Central Valley, where house prices are typically $25,000 to $100,000 cheaper. By 1990, the average price of a house in Livermore, still cheaper than the towns to the west, was $191,000 (*Independent* 1988a).

8. German physicists, led by Werner Heisenberg, did some atomic bomb research during World War II. They came nowhere close to developing a bomb, though the reasons for this are disputed. Jungk (1985) suggested that Heisenberg deliberately impeded the bomb project's progress because he thought the Nazis should not have such a weapon, but later recanted this interpretation (Logan 1993). Jungk's argument has, however, recently been made again by Powers (1993) and Goldberg and Powers (1992).

9. By far the best source on the war years at Los Alamos is Rhodes 1988. Other accounts include books by Easlea (1983), Hacker (1987), and Jungk (1985) and the excellent documentary film by Else (1980). The Hollywood film *Fat Man and Little Boy* covers the same ground but leaves it strewn with factual errors. On the decision to bomb Hiroshima, see Bernstein 1976 and Sherwin 1977.

10. For accounts of the decision to build the H-bomb and the accompanying struggle within the policy and physics communities, see Bernstein 1978; Bundy 1988: 197–229; Herken 1985: 55–58, 66–67; Jungk 1985: 235–248; Schilling 1961; and York 1975a, 1976. On the failure of the Baruch Plan and the crystallization of the cold war, see Bundy 1988; Gaddis 1982; LaFeber 1976; Williams 1962; and Yergin 1977. The Soviet atomic bomb program of these years is brilliantly described by Holloway (1994).

11. My understanding of the origins and early history of the Livermore laboratory has benefited greatly from conversations with Sybil Francis and Barton Bernstein. The latter's paper, "Lawrence, Teller, and the Quest for the Second Lab," is an authoritative but, as yet, unpublished account. See also Lawrence Livermore National Laboratory (1982: 2–16); York (1975b: 11–13, 1987: 65–67).

12. All of these men went on to distinguished careers in the fields of weapons design and military policy. York later became a member of Eisenhower's science advisory committee and Jimmy Carter's chief negotiator for a comprehensive test ban treaty. Harold Brown went on to become director of the Livermore laboratory (1960–1961) and secretary of defense for Jimmy Carter. John Foster was also director of the laboratory (1961–1965) and then accepted a senior position at TRW. In 1990, he was one of three members of a panel appointed by George Bush to investigate allegations of safety problems in the U.S. nuclear arsenal.

13. Los Alamos scientists felt the same way about Livermore. One Los Alamos scientist told me that the levels of classification were "confidential," "secret," "top secret," and, the strictest of all, "hide from Livermore."

14. There is little published information for those seeking an overview of the laboratory and its activities. Places to begin, apart from the laboratory publications and newspaper articles I have mainly used for this section, are Broad 1985, Cochran et al. 1987: 44–52, and the laboratory's *Energy and Technology Review* (1990). An excellent account is given in the unpublished background paper prepared by the Senate Policy Committee of UC Berkeley (1984). A brief, and highly critical, overview is given in Darnovsky 1982.

15. The fence was so easy to scale that I once watched some antinuclear activists climb over to plant trees. On another occasion an antinuclear activist succeeded in getting into the director's building. Many scientists joked about laboratory security. One popular joke is that the laboratory's security officers draw lots to see who will get the one bullet for the day. When I first arrived in Livermore, not yet understanding which parts of the laboratory were off-limits to me, I accidentally gained admittance to a red badge area even though I had no red badge, so lax were security procedures. The one part of the laboratory said to be well guarded is the plutonium facility, which is rumored to contain over 400 pounds of plutonium. I was told that it was guarded by men armed with submachine guns and rehearsed in counterterrorist techniques.

16. Although some laboratory buildings are informally known by names that reflect their function, formally they are not named but numbered. All buildings

have three-digit numbers, all trailers four-digit numbers. The first digit of a building or trailer number is on an east-west axis, the second digit on a north-south axis. In principle, this is supposed to make it easy to find any building or trailer.

There are comparatively few formal buildings because construction is often held up by red tape, sometimes even needing congressional approval. Doing science out of trailers wherever possible enables the laboratory to get on with new projects more quickly. There is also a story, not to be taken seriously I think, that the laboratory favors trailers because they can easily be moved around, thus confusing Soviet spy satellites.

17. This figure comes from a pie chart and a table used by the laboratory in briefings, reference numbers L073 and L045A, respectively. The public relations department's 1989 pamphlet, simply titled "Lawrence Livermore National Laboratory," gives a slightly lower figure. An earlier pamphlet, "Lawrence Livermore Laboratory: Background and Current Research," written in 1980, says that 40% of the laboratory staff work on nuclear weapons.

18. Others that support the 76% figure are Cochran et al. 1987: 48; Gustafson 1990; Hufbauer, Johnson, and Kohn 1990; and Stowsky and Laird 1992.

19. In recent years, at least one laboratory employee, Dr. Ching Wang, has filed suit for racial discrimination (see SPSE Newsletter 1992a, 1992b).

20. An attempt by the laboratory's Society for Professional Scientists and Engineers (SPSE) to strengthen their position by unionizing was voted down by laboratory employees in 1983. The union drive was strenuously opposed by the laboratory's management. For more on this campaign, see Rogers 1979; *Valley Times* 1983.

21. Three notable exceptions to the rule that senior managers have Ph.D.'s are Roy Woodruff, who became associate director for weapons systems; Carl Haussmann (now retired), who became associate director at large; and John Nuckolls, who became director of the laboratory in 1988. Sybil Francis (pers. comm.) points out that it was easier in the past to become a senior manager without a Ph.D.

22. Brian Easlea (1983: 171), speaking of "the well-known . . . hierarchy of prestige that exists within the natural sciences," says the highest-ranking are the "hardest"—those that, like physics, "require greater penetrating power" because they analyze nature in terms of its smallest constituent parts: atoms and their components. Chemistry is "softer" because it only penetrates to the molecular level. Some physicists who do not work on weapons look down on weapons physics, saying that it is too much like engineering to be taken very seriously. (Physicists often speak of engineering as being "too easy" to be interesting.)

23. The exception is Roger Batzel, who directed the laboratory from 1971 to 1988. Batzel has a Ph.D. in chemistry.

24. In the late 1980s the only female senior managers were Mary Woodruff, who resigned as the laboratory's only female associate director just before I arrived in Livermore; Mary Spaeth, who directed the atomic vapor laser isotope separation facility (AVLIS) while I was doing fieldwork, and Carol Alonso, the deputy leader

of A Division. In 1988, a study by the Laboratory Women's Association suggested that female employees were, on average, paid $12,000 a year less than their male counterparts. In 1990, Jeanne Kramer, a technician who claimed she had fallen $25,000 a year behind male colleagues who started working for the laboratory at the same time she did, filed suit against the laboratory (Jeffers 1990a; SPSE Newsletter 1992b). There have also been complaints about computers that flash pictures of naked women on their screens, pinups of naked women in laboratory machine shops (which the laboratory formally outlawed a few years before I got to Livermore), and technicians watching X-rated films on laboratory diagnostic equipment (A. Smith 1990c).

25. Most contemporary nuclear weapons are two-stage devices. The first stage, designed by B Division at Livermore, is the "primary." It derives its explosive energy from the fissioning of uranium-235 or plutonium-239 atoms. The basic problem in primary design is to create a critical mass quickly and efficiently before the nuclear reaction blows the fissioning material apart. This gives designers a few hundredths of microseconds. If the mass of uranium or plutonium approaches criticality too slowly, an immature chain reaction will blow apart the fissioning material prematurely, thus diminishing the reaction's explosive yield and wasting uranium or plutonium, both of which are difficult and expensive to create. Although the bombs dropped on Hiroshima and Nagasaki were one-stage fission bombs, today fission devices tend to be used not as bombs in themselves but as triggers to ignite a much more powerful fusion reaction in the "secondary," the addition of which transforms an atomic bomb into a hydrogen bomb. Secondaries, designed by A Division at Livermore, derive most of their explosive power from the fusion of deuterium and tritium nuclei, that is, from the process that powers the sun. The secondary designers' challenge is, at temperatures of hundreds of millions of degrees, to control and direct the energy from the exploding primary to compress and ignite the deuterium and tritium in the secondary before it is destroyed by the extraordinary temperatures and pressures of the reaction. For more detailed explanations of the physics of nuclear weapons, see Cochran et al. 1984: 22-36; Glasstone and Dolan 1977: 1-25; Hansen 1988; Morland 1979; Postol 1987; and Tsipis 1983: 13-43.

26. The definitive source on Livermore's X-ray laser program is Broad 1992. See also Blum 1988; Broad 1985, 1988b; Moseley 1989.

27. The demise of the X-ray laser program is described in greater detail in chapter 7.

28. For an overview of the Free Electron Laser program, see Briggs 1989, and the special 1986 edition of Energy and Technology Review devoted to the free electron laser (FEL).

29. For more information on Brilliant Pebbles, see Biddle 1987; Broad 1992: 245-267; Canavan and Teller 1990; and Speed 1990.

30. For a book-length portrait of O Group, see Broad 1985. For a less flattering perspective, see Moseley's (1989) interview with Peter Hagelstein, a dis-

gruntled former member of O Group. See also Stober 1989*a*, and Stober and Klein 1992.

31. On the Nova laser, see the laboratory's booklet "Inertial Confinement Fusion." For accounts of the defense applications of laser fusion, see Hogan and Tobin 1989 and Morrison 1985: 36. I have heard laboratory scientists describe the laser fusion program as "primarily military" and "primarily civilian," depending on the audience. As Livermore's former associate director for lasers, John Emmett, said, "If you don't like the program, you say it's 100 percent military. If you like it, then it's 100 percent energy. The House Armed Services Committee is our authorizing agent. As far as they are concerned, this is weapons work and any energy is gravy" (Senate Policy Committee 1984: 39). In a 1989 interview with the *Valley Times*, Erik Storm, the scientist in charge of the Nova laser fusion facility, presented it as primarily an energy research project (Rogers 1989*a*). The laboratory is now planning a more powerful follow-on to Nova called the National Ignition Facility (NIF). See Broad 1994 and Gusterson 1995*b* for discussions of the NIF, which has become controversial because of its expense and military applications.

32. For progress reports on what is left of the program, see Henning 1990; Hooper and Allen 1990; and Logan 1989. The cost estimate for the tandem mirror facility is from Wrubel 1990.

33. The environmental restoration program tends to be regarded as low-status by many Livermore scientists. Nevertheless, helped by DOE's new nationwide emphasis on environmental cleanup, the number of people assigned to environmental work at the laboratory doubled between 1987 and 1990, and the laboratory's budget for environmental protection increased from $10 million in 1986 to $50 million in 1990 (A. Smith 1990*a*).

34. It would be wrong to say that no anthropologists did fieldwork in the United States until recently. However, the numbers and the disciplinary legitimacy of anthropologists writing about American culture began to increase from the 1970s. Still, looking for the equivalent at home of the people they studied abroad, anthropologists tended to concentrate on the poor, the powerless, and the marginal. (See, e.g., Daner 1976; Hostetler and Huntington 1980; Keiser 1969; Liebow 1993; Partridge 1985; Spradley 1988; Stack 1974; Whyte 1981.) Studying groups living in small-scale, localized settings, it was relatively easy for anthropologists to adapt their traditional methodology to fieldwork in their midst. More recently anthropologists have begun to give some thought to the methodological issues involved in studying elites in the United States. (See, e.g., Hoffmann 1980; Marcus 1983; Nader 1974; and Spector 1980.) For descriptions of ethnographic research conducted among American elites, see Brasset 1989; Marcus 1983, 1992; Rose 1989; Traweek 1988; Weatherford 1981; and the 1993 special issue of the *Journal of Contemporary Ethnography* 22(1). Recent years have also seen new attempts to characterize overarching processes and values regulating American culture and society (Arens and Montague 1976; Bellah et al. 1985; Di Leonardo 1984).

35. For a brief discussion of the methodological difficulties inherent in the anthropological study of the cold war, see Pitt 1989. Pitt recommends substituting discourse analysis and historical analysis for participant observation, arguing that the real contribution of anthropology to the study of the cold war is its body of theory.

36. There is a growing literature on approaches to discourse analysis. Two primers in line with the pragmatic approach favored here are Fairclough 1989 and Wilson 1990. For examples of (rather than primers on) discourse analysis, all of which have influenced my own approach, see Barthes 1972, 1979; Cohn 1987; Der Derian 1987; Der Derian and Shapiro 1989; Foucault 1973, 1979, 1980*a*; Gray 1997; Haraway 1991; Keller 1985; Martin 1987, 1990; Radway 1991; Ross 1991; Said 1979; Scarry 1985; and Shapiro 1988.

37. Some of these newspapers tended to rotate reporters in and out of the laboratory beat quite quickly so that they did not get a chance to know the laboratory in depth. Others had reporters who understood the laboratory as deeply as any outsider can. John Miller of the *Oakland Tribune* and Dan Stober of the *San Jose Mercury News* were in the latter category, as were the *Valley Times'* Keith Rogers and the *Independent's* Bob Several, both of whom had covered the laboratory for many years. I am greatly indebted to their reporting for my own understanding of the laboratory.

38. A survey of laboratory employees showed that, while 91% believed the information they read in *Newsline*, only 53% thought the newspaper presented both sides of issues. Following this survey, in 1990, the laboratory tried to shake up the newspaper a little and make it more responsive to employees' needs (Rogers 1990*c*).

39. SANE/Freeze was an outgrowth of the Nuclear Freeze Campaign of the early and mid-1980s. As the freeze movement went into decline, it merged with the older peace group, the Committee for a SANE Nuclear Policy. Hence the rather cumbersome and, to some, mystifying name of the organization. Since the end of the cold war, the group has renamed itself California Peace Action.

40. For an account of that day, see Gusterson 1989.

41. There were three other occasions when weapons scientists and activists were brought together by my fieldwork. On one, a very few activists came to a barbecue at my house in Livermore, at which most guests were laboratory employees, to celebrate the Livermore rodeo. For the most part, the employees did not mingle with the activists. On the second occasion, some activists, desperately in need of a place to spend the night before a protest at the laboratory, were permitted to sleep on our living room floor by my housemate, a laboratory employee. He made them coffee the next morning and, politely declining their joking requests for a ride to the laboratory, left for work. Finally, just before I left Livermore, I threw a big party to which I invited most of the people I had interviewed on both sides. Forty or fifty people, split fairly evenly between both camps, arrived and succeeded in spending a peaceful afternoon in one another's company.

CHAPTER 3. BECOMING A WEAPONS SCIENTIST

1. Classic texts here include Caldicott 1978, 1986; Glendinning 1987; Kull 1986, 1988; Lifton 1982*a*, 1983; Lifton and Markusen 1990; Mack 1985, 1988; and Macy 1983.

2. For the interviewees at the laboratory for whom I have data on religious affiliation, the distribution is as follows: 20% Catholics, 14% atheists, 12% Unitarians (a disproportionately large number because I attended the Unitarian church frequently), 10% agnostics, 10% Evangelicals, 8% Presbyterians, 6% Jews, 6% Buddhists, 2% Episcopalians, 2% Baptists, 2% Lutherans, 2% Methodists, 2% Mormons, and 2% New Age.

3. Faye Ginsburg's (1989) excellent ethnographic study of the pro-life and pro-choice movements in North Dakota offers a close parallel to the perspective adopted here. For example, Ginsburg found that, although the pro-life movement is widely associated in media accounts with the rise of the New Right in the 1980s, in fact its partisans had diverse political commitments, many of them to the Left. Eschewing conventional Left-Right distinctions, Ginsburg analyzed the two movements in terms of two opposed narratives of the female life cycle, showing how these narratives articulate personal life histories with broader social historical changes.

4. My switch from looking for a binding homogeneity to seeking ways in which diverse types are integrated recapitulated in miniature the evolution of anthropological theory itself in the twentieth century—an evolution from, in Durkheimian terms, a preoccupation with "mechanical solidarity" to an interest in "organic solidarity." For example, ritual analysis has evolved from functionalist accounts representing rituals as cultural cloning devices to analyses that emphasize the complex and contradictory ways in which rituals mediate social conflicts; and psychological anthropology has moved from searching for a culture's "basic personality" and "modal personality" to inquiries into the integration of different personalities and emotions within the framework of a common culture (Wallace 1970).

5. For similar arguments about the social construction of emotion and/or the ideological importance of structures of feeling, see Foucault 1979, 1980*a;* Hochschild 1983; Levy 1973, 1984; Lutz 1988; M. Rosaldo 1980; Schweder 1991; Solomon 1984.

6. During the Reagan presidency, federal R&D funds allocated to the military increased by 172% (Henderson 1989: 35). In 1980, the proportion of all federal R&D funds going to the military was 48%, but by 1985, it had shifted to 64%; by 1988, it was 67% (Abbotts 1991: 13; FAS 1986: 7; Norman 1990). Much of the increase can be attributed to the Strategic Defense Initiative.

7. Lloyd Dumas estimated 25% to 30% (FAS 1986: 7); David Gold (1991: 39), 20%; and Randall Forsberg (1980: 266), 40%. Other sources put the proportion of scientists and engineers doing military research still higher. For example,

Charles Schwartz (1989), claims that about 40% of physicists, 40% of electrical engineers, and 65% of aeronautical engineers work primarily on military projects. According to the Congressional Budget Office, in 1981, at the beginning of the Reagan defense buildup, 47% of aeronautical engineers, 30% of mathematicians, 24% of physicists, 18% of electrical engineers, and 12% of mechanical engineers worked on military research (FAS 1986: 7).

8. See, e.g., Blum 1987a, Dickson 1984, FAS 1986, Schwartz 1989. Critics were particularly concerned about the large quantities of research funding earmarked for SDI in the early 1980s and about the Reagan administration's decision to funnel more basic research funding through the Pentagon rather than through civilian agencies such as the National Science Foundation. In the 1980s, even university researchers found the alternatives to military funding drying up (Kistiakowsky 1989a, 1989b).

9. The laboratory has nothing like a university tenure system. Its policy has so far been more or less to guarantee employment to all its scientists and engineers as long as their work is competent and their security clearance in order. It remains to be seen whether such a policy can be maintained in a post–cold war era in which the laboratory may sustain substantial budget cuts. So far, when the laboratory has had to make budget cuts (e.g., in 1973 and 1990), managers have dealt with the problem by enticing volunteers with generous terms for early retirement rather than by selecting employees for layoffs. When particular projects at the laboratory are terminated, participating scientists and engineers either find themselves new assignments or are reassigned by managers. The better scientists and engineers within the laboratory have more freedom to choose the project to which they move.

10. Rosenthal is similarly struck by the stark divergence of opinion about weapons physics. One scientist tells her that bomb design is "as exciting as designing a new toothbrush." A weapons designer replies, "I kind of feel sorry for the people who think [weapons] design work is sterile" (Rosenthal 1990: 57). Theodore Taylor, a weapons designer who eventually quit the Los Alamos laboratory, has said that the magnitude of the forces he was working with and the design challenges involved in weapons work made his job "addictive." Even now, many years after he quit, he says he often has ideas for new weapons designs that it pains him not to be able to pursue (Lifton and Markusen 1990: 134–135).

11. Code developers are computationally oriented physicists who specialize in writing the enormous computer codes that simulate a variety of complex phenomena: the interaction of atoms in a chain reaction, the fireball and blast wave of a nuclear explosion, the greenhouse effect, nuclear winter scenarios, the effect of airflow on planes and missiles, and so on. For a discussion of applications for such codes, see the special issue of *Energy and Technology Review* (September–October 1993).

12. After many years during which the issue was largely neglected, there has in the last decade been an explosion of literature exploring the ethics of nuclear

deterrence and of nuclear weapons work as a vocation for individuals. See, e.g., Dyson 1984; Hardin et al. 1985; Hollenbach 1983; Johnson 1984; Kavka 1987; Kenny 1985; Lackey 1984; National Conference of Catholic Bishops 1983; Novak 1983; Nye 1986; O'Brien and Langan 1986; Russett 1984; Shaw 1984; United Methodist Council of Bishops 1986; Walzer 1977; Wohlstetter 1983. See also the special 1985 issue of the journal *Ethics* (vol. 95, no. 3) on nuclear deterrence.

13. The phrase comes from Joseph Nye's (1986: 49) summary of the deontological position.

14. Kenney (1985), Perkins (1985), and Schell (1982) offer examples of the deontological argument.

15. The best-known exponents of the consequentialist point of view are Dworkin (1985), Nye (1986), and Wohlstetter (1983). For an interesting attempt to cross-fertilize deontological and consequentialist logic, see Kavka 1987.

16. The only time I heard anything resembling a deontological argument in favor of nuclear weapons was when I eavesdropped on an argument between a born-again Christian weapons scientist, Bible in hand, and an ecumenical group of Christian protestors blockading the front gate of the laboratory. The scientist argued that God had created a universe where nuclear weapons were possible and had given humans the understanding to make them. He also suggested that nuclear weapons might be part of God's plan to cleanse the earth with fire, as prophesied in the Book of Revelation. For a fine exploration of this point of view, which Caputi (1991) calls "necroapocalyptic fundamentalism," see Mojtabai's (1986) study of "endtime" thinking in Texas in the 1980s.

17. For examples of this perspective, see DeWitt 1989*a*, 1989*b*; Everett 1989; Glendinning 1987; Lifton 1982*a*, 1982*b*; Lifton and Markusen 1990; Macy 1983; Rosenthal 1990.

18. See, for example, the statements in Cabasso and Moon 1985.

19. In his review of Rosenthal's book, Peter Carey (1990) asks,

> Why should arms-makers have something interesting to say about the values of the age? They aren't philosophers. They're simply filling orders from the government. It is Hamlet, not the gravedigger, who makes the wonderful graveside speech on the future of mankind. As Hamlet says of the gravedigger, who sings while at his morbid task, "'Tis e'en so, the hand of little employment has the daintier sense."

20. Gordon McClure (1992), a lapsed weapons scientist at Sandia National Laboratory in Albuquerque, has also written about this sense that one did not publicly discuss the ethics of weapons work: "If an employee had any doubts, he discussed his doubts at his peril. One did not even discuss such doubts with co-workers." McClure argues, however, that employees did not even consider such questions in private: "The types of people that the labs hire are not at all inclined to consider policy questions, they are detail people. They are carefully selected to solve assigned problems using existing science." It is, of course, difficult to know what questions others are asking themselves in private, especially if there is a public

taboo against articulating certain thoughts. Still, the description of weapons scientists as "detail people" may work better for Sandia, an engineering laboratory, than for Livermore, a physics laboratory.

21. See Bellah et al. 1985; Du Bois 1955; Hsu 1972; Inkeles 1979; Moffatt 1988; Riesman et al. 1950; Slater 1970; Spindler and Spindler 1983; Tocqueville 1956; Varenne 1977; Weber 1958.

22. For discussion of the ways behavioral commitments can shape ideology and beliefs, see Festinger 1964, Nisbett and Ross 1980, and Cialdini 1988. Whereas most of us tend to presume that people's beliefs constrain and enable their behavioral choices, these psychologists, drawing on attribution theory, argue that the reverse is often the case. Without belaboring the point, there are clear parallels between the rise of attribution theory in social psychology in the 1980s and the rise of practice theory in anthropology—a development that has strongly influenced my analysis in this book.

23. This interest in some sort of connection with the Soviets was not unique. While I was doing my fieldwork a number of Livermore's warhead designers were learning Russian and developing an interest in Russian culture.

24. A senior manager told me that one of the most important conversations of his life took place on a hill overlooking Berkeley when the physicist (and laboratory co-founder) Ernest Lawrence told him shortly after World War II that nuclear weapons at last offered humanity the means to make war obsolete. Birgit Brock-Utne (1989: 18–19) points out that this argument was in use long before nuclear weapons existed. For example, Alfred Nobel, the inventor of dynamite, in an exchange of letters with a contemporary peace activist, called himself a pacifist and said he was doing more for peace with his weapons than traditional pacifists were with their speeches.

25. The exception was Richard, an Evangelical Christian weapons scientist who told me, "What scares me more than the weapons themselves is that my colleagues think they'll never be used. That's a form of denial. That's worshipping the human race."

26. For an extended analysis of this finding, see Gusterson 1991a.

27. For an interesting profile of female missile launchers, most of whom give the same kinds of reasons for doing their work as the weapons scientists do, see Tobias 1988. Bartimus and McCartney (1991: 261–288) also provide an interesting discussion of missile launchers' ethical thinking and of the psychological mechanisms that enable them to live with their job.

28. For a strikingly similar line of reasoning by a Quaker working at Sandia National Laboratories, see the profile of Ted Church by Bartimus and McCartney (1991: 81–85). The Livermore scientist and lay (Lutheran) minister John Futterman has also made similar arguments in his unpublished manuscript (1992).

29. For a breakdown of the religious affiliations of those interviewees for whom I have data, see note 2, above.

30. For more on the recent relationship between the Christian church in America and nuclear weapons, see Chernus 1991; Davidson 1983; Garrison 1982; Kurtz 1988: 219–236; Mehan, Nathanson, and Skelly 1990; Mojtabai 1986; Murnion and Hesburgh 1983; National Conference of Catholic Bishops 1983; Novak 1983; United Methodist Council of Bishops 1986; Wallis 1983. See also the Christian magazine *Sojourners*, which has published a number of articles giving the Christian case for the abolition of nuclear weapons.

31. See, e.g., Biagioli 1993; Bijker and Law 1992; Bijker, Hughes, and Pinch 1990; Hughes 1983; Latour 1987; and MacKenzie 1990.

32. For the classic articulation of the notion of ideological apparatuses, see Althusser 1971. While I do not share Althusser's rigid, mechanical, and deterministic view of the church, the media, and the educational system as perfectly interlocking components of an indoctrination system dominated by and serving the state, nevertheless his work is important in identifying and analyzing the range of institutions that, in concert with the state, act to produce the ideological identity of individual citizens. For a stinging critique of the determinism in Althusser's approach, see Thompson 1978.

33. The symbiosis of Christian church and nuclear state is also strikingly symbolized in the person of Bob Nelson, an Episcopal priest who, as deputy manager of Nevada Operations for the DOE, oversaw a number of nuclear tests. In an interview with the *New York Times* (1989) he described himself as "the only priest I know who fires nuclear weapons."

34. Throughout most of the cold war, American policy called for nuclear retaliation against a Soviet nonnuclear attack on Western Europe. The argument used to justify this policy was that since Soviet and Warsaw Pact conventional forces in Europe were superior to NATO's, the willingness to use nuclear weapons first was vital in deterring or reversing a Soviet invasion of Western Europe (Freedman 1983: 76–90, 283–329, 372–386). In the early 1980s, the American first use policy came under attack from a number of directions. First, the mainline American theological community, particularly the Catholic bishops, strongly condemned any role for nuclear weapons beyond that of deterring their use by others (National Conference of Catholic Bishops 1983). Second, a prominent group of retired American cold warriors—McGeorge Bundy, George Kennan, Robert McNamara, and Gerard Smith—made a widely publicized (in defense intellectual circles) plea for an American no first use policy (Bundy et al. 1982; Bundy et al. 1986; McNamara 1986). Third, the burgeoning European antinuclear movement of the early 1980s argued that the use of nuclear weapons against a Soviet invasion would entail the destruction rather than the defense of Europe (Coates 1981; Cox 1982; Thompson 1981, 1982b, 1985). Finally, a number of defense analysts began to question the traditional assumption of Soviet conventional military superiority in Europe (Mearsheimer 1982; Smith 1981). In the meantime the Soviets offered to negotiate a bilateral no first use

agreement and announced unilaterally that they would not be the first to use nuclear weapons.

35. For an analysis of the drafting and political consequences of the Catholic bishops' pastoral letter, see Mehan, Nathanson, and Skelly 1990. Evans (1989) claims that over 10 million Catholic Americans changed their position on the arms race thanks to the pastoral letter. Four Catholic bishops who were particularly outspoken in their opposition to U.S. nuclear weapons policy were Thomas Gumbleton, Walter Sullivan, Raymond Hunthausen (who encouraged Catholics in Seattle to withhold taxes from the U.S. government), and Leroy Mathieson (who appealed to defense workers in Texas to quit their jobs). They are interviewed in Wallis 1983 (pp. 28–40). Mathieson is also profiled in Mojtabai 1986.

36. Some Catholic scientists from Livermore did, however, as mentioned above, participate in a series of dialogues, organized by Bishop Cummins of Oakland, with antinuclear Catholics. Livermore's Methodist church also held a series of low-key discussions on peace issues, including nuclear weapons policy, while I lived in Livermore.

37. The religious community of Livermore did not refuse all contact with the walkers. Several churchgoing families, including some laboratory employees, invited protestors to spend the night in their homes. Also in 1989, Livermore's Unitarian Church invited the walkers to a foot-washing ceremony. Still, Livermore's churches did not welcome the walkers as other churches of the same denominations did in neighboring towns, and, by all accounts, when the possibility of offering hospitality to the walkers was discussed at Livermore church board meetings, it proved divisive. The peace pilgrimages attracted about 60 participants in 1988 and about 20 in 1989. Each year the Good Friday protest—a regular fixture for the Bay Area religious peace community—attracted about 400 participants, roughly 50 of whom were arrested for civil disobedience each time (Bodovitz 1989c; Rogers 1988b).

38. I cannot name the ministers' denominations because this would be tantamount to naming them as individuals. However, all three belonged to substantial churches affiliated with the National Council of Churches.

39. See Mojtabai 1986 for a fascinating exploration of "endtime" thinking in Texas in the 1980s. Many of Mojtabai's interviewees connected nuclear weapons with biblical prophecies of Armageddon, but expected true believers to be "raptured" to heaven shortly before the holocaust. I heard no one in Livermore speak of the "rapture."

CHAPTER 4. SECRECY

1. A good overview of government secrecy in the United States is given by Rourke (1977). For accounts of attempts by the government to tighten U.S. secrecy laws over the last two decades, especially in the 1980s, see Adler 1985; Chalk 1983; Dickson 1984: 137–162; Halperin 1985; and Unger 1982.

2. Since some sigmas effectively require the individual to have others, it is not completely true to say they are not ranked. However, the numbers of the sigmas do not denote rank in the sense that "lieutenant," "sergeant," and "captain," for example, denote rank in the military.

3. For theoretical discussion of the concept of "taboo," see Douglas 1984 and Radcliffe-Brown 1968. The notion of practical consciousness—a consciousness made real in everyday actions and interactions but less self-conscious than a formal ideology—is best articulated by Williams (1977).

4. Although the laboratory map represents the boundary between red and green areas as fixed, in fact, red areas sometimes have green moments (and, less commonly, vice versa). Thus, for example, the control room of the Nova laser facility, which is in a red area, may be declared off-limits to those without green badges when certain kinds of experiments are being performed and sensitive data are appearing on the many computer screens in the control room.

5. With its red, yellow, and green badges, the laboratory badge system is a semiotic code based on the cognitive and emotional reflexes established by traffic lights. In American society, the color red is used to symbolize danger, while green is the color of life and fertility. There may also be a faint stigma attached to red badges thanks to Nathaniel Hawthorne's novel *The Scarlet Letter*.

6. The requirement to list even those arrests for which charges were dropped may be waived as the result of a recent court challenge to the policy (Tom Ramos, pers. comm.).

7. The quotation comes from page 8 (question 25) of OPM Standard Form 86, "Questionnaire for Sensitive Positions (For National Security)."

8. For the government to gain access to many of these files, the scientist being investigated must sign a release form. In 1987 the government added these sentences to the release form: "I release any individual, including records custodians, from all liability for damages that may result to me on account of compliance or any attempts to comply with this authorization. This release is binding, now and in the future, on my heirs, assigns, associates, and personal representatives of any nature" (Office of Personnel Management Standard Form 86, p. 10). Two hundred and fifty Livermore scientists, concerned that they would have no means of redress against anyone who deliberately misrepresented their past records, protested this clause. Warned that this might jeopardize their clearances, they signed under duress but in 1992 succeeded in winning the removal of the clause (*Newsline* 1990a; Smith 1990e; *SPSE Newsletter* 1992c).

9. For obvious reasons the U.S. government is concerned about contacts with foreigners. Once scientists have Q clearances, they are supposed to report to the Laboratory Safeguards and Security Office any conversations they have with foreigners from countries deemed to be sensitive. They must also request government permission to visit countries, such as Russia, where they might be recruited as spies or countries, such as Afghanistan, where they might be in physical danger.

10. Despite the apparent exhaustiveness of the government's Q clearance investigations, there have been allegations that slipshod implementation of security regulations enabled foreign spies to gain access to the Livermore and Los Alamos laboratories. In 1988, the General Accounting Office (GAO) released a report claiming that scientists from a number of countries with existing or incipient nuclear weapons programs had visited U.S. nuclear weapons laboratories under inappropriate circumstances. The countries included the USSR, China, Israel, Pakistan, and India. According to the GAO report, a retrospective search of the visitors' names showed that some were on U.S. government lists of known or suspected spies (Wald 1990). According to the report, of 176 visitors to American weapons laboratories from Communist countries in 1986 and 1987, only six were checked before their visits. During this period, 60 visitors from Communist countries came to Livermore, but only three received background checks beforehand (*Valley Times* 1988). The report alleged that a group of Soviet scientists were taken into classified areas of Livermore's laser program in 1987, even though the Department of Energy had expressly forbidden that particular delegation to enter classified areas. The laboratory denied the charge, saying that they took the scientists into a room that was sometimes "green" and sometimes not and that the Soviet scientists saw no classified information (Brewer 1988).

The following year, in 1989, a prominent arms control scholar revealed that American nuclear weapons scientists had illegally assisted France's nuclear weapons program (Ullman 1989). And, in 1990, the media publicized an FBI investigation that attributed China's rapid perfection of the neutron bomb to successful espionage at Livermore (Stober 1990a).

11. I was also told about one man who lost his Q clearance after he married a woman from the People's Republic of China. On the first day he came into work after the wedding, he was, to his surprise, met at the front gate by security agents who removed his green badge, supervised his packing of personal belongings in his office, and then escorted him out of the green area.

12. For a profile of Perry, see Everett 1989.

13. Studies of secret societies include Bok 1989: 45–58; Brandt 1980; Cohen 1971; Herdt 1987; Hiatt 1979; Kaiser 1980; Laguerre 1980; and Schaefer 1980.

14. I have borrowed this term from Richard Schaefer's (1980) Goffmanesque analysis of the Ku Klux Klan.

15. On "ideal types," see Weber 1949.

16. It is a common misconception that anarchists are nihilists whose main political goal is the creation of chaos (i.e., anarchy) and whose tactics include violence and terror. The anarchists I knew (who were very active in the radical wing of the Bay Area antinuclear movement) were militantly *nonviolent*, and their main goal was not the destruction of order but the undermining of hierarchical and technocratic authority. Envisaging a Rousseauian kind of total democracy, they sought in their own community to eliminate hierarchy, to minimize role differ-

entiation, and to make all decisions by consensus. For a good, if dated, overview of anarchism, see Woodcock 1962.

17. For a somewhat similar analysis of the effects of polygraph tests on new CIA employees, see Kaiser 1980.

18. For those readers who find this improbable, it was revealed that the Department of Energy has been eavesdropping (with illegally acquired equipment) on more than 200 telephone lines at the Hanford nuclear weapons facility in Washington (*Boston Globe* 1991; Pear 1992). It is known that the new telephone system installed at the Livermore laboratory in 1989 includes a computer system that tracks the origin, destination, and duration of every call at the laboratory (Stober 1989*b*).

19. For a similar argument that new government regulations restricting the sharing of certain kinds of commercial secrets with foreigners have led to excessive self-surveillance and self-censorship among university scientists, see Park 1985.

20. A 1990 survey at the Livermore laboratory found that 63% of lab employees feared reprisals for whistle-blowing (Miller 1990). Roy Woodruff, the associate director in charge of weapons programs at Livermore for much of the 1980s, claims that he was subjected to unnecessary and deliberately harassing security investigations (for example, into allegations that he mishandled secret documents) when he resigned his position and filed a complaint following a row with the laboratory director, Roger Batzel, over the direction of weapons research at the laboratory (Broad 1990*b*). For the story of a Los Alamos employee allegedly stripped of his clearance for criticizing one of that laboratory's laser programs, see the *New Mexican* (1992*a*). For the story of a DOE employee who appears to have been stripped of her clearance to punish her for complaining about discrimination in the department, see the *New Mexican* (1992*b*). Arguably Oppenheimer himself is the ultimate, and original, example of a scientist losing his clearance as punishment for political deviance. Despite his wartime role as leader of the Manhattan Project, he lost his clearance in 1954 when his politics came under question after he advised the government not to develop the hydrogen bomb (see Bernstein 1990; Major 1971; Stern 1969).

21. Laser fusion offers a bizarre example of "overclassification." In the United States in the 1980s most laser fusion physics was, because of its relevance to weapons physics, classified even though little similar information was classified in the Soviet Union. Consequently, articles that were freely available in the Soviet Union were classified in the United States, and there were situations in which Soviet scientists gave talks that upset U.S. classification officers because they revealed to uncleared American scientists information those scientists were not supposed to know in case they shared it with the Soviets (DeVolpi et al. 1981: 176).

22. I have borrowed the idea of a separate laboratory self from Lifton and Markusen (1990).

23. Chalk (1985), Hull (1985), McMullin (1985), and Zuckerman (1967: 99–122) survey the historical and contemporary relationship between science and secrecy. Secrecy goes against the grain of science's romantic view of itself as the free and open debate of truth-claims. This view is best articulated by Merton (1973).

24. Trident II, the warhead for which was designed at Los Alamos, has been criticized as unsafe on three grounds. First, the warhead contains ordinary high explosive rather than the less accident-prone insensitive high explosive. Second, the missile uses 1.1 class propellant fuel, which is easier to detonate by accident than the alternative 1.3 class propellant. (The safer propellant was not used because it yields a lower specific impulse and would therefore have reduced the missile's range by 100 or so nautical miles.) Third, the missile is designed so that the fuel is surrounded by nuclear warheads. This design choice, made to save space, is unusual in ballistic missiles, and it increases the chance of an explosive interaction between the fuel and the warheads (Drell, Townes, and Foster 1991; J. Smith 1990a). These safety concerns became public thanks to a leak to the *Washington Post* from a highly placed scientist at Livermore (J. Smith 1990b). This reminds us that while the culture of secrecy at Livermore places impediments in the way of formulating and pursuing unorthodox ethical, technical, or political concerns, we should not presume that discipline at the laboratory is seamlessly perfect.

25. The definitive source on the X-ray laser affair is Broad 1992—a book that grew out of Broad's (1988b) *New York Times Magazine* article. See also Blum 1988 and Broad 1985, an earlier, less critical portrait of SDI research at Livermore.

26. For overviews of the thinking of Manhattan Project scientists on the implications of their work while it was under way, see Else 1980; Rhodes 1988; and Sherwin 1985. For an account by a distinguished Manhattan Project participant, who says "the thought that the bomb would be used on a city without warning never occurred to me," see Peierls 1985. One of the few scientists at Los Alamos itself who wanted a discussion of the implications of the scientists' work and of the danger of a postwar arms race was Niels Bohr; his attempts are described in Wilson 1985. Only one scientist decided to quit the Manhattan Project: see Rotblat 1985 for an autobiographical account of that decision.

27. Garretson is referring to Frederick Turner's (1963) famous study of the cultural significance of the frontier in American history.

28. The most influential theoretical formulation of this point of view in anthropology is that of Collier and Yanagisako (1987a, 1987b).

29. See Enloe 1990: 93–123 for a similar argument about diplomatic wives.

30. Opinion polls showed, for example, that 25% fewer women than men supported America's 1991 war against Iraq (Hulbert 1991; Tavris 1990).

31. Bartimus and McCartney (1991: 228–260) describe the painful tensions in a Wyoming family when one of its women, Lindi Kirkbride, decided to join a local antinuclear group. Kirkbride said, "I was scared to death because I was breaking the family rule by speaking out, by going against the views of my father-in-law,

who was very much in support of the missiles and was the patriarch of the family. . . . To me that was the scariest thing of all—scarier than the missiles" (p. 247).

32. Taylor himself discusses the effect of his family on his attitude to weapons work in an interview in the film *Turning of the Tide* (Payne 1990). In the film he says that the criticism of his wife and mother were among the main reasons for his eventual renunciation of nuclear weapons work.

33. Another poignant story about the estranging effects of secrecy on families was told to me by a woman whose relationship with her father had always been difficult. Her father was a truck driver, and, some years earlier, as a young woman, she asked if she could join him on a trip during her vacation in an attempt to establish a closer relationship. He refused and would not explain why. For some years after this they had no contact, and it was only when they started talking again that he told her his cargo had been a nuclear warhead, which he was not allowed to disclose to her. Ironically, the daughter now has a clearance of her own and works at Livermore, where the warhead her father drove was designed.

CHAPTER 5. BODIES AND MACHINES

1. Morris Berman (1989) argues that the polarity of mind and body is the "basic fault" in Western civilization. Recent years have seen a number of critiques of Western science, mainly by feminist writers, that seek to problematize the dichotomous mind-set of Western science, particularly the polarity of mind and body (Griffin 1989; Haraway 1991; Harding 1986, 1991; Keller 1983, 1985, 1992; Merchant 1980). There have also been critiques of the conventional Christian split between mind and body, spirit and matter, from within the theological community. See, for example, Matthew Fox (1983), whose genealogical approach to Christian theology attempts to retrieve subjugated knowledges from earlier periods of Christian history in the service of a monistic pantheism that unifies the worlds of spirit and flesh. See also Pagels 1979.

2. For examples of the focus on discourse in the legitimation of nuclear weapons, see Aubrey 1982; Chilton 1985, 1989; Cohn 1987; Dillon 1989; Falk 1989; Gregory 1989; Gusterson 1991*b*, 1991*c*; Hilgartner, Bell, and O'Connor 1982; Hook 1985*a*, 1985*b*; Luke 1989; Manoff 1989; Mehan, Nathanson, and Skelly 1990; Nash 1981; Nathanson 1988; Taylor 1990, 1992, 1993; Wertsch 1987; the 1988 special issue of *Multilingua* (vol. 1–2) on nuclear discourse; and the 1984 special issue of *Diacritics* (summer) on nuclear criticism—particularly Derrida's piece.

For examples of psychological analyses focusing on repression, denial, and other "dysfunctional" processes in the psyches of nuclear weapons professionals, see Frank 1982; Holt 1984; Kovel 1983; Kull 1986, 1988; Levine, Jacobs, and Rubin 1988; Lifton 1982*a*; Lifton and Markusen 1990; Mack 1984, 1985, 1988; Rowe 1985; Steiner 1989; and Volkan 1985, 1988.

3. Key texts in this interpretive turn include Clifford 1988; Clifford and Marcus 1986; Crapanzano 1985; Geertz 1973, 1980, 1983, 1988; Marcus and Cushman 1982; and Rabinow 1977.

4. On the recent return of the body to anthropology, see Asad 1983; Comaroff 1985; Csordas 1990, 1994; Davis-Floyd 1992; Feldman 1991; Martin 1987, 1990, 1994; Rosaldo 1990; Scheper-Hughes and Locke 1987; Stoller 1989; and Taussig 1980. For an analysis of the importance of the body to social theory in general, see Turner 1984 and Johnson 1987.

5. Footage of the immediate aftermath of the bombings, shot by Akirir Iwasaki, was promptly impounded at the end of the war (Hook 1988). More recently, antinuclear activists, upset that Hiroshima and Nagasaki went unmentioned in exhibits at Los Alamos' Bradbury Science Museum, threatened a lawsuit and won the right to mount their own exhibit in the museum, including photographs of Hiroshima and Nagasaki.

6. In arguing that nuclear weapons entail dimensions of both sovereign and disciplinary power, I am diverging from Foucault's own view on this matter. In a tantalizingly brief discussion at the end of *The History of Sexuality*, Vol. I, Foucault presents nuclear weapons as a culmination of the development of "bio-power," saying "the atomic situation is now at the end of this process [of development of bio-power and techniques of discipline]: the power to expose a whole population to death is the underside of the power to guarantee an individual's continued existence" (Foucault 1980*a*: 137).

I agree that nuclear weapons, by virtue of their genocidal potential, fit with the evolution of "bio-power." But they also, at the same time, embody a return to some of the privileges and habits of sovereign power. In this vein, Dahl (1985) and R. Falk (1982) suggest—although not specifically in reference to Foucault's theories—that the invention of nuclear weapons interrupted the progressive encroachment of civil society on the state's war-making prerogatives and apparatuses and its absorption into them. Dahl and Falk argue that nuclear weapons in some ways return us to the old situation in which the sovereign can annihilate his (or her) subjects without liberal rituals of consent. Scarry (1985: 139–157) makes a similar point in arguing that nuclear war resembles torture more than war precisely because participants in a nuclear war have no chance to consent to the injuries, or risk of injuries, to their bodies. See also Scarry 1991 on this point.

7. Despite the best efforts of American scientists to document the effects of the atomic bombings in meticulous detail, there is still considerable uncertainty about the precise casualty figures. Taking Hiroshima first, Bernstein (1976*a*: vii) estimates casualties at 70,000. The Committee for the Compilation of Materials on the Damage Caused by the Atomic Bombs in Hiroshima and Nagasaki (1981: 113) estimates 118,000. Bundy (1988: 80) puts the number at 130,000, Rhodes (1988: 734) puts it at 140,000, and Postol (1987: 519) says it could be anywhere between 40,000 and 170,000. For Nagasaki, Bernstein (1976: vii) puts the dead at 40,000. Rhodes (1988: 740) and the Committee for the Compilation of Materials

(1981: 114) both estimate about 70,000 dead, and Postol (1987: 519) says the number could be anywhere between 20,000 and 40,000.

8. For more information on this enterprise, see Caulfield 1989; Committee for the Compilation of Materials 1981; Glasstone and Dolan 1977; Lindee 1990; Neel, Beebe, and Miller 1985; and Postol 1987.

9. There was a flood of articles in the American media about these human radiation experiments when they first came to light at the end of 1993. The article that started it all was Welsome's (1993).

10. Hamilton also claims that the organs of a number of workers have been removed and examined at Los Alamos without the knowledge or permission of their relatives and without the prior consent of the workers who died. Further, he says that Los Alamos has mysteriously lost the remains and the test results of a number of workers whose relatives are suing the government for negligence in regard to their deaths. Many of these worked at the Fernald facility, where uranium was produced, and the Rocky Flats plant, where plutonium triggers were produced. Both facilities were closed by DOE in the late 1980s following revelations that they were violating official health and safety regulations. Bartimus and McCartney (1991: 182–207) tell the story of Don Gabel, a Rocky Flats worker who died of brain cancer, whose brain was mislaid at Los Alamos.

11. Some footage of this gruesome experiment can be seen in the documentary film *Dark Circle* (Irving 1982). The documentary footage is also incorporated into a fictionalized re-creation of the events in the Hollywood film *Nightbreaker* (Markle 1989).

12. Such photographs can be found in Glasstone and Dolan 1977—a canonical reference book for nuclear weapons scientists and other nuclear weapons experts.

13. The comparison between Freud and Radcliffe-Brown is also made by Kuper (1983: 64). For examples of analyses of scientists' jokes, see Gilbert and Mulkay 1984: 172–187; and Katz 1981. In her study of surgeon's jokes—a genre that we might expect to be quite similar to weapons scientists' jokes since both groups place the body in jeopardy—Katz points out that surgeons like to tell two kinds of jokes: those that denigrate their patients and those about an operation going wrong.

14. A half-life is the amount of time it takes for half of a given quantity of a radioactive substance to decay into another (usually nonradioactive) substance. After one half-life, only one-half of the material remains. After two half-lives, only one-fourth remains, and so on.

15. For more information about this "natural fission reactor," see Cowan 1976.

16. For example, one highly placed scientist who was partly responsible for overseeing the safety of nuclear tests at the Nevada Test Site told me that he really did not know anything about fatal doses of radiation or the different cancers associated with different kinds of radiation. In view of the nature of his responsibilities, I was taken aback by this. On another truly remarkable occasion, a spokesperson for the laboratory's Environmental Protection Department assured a Livermore town meeting that a recent approximately 300,000-curie release of

tritium at South Carolina's Savannah River nuclear facility was within safety limits. When I pressed her on this after the meeting, she told me she did not know anything about the safety and danger levels of tritium (a substance routinely handled at the laboratory) but had interpreted a nod from one of her colleagues in the audience as meaning that the release was safe. When I questioned the colleague, he told me his nod was only to confirm that the release, mentioned in a citizen's question at the meeting, had indeed happened.

17. The hearing was on May 9, 1989. These details come from my fieldnotes and from Bodovitz 1989*b*.

18. For further discussions within medical anthropology of this phenomenon of learned mistrust of one's own body, see Davis-Floyd 1992; Farmer and Kleinman 1989; Martin 1987; and Taussig 1980.

19. For classic discussions of totemism in the anthropological literature, see Durkheim 1915; Leach 1967; and Lévi-Strauss 1961. For further discussion of the uses of machinery in the building of scientific reputations, see Hughes 1990; Latour 1987; and Traweek 1988: 46–73.

20. Turkle's argument, particularly the phrase that machines are "good to think with," is itself an appropriation of and a play on older structuralist works that presented animals in very much the same light: as entities that provide mirrors and foils for the construction of human identity. For examples of this literature, see Leach 1964; Lévi-Strauss 1961, 1965; and Tambiah 1969.

21. Caputi (1991) is also struck by the exchange of human and mechanical characteristics in nuclear discourse, and my analysis here draws strongly on hers, as well as on the work of Cohn (1987) and Scarry (1985).

22. For a theoretical discussion of the way metaphors work and of strategies for analyzing them, see Lakoff 1987. Other works that focus on metaphors in scientific discourse are Cohn 1987; Davis-Floyd 1992; Gray 1997; Haraway 1991, 1992; Keller 1985, 1992; and Martin 1987, 1990, 1994.

23. The notion that machines might substitute for or replicate human life underlies the computer scientists' quest for artificial intelligence and the genetic engineers' invasion of the human genome. (A fragment of the human genome project is, incidentally, carried out by the Livermore laboratory's biomedical division.) The Western scientist's pursuit of artificial or mechanical life is, of course, the fundamental drama in Mary Shelley's dark parable for the scientific age, *Frankenstein*. For a lapsed scientist's reflections on the Frankenstein parable, see Easlea 1983. Klaus Theweleit (1987) has also written about the "utopia of the body machine."

CHAPTER 6. TESTING, TESTING, TESTING

1. See, for example, Jon Else's documentary film *The Day After Trinity* as well as the recent Hollywood depiction of the Manhattan Project, *Fat Man and Little Boy*. See also Rhodes 1988 and Jungk 1985.

2. In the usage of nuclear weapons designers there is a difference between a "bomb" and a "device": a "device" is a prototype designed for an experimental test, whereas a "bomb" is a finished product assigned to the military for potential combat use. Los Alamos scientists referred to the first nuclear bomb, tested at Alamogordo in New Mexico, as "the gadget." The term "device" is also part of a wider euphemistic lexicon developed by the nuclear weapons community in which phenomena that appear to the lay person as "bombs," "explosions," "civilian deaths," and "destruction of cities" are referred to as "devices," "events," "collateral damage," and "countervalue attacks," respectively.

3. Hansen (1988: 11) puts the number of components in a modern nuclear weapon at "over 4,000." My interviewees usually said "about 5,000."

4. In 1988 there were about 240 members of A and B divisions, the two weapons design divisions at Livermore. By 1993 this number had fallen to about 210 (Medalia 1994: 32). Although I use the term "designer" as if it were unproblematic, this is far from the case, since some people claimed that computer code developers, though members of A and B divisions, were not "real" designers, and others said that only those who had had overall responsibility for a test were "real" designers.

5. In his autobiography, Herb York, Livermore's first director, also stresses Livermore's entrepreneurial freedom to test outside formal military requirements (York 1987: 75–77, 87).

6. Once the design process enters phase 3, the laboratory is working on a prototype for what will usually become a finished weapon. At this point the weapon receives a "B" number if it is to be a bomb and a "W" number if it is to be a missile warhead. The MX warhead, for example, was the W-87, meaning that it was the 87th warhead to be designed and tested. All tests carried out to perfect the warhead were called W-87 tests.

7. For an explanation of the basic physics of a nuclear weapon and of the relationship between the primary and the secondary within a bomb, see Chapter 2, note 25.

8. My description of the preparation for a nuclear test is heavily indebted to Broad 1986; 1992: 74–75 and Cochran et al. 1987: 44–53. Estimates of the cost of nuclear testing are notoriously problematic. The figures used here are drawn from Broad 1992: 91; Norris and Arkin 1991; and Rogers 1990f.

9. According to official Energy Department figures, roughly 16% of U.S. underground tests have vented radiation, most of them in the 1960s (DOE INV-209 [Rev. 11]). Some antinuclear scientists put the proportion of tests that vented closer to a third (Cochran et al. 1987: 45). Some of the worst accidents in the last 25 years include the 1970 Baneberry test, which sent a radioactive cloud 8,000 feet into the air, contaminating northern Nevada, Utah, and, eventually, Canada (thus putting the United States in technical breach of the Limited Test Ban Treaty); the 1980 Riola test, which vented radioactivity that was later detected in California; and the 1986 Mighty Oak weapons effects test, which contaminated

workers and vented gas into the atmosphere (Hanrahan 1988; Kaplan 1982: 69–71; Soble 1984). For evidence that participation in nuclear testing has caused elevated levels of cancer among workers at the Nevada Test Site, see Schneider 1989.

10. American public concern was initially sparked by the Bravo test of 1954, which contaminated a Japanese fishing boat, *The Lucky Dragon*, killing one crew member and causing radiation sickness among the others (Divine 1978: 4–7). O'Rourke (1986) and Alcalay (1988) claim that the Bravo test also involved the deliberate use of the inhabitants of the Rongelap Atoll as human guinea pigs to explore the short- and long-term effects of radiation on the human body. The United States also conducted atmospheric nuclear tests at the Nevada Test Site in the 1940s, 1950s, and early 1960s. Gallagher (1993) and Rosenberg (1980) describe the adverse effects of these tests on the health of "downwinders" in Utah and American soldiers forced to conduct maneuvers in and around the mushroom clouds at Nevada.

11. On the history of SANE, see Boyer 1984; Katz 1980; McCrea and Markle 1989; and Wittner 1984.

12. One senior manager at Livermore told me that 12% of the laboratory's designers quit during the moratorium, and laboratory managers had expected another 12% to quit if the moratorium lasted another year.

13. The first American underground test was the Rainier test in 1957 at the Nevada Test Site. Staged by the Livermore laboratory at Edward Teller's suggestion, it demonstrated the feasibility of underground testing should atmospheric testing be banned. The test immediately became the subject of public controversy when the AEC, arguing that underground nuclear tests could not easily be detected (and therefore should not be banned), claimed that the Rainier test had not been detected by seismologists more than 250 miles away. There ensued an uproar in which a number of scientists took evidence to the contrary to the Senate Foreign Relations Committee. The AEC finally conceded that the test had been detected as far away as 2,300 miles, in Alaska (Gilpin 1962: 181–182).

14. In "dial-a-yield" weapons the explosive yield is varied by changing the fissile "pit" at the core of the weapon, by adjusting the timing of the neutron generator, or by varying the amount of tritium used to boost the fission reaction in a boosted fission weapon (Cochran et al. 1984: 28–36).

15. In one of the less-known instances of superpower cooperation in the cold war, this technology was secretly shared with the Soviet Union once it was developed (Smoke 1987: 299).

16. According to Article VI of the Non-Proliferation Treaty, in exchange for other countries' renunciation of the right to acquire nuclear weapons, the superpowers undertook to "pursue negotiations in good faith on effective measures relating to cessation of the nuclear arms race at an early date and to nuclear disarmament, and on a treaty on general and complete disarmament." Article VI was, however, ignored by the superpowers throughout the cold war.

17. For the texts of these treaties, as well as a rigorous discussion of their technical and political significance, see Blacker and Duffy 1984.

18. Agnew's claim became controversial on a number of levels. Some, such as York himself, disputed its accuracy, saying that Agnew was exaggerating his own influence (York 1987: 285–287). Others argued that it showed the improper and undemocratic influence of the nuclear weapons laboratories, which were able to use their technical authority to advance their political agenda. Meanwhile the remark stirred controversy at the University of California, which manages the laboratories on behalf of the Department of Energy: some UC faculty members argued that the university was implicated in improper political lobbying (York 1987: 286).

19. New weapons such as the MX warhead were designed so that the conventional explosive in the implosion mechanism was a new kind of insensitive high explosive (IHE) less likely to detonate in an accident. Since IHE is heavier and less energetic than ordinary conventional explosive, this created all kinds of ancillary design challenges for designers seeking to squeeze a large number of warheads onto the top of a missile. Before IHE was introduced U.S. nuclear weapons were involved in a number of accidents, two of which produced nonnuclear explosions that scattered plutonium over a wide area. For more details on U.S. nuclear weapons accidents in the past, see Barasch 1983: 41–42; Hansen 1990; J. Smith 1990a; Williams and Cantelon 1984: 239–245; and Wilson 1983: 196–202.

20. The Soviet nuclear test site in Kazakhstan was the target of a substantial antinuclear movement in the USSR in the late 1980s, although it was given little publicity in the United States. This movement, named the Nevada-Semipalatinsk movement to make clear the mutual dependence of the Soviet and American nuclear testing programs and the solidarity of the Soviet and American antinuclear movements, had emerged to protest the health and environmental effects of Soviet nuclear testing. The movement was led by the well-known Kazakh poet (originally trained as an engineer) Olzhas Suleimenov. In October 1990, the Republic of Kazakhstan passed a Declaration of Sovereignty that included a clause prohibiting all nuclear testing within its borders immediately. The test site was officially closed on August 29, 1991—much earlier than Gorbachev had intended. Little has been written about the Nevada-Semipalatinsk movement in English. For sketchy accounts of its history and achievements, see Brown 1991; Carter 1990; and Zheutlin 1990.

21. Although some laboratory scientists were heavily involved in research for the Strategic Defense Initiative, others produced studies pointing out flaws in the strategic rationales used to legitimate many SDI weapons (see, e.g., Speed 1990).

22. Although it is not an arms control measure, Livermore scientists point out that the laboratory, having designed the warhead for the MX missile, also conducted the basing study that concluded that the "dense pack" basing mode planned for the missile was ill-conceived. Two Livermore employees, John Harvey and

Barry Fridling, also published an article criticizing the idea that the MX could be based on mobile trains (Harvey and Fridling 1988–1989).

23. The Threshold Test Ban Treaty, signed in 1974, forbids nuclear explosions stronger than 150 kilotons. When the Reagan administration made its claim that the Soviets were in breach of the treaty, there were ambiguous data about the yields of some recent Soviet nuclear tests. The data could be interpreted as showing that the Soviets were complying with the 150-kiloton limit on nuclear tests but could also be interpreted as showing that the Soviets had breached the limit on a few occasions. Interpretation of the seismic data was complicated by the fact that the geology of the Soviet test site was different from the geology of the American test site in Nevada, giving stronger seismic signals of explosions than would be the case in Nevada. American scientists were unsure how to factor this difference into their calculations of Soviet explosive yields. Whereas the Reagan administration claimed that the Soviets had breached the treaty, the position of Livermore scientists was that they could not be sure that the Soviets were definitely in compliance with the treaty, but neither could they be sure that the Soviets had broken it and that, in any case, any Soviet violation could only be marginal. This is what Batzel and Nordyke testified to the Senate Foreign Relations Committee.

See also J. Smith 1985 for details of the weapons laboratories' concern when President Reagan erroneously claimed that the Soviets could afford to suspend nuclear testing in 1985 because they had just completed an accelerated testing program.

24. For similar arguments that the Livermore laboratory promotes weapons design and testing out of institutional self-interest, see Broad 1985; Marsh 1983a; and J. Smith 1985. For a very different argument, namely, that the pace of nuclear testing has been driven entirely by the political relationship between the superpowers and not by technical requirements or by the self-interest of the laboratories, see Rhodes 1994.

25. Following the end of the cold war, laboratory managers gave primary emphasis to a new reason for continued testing: to improve the safety of the nuclear stockpile. This followed the revelation in 1990 that design flaws in three American warheads—the W-79 artillery shell, the W-88 Trident warhead, and the short-range attack missile-A—created the possibility of accidental explosions in certain extreme situations (Drell, Townes, and Foster 1991; J. Smith 1990a). A warhead is unsafe if it goes off when it is not supposed to and unreliable if it does not go off when it is supposed to. The government defines reliability in such a way that if a weapon certified at 100 kilotons only produced an 80-kiloton yield, then it would be deemed unreliable.

26. This letter is reproduced in Appendix K of Kidder 1987.

27. Kidder was alluding here to a controversy from two years earlier regarding allegations that the laboratories were deliberately designing weapons that might

need reliability testing. Batzel inadvertently touched off the controversy when he testified to Congress in 1985 that "these weapons were designed under the assumption that nuclear testing would continue, so that if any problem ever arose in the stockpile, a nuclear test could be performed to help certify that the weapon would continue to work as it was designed to. . . . The designs would have been very different if the guidelines from the government had placed primary emphasis on stockpile longevity" (quoted in Markey 1985; see also Rogers 1985). Designers refer to highly reliable weapons as "wooden bombs." As the name implies, "wooden bombs" are not very exciting, and designers have been more interested in designing weapons that push the edge of the envelope.

28. Cochran et al. (1987: 44) quote an estimate by Farooq Hussain of a dozen reliability tests over thirty-five years. Livermore scientists told me that most American reliability tests were carried out in the 1980s.

29. For a more detailed exploration of the issues at stake here, see the contending Livermore reports by Kidder (1987) and Miller et al. (1987). The issue is reprised by Fetter (1987–1988, 1988a, 1988b), who argues that stockpile reliability can be assured with high confidence under a test ban. For a rebuttal of his argument by two Livermore scientists (one of whom was a co-author of the original report that largely sparked the whole debate), see Immele and Brown 1988.

30. In science and technology studies, recent years have seen a veritable explosion of books and articles making the case that scientific knowledge is not a store of accumulated, proven facts but a corpus of more or less contestable constructions of the world. Within this literature all scientific and technical judgments are seen as, to some degree, political and potentially contestable. Important contributions to this literature include Bijker, Hughes and Pinch 1990; Bloor 1991; Collins 1985; Feyerabend 1988; Haraway 1990, 1991; Harding 1986; Latour 1987, 1988; Latour and Woolgar 1979; and Pickering 1984, 1992. This perspective can be traced back to the seminal works of Kuhn (1962) and Fleck (1979).

31. The phrase "incitement to discourse" comes from Foucault (1980a: chap. 1). Foucault points out that discourse is most insidiously controlled by defining the questions asked rather than the answers given.

32. For a little-read but interesting book arguing that science is saturated with elements of myth and ritual, see Reynolds 1991. For other attempts to apply ritual theory to scientific practices, see Abir-Am 1992, Davis-Floyd 1992, and Lynch 1988. Gusterson (1992) evaluates Abir-Am's article and discusses more generally the notion of applying ritual theory to science.

33. Mary Pratt (pers. comm.) points out that processes of initiation often involve breaking taboos. For example, the Ilongots of the Philippines take heads in order to come of age (R. Rosaldo 1980), and Hell's Angels traditionally taste menstrual blood in their initiation rituals. In the case of weapons scientists, the "nuclear taboo"—the tradition that nuclear weapons are too terrible to explode—is broken, albeit in a carefully controlled way.

34. For more on the notion of "symbolic capital" and on strategies for trading it, see Bourdieu 1977*a*, 1977*b*, 1984.

35. Paul Chilton (pers. comm.) points out that this passage is a high-tech variant of the classic mythological quest narrative: a lost object triggers a dangerous and heroic journey to the underworld, where a riddle is solved, thus restoring order to the world and establishing the status of the hero(es).

36. For further exploration of religious imagery in American nuclear culture, see Chernus 1989, 1991.

37. On physicists' predilection for giving their experimental equipment sexualized names, see Traweek 1992.

38. One of the more bizarre contributions to this debate is a cartoon, drawn by the physicist Gamow, depicting Teller's and Ulam's contributions to the H-bomb. I saw the cartoon at the National Atomic Museum in Albuquerque, where the accompanying text explained that Teller "wears an Indian necklace, which according to Gamow is the symbol for the womb." One Livermore scientist also told me a story about the American physicist John Wheeler visiting Zeldovich, one of the creators of the Soviet H-bomb. Wheeler presented Zeldovich with "male" and "female" salt and pepper shakers, explaining that the female one represented Teller and the male one Zeldovich, whose H-bomb design was considered more elegant than Teller's.

39. Keller (1992) has made the same broad argument. For a similar argument applied to the rituals of nonliterate societies, see Bettelheim 1971.

40. See Cohn 1987 for a piece that takes some of Easlea's data and reworks the analysis within this framework of language as constitutive of, rather than simply symptomatic of, subjective reality. One advantage of this more sociological perspective in the present context is that it does not matter whether speakers invented a circuit of metaphors themselves or inherited it from other social groups with whom they share it; this is because the analytical focus within the framework of this perspective is not on the unconscious motivation of speakers but on the social effects of shared linguistic conventions whose use binds together communities of speakers.

CHAPTER 7. CRISIS

1. An anecdote illustrates the point: one veteran protestor recalled for me that for a long time the only people who criticized the laboratory's work were a handful of Christians who occasionally held low-key vigils at the laboratory gates. In 1960 one of their number found the address of Director Harold Brown in the local telephone book and went to pay him an unannounced visit one weekend. Reportedly, Brown, who was teaching his son to swim in the backyard swimming pool, invited the protestor to come and have some lemonade by the pool and discuss nuclear weapons. The visit was, so I was told, quite cordial.

2. For the definitive study of nuclear war-fighting talk in the Reagan administration, see Scheer 1982. For critical accounts of the rise of the "Second Cold War," see Halliday 1983 and Sanders 1983.

3. The "Call to Halt the Arms Race" is reprinted in Appendix A of Waller 1987, a history of the freeze in Congress written by a congressional staffer who worked on its behalf. Pam Solo (1988), another insider in the Nuclear Freeze Campaign, has also written a history of the campaign. For a detailed exposition of the idea of a nuclear freeze, see Forsberg 1982. Kennedy and Hatfield (1982) give the definitive popular articulation of the rationale for a freeze. There are now a number of edited volumes evaluating the freeze: Miller (1984) is largely sympathetic to the Freeze; Payne and Gray (1984) and Garfinkle (1984) are not; the essays in Cole and Taylor's volume (1983) are more heterogeneous in perspective.

4. On the success of the antinuclear movement in reframing the nuclear weapons debate, see Mehan and Skelly 1988; and Mehan, Nathanson and Skelly 1990.

5. Different polls produced slightly different numbers. Lou Harris (1984) found 76% supporting a bilateral freeze. Solo (1988: 84) cites an ABC News/ *Washington Post* poll, taken in April 1982, that found 81% support for a freeze. Milburn, Watanabe, and Kramer (1986) cite a different ABC/*Washington Post* poll, this one from 1983, finding 83% support for a freeze, and their own Massachusetts poll found 81% support with surprisingly little variation by political affiliation, ethnicity, income, education, or religion. McCrea and Markle (1989: 140) cite a range of polls putting support for a freeze at between 70 and 80% between 1982 and 1984.

6. For a more extended exploration of the New Age faction of the peace movement, see Wright 1989. For a critical portrait of Beyond War, see Faludi 1987.

7. Although the term "civil disobedience" may be more familiar than "direct action," I often use the latter because it is the term preferred by most of those I knew in this wing of the movement. Those who insisted on calling what they did "direct action" rather than "civil disobedience" disliked the implication of token gesturing in the word "civil," and they resented calling their own actions "disobedience" since they felt that it was the government, not them, that was disobeying the law—the international law against planning genocide under which the Nazis were tried at Nuremburg. Some protestors even called their actions "divine obedience," though the term did not catch on.

8. My understanding of the Livermore Action Group mainly comes from an excellent pair of articles and a book by Barbara Epstein (1985, 1988, 1991) and from Schaeffer (1989). Epstein, an activist and a professional historian, writes as an insider with a complex sociological understanding of the movement in which she participated. LAG's internal conversations can be followed in its newspaper *Direct Action*, of which there are 25 issues. A fine documentary film about the June 21, 1982, LAG protest is Peter Adair's *Stopping History*.

9. Knowing accurate numbers of demonstrators at any protest is notoriously difficult. Even the number of arrests is often disputed, as in this instance: the laboratory estimated a total crowd of a little over 4,100 with 1,216 arrests, while LAG estimated a total crowd of around 5,000 with "over 1,300" arrests.

10. The laboratory puts the number of arrests at 1,029. Diehl (1988) puts the number at "about 1,200." Cabasso and Moon (1985: 4) say 1,008 people were arrested on June 20, and arrests over the next few days brought the total number to 1,066.

11. There were seven antinuclear political action committees active in the 1984 election. They raised almost $5.5 million among them. Of this, $3.75 million was raised by the freeze political action committee, Freeze Voter '84 (Solo 1988: 169).

12. One senior arms control adviser in the Reagan administration told me privately that their strategy in the INF talks was to offer the Soviets conditions they could not be expected to accept so as to maintain the process of negotiation without the encumbrance of agreement. He said the policy backfired horribly when the Soviets simply accepted the American position. For a study of the first Reagan administration's reluctance during the early stages of the INF talks to make the compromises that are usually necessary to achieve an arms control agreement, see Talbot 1984.

13. The statistics in this paragraph come from the APT itself. The *Las Vegas Review-Journal* put the number of arrests for the 1988 action at 2,050 (Weier 1988). The numbers of arrests are potentially misleading in that they contain a large number of repeat arrests: since the police released everyone they arrested each day without charging them, and since these protests went on for a week, many people were arrested several times each during the week. For accounts of the protests see Jenkins 1988 and the fine opening chapters of Solnit 1994.

14. Although I speak of the environmental and antinuclear movements as if they are distinct, in fact many leaders of the former were also active in the latter, and they regarded the distinction between the two as artificial. However, some people in Livermore who supported Tri-Valley CAREs told me that they disagreed with CAREs' opposition to the laboratory's weapons work but were willing to work with the group anyway because they were so distressed by the laboratory's environmental record, and this was CAREs' main focus.

15. For a brief history of CAREs, see Tompkins 1990. Media revelations of health and environmental problems in the nuclear weapons complex focused mainly on the Hanford plutonium production facility in Washington State, the Fernald uranium facility in Ohio, the Savannah River tritium reactors in South Carolina, and the Rocky Flats plutonium pit facility in Colorado. While reporting on these facilities, particularly in the *New York Times*, emboldened local journalists to seek out analogous environmental stories in Livermore, local forces were also at work: for example, two local journalists told me that by the late 1980s the publishers of the *Tri-Valley Herald* were increasingly inclined to resent the laboratory as a bastion of local antigrowth sentiment and as an institution that took

up a square mile of prime real estate without even paying local taxes. Accordingly, they were said to have encouraged their reporters to cover the laboratory's problems more aggressively.

16. Laboratory officials insisted that the solvents, trichloroethylene and perchloroethylene, were the legacy of the naval air force base that had occupied the site before the laboratory and were not a result of the laboratory's nuclear weapons work. The benzene contamination occurred when gasoline leaked into the ground from underground storage tanks between the early 1950s and 1979. The highest levels of contamination, widely cited in the media, were characteristic of very few spots at the laboratory (Stober 1990*a*).

17. In the early 1990s Livermore was dropped from Stark's territory in the course of redistricting. Its next congressman was a Republican, Bill Baker.

18. See GAO Report B-229072.

19. For media accounts of the Snowstorm controversy, see Iwata 1988*a*, 1988*c*; Kiernan 1988*a*; and Sirica 1988. Nuckolls became director of the laboratory after the termination of Operation Snowstorm, but he did investigate and defend the laboratory's actions: see Nuckolls 1988.

20. The laboratory responded to this slew of drug problems by instituting mandatory drug testing for those employees working in the plutonium facility and for any employee suspected by their supervisor of using drugs. The laboratory also offered to pay 80% of the rehabilitation costs for any employee attending a substance-abuse treatment center (Rogers 1989*c*).

21. The Woodruff affair was also investigated by the GAO. The resulting report (B-293094) was not very critical of the laboratory, but there were later allegations that the GAO investigation was itself improper since one of the investigators was seeking employment at the laboratory while investigating its conduct. The definitive account of the entire affair is Broad 1992*a*.

22. For examples of arguments on both sides of this controversy, see Hecker and Nuckolls 1990 and Hufbauer, Johnson, and Kohn 1990.

CHAPTER 8. A DIFFERENT REALITY

1. Two histories of earlier phases of the American peace movement that evoke its essentially middle-class character, though without focusing explicitly on it, are DeBenedetti 1980 and Wittner 1984. For a book-length portrait of the antinuclear movement of the 1980s that foregrounds its middle-class aura, see Loeb 1987. See also Peattie 1986. For studies of the movement against the Vietnam War that emphasize the socially advantaged background of most protestors, see Erikson 1968 and Solomon and Fishman 1970.

2. Quoted in Ehrenreich (1989: 149).

3. On the notion of cultural capital, see Bourdieu 1984.

4. There are both left- and right-wing versions of "new class" theory, the principal difference being that the Left sees in the new class a constituency for

humane social change while the Right sees in them a group of elitist troublemakers disguising their own self-interest beneath a professed concern for others. Alvin Gouldner (1979) is, along with Alaine Touraine (1981), one of the best-known exponents of the Left perspective. Irving Kristol, Seymour Martin Lipset, Michael Novak, and Daniel Moynihan are among those who have articulated the Right perspective. For a rigorous, if ultimately unsympathetic, overview of their thinking, see Ehrenreich 1989: 144–195. A briefer, but sympathetic, synopsis of the Right perspective is given by Berger (1994).

5. Book-length examples of this popular literature include Caldicott 1978; Ground Zero 1982; Kennedy and Hatfield 1982; Powers 1982; Scheer 1982; Schell 1982, 1986; and Thompson and Smith 1981. These years also saw a proliferation of articles on nuclear weapons policy for the educated lay person in newspapers and magazines such as *Atlantic*, the *New Republic*, and the *New Yorker* (where Jonathan Schell's *The Fate of the Earth* appeared as a series of articles before its publication as a book).

6. The most eloquent statements from this time of a sense of inevitable impending catastrophe are Ellsberg 1981 and Thompson 1981, 1982*a*.

7. One minority group that did participate to some extent in the movement was the Asian community, which had its own group, Bay Area Asians for Nuclear Disarmament (BAAND), in the 1980s. Its members were, like white followers of the movement, largely middle class, and the movement had a special resonance for them because of the bombing of Hiroshima and Nagasaki.

8. The movement of the 1950s against nuclear testing is most comprehensively described by Divine (1978) and Wittner (1984). See also Gilpin 1962; Holgate 1991; Katz 1980; and McCrea and Markle 1989. Boyer (1984, 1985) describes the wave of concern in the late 1940s that preceded the mass movement of the late 1950s and then the long period of quiescence that followed.

9. For more on the women's peace movement, see Blackwood 1984; Krasniewicz 1992; Mehan and Wills 1988; and Wilson 1988.

10. For portraits of religious antinuclear activists, see Loeb 1987; Mojtabai 1986; Totten and Totten 1984; and Wallis 1983.

11. In her ethnographic study of a nuclear reprocessing plant in France, Françoise Zonabend (1993: 7) similarly notices "the absence of disaster dreams. Of the people I interviewed, all but two assured me that they never had such dreams, as if everyone here unconsciously forbids him or herself to dream about a nuclear apocalypse." Unlike me, however, Zonabend seems to assume that it is "natural" to be afraid of nuclear technology and that only the absence of nuclear nightmares requires explanation. For a different view of nuclear fear, see Weart 1988.

12. I do not want to give the impression that these protests *only* contain images of death. Many people arrive at protests with images of doves, rainbows, children holding hands, peace signs, and so on. The protests are split between images of death and despair, on the one hand, and images of life and hope, on the other. The

movement, like many of the individuals within it, struggles to integrate the impulses of hope and despair as responses to nuclear weapons.

13. Two Bay Area pioneers of such workshops are Chellis Glendinning (1987) and Joanna Macy (1983), who were active in Psychotherapists for Social Responsibility and Interhelp, respectively. These groups specifically worked on the issue of "psychic numbing" in the nuclear age. Workshop exercises involved, for example, drawing pictures of what one would most fear losing in a nuclear war, or imagining explaining to a child in the next century how nuclear weapons were eliminated from the earth. It is no coincidence that these groups did well in the Bay Area, which has large New Age and psychotherapeutic communities.

14. For a brief description of the BB exercise in practice, see Faludi 1987: 21–22.

15. A. G. Mojtabai (1992) argues that antinuclear narratives are secular variants of Christian apocalyptic narratives about the end of the world. She suggests that antinuclear narratives of the end of the world are less appealing than their Christian counterparts because they present the end as morally meaningless rather than as a redemptive conflagration that forms part of a morally coherent story.

16. Livermore scientists who have reviewed this passage called it exaggerated and technically inaccurate. One accused Caldicott of "inventing something comparable to a small asteroid strike in order to scare herself." The passage is quoted here, regardless of its technical accuracy or inaccuracy, as an example of an influential antinuclear activist's rhetoric.

17. For expositions of this point of view, see Glendinning 1987; Lifton 1982*a*; Lifton and Markusen 1990; and Macy 1983.

18. The general line of argument here is, as many readers will recognize, indebted to Foucault's (1980*a*) argument that the selves of people in the West have, in the last century, been colonized by sexuality under the guise of sexual liberation. Foucault argues that educators, doctors, and psychologists have been among the principal agents encouraging the internalization and confession of sexuality; they have also been the principal agents encouraging the internalization and confession of the bomb.

19. Teller and Sagan were literally paired off with one another in a debate on the arms race in *Discover* magazine: see Sagan 1985 and Teller 1985.

20. Hans Bethe worked on the Manhattan Project and the development of the hydrogen bomb. He was head of the theoretical division at Los Alamos. In the 1980s, when he was a Cornell physics professor, Bethe spoke against SDI and on behalf of a nuclear test ban treaty. Norris Bradbury succeeded Oppenheimer as director of Los Alamos. Carson Mark was head of Los Alamos' theoretical division. Richard Garwin, an IBM physicist who had worked on the hydrogen bomb, has been one of the government's foremost advisers on weapons policy and arms control; he became an outspoken opponent of SDI in the 1980s. Glenn Seaborg, the inventor of plutonium, was chair of the Atomic Energy Commission in the

1950s but became a proponent of a nuclear test ban treaty in the 1980s. Herb York, the Livermore laboratory's first director, headed Jimmy Carter's negotiating team at the comprehensive test ban treaty talks. For more on Ray Kidder, a Livermore scientist who opposed continued nuclear testing in the 1980s, see chapter 6.

21. For Evernden's written arguments that it would be possible to verify at least a very low threshold test ban treaty, see Evernden 1982, 1986. Evernden, who works for the U.S. Geological Survey, spoke to the press on behalf of the Nuclear Freeze Campaign, which specifically deployed him to counter arguments that it would be impossible to verify stringent restrictions on nuclear testing.

22. Sagan and Turco were two well-known scientists in a group of five that produced the original study arguing that even a "small" nuclear war would probably produce an environmental catastrophe, a "nuclear winter," for the entire planet. Most scientists now agree that the original study was deeply flawed, but the general idea of nuclear winter still stands, even though there is disagreement about the magnitude of the effect in the event of a major nuclear exchange. For the original study, see Turco et al. 1983. For a more recent account by Sagan, see Sagan 1986.

23. For this group's best-known collective statement of the need to deescalate the arms race, see Bundy et al. 1982. For their individual critiques of the arms race, see Kennan 1983 and McNamara 1986. Talbot (1984) explores their recruitment to the freeze.

24. The argument that nuclear weapons violate international law has been developed by Boyle (1988). One of its most influential supporters in northern California is Frank Newman, a former California State Supreme Court justice who now teaches law at UC Berkeley. The late 1980s also saw unsuccessful attempts by Congressman Ron Dellums to obtain court injunctions declaring unconstitutional the official U.S. policy that the president can use nuclear weapons without congressional approval. (Scarry 1991: note 33). See Scarry 1991 for an argument that the president's ability to launch a nuclear attack without congressional or popular approval violates the Second Amendment guaranteeing all citizens the right to bear arms (and hence participatory control over the collective use of violence).

25. Behar (1991) makes a similar argument that, in the contemporary era, doctors have appropriated the roles of priest and minister. For an extended analysis of the doctors' effectiveness in mobilizing their expanded authority in the nuclear arms debate, see Neale 1988.

26. For examples of such claims about children, see the documentary film *Growing Up in the Nuclear Shadow: What the Children Have to tell Us* (Verdon-Roe, Thiermann, and Thiermann 1983) and the written texts by Coles (1985); Goodman et al. (1983); Lifton (1982*a*: 48–56); and Mack and Snow (1986).

27. Forsberg's best-known writings are Forsberg 1982, 1984.

28. It is easy to forget the importance of children in the antinuclear movement. An important national figure in the antinuclear movement of the early 1980s was

Samantha Smith who, when not yet a teenager, wrote a letter to Yuri Andropov asking why the superpowers could not end the arms race. She received national media coverage when she met Andropov at the Kremlin, after which she toured the United States speaking on the peace issue. The antinuclear movement also mobilized children to write letters to Ronald Reagan about their fears of dying in a nuclear war and organized a program called Children as Teachers of Peace. Children were often used in the rhetoric of the movement as embodiments of innocent wisdom—"Why can't the Americans and Russians just make friends, daddy?"—to interrogate the realpolitik of the state and to provide a radically different perspective from which the arms race made no sense.

In northern California itself, the Livermore Action Group included a children's affinity group that participated in civil disobedience, and at one public hearing on the laboratory's environmental record a ten-year-old boy stood up and said, "I am furious at you for dumping your waste. In my house, if someone makes a mess before cleaning up another one, they're in big trouble" (McKenzie 1991*b*).

29. Although some people come to protests simply as individuals, many come as members of "affinity groups," so called because membership is based on some thread of affinity: paganism, residence in a common neighborhood, participation in the men's movement, an interest in liberation theology, and so on. These groups often spend weeks in discussion and rehearsal preparing for a protest. Affinity groups help build a sense of community and, since each is in theory supposed to send a delegate to the "spokescouncil" coordinating any protest, they provide political representation for individuals. Most affinity groups, using a totemic logic, identified themselves with animal, or occasionally plant, names. I found groups called Night Doves, Cattle and Camels, Desert Ducks, Pacific Desert Whales, Wild Turtles, Peace Turtles, Sea Cucumbers, Mustard Seed, Sunflower Brigade, Desert Slugs, White Rose, the Texas Disarmadillos, and Roadrunners. A few groups, such as the Communist Dupes and the Scum of the Earth, made ironic use of their opponents' labels for antinuclear activists. Peter Adair's (1983) documentary film *Stopping History* gives a fine depiction of affinity group processes.

30. This name comes from Dorothy Bryant's feminist science fiction novel, *The Kin of Ata Are Waiting for You.*

31. Gaia, often glossed as the goddess of the earth, was the ancient Greek goddess from whom the other gods and goddesses were born. She is an image of a primordial eco-feminine unity.

32. Recent years have seen an explosion of psychological literature on the different psychologies of men and women. The most important books here have been Bly 1990; Chodorow 1978; Dinnerstein 1977; Gilligan 1982; J. Miller 1973; and Tannen 1991.

33. For theoretical formulations of the point of view that war and gender are both linked and culturally produced, see Brock-Utne 1985; Cohn 1987; Gerzon 1982; Hunter 1991; Reardon 1985; Spretnak 1983; and Starhawk 1980, 1987.

34. Ruddick 1989 is the classic exposition of the maternal position. For a study of a women's peace group in San Diego that organized its activism around notions of maternal politics, see Mehan and Wills 1988.

35. The separatist position is articulated in Strange 1989 and Zanotti 1982, and critiqued in Hunter 1991. For introductions to the thinking behind the women's peace camp movement, see Lederman 1989, McAllister 1982, and Russell 1989*b*. For reports on the best-known women's peace camp, the Greenham Common camp in Britain, see Blackwood 1984; Cook and Kirk 1983; Jones 1989; and Wilson 1988. For accounts of the women's peace camp at Seneca Falls, New York, see Krasniewicz 1992 and Paley 1983. Krasniewicz explores in detail the clash between the androgynous and separatist wings of the women's peace movement.

CHAPTER 9. CONCLUSION: THE END OF AN ERA?

1. Although most Soviet tests were conducted at Semipalatinsk, the Soviet Union also occasionally used a Siberian test site at Novaya Zemlya. Siberian weather conditions made the latter site unusable for most of the year. Should the Russian Republic want to embark on a nuclear testing program in the future, it would have to use this site since Semipalatinsk is located in the Republic of Kazakhstan.

2. The Department of Energy closed the plutonium production facility at Hanford in Washington State, the plutonium "trigger" production facility at Rocky Flats in Colorado, the tritium reactor at Savannah River in South Carolina, the uranium plant in Fernald, Ohio, and the nuclear test site in Nevada. In the late 1980s, DOE planned to rebuild many of the facilities it was closing but has subsequently decided to consolidate the functions from closed facilities in remaining parts of the nuclear weapons complex, which will now operate on a smaller scale and will be more oriented to dismantling than producing weapons.

3. The laboratory did, however, continue its design work on the warhead, the W-89, in order to explore new warhead design concepts involving the recycling of components—particularly the plutonium "pits"—from dismantled older warheads (Lawrence Livermore National Laboratory 1992: 29).

4. The weapons laboratories have argued that, in the absence of underground nuclear testing, a community of weapons scientists must be maintained and the safety and reliability of the arsenal assured through "science-based stockpile stewardship" (SBSS). The SBSS program would include improved computer simulations of nuclear tests and an array of machines designed to simulate different aspects of a nuclear explosion such as the implosion of a plutonium pit and the thermonuclear fusion process. Livermore has requested $1.1 billion to build the National Ignition Facility (NIF)—a laser fusion facility that would simulate thermonuclear fusion at higher energies and densities than the laboratory's existing Nova laser. See Gusterson 1995*b* for a discussion of the implications of and controversy around NIF.

5. Weapons designers have for some years used supercomputer programs and Nova Laser tests to enhance their understanding of nuclear weapons physics but have always subordinated such experiments to nuclear tests themselves. They also used "zero-yield" tests during the Soviet/American nuclear test moratorium of 1958–1960 (Stober 1992a).

BIBLIOGRAPHY

Abbotts, John
    1991   "Time for Rebirth of Civilian R&D." *Bulletin of the Atomic Scientists* 46(9): 12–13.

Abir-Am, Pnina
    1992   "A Historical Ethnography of a Scientific Anniversary in Molecular Biology: The First Protein X-ray Photograph (1984, 1934)." *Social Epistemology* 6(4): 323–355.

Adair, Peter
    1983   *Stopping History.* San Francisco: Adair and Armstrong Films.

Adler, Allan
    1985   "Unclassified Secrets." *Bulletin of the Atomic Scientists* 41, no. 3 (March): 26–28.

Adorno, Theodor, Else Frenkel-Brunswik, Daniel Levinson, and R. Sanford
    1950   *The Authoritarian Personality.* New York: Harper and Brothers.

AEC Meeting 1377 (28 May 1958)
    1984   In *The American Atom: A Documentary History of Nuclear Policies from the Discovery of Fission to the Present, 1939–1984,* ed. Robert Williams and Philip Cantelon, 191–196. Philadelphia: University of Pennsylvania Press.

Agnew, Harold
    1981   Interview. *Los Alamos Science Magazine* 2, no. 2 (Summer/Fall): 152–159.

Albro, Edward
    1990a   "Merchants Fret over Initiative." *Livermore Valley Herald,* 6 May.
    1990b   "Council Lambastes Initiative." *Livermore Valley Herald,* 25 April.
    1991a   "Is the Party Over at Livermore Lab?" *Tri-Valley Herald,* 9 June.

Albuquerque Journal
  1989   "KAFB Accidents Involved N-Weapons, Witness Says." 10 Oc-
            tober.
Alcalay, Glenn
  1988   "Human Guinea Pigs for Nuclear Testing: The Bravo Cover-up."
            CovertAction 29: 15–17.
Aldridge, Robert
  1983   *First Strike! The Pentagon's Strategy for Nuclear War.* Boston: South
            End Press.
Alexander, Frederic
  1963   *The History of Sandia Corporation Through 1962.* Albuquerque: The
            Corporation.
Allison, Graham
  1971   *Essence of Decision: Explaining the Cuban Missile Crisis.* Boston: Little,
            Brown.
  1977   "Questions About the Arms Race: Who's Racing Whom? A Bu-
            reaucratic Perspective." In *American Defense Policy*, 4th ed., ed. John
            Endicott and Roy Stafford, 424–441. Baltimore: John Hopkins
            University Press.
Allison, Graham, Albert Carnesale, and Joseph Nye (eds.)
  1985   *Hawks, Doves, and Owls: An Agenda for Avoiding Nuclear War.* New
            York: W. W. Norton.
Allison, Graham, and Morton Halperin
  1972   "Bureaucratic Politics: A Paradigm and Some Policy Implications."
            World Politics 24 (Spring): 40–80.
Althusser, Louis
  1971   "Ideology and Ideological State Apparatuses: Notes Towards an
            Investigation." In Althusser, *Lenin and Philosophy and Other Essays*,
            121–173. New York: Monthly Review Press.
Arens, W., and Susan Montague (eds.)
  1976   *The American Dimension: Cultural Myths and Social Realities.* Sher-
            man Oaks, Calif.: Alfred.
Arkin, William
  1992   "Little Nuclear Secrets." *New York Times*, 9 September.
Armantrout, Janet
  1990   "Rumblings of Discontent at Lab." *Independent*, 21 February.
Asad, Talal
  1983   "Notes on Body Pain and Truth in Medieval Christian Ritual."
            Economy and Society 12: 287–327.
Ashley, Richard
  1986   "The Poverty of Neorealism." In *Neorealism and Its Critics*, ed.
            Robert Keohane, 255–300. New York: Columbia University Press.

1987   "The Geopolitics of Geopolitical Space: Towards a Critical Social
            Theory of International Politics." *Alternatives* 12 (October): 403–
            434.
Atomic Energy Act
1954   Atomic Energy Act. Abridged version printed in Appendix C in
            Alexander DeVolpi, Gerald Marsh, Ted Postol, and George Stan-
            ford, *Born Secret: The H-Bomb, the Progressive Case, and National
            Security.* New York: Pergamon Press. Pp. 258–261.
Aubrey, Crispin (ed.)
1982   *Nukespeak: The Media and the Bomb.* London: Comedia.
Barasch, Marc Ian
1983   *The Little Black Book of Atomic War.* New York: Dell.
Barash, David, and Judith Lipton
1985   *The Caveman and the Bomb: Human Nature, Evolution, and Nuclear
            War.* New York: McGraw-Hill.
Barnet, Richard
1991   "The Uses of Force." *New Yorker,* 29 April, 82–95.
Barthes, Roland
1972   *Mythologies.* New York: Hill and Wang.
1979   *The Eiffel Tower.* New York: Hill and Wang.
Bartimus, Tad, and Scott McCartney
1991   *Trinity's Children: Living Along America's Nuclear Highway.* New
            York: Harcourt Brace Jovanovich.
Baudrillard, Jean
1983   *Simulations.* New York: Semiotext(e).
Beeman, William O.
1989   "Anthropology and the Myths of American Foreign Policy." In *The
            Anthropology of War and Peace: Perspectives on the Nuclear Age,* ed.
            Paul Turner and David Pitt, 49–65. South Hadley, Mass.: Begin
            and Garvey.
Behar, Ruth
1991   "Death and Memory: From Santa Maria Del Monte to Miami
            Beach." *Cultural Anthropology* 6(3): 346–384.
Bellah, Robert, Richard Madsen, William Sullivan, Ann Swidler, and Steven
    Tipton
1985   *Habits of the Heart: Individualism and Commitment in American Life.*
            Berkeley, Los Angeles, and London: University of California Press.
Benedict, Ruth
1934   *Patterns of Culture.* Boston: Houghton Mifflin.
Berger, Peter
1994   Furtive Smokers—and What They Tell Us About America. *Com-
            mentary* (June): 21–26.

Berger, Peter, and Thomas Luckmann
　1967　　*The Social Construction of Reality: A Treatise in the Sociology of Knowledge*. New York: Anchor Books.
Berman, Morris
　1989　　*Coming to Our Senses: Body and Spirit in the Hidden History of the West*. New York: Simon and Schuster.
Bernstein, Barton
　1976　　*The Atomic Bomb: The Critical Issues*. Boston: Little, Brown.
　1978　　"Energy and Conflict: The Life and Times of Edward Teller." *Bulletin of the Atomic Scientists* 34(3): 51–53.
　1990　　"The Oppenheimer Loyalty-Security Case Reconsidered." *Stanford Law Review* 42 (Summer): 1383–1484.
Bettelheim, Bruno
　1971　　*Symbolic Wounds: Puberty Rites and the Envious Male*. New York: Collier.
Biagioli, Mario
　1993　　*Galileo, Courtier: The Practice of Science in the Culture of Absolutism*. Chicago: University of Chicago Press.
Biddle, Wayne
　1987　　Star Wars: The Dream Diminished. *Discover*, July, 26–38.
Bijker, Wiebe, Thomas Hughes, and Trevor Pinch
　1990　　*The Social Construction of Technological Systems*. Cambridge: MIT Press.
Bijker, Wiebe, and John Law (eds.)
　1992　　*Shaping Technology/Building Society: Studies in Sociotechnical Change*. Cambridge: MIT Press.
Blacker, Coit, and Gloria Duffy (eds.)
　1984　　*International Arms Control: Issues and Agreements*. Stanford: Stanford University Press.
Blackwood, Caroline
　1984　　*On the Perimeter*. London: Penguin Books.
Blight, James
　1987　　"Toward a Policy-Relevant Psychology of Avoiding Nuclear War." *American Psychologist* 42(1): 12–29.
Bloor, David
　1991　　*Knowledge and Social Imagery*. 2d ed. Chicago: University of Chicago Press.
Blum, Deborah
　1987*a*　"Scientists March to a Military Beat." *Sacramento Bee*, 12 July.
　1987*b*　Nuclear Labs: Bulwark Against Test Bans. *Sacramento Bee*, 2 August.

1988   "Weird Science: Livermore's X-ray Laser Flap." *Bulletin of the Atomic Scientists* 44(6): 7–13.

Blumberg, Stanley, and Louis Panos

1990   *Edward Teller: Giant of the Golden Age of Physics.* New York: Scribner's.

Bly, Robert

1990   *Iron John.* Palo Alto: Addison-Wesley.

Bodovitz, Sandra

1988*a*   "A Dukakis Victory Could Shake Up Lab." *Tri-Valley Herald,* 7 November.

1988*b*   "Suspect Story Prompts Officials to Pull Lab's Weekly Newspaper." *Tri-Valley Herald,* 14 October.

1988*c*   "Mayor to View Lab Sewage Alarm System." *Tri-Valley Herald,* 28 July.

1989*a*   "Sandia to Keep Nuclear Emphasis." *Tri-Valley Herald,* 9 May.

1989*b*   "Livermore Burns over Incinerator Plan; Lab Says It's Safe." *Tri-Valley Herald,* 21 May.

1989*c*   "Protest Blocks Lab Gate." *Tri-Valley Herald,* 25 March.

1989*d*   "Livermore Group Given EPA Grant." *Tri-Valley Herald,* 4 February.

1989*e*   "Questions Dog Lab's Neighbors." *Tri-Valley Herald,* 24 July.

1989*f*   "Stark Tells Laboratory to Get Out." *Tri-Valley Herald,* 12 March.

1989*g*   "Stark: I Wouldn't Mind if Lab Left." *Tri-Valley Herald,* 17 March.

1989*h*   "Livermore Wants Lab to Pay for Road Work." *Tri-Valley Herald,* 27 May.

Bok, Sissela

1989   *Secrets: On the Ethics of Concealment and Revelation.* New York: Vintage.

Bordo, Susan

1990   "'Material Girl': The Effacements of Postmodern Culture." *Michigan Quarterly Review* 29(4): 653–677.

Boston Globe

1991   "Wiretap Devices at Nuclear Facility." 1 August.

Bourdieu, Pierre

1977*a*   *Outline of a Theory of Practice.* New York: Cambridge University Press.

1977*b*   "Symbolic Power." In *Identity and Structure: Issues in the Sociology of Education,* ed. Dennis Gleeson, 112–119. Nafferton, England: Nafferton Press.

1984   *Distinction: A Social Critique of the Judgment of Taste.* Cambridge: Harvard University Press.

Boyer, Paul
    1984   "From Activism to Apathy: The American People and Nuclear Weapons, 1963–1980." *Journal of American History* 70: 820–844.
    1985   *By the Bomb's Early Light: American Thought and Culture at the Dawn of the Atomic Age.* New York: Pantheon.

Boyle, Francis Anthony
    1988   *Defending Civil Resistance Under International Law.* Dobbs Ferry, N.Y.: Transnational Publishers.

Bracken, Paul
    1983   *The Command and Control of Nuclear Forces.* New Haven: Yale University Press.

Brandt, Elizabeth
    1980   "On Secrecy and the Control of Knowledge: Taos Pueblo." In *Secrecy: A Cross-Cultural Perspective*, ed. Stanton Tefft, 123–146. New York: Human Sciences Press.

Brasset, Donna
    1989   "U.S. Military Elites: Perceptions and Values." In *The Anthropology of War and Peace: Perspectives on the Nuclear Age*, ed. Paul Turner and David Pitt, 32–48. South Hadley, Mass.: Begin and Garvey.

Brewer, Boni
    1988   "Lab Denies Breaches in Security." *Valley Times*, 14 October.
    1989   "Stark Threatens to Sue Lab Over Toxics Incinerator." *Valley Times*, 18 January.

Briggs, Richard
    1989   "Induction Acclerators and Free-Electron Lasers at LLNL." LLNL Document no. UCID-21639.

Broad, William
    1985   *Star Warriors: A Penetrating Look into the Lives of the Young Scientists Behind Our Space Age Weaponry.* New York: Simon and Schuster.
    1986   "Bomb Tests: Technology Advances Against Backdrop of Wide Debate." *New York Times*, 15 April.
    1988*a*   "Seismic Data Reveal 117 Secret U.S. Nuclear Tests." *Valley Times*, 17 January.
    1988*b*   "Beyond the Bomb: Turmoil in the Labs." *New York Times Magazine*, 9 October.
    1990*a*   "Crown Jewel of 'Star Wars' has Lost Its Luster." *New York Times*, 13 February.
    1990*b*   "Bitter Dispute at Weapons Lab Is Settled with Job Switch." *New York Times*, 23 May.
    1992   *Teller's War: The Top Secret Story Behind the Star Wars Deception.* New York: Simon and Schuster.

1994   "Vast Laser Would Advance Fusion and Retain Bomb Experts."
            New York Times, 21 June.

Brock-Utne, Birgit
    1985   *Educating for Peace: A Feminist Perspective.* New York: Pergamon
            Press.
    1989   "A Feminist Perspective on Peace Studies." Paper delivered at joint
            convention of the International Studies Association and the British
            International Studies Association, London, 28 March–1 April.

Brodie, Bernard
    1946   *The Absolute Weapon: Atomic Power and World Order.* New York:
            Harcourt Brace.

Brown, Paul
    1989   "Ethics and Nuclear Weapons Research." Unpublished paper
            written at Lawrence Livermore National Laboratory under con-
            tract no. W-7405-ENG-48.

Brown, Bess
    1991   "The Strength of Kazakhstan's Antinuclear Lobby." *Report on the
            USSR*, 25 January, 23–24.

Bryant, Dorothy
    1976   *The Kin of Ata Are Waiting for You.* New York: Random House/
            Berkeley: Moon.

Budwine, Robert
    1990   "Weapons Research Must Continue." *Tri-Valley Herald*, 21 Sep-
            tember.

Bull, Hedley
    1977   *The Anarchical Society.* New York: Columbia University Press.

Bundy, McGeorge
    1988   *Danger and Survival: Choices About the Bomb in the First Fifty Years.*
            New York: Vintage.

Bundy, McGeorge, George Kennan, Robert McNamara, and Gerard Smith
    1982   "Nuclear Weapons and the Atlantic Alliance." *Foreign Affairs* 60,
            no. 4 (Spring): 753–768.

Bundy, McGeorge, Morton Halperin, William Kaufmann, George Kennan, Rob-
    ert McNamara, Madalene O'Donnell, Leon Sigal, Gerard Smith, Richard
    Ullman, and Paul Warnke
    1986   "Back from the Brink." *Atlantic Monthly*, August, 35–41.

Butterfield, Arline
    1983   "Valley Pastors Tell What They Learned in Jail: Penal System
            Called Dehumanizing." *Valley Times*, 10 July.

Cabasso, Jackie, and John Burroughs
    1995*a* "Beyond the NPT: Abolition 2000!" Western States Legal Foun-
            dation Special Report.

1995*b*   "End Run Around the NPT." *Bulletin of the Atomic Scientists* 51(5): 27–29.

Cabasso, Jackie, and Susan Moon

1985   *Risking Peace: Why We Sat in the Road.* Berkeley: Open Books.

Caldicott, Helen

1978   *Nuclear Madness.* New York: Bantam.

1986   *Missile Envy: The Arms Race and Nuclear War.* New York: Bantam.

Campbell, David

1992   *Writing Security: United States Foreign Policy and the Politics of Identity.* Minneapolis: University of Minnesota Press.

Canavan, Gregory, and Edward Teller

1990   "Strategic Defence for the 1990s." *Nature* 344 (April 19): 699–704.

Caputi, Jane

1991   "The Metaphors of Radiation—or Why a Beautiful Woman is Like a Nuclear Power Plant." *Women's Studies International Forum* 14(5): 423–442.

Carey, Peter

1990   "Nuclear Weapons Work Has Ordinary Side." *San Jose Mercury News,* 29 July.

Carnesale, Albert, and Richard Haass

1987   *Superpower Arms Control: Setting the Record Straight.* Cambridge: Ballinger.

Carr, E. H.

1964   *The Twenty Years Crisis: 1919–1939.* New York: Harper Torchbooks.

Carter, Luther

1990   "Soviet Nuclear Testing: The Republics Say No." *Science,* 16 November, 903–904.

Caulfield, Catherine

1989   *Multiple Exposures: Chronicles of the Radiation Age.* New York: Harper and Row.

Certeau, Michel de

1984   *The Practice of Everyday Life.* Berkeley, Los Angeles, and London: University of California Press.

Chalk, Rosemary

1983   "Security and Scientific Communication." *Bulletin of the Atomic Scientists* 39(7): 19–23.

1985   "Overview: AAAS Project on Secrecy and Openness in Science and Technology." *Science, Technology, and Human Values* 10(2): 28–35.

Chen, Edwin

1989   "U.S. A-Arms Plants Badly Contaminated, Panel Says; Cleanup May Cost $100 Billion." *Los Angeles Times,* 21 December.

Chernus, Ira
> 1989   *Dr. Strangegod: On the Symbolic Meaning of Nuclear Weapons.* Columbia: University of South Carolina Press.
> 1991   *Nuclear Madness: Religion and the Psychology of the Nuclear Age.* Albany: State University of New York Press.

Chilton, Paul (ed.)
> 1985   *Language and the Nuclear Arms Debate: Nukespeak Today.* London: Francis Pinter.
> 1989   "Safe as Houses?" *Peace Review* 1(2): 12–17.

Chodorow, Nancy
> 1978   *The Reproduction of Mothering: Psychoanalysis and the Sociology of Gender.* Berkeley, Los Angeles, and London: University of California Press.

Chomsky, Noam
> 1988   *The Culture of Terrorism.* Boston: South End Press.

Cialdini, Robert
> 1988   *Influence: Science and Practice.* Glenview, Ill.: Scott Foresman.

Clifford, James
> 1981   "On Ethnographic Surrealism." *Comparative Studies in History and Society* 23: 539–564.
> 1988   *The Predicament of Culture: Twentieth Century Ethnography, Literature, and Art.* Cambridge: Harvard University Press.

Clifford, James, and George Marcus
> 1986   *Writing Culture: The Poetics and Politics of Ethnography.* Berkeley, Los Angeles, and London: University of California Press.

Coates, Ken
> 1981   "European Nuclear Disarmament." In *Protest and Survive,* ed. E. P. Thomspon and Dan Smith, 189–213. New York: Monthly Review Press.

Cochran, Thomas, William Arkin, and Milton Hoenig
> 1984   *Nuclear Weapons Databook.* Vol. I. Cambridge: Ballinger.

Cochran, Thomas, William Arkin, Robert Norris, and Milton Hoenig
> 1987   *Nuclear Weapons Databook.* Vol. II. Cambridge: Ballinger.

Cohen, Abner
> 1971   "The Politics of Ritual Secrecy." *Man* 6(3): 427–448.
> 1980   "Drama and Politics in the Development of a London Carnival." *Man* 15: 65–87.

Cohn, Carol
> 1987   "Sex and Death in the Rational World of Defense Intellectuals." *Signs* 12(4): 687–718.

Cole, Paul M., and William J. Taylor (eds.)
> 1983   *The Nuclear Freeze Debate: Arms Control Issues for the 1980s.* Boulder, Colo.: Westview Press.

Coles, Robert
 1985 "Children and the Bomb." *New York Times Magazine*, 8 December.
Collier, Jane, and Sylvia Yanagisako
 1987*a* "Introduction." In *Gender and Kinship: Essays Toward a Unified Analysis*, ed. Jane Collier and Sylvia Yanagisako, 1–13. Stanford: Stanford University Press.
 1987*b* "Toward a Unified Analysis of Gender and Kinship." In *Gender and Kinship: Essays Toward a Unified Analysis*, ed. Jane Collier and Sylvia Yanagisako, 14–50. Stanford: Stanford University Press.
Collins, H. M.
 1985 *Changing Order: Replication and Induction in Scientific Practice.* Beverly Hills: Sage.
Comaroff, Jean
 1985 *Body of Power, Spirit of Resistance.* Chicago: University of Chicago Press.
Committee for the Compilation of Materials on the Damage Caused by the Atomic Bombs in Hiroshima and Nagasaki (eds.)
 1981 *Hiroshima and Nagasaki: The Physical, Medical, and Social Effects of the Atomic Bombings.* New York: Basic Books.
Cook, Alice, and Gwyn Kirk
 1983 *Greenham Women Everywhere: Dreams, Ideas, and Actions from the Women's Peace Movement.* Boston: South End Press.
Cowan, George A.
 1976 "A Natural Fission Reactor." *Scientific American*, July, 36–47.
Cox, John
 1982 "A 'Limited' Nuclear War." In *Exterminism and Cold War*, ed. New Left Review, 175–184. London: Verso.
Craig, Paul
 1988 "Nuclear Weapons Testing Constraints: Which Way Lies Progress?" Mimeographed paper.
Crapanzano, Vincent
 1985 *Tuhami: Portrait of a Moroccan Mystic.* Chicago: University of Chicago Press.
Csordas, Thomas
 1990 "Embodiment as a Paradigm for Anthropology." *Ethos* 18(1): 5–47.
 1994 *Embodiment and Experience: The Existential Ground of Culture and Self.* Cambridge: Cambridge University Press.
Daalder, Ivo
 1987 "The Limited Test Ban Treaty." In *Superpower Arms Control:*

    Setting the Record Straight, ed. Albert Carnesale and Richard Haass,
    9–39. Cambridge: Ballinger.

daCosta, Robert
    1990   "This Quarter Reasoning." *A&DS* (August): 3–6.

Dahl, Robert
    1985   *Controlling Nuclear Weapons: Democracy versus Guardianship.* New
            York: Syracuse University Press.

Daner, Francine
    1976   *The American Children of Krsna: A Study of the Hare Krsna Movement.*
            New York: Holt, Rinehart, and Winston.

Darnovsky, Marcy
    1982   "Lawrence Livermore Laboratory." In *Nuclear California: An In-
            vestigative Report*, ed. David Kaplan, 95–99. San Francisco: Center
            for Investigative Reporting.

Davidson, Donald L.
    1983   *Nuclear Weapons and the American Churches: Ethical Positions on
            Modern Warfare.* Boulder, Colo.: Westview Press.

Davis, Bob
    1990   "After Years of Secrecy, Nuclear Arms Plants Show Off Technol-
            ogy." *Wall Street Journal*, 4 December.

Davis-Floyd, Robbie
    1992   *Birth as an American Rite of Passage.* Berkeley, Los Angeles, and
            Oxford: University of California Press.

Dearborn, David
    1990   "My Life as a Weapons Scientist." Talk to visiting group from
            Stanford University, Lawrence Livermore National Laboratory
            Visitors Center, 6 August.

DeBenedetti, Charles
    1980   *The Peace Reform in American History.* Bloomington: Indiana Uni-
            versity Press.

Department of Energy (Office of Safeguards and Security)
    1989   "Criteria for Determining Eligibility for Access to Classified Mat-
            ter or Significant Quantities of Special Nuclear Material." 54 FR
            5376, 2 February.

Der Derian, James
    1987   *On Diplomacy: A Genealogy of Western Estrangement.* Oxford: Basil
            Blackwell.

Der Derian, James, and Michael Shapiro (eds.)
    1989   *International/Intertextual Relations.* Lexington: Lexington Books.

Derrida, Jacques
    1978   *Writing and Difference.* London: Routledge and Kegan Paul.

1984   "No Apocalypse, Not Now (Full Speed Ahead, Seven Missiles, Seven Missives)." *Diacritics* 20: 20–32.

Deutsch, Karl W., and David Singer

1964   "Multipolar Power Systems and International Stability." *World Politics* 16(3): 390–406.

DeVolpi, Alexander, Ted Postol, Gerald Marsh, and George Stanford

1981   *Born Secret: The H-Bomb, The Progressive Case, and National Security.* New York: Pergamon.

DeWitt, Hugh

1986   "Labs Drive the Arms Race." In *Assessing the Nuclear Age*, ed. Len Ackland and Steven McGuire, 101–106. Chicago: Educational Foundation for Nuclear Science.

1989a   "The Nuclear Arms Race as Seen by a Nuclear Weapons Lab Staff Member." *SANA Update: Scientists Against Nuclear Arms Newsletter* 74: 2–4.

1989b   "At Peace with the Bomb." *Progressive* 53(9): 26–27.

1990   "Moral Issues Faced by Scientists in Nuclear Weapons Work." Respondent paper at 40th Pugwash Conference on Science and World Affairs, Egham, U.K. 15–20 September.

De Wolk, Roland

1989   "Toxic Waste Dumps, Secrecy Sour Town's Relationship to the Facility." *Oakland Tribune*, 13 August.

1990   "Gardener [*sic*] Wants to Keep UC Link to Labs." *Oakland Tribune*, 15 September.

Diacritics

1984   Special issue on Nuclear Criticism, no. 20 (Summer).

Di Leonardo, Michaela

1984   *The Varieties of Ethnic Experience: Kinship, Class, and Gender among California Italian-Americans.* Ithaca: Cornell University Press.

Dickson, David

1984   *The New Politics of Science.* New York: Pantheon.

Diehl, Patrick

1988   "Action History of Livermore Action Group." Mimeographed paper.

Dillon, G. M.

1989   "Modernity, Discourse, and Deterrence." *Current Research on Peace and Violence* 12(2): 90–104.

Dillon, John

1989a   "Developers, Lab Employees Boost Candidates." *Valley Times*, 28 September.

1989b   "Livermore Votes No Lab Waste Permit." *Valley Times*, 15 November.

Dinnerstein, Dorothy
   1977   *The Mermaid and the Minotaur*. New York: Harper and Row.
Divine, Robert A.
   1978   *Blowing on the Wind: The Nuclear Test Ban Debate 1954–1960*. New
             York: Oxford University Press.
Douglas, Ann
   1977   *The Feminization of American Culture*. New York: Knopf.
Douglas, Mary
   1984   *Purity and Danger: An Analysis of the Concepts of Pollution and Taboo*.
             New York: Ark Books.
Douglas, Mary, and Aaron Wildavsky
   1982   *Risk and Culture: An Essay on the Selection of Technological and En-
             vironmental Dangers*. Berkeley, Los Angeles, and London: Univer-
             sity of California Press.
Downey, Gary
   1986   "Risk in Culture: The American Conflict Over Nuclear Power."
             Cultural Anthropology 1: 388–412.
Doyle, Michael
   1989   "U.S. Probe Accuses Livermore Lab Officials of Gift Abuses."
             Oakland Tribune, 19 February.
Doyle, Michael W.
   1983   "Kant, Liberal Legacies, and Foreign Affairs." *Philosophy and Public
             Affairs* 12(3–4): 205–235, 323–353.
Drell, Sidney
   1991   "Safety Concerns and the U.S. Nuclear Arsenal." Defense and
             Arms Control Seminar Presentation, MIT, 24 April.
Drell, Sidney, Charles Townes, and John Foster
   1991   "How Safe Is Safe?" *Bulletin of the Atomic Scientists* 47(3): 35–
             40.
Dreyfus, Hubert, and Paul Rabinow
   1983   *Michel Foucault: Beyond Structuralism and Hermeneutics*. Chicago:
             University of Chicago Press.
Du Bois, Cora
   1955   "The Dominant Value Profile in American Culture." *American
             Anthropologist* 57: 1232–1239.
Durkheim, Emile
   1915   *The Elementary Forms of the Religious Life*. New York: Macmillan.
Dyson, Freeman
   1984   *Weapons and Hope*. New York: Harper Colophon.
Easlea, Brian
   1983   *Fathering the Unthinkable: Masculinity, Scientists, and the Arms Race*.
             London: Pluto Press.

Ehrenreich, Barbara
    1984   *The Hearts of Men: American Dreams and the Flight from Commitment.* Garden City, N.Y.: Anchor.
    1989   *Fear of Falling: The Inner Life of the Middle Class.* New York: Harper Perennial.
Ellsberg, Daniel
    1981   "Call to Mutiny." In *Protest and Survive*, ed. E. P. Thompson and Dan Smith, i–xxviii. New York: Monthly Review Press.
Else, Jon
    1980   *The Day After Trinity.* San Jose: KTEH-TV.
Elshtain, Jean Bethke
    1987   *Women and War.* New York: Basic Books.
    1990   "Why Worry About the Animals?" *Progressive* 54(3): 17–23.
Energy and Technology Review
    1986   "The Free Electron Laser Program." December.
    1990   "The State of the Laboratory." July/August.
Enloe, Cynthia
    1983   *Does Khaki Become You? The Militarization of Women's Lives.* Boston: South End Press.
    1990   *Bananas, Beaches, and Bases: Making Feminist Sense of International Politics.* Berkeley, Los Angeles, and Oxford: University of California Press.
    1993   *The Morning After: Sexual Politics at the End of the Cold War.* Berkeley, Los Angeles, and Oxford: University of California Press.
Epstein, Barbara
    1985   "The Culture of Direct Action." *Socialist Review* 82–83: 31–61.
    1988   "The Politics of Prefigurative Community: The Non-Violent Direct Action Movement." In *Reshaping the U.S. Left: Popular Struggles in the 1980s*, ed. Mike David and Michael Spriker, 63–92. London: Verso Books.
    1991   *Political Protest and Cultural Revolution: Nonviolent Direct Action in the 1970s and 1980s.* Berkeley, Los Angeles, and Oxford: University of California Press.
Erikson, Erik
    1968   *Identity: Youth and Crisis.* New York: W. W. Norton.
Ethics
    1985   Special Issue: Ethics and Nuclear Deterrence. *Ethics* 95(3).
Evan, William, and Stephen Hilgartner (eds.)
    1987   *The Arms Race and Nuclear War.* Englewood Cliffs, N.J.: Prentice-Hall.
Evans, David
    1989   "Nuclear Deterrence and Morality: One Expert's Journey." *Chicago Tribune*, 15 December.

Evans-Pritchard, E. E.
  1937   *Witchcraft, Oracles and Magic Among the Azande*. Oxford: Oxford
            University Press.

Everett, Melissa
  1989   "A Dyed-in-the-Wool Democrat: Bill Perry." In *Breaking Ranks*,
            ed. Melissa Everett, 125–144. Philadelphia: New Society Pub-
            lishers.

Evernden, Jack
  1982   "The Verification of a Comprehensive Test Ban." *Scientific Amer-
            ican*, October, 47–55.

  1986   "Politics, Technology and the Test Ban." In *Assessing the Nuclear
            Age*, ed. Len Ackland and Steven McGuire, 181–188. Chicago:
            Educational Foundation for Nuclear Science.

Ezrahi, Yaron
  1990   *The Descent of Icarus: Science and the Transformation of Contemporary
            Democracy*. Cambridge: Harvard University Press.

Fairclough, Norman
  1989   *Language and Power*. New York: Longman.

Falk, Jim
  1989   "The Discursive Shaping of Nuclear Militarism." *Current Research
            on Peace and Violence* 12(2): 53–76.

Falk, Richard
  1982   "Nuclear Weapons and the End of Democracy." *Praxis Interna-
            tional* 2(1): 1–11.

Faludi, Susan
  1987   "Inner Peaceniks." *Mother Jones*, April, 20–53.

Farmer, Paul, and Arthur Kleinman
  1989   "AIDS as Human Suffering." *Daedalus* (Spring): 135–160.

FAS (Federation of American Scientists)
  1986   "The Militarization of R&D." *Public Interest Report: Journal of the
            Federation of American Scientists*, Special Issue on DoD and R&D,
            39, no. 7 (September).

Feldman, Allen
  1991   *Formations of Violence*. Chicago: University of Chicago Press.

Festinger, L.
  1964   *Conflict, Decision, and Dissonance*. Stanford: Stanford University
            Press.

Fetter, Steve
  1987–   "Stockpile Confidence Under a Nuclear Test Ban." *International
  1988   Security* 12(3): 132–167.

  1988a   "Correspondence: The Author Replies." *International Security*
            13(1): 210–215.

  1988b   *Toward a Comprehensive Test Ban*. Cambridge: Ballinger.

Feyerabend, Paul
  1988   *Against Method.* New York: Routledge.
Fleck, Ludwig
  1979   *The Genesis and Development of a Scientific Fact.* Chicago: University of Chicago Press.
Forsberg, Randall
  1980   "Military R&D: A Worldwide Institution." *Proceedings of the American Philosophical Society* 124(4).
  1982   "A Bilateral Nuclear Weapons Freeze." *Scientific American* 247(5): 52–61.
  1984   "The Freeze and Beyond: Confining the Military to Defense as a Route to Disarmament." *World Policy Journal* 1(2): 285–318.
Forsyth, Jim
  1990   "Stop Nuclear Testing Now." *Tri-Valley Herald,* 7 August.
Foucault, Michel
  1973   *The Order of Things: An Archaeology of the Human Sciences.* New York: Vintage Books.
  1979   *Discipline and Punish: The Birth of the Prison.* New York: Vintage Books.
  1980a   *The History of Sexuality.* Vol. 1. *An Introduction.* New York: Vintage Books.
  1980b   *Power/Knowledge.* New York: Pantheon Books.
Fox, Matthew
  1983   *Original Blessing.* Santa Fe, New Mex.: Bear.
Frank, Jerome
  1982   *Sanity and Survival in the Nuclear Age: Psychological Aspects of War and Peace.* New York: Random House.
Frankel, Sara
  1990   "Peace Groups: Good News, Bad News." *San Francisco Examiner,* 16 March.
Franklin, H. Bruce
  1988   *War Stars: The Superweapon and the American Imagination.* New York: Oxford University Press.
Freedman, Lawrence
  1983   *The Evolution of Nuclear Strategy.* New York: St. Martin's Press.
Freiberger, Paul
  1990   "High-Tech Firms Seek Shift from Military Markets to Civilian R&D." *San Francisco Examiner,* 14 March.
Freud, Sigmund
  1989   *The Psychopathology of Everyday Life.* New York: W. W. Norton.
Fromm, Erich
  1942   *The Fear of Freedom.* London: K. Paul, Trench, Trubner.

Furman, Necah
   1990   *Sandia National Laboratories: The Postwar Decade.* Albuquerque: University of New Mexico Press.
Futterman, John
   1992   "Obscenity and Peace." In John Futterman, *The Bomb and the Cross: Notes on American Icons.* Unpublished manuscript.
Gaddis, John Lewis
   1982   *Strategies of Containment: A Critical Appraisal of Postwar American National Security Policy.* New York: Oxford University Press.
   1986   "The Long Peace: Elements of Stability in the Post-War International System." *International Security* 10: 99–142.
Gallagher, Carole
   1993   *American Ground Zero: The Secret Nuclear War.* Cambridge: MIT Press.
Galvin, Robert, et al.
   1995   *Alternative Futures for the Department of Energy National Laboratories.* Report prepared by the Secretary of Energy Advisory Board.
Garfinkle, Adam
   1984   *The Politics of the Nuclear Freeze.* Philadelphia: Foreign Policy Research Institute.
Garretson, Lucy
   1976   *American Culture: An Anthropological Perspective.* Dubuque, Iowa: W. C. Brown.
Garrison, Jim
   1982   *The Darkness of God: Theology After Hiroshima.* Grand Rapids, Mich.: Eerdmans.
Geertz, Clifford
   1973   *The Interpretation of Cultures.* New York: Basic Books.
   1980   *Negara: The Theater State in Nineteenth-Century Bali.* Princeton: Princeton University Press.
   1983   *Local Knowledge.* New York: Basic Books.
   1988   *Works and Lives: The Anthropologist as Author.* Stanford: Stanford University Press.
Gerzon, Mark
   1982   *A Choice of Heroes: The Changing Face of American Manhood.* Boston: Houghton Mifflin.
Giddens, Anthony
   1979   *Central Problems in Social Theory.* Berkeley, Los Angeles, and London: University of California Press.
   1984   *The Constitution of Society: Outline of the Theory of Structuration.* Cambridge: Polity Press.

Gilbert, Nigel, and Michael Mulkay
    1984   *Opening Pandora's Box: A Sociological Analysis of Scientists' Discourse.*
        Cambridge: Cambridge University Press.

Gilligan, Carol
    1982   *In a Different Voice: Psychological Theory and Women's Development.*
        Cambridge: Harvard University Press.

Gilmore, David
    1990   *Manhood in the Making.* New Haven: Yale University Press.

Gilpin, Robert
    1962   *American Scientists and Nuclear Weapons Policy.* Princeton: Princeton
        University Press.
    1981   *War and Change in World Politics.* Cambridge: Cambridge Univer-
        sity Press.

Ginsburg, Faye
    1989   *Contested Lives: The Abortion Debate in an American Community.*
        Berkeley, Los Angeles, and Oxford: University of California Press.

Glaser, Charles
    1991   *Analyzing Strategic Nuclear Policy.* Princeton: Princeton University
        Press.

Glasstone, Samuel, and Philip Dolan
    1977   *The Effects of Nuclear Weapons.* Washington, D.C.: Department of
        Defense and Energy Research and Development Administration.

Glendinning, Chellis
    1987   *Waking Up in the Nuclear Age.* Philadelphia: New Society.

Gluckman, Max
    1954   *Rituals of Rebellion in South-East Africa.* Manchester: Manchester
        University Press.

Goffman, Erving
    1961   *Asylums: Essays on the Social Situation of Mental Patients and Other
        Inmates.* New York: Doubleday.

Gold, David
    1991   "Military R&D a Poor Scapegoat for Flagging Economy." *Bulletin
        of the Atomic Scientists* 47(1): 38–43.

Goldberg, Stanley, and Thomas Powers
    1992   "Declassified Files Reopen 'Nazi Bomb' Debate." *Bulletin of the
        Atomic Scientists* 48(7): 32–40.

Goodman, L. A., J. E. Mack, W. R. Beardslee, and R. M. Snow
    1983   "The Threat of Nuclear War and the Nuclear Arms Race: Ado-
        lescent Experience and Perceptions." *Political Psychology* 4(3): 501–
        530.

Gordon, Larry
    1990   "UC President Asks Renewal of Pacts for Weapon Labs." *Los
        Angeles Times,* 14 September.

Gouldner, Alvin
  1979   *The Future of Intellectuals and the Rise of the New Class.* New York:
            Oxford University Press.
Gray, Chris
  1997   *Postmodern War: Computers as Myths and Metaphors and the U.S.
            Military 1940–1950.* New York: Guilford Press.
Greb, G. Allen, and Warren Heckrotte
  1983   "The Long History: The Test Ban Debate." *Bulletin of the Atomic
            Scientists* 39(7): 36–42.
Green, Marian
  1983   "Protestors Will Have Long Wait, Says Judge." *Valley Times,* 29
            June.
Gregory, Donna
  1989   "The Dictator's Furnace: Metaphor and Alchemy in National Se-
            curity Discourse." *Current Research on Peace and Violence* 12(2):
            47–52.
Griffin, Susan
  1989   "Ideologies of Madness." In *Exposing Nuclear Phallacies,* ed. Diana
            Russell, 75–83. New York: Pergamon Press.
Ground Zero
  1982   *Nuclear War: What's in It for You?* New York: Pocket Books.
Gustafson, John
  1990   "Labs Tackle the Four 'E's' Plus National Security." *UC Focus,*
            May.
Gusterson, Hugh
  1989   "Knock Knock." *Nuclear Times* 7(3): 18–19.
  1991*a*   "Orientalism and the Arms Race: An Analysis of the Neocolonial
            Discourse on Nuclear Non-Proliferation." *Working Papers and
            Proceedings of the Center for Psychosocial Studies* (Chicago) No. 47.
  1991*b*   "Nuclear War, the Gulf War, and the Disappearing Body." *Journal
            of Urban and Cultural Studies* 2(1): 45–55.
  1991*c*   "Endless Escalation: The Cold War as Postmodern Narrative."
            Tikkun 6, no. 5 (September/October): 45–46, 90–92.
  1992   "The Rituals of Science: Comment on Abir-Am." *Social Episte-
            mology* 6(4): 373–387.
  1993*a*   "Exploding Anthropology's Canon in the World of the Bomb:
            Ethnographic Writing on Militarism." *Journal of Contemporary
            Ethnography* 22(1): 59–79.
  1993*b*   "Realism and the International Order After the Cold War." *Social
            Research* 60(2): 279–300.
  1995*a*   "Becoming a Weapons Scientist." In *TechnoScientific Imaginaries,*
            ed. George Marcus, 255–274. Chicago: University of Chicago
            Press.

1995*b*   "Nif-ty Exercise Machine." *Bulletin of the Atomic Scientists* 51(5):
             22–26.
Habermas, Jurgen
   1981   *Theory of Communicative Action.* Boston: Beacon Press.
Hacker, Barton
   1987   *The Dragon's Tail: Radiation Safety in the Manhattan Project.* Berke-
             ley, Los Angeles, and London: University of California Press.
Haddock, Vicki
   1990   "Defense Cuts? Not in *My* District." *San Francisco Examiner,* 15
             March.
Hafferty, Frederic
   1991   *Into the Valley: Death and the Socialization of Medical Students.* New
             Haven: Yale University Press.
Halperin, Morton
   1985   "Secrecy and National Security." *Bulletin of the Atomic Scientists*
             41(7): 114–117.
Halliday, Fred
   1983   *The Making of the Second Cold War.* London: Verso Books.
Hamilton, Minard
   1991   "Body Snatchers." *Mother Jones* 16, no. 4 (July/August): 15–16.
Hanrahan, John
   1988   "Cracking Up at the Test Site." *Nuclear Times* 7(2): 6–7.
Hansen, Chuck
   1988   *U.S. Nuclear Weapons: The Secret History.* New York: Orion Books.
   1990   "1,000 More Accidents Declassified." *Bulletin of the Atomic Scientists*
             46(5): 9, 41.
Haraway, Donna
   1990   *Primate Visions: Gender, Race and Nature in the World of Modern
             Science.* New York: Routledge.
   1991   *Simians, Cyborgs, and Women: The Reinvention of Nature.* New York:
             Routledge.
   1992   "The Promises of Monsters: A Regenerative Politics for Inappro-
             priate/d Others." In *Cultural Studies,* ed. Lawrence Grossberg,
             Cary Nelson, and Paula Treichler, 295–337. New York: Rout-
             ledge.
Hardin, Russell, et al.
   1985   *Nuclear Deterrence: Ethics and Strategy.* Chicago: University of Chi-
             cago Press.
Harding, Sandra
   1986   *The Science Question in Feminism.* Ithaca: Cornell University Press.
   1991   *Whose Science, Whose Knowledge? Thinking from Women's Lives.* Ith-
             aca: Cornell University Press.

Harper's
    1992   "Government Secrets, Backward and Forward." *Harper's*, October, 20.
Harris, Louis
    1984   "Public Attitudes Toward the Freeze." In *The Nuclear Weapons Freeze and Arms Control*, ed. Steven Miller, 39–40. Cambridge: Ballinger.
Harvard Nuclear Study Group (Albert Carnesale, Paul Doty, Stanley Hoffmann, Samuel Huntington, Joseph Nye, Scott Sagan)
    1983   *Living With Nuclear Weapons*. Cambridge: Harvard University Press.
Harvey, John, and Barry Fridling
    1988–1989 "On the Wrong Track? An Assessment of MX Rail Garrison Basing." *International Security* 13, no. 3 (Winter): 113–141.
Haun, Marianna
    1991   "A Tree Glows in Livermore." *Tracy Press*, 5 June.
Hecker, Siegfried, and John Nuckolls
    1990   "Managing the Labs Is a Public Service." *UC Focus*, May.
Heller, Arnie
    1989   "May Reviews His Career, Prospects for Arms Control." *Livermore Laboratory Newsline*, 25 January, 4.
Henderson, Breck
    1989   "U.S. Defense Budget Cuts Could Imperil Nation's Research and Development Effort." *Aviation Week and Space Technology*, December 12, 35.
Henning, C. D.
    1990   "The International Thermonuclear Experimental Reactor." *Energy and Technology Review* (July/August): 46–47.
Herdt, Gil
    1987   *Guardians of the Flutes: Idioms of Masculinity*. New York: Columbia University Press.
Herken, Gregg
    1985   *Counsels of War*. New York: Knopf.
Hersey, John
    1946   *Hiroshima*. New York: Modern Library.
Hiatt, L. R.
    1979   "Queen of the Night, Mother-Right, and Secret Male Cults." In *Fantasy and Symbol: Studies in Anthropological Interpretation*, ed. R. H. Hook, 247–266. New York: Academic Press.
Hilgartner, Stephen, Richard Bell, and Rory O'Connor
    1982   *Nukespeak: The Selling of Nuclear Technology in America*. New York: Penguin.

Hochschild, Arlie

1983   *The Managed Heart: The Commercialization of Human Feeling.* Berkeley, Los Angeles, and London: University of California Press.

Hoffmann, Joan Eakin

1980   "Problems of Access in the Study of Social Elites and Boards of Directors." In *Fieldwork Experience: Qualitative Approaches to Social Research*, ed. William Shaffir, Robert Stebbins, and Allan Turowetz, 45–56. New York: St. Martin's Press.

Hoffmann, Stanley

1978   *Primacy or Word Order: American Foreign Policy since the Cold War.* New York: McGraw-Hill.

1986   "On the Political Psychology of Peace and War: A Critique and an Agenda." *Political Psychology* 7(1): 1–21.

Hogan, William, and Michael Tobin

1989   "Overview of Defense Applications of ICF." Lawrence Livermore National Laboratory report no. UCID-21837.

Holgate, Laura S. Hayes

1991   "Fallout in the Fifties: The Beginnings of Environmentalism as Arms Control." *Breakthroughs* 1(2): 14–19.

Hollenbach, David

1983   *Nuclear Ethics: A Christian Moral Argument.* New York: Paulist Press.

Holloway, David

1994   *Stalin and the Bomb: The Soviet Union and Atomic Energy, 1936–1956.* New Haven: Yale University Press.

Holt, Robert R.

1984   "Can Psychology Meet Einstein's Challenge?" *Political Psychology* 5(2): 199–225.

1986   "Bridging the Rift in Political Psychology: An Open Letter to Stanley Hoffmann." *Political Psychology* 7(2): 235–244.

Homans, George

1941   "Anxiety and Ritual: The Theories of Malinowski and Radcliffe-Brown." *American Anthropologist* 43: 164–172.

Honicker, Clifford

1989   "The Hidden Files." *New York Times Magazine*, 19 November.

Hook, Glen

1985*a*   "Making Nuclear Weapons Easier to Live with: The Political Role of Language in Nuclearization." *Bulletin of Peace Proposals* (Winter): 67–77.

1985*b*   "The Nuclearization of Language: Nuclear Allergy as Metaphor." *Journal of Peace Research* 21(3): 259–275.

1988   "Censorship and Reportage of Atomic Damage in Hiroshima and Nagasaki." *Multilingua* 7(1–2): 133–156.

Hooper, B., and S. Allen

1990   "Microwave Tokamac Experiment." *Energy and Technology Review* (August): 44–45.

Horton, Robin

1967   "African Traditional Thought and Western Science." *Africa* 37(1/2): 50–71; 155–187.

Hostetler, John, and Gertrude Huntington

1980   *The Hutterites in North America.* New York: Holt, Rinehart, and Winston.

Hsu, Francis

1972   "American Core Values and National Character." In *Psychological Anthropology*, ed. Francis Hsu, 209–230. Cambridge: Schienkman.

Hufbauer, Karl, Oliver Johnson, and Walter Kohn

1990   "Managing the Labs Is a Historic Anomaly." *UC Focus*, May.

Hughes, Thomas

1983   *Networks of Power: Electrification in Western Society, 1880–1930.* Baltimore: Johns Hopkins University Press.

1990   "The Evolution of Large Technological Systems." In *The Social Construction of Technological Systems*, ed. Wiebe Bijker, Thomas Hughes, and Trevor Pinch, 51–82. Cambridge: MIT Press.

Hulbert, Ann

1991   "Mothers and Battles." *New Republic*, 1 April, 46.

Hull, David

1985   "Openness and Secrecy in Science: Their Origins and Limitations." *Science, Technology, and Human Values* 10(2): 4–13.

Hunter, Anne E. (ed.)

1991   *On Peace, War, and Gender: A Challenge to Genetic Explanations.* New York: Feminist Press.

Huyghe, Bernard

1986   "Toward a Structural Model of Violence: Male Initiation Rituals and Tribal Warfare." In *Peace and War: Cross-Cultural Perspectives*, ed. Mary LeCron Foster and Robert Rubinstein, 25–48. New Brunswick, N.J.: Transaction.

Immele, John

1984   "A Missile Deal for Europe—and Beyond." *Washington Post*, 13 January.

Immele, John, and Paul Brown

1988   "Correspondence." *International Security* 13(1): 196–210.

Independent
1988*a* "Lower Cost of Homes, Rural Lifestyle in Central Valley Drawing Lab Employees." 1 June.
1988*b* "Livermore to Fight East Avenue Closure." 11 May.
1988*c* "Lobbyist Hired to Deal with the Labs." 15 June.
1989 "Lab Says Security Violations a Matter of Interpretation." 6 December.

Inkeles, Alex
1979 "Continuity and Change in the U.S. National Character." In *The Third Century: America as a Post-Industrial Society*, ed. Seymour Lipset, 389–416. Stanford: Hoover Institution Press.

Irving, Carl
1991 "UC Faculty Opposes Weapons Lab Ties." *San Francisco Examiner*, 5 June.

Irving, Judy
1982 *Dark Circle*. New York: New Yorker Films.

Iwata, Edward
1988*a* "Lab Drug Probe's Abrupt End." *San Francisco Chronicle*, 15 June.
1988*b* "Drugs at Livermore—More Reports." *San Francisco Chronicle*, 17 June.
1988*c* "Who's Running Livermore Lab, Demo Wonders." *San Francisco Chronicle*, 8 July.

Jeffers, Michelle
1989 "Brown Tops in Fund-raising for City Races." *Tri-Valley Herald*, 1 October.
1990*a* "Veteran Technician Sues Lab, Claims Discrimination." *Valley Times*, 23 June.
1990*b* "Panel Urges Continued UC Management." *Valley Times*, 9 June.

Jendreson, Malcolm D., et al.
1989 "Report of the Advisory Committee on the University's Relationship with the Department of Energy Laboratories." University of California Academic Senate. Unpublished report.

Jenkins, Robin
1988 "Hundreds Arrested at Nevada." *Nuclear Times* 6(5): 8–9.

Jervis, Robert
1984 *The Illogic of American Nuclear Strategy*. Ithaca: Cornell University Press.
1989 *The Meaning of the Nuclear Revolution: Statecraft and the Prospect of Armageddon*. Ithaca: Cornell University Press.

Johnson, K. D.
    1984   "The Morality of Nuclear Deterrence." In *The Nuclear Crisis Reader*, ed. Gwyn Prins, 141–153. New York: Vintage Books.

Johnson, Mark
    1987   *Body in the Mind: The Bodily Basis of Meaning, Imagination, and Reason.* Chicago: University of Chicago Press.

Jones, Lynne
    1989   "On Common Ground: The Women's Peace Camp at Greenham Common." In *Exposing Nuclear Phallacies*, Diana E.H. Russell, 198–215. New York: Pergamon Press.

Jungk, Robert
    1985   *Brighter Than a Thousand Suns: A Personal History of the Atomic Scientists.* London: Pelican Books.

Kaiser, Fred
    1980   "Secrecy, Intelligence, and Community: The U.S. Intelligence Community." In *Secrecy: A Cross-Cultural Perspective*, ed. Stanton Tefft, 273–296. New York: Human Sciences Press.

Kaku, Michio, and Daniel Axelrod
    1987   *To Win a Nuclear War: The Pentagon's Secret War Plans.* Boston: South End Press.

Kang, David
    1987   "Bumpkins and Eggheads: A Cultural Look at Livermore in the 1950s." Honors thesis, Anthropology Department, Stanford University.

Kaplan, David
    1982   "Broken Arrows: Where the Bombs Are." In *Nuclear California: An Investigative Report*, ed. David Kaplan, 53–64. San Francisco: Center for Investigative Reporting.

Katz, M.
    1980   *Ban the Bomb: A History of SANE, the Committee for a Sane Nuclear Policy, 1957–1985.* Westport, Conn.: Greenwood Press.

Katz, Pearl
    1981   "Ritual in the Operating Room." *American Ethnologist* 20: 335–350.

Kavka, Gregory
    1987   *Moral Paradoxes of Nuclear Deterrence.* New York: Cambridge University Press.

Kazin, Michael
    1983   "Politics and the New Peace Movement." *Socialist Review* (January–February): 109–121.
    1984   "The Freeze: From Strategy to Social Movement." In *Search for*

Sanity: The Politics of Nuclear Weapons and Disarmament, ed. Paul Joseph and Simon Rosenblum, 445–461. Boston: South End Press.

Keeley, James F.

1990   "Toward a Foucauldian Analysis of International Regimes." *International Organization* 44 (Winter): 83–105.

Keen, Sam

1986   *Faces of the Enemy.* New York: Harper and Row.

Keiser, L.

1969   *The Vicelords: Warriors of the Streets.* New York: Holt, Rinehart, and Winston.

Keller, Evelyn Fox

1983   *A Feeling for the Organism: The Life and Work of Barbara McClintock.* New York: Freeman.

1985   *Reflections on Gender and Science.* New Haven: Yale University Press.

1992   *Secrets of Life, Secrets of Death: Essays on Language, Gender, and Science.* New York: Routledge Press.

Kennan, George

1983   *The Nuclear Delusion: Soviet-American Relations in the Atomic Age.* New York: Pantheon Books.

Kennedy, Edward, and Mark Hatfield

1982   *Freeze: How You Can Help Prevent Nuclear War.* New York: Bantam Books.

Kenny, Anthony

1985   *The Logic of Deterrence.* Chicago: University of Chicago Press.

Keohane, Robert

1984   *After Hegemony: Cooperation and Discord in the World Political Economy.* Princeton: Princeton University Press.

1986   (ed.) *Neorealism and Its Critics.* New York: Columbia University Press.

Kidder, Ray

1987   "Maintaining the U.S. Stockpile of Nuclear Weapons During a Low-Threshold or Comprehensive Test Ban." Lawrence Livermore National Laboratory, document no. UCRL-53820.

Kiernan, Vincent

1988*a*   "Lab a 'Whipping Boy.'" *Tri-Valley Herald,* 16 June.

1988*b*   "Concern over Lab Badges." *Tri-Valley Herald,* 1 April.

King, Donald

1982   "How Livermore Employees View Morality of Jobs." *Tri-Valley Herald,* 11 July.

Kistiakowsky, Vera

1989a   "Military Funding of University Research." *Annals of the American Academy of Political and Social Science* 502 (March): 141.

1989b   "Keep Pentagon Out of Civilian Economy." *Bulletin of the Atomic Scientists*, 45(3): 5.

Klein, Bradley

1988   "After Strategy: The Search for a Post-Modern Politics of Peace." *Alternatives* 13: 293–318.

Kolodziej, Edward

1992   "Renaissance in International Security Studies? Caveat Lector!" *International Studies Quarterly* 36: 421–438.

Konner, Melvin

1987   *On Becoming a Doctor: A Journey of Initiation in Medical School.* New York: Viking.

Kopit, Arthur

1984   *End of the World with Symposium to Follow.* New York: Samuel French.

Kovel, Joel

1983   *Against the State of Nuclear Terror.* Boston: South End Press.

Krasner, Stephen

1983a   "Structural Causes and Regime Consequences: Regimes as Intervening Variables." In *International Regimes*, ed. Stephen Krasner, 1–21. Ithaca: Cornell University Press.

1983b   (ed.) *International Regimes.* Ithaca: Cornell University Press.

Krasniewicz, Louise

1992   *Nuclear Summer: The Clash of Communities at the Seneca Women's Peace Encampment.* Ithaca: Cornell University Press.

Kuhn, Thomas

1962   *The Structure of Scientific Revolutions.* Chicago: University of Chicago Press.

Kull, Steven

1985   "Nuclear Nonsense." *Foreign Policy* 58: 28–52.

1986   "Mind-Sets of Defense Policy-Makers." *Psychohistory Review* 14(3): 21–37.

1988   *Minds at War: Nuclear Reality and the Inner Conflicts of Defense Policymakers.* New York: Basic Books.

Kunda, Gideon

1992   *Engineering Culture.* Philadelphia: Temple University Press.

Kuper, Adam

1983   *Anthropology and Anthropologists: The Modern British School.* New York: Routledge and Kegan Paul.

Kurtz, Lester
    1988   *The Nuclear Cage; A Sociology of the Arms Race.* Englewood Cliffs, N.J.: Prentice-Hall.

Lackey, Douglas
    1984   *Moral Principles and Nuclear Weapons.* Totowa, N.J.: Rowan and Allanheld.

Laclau, Ernesto, and Chantal Mouffe
    1985   *Hegemony and Socialist Strategy: Towards a Radical Democratic Politics.* London: Verso Books.

LaFeber, Walter
    1976   *America, Russia, and the Cold War, 1945–1975.* New York: John Wiley and Sons.

Laguerre, Michel S.
    1980   "Bizango: A Voodoo Secret Society in Haiti." In *Secrecy: A Cross-Cultural Perspective*, ed. Stanton Tefft, 147–160. New York: Human Sciences Press.

Lakoff, George, and Mark Johnson
    1980   *Metaphors We Live By.* Chicago: University of Chicago Press.

Lanouette, William
    1992   *Genius in the Shadows: A Biography of Leo Szilard, the Man Behind the Bomb.* Chicago: University of Chicago Press.

Latour, Bruno
    1987   *Science in Action: How to Follow Scientists and Engineers Through Society.* Cambridge: Harvard University Press.
    1988   *The Pasteurization of France.* Cambridge: Harvard University Press.

Latour, Bruno, and Steve Woolgar
    1979   *Laboratory Life: The Social Construction of Scientific Facts.* Beverly Hills, Calif.: Sage.

Lawrence Livermore National Laboratory
    1982   *Thirty Years of Technical Excellence.* Livermore: Lawrence Livermore National Laboratory Communications Resources Office.
    1992   "Preparing for the 21st Century: 40 Years of Excellence." Lawrence Livermore National Laboratory Publication no. UCRL-AR-108618.

Leach, Edmund
    1964   "Animal Categories and Verbal Abuse." In *New Directions in the Study of Language*, ed. E. H. Lennenberg, 23–63. Cambridge: MIT Press.
    1967   (ed.) *The Structural Study of Myth and Totemism.* London: Tavistock.

Lederman, Rachel
    1989   "Looking Back: The Women's Peace Camps in Perspective." In

Exposing Nuclear Phallacies, ed. Diana E. H. Russell, 244–256. New York: Pergamon Press.

Levertov, Denise

1988   "Making Peace." In *Women on War: Essential Voices from a Brilliant International Assembly*, ed. Daniela Gioseffi, 326–327. New York: Touchstone Books.

Lévi-Strauss, Claude

1961   *Totemism*. Boston: Beacon Press.

1965   "The Bear and the Barber." In *Reader in Comparative Religion*, ed. William Lessa and Evon Vogt, 289–297. New York: Harper and Row.

1966   *The Savage Mind*. Chicago: University of Chicago Press.

Levine, Howard B., Daniel Jacobs, and Lowell J. Rubin (eds.)

1988   *Psychoanalysis and the Nuclear Threat: Clinical and Theoretical Studies*. Hillsdale, N.J.: Analytic Press.

Levy, Larry

1990   "Decade to Disarm: Global Action to End the Arms Race March 29–April 2, 1990." *Test Banner* 3(1): 8–9.

Levy, Robert

1973   *The Tahitians: Mind and Experience in the Society Islands*. Chicago: University of Chicago Press.

1984   "Emotion, Knowing, and Culture." In *Culture Theory: Essays on Mind, Self, and Emotion*, ed. Richard Schweder and Robert LeVine, 214–237. New York: Cambridge University Press.

Liebow, Elliott

1993   *Tell Them Who I Am: The Lives of Homeless Women*. New York: Penguin.

Lifton, Robert Jay

1982*a*   "Imagining the Real." In *Indefensible Weapons: The Political and Psychological Case Against Nuclearism*, ed. Robert Lifton and Richard Falk, 3–125. New York: Basic Books/Harper Colophon.

1982*b*   "Beyond Psychic Numbing: A Call to Awareness." *American Journal of Orthopsychiatry* 52: 619–629.

1983   *The Broken Connection: On Death and the Continuity of Life*. New York: Basic Books/Harper Colophon.

Lifton, Robert Jay, and Eric Markusen

1990   *The Genocidal Mentality: Nazi Holocaust and Nuclear Threat*. New York: Basic Books.

Lindee, Susan

1990   "Radiation, Mutation, and Species Survival: The Genetics Studies of the Atomic Bomb Casualty Commission in Hiroshima and Nagasaki, Japan." Ph.D. dissertation, Cornell University.

Linenthal, Edward Tabor
  1989   *Symbolic Defense: The Cultural Significance of the Strategic Defense Initiative.* Urbana: University of Illinois Press.
Link, Terry
  1990   "Professors Oppose UC's Ties with Labs." *Oakland Tribune,* 14 March.
LLNL Women's Association
  1988   *LLLWA Salary Study Committee Report.* 26 July.
Loeb, Paul
  1986   *Nuclear Culture: Living and Working in the World's Largest Atomic Complex.* Philadelphia: New Society Publishers.
  1987   *Hope in Hard Times: America's Peace Movement and the Reagan Era.* Lexington: Lexington Books.
Logan, G.
  1989   "Magnetic Fusion Energy." *Energy and Technology Review* (July–August): 38–39.
Logan, Jonathan
  1993   "Bomb Maker or Bomb Breaker?" *Boston Globe,* 7 March.
Luke, Timothy W.
  1989   "'What's Wrong With Deterrence?' A Semiotic Interpretation of National Security Policy." In *International/Intertextual Relations: Postmodern Readings of World Politics,* ed. James Der Derian and Michael Shapiro, 207–229. Lexington: Lexington Books.
Lutz, Catherine A.
  1988   *Unnatural Emotions: Everyday Sentiments on a Micronesian Atoll and Their Challenge to Western Theory.* Chicago: University of Chicago Press.
Lynch, Michael
  1988   "Sacrifice and the Transformation of the Animal Body into a Scientific Object: Laboratory Culture and Ritual Practice in the Neurosciences." *Social Studies of Science* 18(2): 265–289.
Lyotard, Jean-François
  1984   *The Post-Modern Condition: A Report on Knowledge.* Minneapolis: University of Minnesota Press.
McAllister, Pam (ed.)
  1982   *Reweaving the Web of Life: Feminism and Nonviolence.* Philadelphia: New Society Publishers.
McClatchy News Service
  1994   "History Has Glow in Desert." *Tri-Valley Herald,* 13 November.
McClure, Gordon
  1992   "State's Labs Have Had No Experience in Policy Making." *Albuquerque Journal,* 16 April.

McCrea, Frances, and Gerald Markle
  1989   *Minutes to Midnight: Nuclear Weapons Protest in America*. Newbury
          Park, Calif.: Sage.
Mack, John
  1983   "Nationalism and the Self." *Psychohistory Review*, (Spring): 47–69.
  1984   "Resistance to Knowing in the Nuclear Age." *Harvard Educational
          Review* 54: 260–270.
  1985   "Toward a Collective Psychopathology of the Nuclear Arms Com-
          petition." *Political Psychology* 6(2): 291–321.
  1986   "Nuclear Weapons and the Dark Side of Humankind." *Political
          Psychology* 7(2): 223–233.
  1988   "The Enemy System." *The Lancet*, 13 August, 385–387.
  1989   "Psychoanalysis in Germany 1933–1945: Are There Lessons for
          the Nuclear Age?" *Political Psychology* 10(1): 53–61.
Mack, John, and Roberta Snow
  1986   "Psychological Effects on Children and Adolescents." In *Psychology
          and the Prevention of Nuclear War*, ed. Ralph K. White, 16–33. New
          York: New York University Press.
McKenzie, Aline
  1991*a*   "UC Countersues the DOE." *Valley Times*, 15 June.
  1991*b*   "DOE Listens to Public as Part of Waste Study." *Valley Times*, 9
          January.
MacKenzie, Donald
  1990   *Inventing Accuracy: A Historical Sociology of Nuclear Missile Guidance*.
          Cambridge: MIT Press.
McLean, Scilla (ed.)
  1986   *How Nuclear Weapons Decisions Are Made*. Basingstoke: Macmillan.
McMullin, Ernan
  1985   "Openness and Secrecy in Science: Some Notes on Early History."
          Science, Technology, and Human Values 10(2): 14–23.
McNamara, Robert
  1986   *Blundering into Disaster: Surviving the First Century of the Nuclear
          Age*. New York: Pantheon.
Macy, Joanna
  1983   *Despair and Personal Power in the Nuclear Age*. Philadelphia: New
          Society Publishers.
Major, John
  1971   *The Oppenheimer Hearing*. New York: Stein and Day.
Malinowski, Bronislaw
  1948   *Magic, Science and Religion and Other Essays*. Boston: Beacon Press.
Mandelbaum, Michael
  1981   *The Nuclear Revolution*. Cambridge: Cambridge University Press.

Manoff, Robert
    1989   "Modes of War and Modes of Social Address: The Text of SDI."
                Journal of Communication 39(1): 59–83.
Marcus, George
    1983   *Elites: Ethnographic Issues.* Albuquerque: University of New Mexico
                Press.
    1992   *Lives in Trust: The Fortunes of Dynastic Families in Late Twentieth-
                Century America.* Boulder, Colo.: Westview Press.
Marcus, George, and Richard Cushman
    1982   "Ethnographies as Texts." *Annual Review of Anthropology* 11: 25–69.
Marcus, George, and Michael Fischer
    1986   *Anthropology as Cultural Critique.* Chicago: University of Chicago
                Press.
Markey, Edward
    1985   Letter to Caspar Weinberger. 4 December.
Markle, Peter
    1989   *Nightbreaker.* Los Angeles: Symphony Pictures.
Marsh, Gerald
    1983a   "Furthermore . . ." *Bulletin of the Atomic Scientists* 39(7): 42–43.
    1983b   "No Evidence of Cheating." *Bulletin of the Atomic Scientists* 39
                (3): 4.
Martin, Emily
    1987   *The Woman in the Body: A Cultural Analysis of Reproduction.* Boston:
                Beacon Press.
    1990   "Toward an Anthropology of Immunology: The Body as Nation-
                State." *Medical Anthropology Quarterly* 4(4): 410–426.
    1994   *Flexible Bodies: Tracking Immunity in American Culture from the Days
                of Polio to the Age of AIDS.* Boston: Beacon Press.
Marx, Karl
    1972   *Capital.* Book 1. London: Everyman Library.
May, Michael
    1986   "A View from the Weapons Labs." In *Assessing the Nuclear Age:
                Selections from the Bulletin of the Atomic Scientists,* ed. Len Ackland
                and Steven McGuire, 95–101. Chicago: Educational Foundation
                for Nuclear Science.
May, Michael, George Bing, and John Steinbruner
    1988   "Strategic Arsenals After START: The Implications of Deep
                Cuts." *International Security* 13(1): 90–133.
Mearsheimer, John
    1982   "Why the Soviets Can't Win Quickly in Central Europe." *Inter-
                national Security* (Summer): 3–39.
    1993   "Back to the Future: Instability in Europe after the Cold War." In

The Cold War and After: Prospects for Peace, ed. Sean Lynn-Jones and Steven Miller, 141–192. Cambridge: MIT Press.

Medalia, John
    1994   *Nuclear Weapons Stockpile Stewardship: The Role of Livermore and Los Alamos Laboratories.* Congressional Research Service Report no. 94-418-F.

Mehan, Hugh, Charles Nathanson, and James Skelly
    1990   "Nuclear Discourse in the 1980s: The Unravelling Conventions of the Cold War." *Discourse and Society*, October.

Mehan, Hugh, and James Skelly
    1988   "Reykjavik: The Breach and Repair of the Pure War Script." *Multilingua* 7(1–2): 35–66.

Mehan, Hugh, and J. Wills
    1988   "MEND: A Nurturing Voice in the Nuclear Arms Debate." *Social Problems* 35(4): 363–383.

Melman, Seymour
    1974   *The Permanent War Economy: American Capitalism in Decline.* New York: Touchstone Books.

Merchant, Carolyn
    1980   *The Death of Nature.* San Francisco: Harper and Row.

Merton, Robert K.
    1973   "The Normative Structure of Science." In Merton, *The Sociology of Science*, 267–278. Chicago: University of Chicago Press.

Meyer, Josh
    1988   "Livermore Lab Still Drug Hive, Panel Is Told." *San Francisco Examiner*, 16 June.

Miall, Hugh
    1987   *Nuclear Weapons: Who's in Charge?* London: Macmillan.

Milburn, Michael A., Paul Y. Watanabe, and Bernard M. Kramer
    1986   "The Nature and Sources of Attitudes Toward a Nuclear Freeze." *Political Psychology* 7(4): 661–674.

Millennium
    1988   Special Issue: Women and International Relations. 17(3).

Miller, Alex
    1989   "Stark Says Lab Is Not a Very Good Neighbor." *Independent*, 15 March.

Miller, Jean Baker
    1973   *Toward a New Psychology of Women.* Boston: Beacon Press.

Miller, George, Paul Brown, and Carol Alonso
    1987   "Report to Congress on Stockpile Reliability, Weapon Remanufacture, and the Role of Nuclear Testing." Lawrence Livermore National Laboratory, document no. UCRL-53822.

Miller, John
   1990   "Lab Doesn't Come Clean, Workers Say." *Oakland Tribune*, 5 June.
Miller, Steven (ed.)
   1984   *The Nuclear Weapons Freeze and Arms Control.* Cambridge: Ball-
            inger.
Mirabella
   1994   "The Whistleblower, the Ethicist, and the Reporter." July, 129–
            131.
Moffatt, Michael
   1988   *Coming of Age in New Jersey.* New Brunswick, N.J.: Rutgers Uni-
            versity Press.
Mojtabai, A. G.
   1986   *Blessed Assurance: At Home with the Bomb in Amarillo, Texas.* Boston:
            Houghton Mifflin.
   1992   "Apocalyptic Now—A Look at Modern Religious Prophecy." *Bos-
            ton Globe*, 27 September.
Monroe, Linda Roach
   1990   "Accident at Nuclear Plant Spawns a Medical Mystery." *Los Angeles
            Times*, 10 September.
Moore, S. F., and Barbara Myerhoff (eds.)
   1977   *Secular Ritual.* Assen: Van Gorcum.
Morgenthau, Hans
   1948   *Politics Among Nations.* New York: Knopf.
Morland, Howard
   1979   "The H-Bomb Secret: To Know How Is to Ask Why." *Progressive*
            43(11): 14–45.
Morrison, David
   1985   "Energy Department's Weapons Conglomerate." *Bulletin of the
            Atomic Scientists* 41(4): 32–37.
Moseley, Bill
   1989   Interview: Peter Hagelstein. *Omni* 11(8): 74–94.
Multilingua
   1988   *Multilingua* (1–2). Special issue on Nuclear Discourse.
Murnion, Philip, and Theodore Hesburgh (eds.)
   1983   *Catholics and Nuclear War.* New York: Crossroad Press.
Nader, Laura
   1974   "Up the Anthropologist: Perspectives Gained from Studying Up."
            In *Reinventing Anthropology*, ed. Dell Hymes, 284–311. New York:
            Vintage Books.
Nash, Henry T.
   1981   "The Bureaucratization of Homicide." In *Protest and Survive*, ed.
            E. P. Thompson and Dan Smith, 149–160. New York: Monthly
            Review Press.

Nash, Terri
  1982   *If You Love This Planet*. Los Angeles: Direct Cinema.
Nathanson, Charles
  1988   "The Social Construction of the Soviet Threat." *Alternatives* 13: 443–483.
National Conference of Catholic Bishops
  1983   *The Challenge of Peace: God's Promise and Our Response*. Washington, D.C.: U.S. Catholic Conference.
Neale, Mary
  1988   "Balancing Passion and Reason: The Physicians Movement Against Nuclear Weapons." Ph.D. dissertation, University of California, San Francisco.
Neel, James V., Gilbert Beebe, and Robert W. Miller
  1985   "Delayed Biomedical Effects of the Bomb." *Bulletin of the Atomic Scientists* 41(7): 72–75.
New Left Review (ed.)
  1982   *Exterminism and Cold War*. London: Verso.
New Mexican
  1992*a*   "Fired LANL Scientist Dealt Another Blow in 5-Year Fight for Vindication." 19 July.
  1992*b*   "Complaining DOE Worker Loses Clearance." 18 May.
New York Times
  1989   "Priest Tells of His role in Nevada Bomb Tests." 8 December.
Newman, Frank
  1990   "UC Should Phase Out Its Role in the Labs." *San Francisco Chronicle*, 19 September.
Newsline
  1990*a*   "Certain Q Clearance Questions Discomfort Some." 18 July.
  1990*b*   "How to Wear and Care for Your Laboratory Badge." 27 June.
NGO Abolition Caucus
  1995   "Statement." Unpublished.
Nisbett, Paul, and Lee Ross
  1980   *Human Inference: Strategies and Shortcomings of Social Judgment*. Englewood Cliffs, N.J.: Prentice-Hall.
Norman, Colin
  1990   "Defense Research after the Cold War." *Science*, 19 January, 272.
Norris, Robert, and William Arkin
  1990   "Hot Dogs." *Bulletin of the Atomic Scientists* 46(10): 56.
  1991   "Known Nuclear Tests Worldwide, 1945 to December 31, 1989." *Bulletin of the Atomic Scientists* 46(3): 57.
Novak, Michael
  1983   *Moral Clarity in the Nuclear Age*. Nashville: Thomas Nelson.

Nuckolls, John
  1988   "Nuckolls Briefs Regents on Snowstorm." *Newsline,* 20 July.
Nuclear Notebook
  1990   "New Bomb Factory to Open Soon at Test Site." *Bulletin of the Atomic Scientists* 46(3): 56.
Nye, Joseph
  1986   *Nuclear Ethics.* New York: Free Press.
Oakland Tribune
  1989   "Pleasanton Panel Urges EIR on Lab Incinerator." 3 May.
O'Brien, William, and John Langan
  1986   *The Nuclear Dilemma and the Just War Tradition.* Lexington: Lexington Books.
O'Connell, Brian
  1980   "Secrecy in Business: A Sociological View." In *Secrecy: A Cross-Cultural Perspective,* ed. Stanton Tefft, 229–244. New York: Human Sciences Press.
O'Connor, John
  1983*a*   "Judge Orders Lewis to Begin Some Arraignments." *Valley Times,* 26 June.
  1983*b*   "Lewis Polled Community on Lab Protests." *Valley Times,* 29 June.
O'Rourke, Dennis
  1986   *Half-Life: A Parable for the Nuclear Age.* Los Angeles: Direct Cinema.
Ortner, Sherry
  1984   "Theory in Anthropology Since the Sixties." *Comparative Studies in Society and History* 26(1): 126–166.
Owen, Bill
  1973   *Suburbia.* San Francisco: Straight Arrow Books.
Pagels, Elaine
  1979   *The Gnostic Gospels.* New York: Random House.
Paley, Grace
  1983   "The Seneca Stories: Tales from the Women's Peace Encampment." *Ms.,* December, 54–62, 108.
Park, Robert L.
  1985   "Intimidation Leads to Self-Censorship in Science." *Bulletin of the Atomic Scientists* 41(3): 22–25.
Parkin, Frank
  1968   *Middle Class Radicalism.* Manchester: Manchester University Press.
Partridge, William
  1985   *The Hippie Ghetto: The Natural History of a Subculture.* New York: Holt, Rinehart, and Winston.
Payne, Karen
  1990   *The Turning of the Tide.* Channel 4, UK.

Payne, Keith, and Colin Gray (eds.)
    1984   *The Nuclear Freeze Controversy.* New York: University Press of
                America.
Pear, Robert
    1992   "Report Says Energy Department Collects Information on Some
                Americans." *New York Times,* 14 June.
Peattie, Lisa
    1986   "The Defense of Daily Life." *International Union of Anthropological
                and Ethnological Sciences Commission on the Study of Peace Newsletter*
                4(1): 3–12.
    1988   "Economic Conversion as a Set of Organizing Ideas." *Bulletin of
                Peace Proposals* 19(1): 11–20.
Peavey, Fran
    1986   *Heart Politics.* Philadelphia: New Society Press.
Peierls, Rudolf
    1985   "Reflections of a British Participant." *Bulletin of the Atomic Scientists*
                41(7): 27–29.
Perkins, Raymond
    1985   "Deterrence Is Immoral." *Bulletin of the Atomic Scientists* 41(2):
                32–34.
Perlman, David
    1988   "Congressman Says Star Wars Charges True." *San Francisco
                Chronicle,* 26 February.
Perry, Bill
    1990   "Devices, Never Bombs." *Diablo,* April.
Phillips, William G.
    1974   "The Classification System." In *None of Your Business: Government
                Secrecy in America,* ed. Norman Dorsen and Stephen Gillers, 61–92.
                New York: Viking Press.
Pickering, Andrew
    1984   *Constructing Quarks: A Sociological History of Particle Physics.* Chi-
                cago: University of Chicago Press.
    1992   *Science as Practice and Culture.* Chicago: University of Chicago Press.
Pinch, Trevor
    1993   "Testing—One, Two, Three . . . Testing: Towards a Sociology of
                Testing." *Science, Technology, and Human Values* 18(1): 25–41.
Pitt, David
    1989   "The International Tribe and the Cold War." In *The Anthropology
                of War and Peace,* eds. Paul Turner and David Pitt, 3–14. South
                Hadley, Mass.: Begin and Harvey.
Posen, Barry
    1984–1985   "Measuring the European Conventional Balance." *International
                Security* (Winter): 47–88.

Postol, Theodore
    1987   "Nuclear War." In *Encyclopedia Americana*, 519–532. Danbury, Conn.: Grolier.

Powers, Thomas
    1982   *Thinking About the Next War*. New York: Mentor Books.
    1993   *Heisenberg's War: The Secret History of the German Bomb*. New York: Knopf.

Prins, Gwyn
    1984   "Introduction: The Paradox of Security." In *The Nuclear Crisis Reader*, ed. Gwyn Prins, ix–xvii. New York: Vintage Books.
    1988   "Perverse Paradoxes in the Application of the Paradoxical Logic of Strategy." *Millennium* 17(3): 539–551.

Rabinow, Paul
    1977   *Reflections on Fieldwork in Morocco*. Berkeley, Los Angeles, and London: University of California Press.

Radcliffe-Brown, A. R.
    1965   "On Joking Relationships." In Radcliffe-Brown, *Structure and Function in Primitive Society*, 90–104. New York: Free Press.
    1968   "Taboo." In *Studies in Social and Cultural Anthropology*, ed. John Middleton, 175–195. New York: Thomas Y. Crowell.

Radway, Janice
    1991   *Reading the Romance: Women, Patriarchy, and Popular Literature*. Chapel Hill: University of North Carolina Press.

Ramos, Tom
    1991   "The Future of Theater Nuclear Forces." *Strategic Review* (Fall): 41–47.

Rapp, Rayna
    1978   "Family and Class in Contemporary America: Notes Toward an Understanding of Ideology." *Science and Society* 42: 278–300.

Reardon, Betty
    1983   *Sexism and the War System*. New York: Teachers College Press.

Reiter, Rayna Rapp
    1975   "Men and Women in the South of France: Public and Private Domains." In *Toward an Anthropology of Women*, ed. Rayna Rapp Reiter, 252–282. New York: Monthly Review Press.

Reynolds, Peter
    1991   *Stealing Fire: The Atomic Bomb as Symbolic Body*. Palo Alto: Iconic Anthropology Books.

Rhodes, Richard
    1988   *The Making of the Atomic Bomb*. New York: Touchstone Books.
    1994   "Atomic Logic: The Bomb in the Post–Cold War World." *Rolling Stone*, 24 February, 30–37, 69.

Riesman, David et al.

1950 *The Lonely Crowd: A Study of the Changing American Character.* New Haven: Yale University Press.

Rogers, Keith

1979 "'Union-busting' Charge Hurled at Lab Brass." *Valley Times,* 3 July.

1980 "A Look at the People in the Bomb Business." *Valley Times,* 13 July.

1982 "Soviets Ready to Discuss Nuclear Freeze." *Valley Times,* 4 March.

1985 "Nuke Tests 'Unnecessary.'" *Valley Times,* 2 October.

1987*a* "DOE Probing Scientists' Nuclear Lobbying." *Valley Times,* 22 May.

1987*b* "Toxic Water Escapes from LLL." *Valley Times,* 18 December.

1988*a* "FBI, Bombing Suspect Mulling Deal." *Valley Times,* 10 April.

1988*b* "Marchers Arrive in Livermore; Protest Set." *Valley Times,* 1 April.

1989*a* "Lab Works on New Energy Source." *Valley Times,* 1 February.

1989*b* "Lab to Improve Minority Hiring Policies." *Valley Times,* 25 May.

1989*c* "Lab Program Aims to End Workers' Drug Problems." *Valley Times,* 24 September.

1989*d* "Lab Downplays Effect on Plants in Spiked Garden." *Valley Times,* 10 September.

1989*e* "Lab Cleanup Projection $310 Million." *Valley Times,* 15 November.

1990*a* "EPA Tells Lab Incinerator's Days Are Over." *Valley Times,* 12 September.

1990*b* "Director of Lab Seeks to Recruit Black Scientists." *Valley Times,* 27 June.

1990*c* "Lab Officials Hope to Jazz up Paper's Image." *Valley Times,* 7 June.

1990*d* "Engineers Criticize Lab Management." *Valley Times,* 8 March.

1990*e* "Lab's Top Execs' Earnings Behind Others in Bay Area." *Valley Times,* 4 March.

1990*f* "Lab Scientists Fear Effect of Test Ban on Weapons." *Valley Times,* 11 March.

1990*g* "Lab Official Was Aware of 'Glove Box' Problem." *Valley Times,* 26 January.

1990*h* "More Information Needed on Issues, Lab Workers Say." *Valley Times,* 1 June.

Rosaldo, Michelle

1974 Woman, Culture, and Society: A Theoretical Overview. In *Woman, Culture, and Society,* ed. Michelle Rosaldo and Louise Lamphere, 17–42. Stanford: Stanford University Press.

1980   *Knowledge and Passion: Ilongot Notions of Self and Social Life.* New York: Cambridge University Press.

1984   "Toward an Anthropology of Self and Feeling." In *Culture Theory: Essays on Mind, Self, and Emotion,* ed. Richard Schweder and Robert LeVine, 137–157. New York: Cambridge University Press.

Rosaldo, Renato

1980   *Ilongot Headhunting, 1883–1974: A Study in Society and History.* Stanford: Stanford University Press.

1989   *Culture and Truth: The Remaking of Social Analysis.* Boston: Beacon Press.

1990   "Others of Invention: Ethnicity and Its Discontents." *Voice Literary Supplement* 82: 27–29.

Rose, Dan

1989   *Patterns of American Culture: Ethnography and Estrangement.* Philadelphia: University of Pennsylvania Press.

Rosenberg, Howard L.

1980   *Atomic Soldiers: American Victims of Nuclear Experiments.* Boston: Beacon Press.

Rosencrance, Richard N.

1986   *The Rise of the Trading State: Commerce and Conquest in the Modern World.* New York: Basic Books.

Rosenthal, Debra

1990   *At the Heart of the Bomb: The Deadly Allure of Weapons Work.* Reading, Mass.: Addison-Wesley.

Ross, Andrew

1991   *Strange Weather: Culture, Science and Technology in the Age of Limits.* New York: Routledge.

Rotblat, Joseph

1985   "Leaving the Bomb Project." *Bulletin of the Atomic Scientists* 41(7): 16–19.

Roth, Evan

1989   "Lab Cleanup Will Cost $1.2 Billion to Meet U.S. Laws." *Valley Times,* 20 January.

Rourke, Francis E.

1977   "The United States." In *Government Secrecy in Democracies,* ed. Itzhak Galnoor, 113–128. New York: New York University Press.

Rowe, Dorothy

1985   *Living with the Bomb.* London: Routledge and Kegan Paul.

Rubin, Lowell

1988   "Melancholia, Mourning, and the Nuclear Threat." In *Psychoanalysis and the Nuclear Threat: Clinical and Theoretical Studies,* ed. Howard Levine, Daniel Jacobs, and Lowell Rubin, 245–258. Hillsdale, N.J.: Analytic Press.

Rubinstein, Robert, and Mary LeCron Foster (eds.)

1988   *The Social Dynamics of Peace and Conflict: Culture in International Society.* Boulder, Colo.: Westview Press.

1989   *Peace and War: Cross-Cultural Perspectives.* New Brunswick, N.J.: Transaction.

Ruddick, Sara

1989   *Maternal Thinking: Toward a Politics of Peace.* New York: Ballantine.

Ruina, Jack

1991   "Will Nuclear Weapons Testing Ever Be Stopped?" Defense and Arms Control Studies Program Seminar, Massachusetts Institute of Technology. 19 March.

Russell, Diana E. H.

1989*a*   "Sexism, Violence, and the Nuclear Mentality." In *Exposing Nuclear Phallacies*, ed. Diana E. H. Russell, 63–74. New York: Pergamon Press.

1989*b*   "The Puget Sound Women's Peace Camp: Interviews with Two Activists." In *Exposing Nuclear Phallacies*, ed. Diana E. H. Russell, 223–235. New York: Pergamon Press.

Russett, Bruce

1984   "Ethical Dilemmas of Nuclear Deterrence." *International Security* (Spring): 36–54.

Sagan, Carl

1985   "Con (The Case Against SDI)." *Discover*, September, 66–74.

1986   "Nuclear War and Climatic Catastrophe: Some Policy Implications." In *The Long Darkness: Psychological and Moral Perspectives on Nuclear Winter*, ed. Lester Grinspoon, 7–62. New Haven: Yale University Press.

Said, Edward

1979   *Orientalism.* New York: Vintage Books.

Saltonstall, David

1992   "Weaning Lab off Weapons Design." *Valley Times*, 9 August.

Sanday, Peggy

1974   "Female Status in the Public Domain." In *Woman, Culture, and Society*, ed. Michelle Rosaldo and Louise Lamphere, 189–206. Stanford: Stanford University Press.

Sanders, Jerry

1983   *Peddlers of Crisis: The Committee on the Present Danger and the Politics of Containment.* Boston: South End Press.

Sapolsky, Harvey

1972   *The Polaris System Development: Bureaucratic and Programmatic Success in Government.* Cambridge: Harvard University Press.

1990   "The Politics of Risk." *Daedalus* 119(4): 83–96.

Scarry, Elaine
   1985   *The Body in Pain: The Making and Unmaking of the World.* New York:
            Oxford University Press.
   1991   "War and the Social Contract: Nuclear Policy, Distribution, and
            the Right to Bear Arms." *University of Pennsylvania Law Review*
            139(5): 1257–1316.
Schaefer, Richard T.
   1980   "The Management of Secrecy: The Ku Klux Klan's Successful
            Secret." In *Secrecy: A Cross-Cultural Perspective,* ed. Stanton Tefft,
            161–177. New York: Human Sciences Press.
Schaeffer, Robert
   1989   "Anti-Nuclear Families." *Nuclear Times* 7(3): 23–24.
Scheer, Robert
   1982   *With Enough Shovels: Reagan, Bush, and Nuclear War.* New York:
            Random House.
Schell, Jonathan
   1982   *The Fate of the Earth.* New York: Avon Books.
   1986   *The Abolition.* New York: Avon Books.
Schelling, Thomas
   1960   *The Strategy of Conflict.* Cambridge: Harvard University Press.
   1966   *Arms and Influence.* New Haven: Yale University Press.
Scheper-Hughes, Nancy, and Margaret Locke
   1987   "The Mindful Body: A Prolegomenon to Future Work in Medical
            Anthropology." *Medical Anthropology Quarterly* 1:1–36.
Schiffman, Josepha
   1991   "Fight the Power: Two Groups Mobilize for Peace." In *Ethnog-
            raphy Unbound: Power and Resistance in the Modern Metropolis,* ed.
            Michael Buroway, 58–79. Berkeley, Los Angeles, and Oxford: Uni-
            versity of California Press.
Schilling, Warner R.
   1961   "The H-Bomb Decision: How to Decide Without Actually Choos-
            ing." *Political Science Quarterly* 76: 24–46.
Schneider, David
   1980   *American Kinship: A Cultural Account.* Chicago: University of Chi-
            cago Press.
Schneider, Keith
   1989   "Nuclear Tests' Legacy of Anger: Workers See a Betrayal or
            Peril." *New York Times,* 14 December.
   1990   "Cost of Cleanup at Nuclear Sites is Raised by 50%." *New York
            Times,* 4 July.
Schwartz, Charles
   1988   "The Political Character of the University of California's Nuclear
            Weapons Laboratories." Briefing paper in information packet for

IGCC conference on the University of California and the weapons laboratories, UC Davis, 21–22 May.

1989   *Information for Students on the Military Aspects of Careers in Physics.* Booklet published by Charles Schwartz, Physics Department, University of California, Berkeley.

Schweder, Richard

1991   *Thinking Through Cultures: Expeditions in Cultural Psychology.* Cambridge: Harvard University Press.

Sea, Geoffrey

1992   "Clinging to Nukes." *San Francisco Bay Guardian,* 6 May.

Seaborg, Glenn

1981   *Kennedy, Krushchev, and the Test Ban.* Berkeley, Los Angeles, and London: University of California Press.

Senate Policy Committee, Berkeley Division of the Academic Senate, University of California

1984   "The University of California, the Lawrence Livermore National Laboratory, and the Los Alamos National Laboratory." Unpublished background paper.

Several, Robert

1990   "No Converts as Lab Hears Anti-Nuclear Leader from USSR." *Independent,* 12 December.

Shapiro, Michael

1988   *The Politics of Representation: Writing Practices in Biography, Photography and Policy Analysis.* Madison: University of Wisconsin Press.

Shaw, William

1984   "Deterrence and Deontology." *Ethics* 92, no. 2 (January): 248–260.

Shelley, Mary

1969   *Frankenstein.* Oxford: Oxford University Press.

Sherwin, Martin

1977   *A World Destroyed: The Atomic Bomb and the Grand Alliance.* New York: Vintage Books.

1985   "How Well They Meant." *Bulletin of the Atomic Scientists* 41(7): 9–15.

Shils, Edward

1956   *The Torment of Secrecy: The Background and Consequences of American Security Policies.* Glencoe, Ill.: Free Press.

Simich, Laura

1987   "Comiso: The Politics of Peace in a Sicilian Town." *IUAES Commission on the Study of Peace Newsletter* 5(3): 5–9.

Sirica, Coimbra M.

1988   "Livermore Lab Was Drug Haven, Investigators Say." *San Francisco Chronicle,* 16 June.

Sivard, Ruth Leger
  1987   *World Military and Social Expenditures 1987–88.* Washington, D.C.: World Priorities.

Sixty Minutes
  1988   "Edward Teller." 21, no. 8, 13 November. CBS News.

Slater, Philip
  1970   *The Pursuit of Loneliness: American Culture at the Breaking Point.* Boston: Beacon Press.

Smith, Alice
  1965   *A Peril and a Hope: The Atomic Scientists' Movement, 1945–1957.* Chicago: University of Chicago Press.

Smith, Andrew
  1990*a*   "New Course Chartered in Age of Peace." *Tri-Valley Herald,* 9 September.
  1990*b*   "Genius, Resources Grace Facility." *Tri-Valley Herald,* 9 September.
  1990*c*   "Lab Groups Angered by Sexual Software." *Tri-Valley Herald,* 15 August.
  1990*d*   "Two Local Sites Make Worst-Case List of EPA." *Tri-Valley Herald,* 30 August.
  1990*e*   "Clearances at Lab to be Reviewed." *Tri-Valley Herald,* 25 July.
  1990*f*   "Lab on Lookout for Spies." *Tri-Valley Herald,* 22 January.
  1990*g*   "Lab Spreads Radiation in Air." *Tri-Valley Herald,* 4 August.
  1990*h*   "Environmentalists Petitioning Against Lab's Incinerator Plan." *Tri-Valley Herald,* 2 February.

Smith, Dan
  1981   "The European Nuclear Theater." In *Protest and Survive,* ed. E. P. Thompson and Dan Smith, 55–69. New York: Monthly Review Press.

Smith, Jeff
  1989   *Unthinking the Unthinkable: Nuclear Weapons and Western Culture.* Bloomington: Indiana University Press.

Smith, Jeffrey
  1985   "Weapons Labs Influence Test Ban Debate." *Science* 229 (13 September): 1067–1069.
  1987   "Firm, Lab Personnel Aid Lobbying Against Nuclear Restrictions." *Washington Post,* 21 May.
  1990*a*   "America's Arsenal of Nuclear Time Bombs." *Washington Post National Weekly Edition,* 28 May–3 June.
  1990*b*   "Nuclear Weapons Safety and Testing: The Technology and Politics." Defense and Arms Control Studies Colloquium, MIT. 3 October.

Smoke, Richard
  1984   "The 'Peace' of Deterrence and the 'Peace' of the Antinuclear War Movement." *Political Psychology* 5(4): 741–748.
  1987   *National Security and the Nuclear Dilemma: An Introduction to the American Experience.* New York: Random House.
Snow, C. P.
  1959   *The Two Cultures and the Scientific Revolution.* Cambridge: Cambridge University Press.
Soble, Ronald
  1984   "62 Radioactive Accidents Mar Test Site's Record." *Los Angeles Times,* 27 November.
Solnit, Rebecca
  1994   *Savage Dreams: A Journey into the Hidden Wars of the American West.* San Francisco: Sierra Club Books.
Solo, Pam
  1988   *From Protest to Policy: Beyond the Freeze to Common Security.* Cambridge: Ballinger.
Solomon, Fredric, and Jacob Fishman
  1970   "Youth and Peace: A Psychosocial Study of Student Peace Protestors in Washington, D.C." In *Encounter: Issues of Human Concern,* ed. Robert Guthrie. Menlo Park, Calif.: Cummings.
Solomon, Robert C.
  1984   "Getting Angry: The Jamesian Theory of Emotion in Anthropology." In *Culture Theory: Essays on Mind, Self, and Emotion,* ed. Richard Schweder and Robert LeVine, 238–254. New York: Cambridge University Press.
Spector, Malcolm
  1980   "Learning to Study Public Figures." In *Fieldwork Experience: Qualitative Approaches to Social Research,* ed. William Shaffir, Robert Stebbins, and Allan Turowetz, 98–109. New York: St. Martin's Press.
Speed, Roger
  1990   "ASATs vs. Brilliant Pebbles." Lawrence Livermore National Laboratory, no. UCRL-ID-103669.
Spindler, George, and Louise Spindler
  1983   "Anthropologists View American Culture." *Annual Review of Anthropology* 12: 49–78.
Spradley, James
  1988   *You Owe Yourself a Drunk: An Ethnography of Urban Nomads.* Washington, D.C.: University Press of America.
Spretnak, Charlene
  1983   "Naming the Cultural Forces that Push Us Toward War." *Journal of Humanistic Psychology* 23(3): 104–114.

SPSE Newsletter
  1992*a*   Editorial. "Ranking Gone Awry." *Livermore Laboratory Society of Professional Scientists and Engineers Newsletter* no. 3, September.
  1992*b*   "Lab Cited for Contempt." *Livermore Laboratory Society for Professional Scientists and Engineers Newsletter* no. 3, September.
  1992*c*   "Security Questionnaire Fixed." *Livermore Laboratory Society of Professional Scientists and Engineers Newsletter* no. 3, September.

Stack, Carol
  1974   *All Our Kin: Strategies for Survival in a Black Community.* New York: Harper and Row.

Starhawk
  1980   *Dreaming the Dark: Magic, Sex, and Politics.* Boston: Beacon Press.
  1987   *Truth or Dare: Encounters with Power, Authority, and Mystery.* San Francisco: Harper and Row.

Staub, Ervin
  1989   "The Evolution of Bystanders, German Psychoanalysis, and Lessons for Today." *Political Psychology* 10(1): 39–52.

Stein, H. F.
  1985   "Psychological Complementarity in Soviet-American Relations." *Political Psychology* 6(2): 249–261.

Stein, Josephine
  1988   "Scientists, Engineers, and the Arms Race." Paper presented at Conference, "Ways Out of the Arms Race," London, England, 2 December.

Steiner, Pamela Pomerance
  1989   "In Collusion with the Nation: A Case Study of Group Dynamics at a Strategic Nuclear Policymaking Meeting." *Political Psychology* 10(4): 647–673.

Stern, Philip
  1969   *The Oppenheimer Case: Security on Trial.* New York: Harper and Row.

Stern, Susan
  1990   "Any Defense Cuts Will Jolt Bay Area." *Oakland Tribune,* 28 January.
  1991   "Scientists Want UC to Keep Control of the Lab." *Oakland Tribune,* 19 July.

Stewart, Kathleen
  1995   "Bitter Faiths." In *Technoscientific Imaginaries: Conversations, Profiles, and Memoirs,* ed. George Marcus, 381–397. Chicago: University of Chicago Press.

Stober, Dan
  1989*a*   "Innovative Band Challenges NASA." *San Jose Mercury News,* 28 November.

1989*b*   "Despite Hang-ups, Huge Phone System on Line." *San Jose Mercury News*, 4 November.

1990*a*   "Chinese Neutron Bomb May Have Local Origin." *San Jose Mercury News*, 21 November.

1990*b*   "Weapons Designers Feel Blows to Budget." *San Jose Mercury News*, 9 September.

1991   "Livermore's Bomb Builders Facing New Era: Bush Arms Plan Ends Lab's Nuclear Project." *San Jose Mercury News*, 1 October.

1992*a*   "A Plea to Retain N-Tests." *San Jose Mercury News*, 23 November.

1992*b*   "Nuclear Labs Designing Small, Smart Weapons: Arms Planners Focus on Third World Uses." *San Jose Mercury News*, 23 March.

Stober, Dan, and Jeffrey Klein

1992   "The American Empire in Space." *San Jose Mercury News West Magazine*, 2 August.

Stoller, Paul

1989   *The Taste of Ethnographic Things: The Senses in Anthropology*. Philadelphia: University of Pennsylvania Press.

Stowsky, Jay, and Burgess Laird

1992   "Conversion to Competitiveness: Making the Most of the National Labs." *American Prospect* (Fall): 91–98.

Strange, Penny

1989   "It'll Make a Man of You: A Feminist View of the Arms Race." In *Exposing Nuclear Phallacies*, ed. Diana E. H. Russell, 104–126. New York: Pergamon Press.

Sylvester, Christine

1994   *Feminist Theory and International Relations in a Postmodern Era*. New York: Cambridge University Press.

Taketomo, Yasuhiko

1988   "Hiroshima and Denial." In *Psychoanalysis and the Nuclear Threat: Clinical and Theoretical Studies*, ed. Howard Levine, Daniel Jacobs, and Lowell Rubin, 259–272. Hillsdale, N.J.: Analytic Press.

Talbot, David

1984   "And Now They Are Doves." *Mother Jones*, May, 26–60.

Talbott, Strobe

1984   *Deadly Gambits: The Reagan Administration and the Stalemate in Nuclear Arms Control*. New York: Knopf.

Tambiah, Stanley

1969   "Animals Are Good to Think and Good to Prohibit." *Ethnology* 8(4): 423–459.

Tannen, Deborah

1991   *You Just Don't Understand: Men and Women in Conversation*. New York: Ballantine.

Taussig, Michael
  1980   "Reification and the Consciousness of the Patient." *Social Science
             and Medicine* 14B: 3–13.
Tavris, Carol
  1990   "The Anti-War Gender Gap Is Back." *Los Angeles Times,* 26 No-
             vember.
Taylor, Bryan C.
  1990   "Reminiscences of Los Alamos: Narrative, Critical Theory, and
             the Organizational Subject." *Western Journal of Speech Communi-
             cation* 54: 395–419.
  1992   "The Politics of the Nuclear Text: Reading Robert Oppen-
             heimer's Letters and Recollections." *Quarterly Journal of Speech*
             78: 429–449.
  1993   *"Fat Man and Little Boy:* The Cinematic Representation of Interests
             in the Nuclear Weapons Organization." *Critical Studies in Mass
             Communication* 10: 367–394.
Teller, Edward
  1962   *The Legacy of Hiroshima.* New York: Doubleday.
  1985   "Pro (The Case for SDI)." *Discover,* September, 66–74.
Test Banner
  1989   "Would You Stay Home for $1,000?" May.
Theweleit, Klaus
  1987   *Male Fantasies, Vol. 1: Women, Floods, Bodies, History.* Minneapolis:
             University of Minnesota Press.
Thiermann, Ian, and Eric Thiermann
  1981   *The Last Epidemic.* Oakland: Educational Film and Video Project.
Thompson, E. P.
  1978   *The Poverty of Theory and Other Essays.* New York: Monthly Review
             Press.
  1981   "A Letter to America." In *Protest and Survive,* ed. E. P. Thompson
             and Dan Smith, 3–52. New York: Monthly Review Press.
  1982*a*   "Notes on Exterminism, the Last Stage of Civilization." In *Ex-
             terminism and Cold War,* ed. New Left Review, 1–34. London:
             Verso Books.
  1982*b*   *Beyond the Cold War: A New Approach to the Arms Race and Nuclear
             Annihilation.* New York: Pantheon Books.
  1985   *The Heavy Dancers: Writings on War, Past and Future.* New York:
             Pantheon Books.
  1986   "The Rituals of Enmity." In *Prospectus for a Habitable Planet,*
             ed. E. P. Thompson and Dan Smith, 11–43. London: Penguin
             Books.
Thompson, E. P., and Dan Smith
  1981   *Protest and Survive.* New York: Monthly Review Press.

Tickner, J. Ann
 1992   *Gender in International Relations: Feminist Perspectives on Achieving International Security.* New York: Columbia University Press.
Tipton, Steven
 1981   *Getting Saved from the Sixties: Moral Meaning in Conversion and Cultural Change.* Berkeley, Los Angeles, and London: University of California Press.
Tobias, Sheila
 1988   "Armed and Dangerous." *Ms.,* August, 62–67.
Tocqueville, Alexis de
 1956   *Democracy in America.* New York: New American Library.
Tompkins, J. H.
 1990   "Whose Livermore Is It Anyway?" Pt. 2. *Diablo,* May.
Totten, Sam, and Martha Totten
 1984   *Facing the Danger: Interviews with 20 Anti-Nuclear Activists.* Trumansburg, N.Y.: Crossing Press.
Touraine, A.
 1981   *The Voice and the Eye: An Analysis of Social Movements.* Cambridge: Cambridge University Press.
Traweek, Sharon
 1988   *Lifetimes and Beamtimes: The World of High Energy Physics.* Cambridge: Harvard University Press.
 1992   "Border Crossings: Narrative Strategies in Science Studies and Among Physicists at Tsukuba Science City, Japan." In *Science as Practice and Culture,* ed. Andy Pickering, 429–465. Chicago: University of Chicago Press.
Tri-Valley Herald
 1988   "Arrest in Lab Car-bombing." 8 April.
 1989   "Do You Know What They Do at Lawrence Livermore National Laboratory?" 23 January.
 1990   "The Companies that Keep Livermore Employed." 22 April.
 1991   "Top Salaries at Lawrence Livermore Lab." 22 February.
Tsipis, Kosta
 1983   *Arsenal: Understanding Weapons in the Nuclear Age.* New York: Touchstone Books.
 1990   "Time for Rebirth of Civilian R&D." *Bulletin of the Atomic Scientists* 46(9): 11–12.
Turco, R. P., O. B. Toon, T. P. Ackerman, J. B. Pollack, and C. Sagan
 1983   "Nuclear Winter: Global Consequences of Multiple Nuclear Explosions." *Science* 222: 1283–1292.
Turkle, Sherry
 1984   *The Second Self: The Human Spirit in a Computer Culture.* New York: Simon and Schuster.

Turner, Bryan

    1984   *The Body and Society.* Oxford: Basil Blackwell.

Turner, Frederick

    1963   *The Significance of the Frontier in American History.* New York: Ungar.

Turner, Paul, and David Pitt

    1989   *The Anthropology of War and Peace: Perspectives on the Nuclear Age.* South Hadley, Mass.: Begin and Garvey.

Turner, Victor

    1967   *The Forest of Symbols: Aspects of Ndembu Ritual.* Ithaca: Cornell University Press.

    1969   *The Ritual Process: Structure and Anti-Structure.* Chicago: Aldine.

    1974   *Dramas, Fields and Metaphors: Symbolic Action in Human Society.* Ithaca: Cornell University Press.

Ullman, Richard

    1989   "The Covert French Connection." *Foreign Policy* 75: 3–33.

Unger, Stephen

    1982   "The Growing Threat of Government Secrecy." *Technology Review* 85 (February–March): 30–39.

United Methodist Council of Bishops

    1986   *In Defense of Creation: The Nuclear Crisis and a Just Peace.* Nashville: Graded Press.

Valley Times

    1983   "Three LLL Groups Reject Union Representation by 3–1." *Valley Times,* 26 June.

    1988   "Labs' Security Lax, Official Testifies." 12 October.

    1990   "Old Nuke Facilities at Livermore May be Shut Down." 15 August.

Van Gennep, Arnold

    1909   *The Rites of Passage.* London: Routledge and Kegan Paul.

Varenne, Herve

    1977   *Americans Together: Structured Diversity in a Midwestern Town.* New York: Teachers College Press.

Vasquez, John

    1983   *The Power of Power Politics.* New Brunswick, N.J.: Rutgers University Press.

Verdon-Roe, Vivienne, Ian Thiermann, and Eric Thiermann

    1983   *In the Nuclear Shadow: What Can the Children Tell Us?* Oakland: Educational Film and Video Project.

Volkan, Vamik

    1988   *The Need to Have Enemies and Allies.* Northvale, N.J.: Jason Aronson.

Wald, Matthew
    1990   "Gaps in Security Are Found in Nuclear Weapons Program." *New York Times,* 21 December.
Walker, Robert
    1986   "Culture, Discourse, Insecurity." *Alternatives* 11(4): 485–504.
Wallace, A. F. C.
    1970   *Culture and Personality.* New York: Random House.
Waller, Douglas C.
    1987   *Congress and the Nuclear Freeze: An Inside Look at the Politics of a Mass Movement.* Amherst: University of Massachusetts Press.
Wallis, Jim (ed.)
    1983   *Peacemakers: Christian Voices from the New Abolitionist Movement.* San Francisco: Harper and Row.
Walt, Stephen
    1991   "The Renaissance of Security Studies." *International Studies Quarterly* 35: 211–239.
Waltz, Kenneth
    1959   *Man, the State and War.* New York: Columbia University Press.
    1979   *Theory of International Politics.* New York: Random House.
Walzer, Michael
    1977   *Just and Unjust Wars: A Moral Argument with Historical Illustrations.* New York: Basic Books.
Weart, Spencer
    1988   *Nuclear Fear: A History of Images.* Cambridge: Harvard University Press.
Weatherford, J. McIver
    1981   *Tribes on the Hill.* New York: Rawson Wade.
Weber, Max
    1946   "Science as Vocation." In *Max Weber: Essays in Sociology,* ed. Hans Gerth and Charles Mills, 129–156. New York: Oxford University Press.
    1949   *The Methodology of the Social Sciences.* Glencoe, Ill.: Free Press.
    1958   *The Protestant Ethic and the Spirit of Capitalism.* New York: Charles Scribners.
Weier, Anita
    1988   "Protest Ends at Test Site." *Las Vegas Review Journal,* 21 March.
Weisman, Jonathan
    1992   "Future of Lab Up in Air." *Tri-Valley Herald,* 9 November.
Welsome, Eileen
    1993   "The Plutonium Experiment." *Albuquerque Tribune,* 15–17 November. (Series of articles reissued as booklet.)

Wendt, Alexander
    1992   "Anarchy Is What States Make of It: The Social Construction of Power Politics." *International Organization* 46: 391–425.

Wertsch, James
    1987   "Modes of Discourse in the Nuclear Arms Debate." *Current Research on Peace and Violence* 10 (2–3): 102–112.

Whyte, William
    1981   *Streetcorner Society: The Social Structure of an Italian Slum.* Chicago: University of Chicago Press.

Williams, Raymond
    1977   *Marxism and Literature.* New York: Oxford University Press.

Williams, Robert C., and Philip Cantelon
    1984   *The American Atom: A Documentary History of Nuclear Policies from the Discovery of Fission to the Present, 1939–1984.* Philadelphia: University of Pennsylvania Press.

Williams, William Appleman
    1962   *The Tragedy of American Diplomacy.* New York: Dell.

Willis, Paul
    1981   *Learning to Labour: How Working Class Kids Get Working Class Jobs.* New York: Columbia University Press.

Wilson, Andrew
    1983   *The Disarmer's Handbook of Military Technology and Organization.* London: Penguin Books.

Wilson, John
    1990   *Politically Speaking: The Pragmatic Analysis of Political Language.* Oxford: Basil Blackwell.

Wilson, Lynn
    1988   "Power and Epistemology: Rethinking Ethnography at Greenham." In *Anthropology for the '90s,* ed. Johnetta Cole, 42–58. New York: Free Press.

Wilson, Robert
    1985   "Niels Bohr and the Young Scientists." *Bulletin of the Atomic Scientists* 41(7): 23–26.

Wittner, Lawrence
    1984   *Rebels Against War: The American Peace Movement, 1941–60.* New York: Columbia University Press.

Wohlstetter, Albert
    1983   "Bishops, Statesmen, and Other Strategists on the Bombing of Innocents." *Commentary,* June, 15–35.

Woodcock, George
    1962   *Anarchism: A History of Libertarian Ideas and Movements.* New York: Meridian Books.

Woodward, Beverly
   1986   "Psychoanalysis and the Nuclear Threat." *Cross Currents* 36(1):
              10–16.
Worsley, Peter
   1989   "The Superpowers and the Tribes." In *Peace and War: Cross-
              Cultural Perspectives*, ed. Mary LeCron Foster and Robert Rubin-
              stein, 293–306. New Brunswick, N.J.: Transaction Books.
Wright, Lawrence
   1989   "Inner Peace." *Rolling Stone*, 16 November, 152–199.
Wrubel, Robert
   1990   "4,000 Bomb Experts, Cheap." *Financial World*, 9 January, 53.
Yanagisako, Sylvia
   1987   "Mixed Metaphors: Native and Anthropological Models of Gender
              and Kinship Domains." In *Gender and Kinship: Essays Toward a
              Unified Analysis*, ed. Jane Collier and Sylvia Yanagisako, 86–118.
              Stanford: Stanford University Press.
Yergin, Daniel
   1977   *Shattered Peace: The Origins of the Cold War and the National Security
              State*. Boston: Houghton Mifflin.
York, Herbert
   1970   *Race to Oblivion: A Participant's View of the Arms Race*. New York:
              Simon and Schuster.
   1975*a*   "The Debate Over the Hydrogen Bomb." *Scientific American* 233
              (October): 106–113.
   1975*b*   "The Origins of the Lawrence Livermore Laboratory." *Bulletin of
              the Atomic Scientists* 31(7): 8–14.
   1976   *The Advisors: Oppenheimer, Teller, and the Superbomb*. San Francisco:
              W. H. Freeman.
   1987   *Making Weapons, Talking Peace: A Physicist's Odyssey from Hiroshima
              to Geneva*. New York: Basic Books.
Young, Nigel
   1987   "The Contemporary European Anti-Nuclear Movement." In *The
              Arms Race and Nuclear War*, ed. William M. Evan and Stephen
              Hilgartner, 235–242. Englewood Cliffs, N.J.: Prentice-Hall.
Zagotta, William
   1990   "A Perspective on Eliminating Nuclear Weapons Testing." *Tri-
              Valley Herald*, 22 July.
Zamora, Tom
   1992   "New Jobs for Old Labs?" *Bulletin of the Atomic Scientists* 48(9):
              14–21.
Zanotti, B.
   1982   "Patriarchy: A State of War." In *Reweaving the Web of Life: Fem-*

inism and Nonviolence, ed. Pam McAllister, 16–19. Philadelphia: New Society Publishers.

Zheutlin, Peter

    1990   "Nevada, U.S.S.R." *Bulletin of the Atomic Scientists* 46(2): 1–12.

Zonabend, Françoise

    1993   *The Nuclear Peninsula*. Cambridge: Cambridge University Press.

Zuckerman, Solly

    1967   *Scientists and War: The Impact of Science on Military and Civil Affairs*. New York: Harper and Row.

    1983   *Nuclear Illusion and Reality*. New York: Vintage Books.

Zur, Ofer

    1987   "The Psychohistory of Warfare: The Co-evolution of Culture, Psyche, and the Enemy." *Journal of Peace Research* 24(2): 125–134.

INDEX

Designer: UC Press Staff
Compositor: Braun-Brumfield, Inc.
Text: Janson
Display: Janson